My Disney STARS AND HEROES S

STARTER

Teacher's Book with Teacher's Portal Access Code

Michelle Worgan

Pearson Education Limited
KAO Two
KAO Park
Hockham Way
Harlow, Essex
CM17 9SR
England
and Associated Companies throughout the world.

pearsonenglish.com
© Pearson Education Limited 2022

© 2022 Disney Enterprises, Inc. All rights reserved. Pixar properties © Disney/Pixar

The right of Michelle Worgan to be identified as the author of this Work has been asserted by her in accordance with the Copyright, Designs and Patents Act 1988.

All rights reserved; no part of this publication may be reproduced, stored in a retrieval system, or transmitted in any form or by any means, electronic, mechanical, photocopying, recording, or otherwise without the prior written permission of the Publishers.

First published 2022
Second impression 2024
ISBN: 978-1-292-44177-1
Set in Arta Bold 10/12pt

Printed in the United Kingdom by Ashford Press

Image Credits
123RF.com: Ababaka 121, Agencyby 7, 22, 25, 107, Anna Trefilova 117, Asife 157, Belchonock 63, Christian Schnoor 181, Davide guidolin 181, Dmitry Lobanov 139, 139, Erstudiostok 67, Gelpi 16, 99, Happymay 135, Jacek Chabraszewski 16, 26, 31, 99, 171, Jacob Laugesen 45, Kirill Ryzhov 53, Lacheev 89, Marctran 197, Martin Lisner 181, Olga Yastremska 117, 127, Parinya Agsararattananont 125, Parinya Binsuk 67, Pavel Losevsky 143, Phasin Sudjai 18, 103, Photoallel 127, Photomelon 63, Pixelrobot 63, Piyawat Nandeenopparit 195, Roman Gorielov 121, Ruslan Kudrin 127, Samuel Sequeira 117, Sasi Ponchaisan 197, Sayfutdinov 49, Serezniy 71, Stuart Porter 171, Thomas Gowanlock 127, Vejaa 71, Vitalily73 117;

Getty Images: Armin Staudt/EyeEm 91, Caziopeia 153, Christopher Hope-Fitch 89, Daniel Kaesler/EyeEm 69, Denise Crew 55, Domin_domin 117, Emholk 7, 22, 25, 107, FatCamera 17, 101, FredFroese 87, Hakase_ 179, Iurii Garmash 189, Jade Albert Studio, Inc/DigitalVision 51, Jallfree 51, James Hager/robertharding 171, Jaroon 6, 20, 21, 46, JBryson 141, 193, Jose Luis Pelaez Inc 123, 175, 195, Juanmonino 153, Kali9 125, Kei Kobayashi/EyeEm 181, Kirin_photo 53, Krisikorn Tanrattanakunl/EyeEm 87, Lurii Garmash 201, Marin Tomas 189, 201, Martin Ruegner 135, Maurizio siani 71, Michael Marsh/stocks photography 145, Milan_Jovic 199, Nastasic 89, Nata_Snow 89, Nisha Sharma/EyeEm 55, Peter Dazeley 125, Pinstock 71, Rastko Belic/EyeEm 63, RazoomGames 53, Rubberball/Nicole Hill 197, Stretch Photography 161, Tagphoto 163, Tambako the Jaguar 181, Thatsaphon Saengnarongrat/EyeEm 175, Westend61 163, Yevtony 179; **Pearson Education Ltd:** Coleman Yuen/Pearson Education Asia Ltd 135, Rafal Trubisz/Pearson Central Europe SP. Z.O.O 69, Jules Selmes 16, 26, 31, 99, 139, 139, 163, 175, Trevor Clifford 171; **Shutterstock**: 2347286 135, A3pfamily/Shutterstock 53, Africa Studio 45, Aleksandar Bunevski 127, Anatoliy Karlyuk 18, 103, Andrea Slatter 85, ANDREI_SITURN 179, Andrey Burstein 53, Andrii Velykyi 157, ArtMediaFactory 181, B Calkins 181, Bmaki/Shutterstock 63, Danny Smythe/Shutterstock 153, Dmitrijs Mihejevs 181, Dmitry Lobanov 16, 26, 31, 99, George Filyagin 81, Herjua 125, Irin-k 145, Jareerat 181, Jasper Suijten 135, Jihan Nafiaa Zahri 193, Jim Barber/Shutterstock 199, Karkas 117, Kriangkrainetnangrong 171, L Julia 6, 20, 21, 46, LeNi/Shutterstock 153, Leonid Andronov 189, 201, Lifestyle Graphic 22, Lopolo 123, Ludmila Ivashchenko 127, Luis Molinero 33, Lukas Gojda 81, Lunatictm 81, 91, Mai Groves 33, Marharyta Gangalo 159, Martina_L/Shutterstock 117, MIA Studio 141, Mikhail Turov 117, MNStudio 179, Morrowind 85, Mubus7 189, 201, Nata-Lia 163, Netrun78 7, 22, 25, 107, Nexus 7 153, 181, Nikshor 91, Novak.elcic 135, Olga Sapegina 16, 26, 31, 99, Pavel L Photo and Video 143, Photographee.eu 73, PV productions 199, Robert Kneschke 161, Ruslan Kudrin 117, Samuel Borges Photography 7, 22, 25, 107, Santiago Cornejo 189, 201, Sergey Novikov 39, Sergiy1975 63, SergiyN 171, Shippee 53, Stockcreations 153, Subbotina Anna 7, 22, 25, 107, Sunny Forest 7, Sunny Forest/Shutterstock 22, 25, 107, Tamapapat 189, 201, Tom Wang 159, Tosaphon C 171, TTphoto 171, TY Lim 49, Valentyn Volkov 163, Wavebreakmedia 89, Xiaorui 117, Yellow Cat 81, Yuganov Konstantin 39, Yuliia D 175, Zelfit 199.

Illustrations
Emma Randall/Plum Pudding: pp.31, 208

Cover illustrations © 2022 Disney Enterprises, Inc. All rights reserved. Pixar properties © Disney/Pixar

Contents

Scope and Sequence	4
Welcome to *My Disney Stars and Heroes!*	6
Component overview	12
Unit tour and *Teaching with …* sections	14
Teaching with the videos	15
Teaching with the picture cards / word cards	16
Teaching with songs and chants	17
Teaching with stories and story cards	19
Online modules: Phonics	20
Facilitating communication and speaking	21
Teaching the Personal and Social Skills	23
Teaching cross-curricular content	25
Reviewing material and measuring progress	27
Online modules: Big Projects	27
Teaching with the posters	28
Classroom management	29
Teacher's Book tour	30
Say hello!	32
Welcome!	34
1 My family	40
2 My room	58
3 My school	76
4 My body	94
5 My clothes	112
6 Nature	130
7 Food	148
8 Animals	166
9 In the city	184
Videoscript	202
Workbook audioscript	203
Games Bank	206
My teacher progress journal	208

Scope and Sequence

Say hello! — page 4 | Character names — I'm … | Hello, Stars and Heroes song — Hi, hello

	Vocabulary	Grammar and communication	Story	Personal and Social Skills	Cross-curricular
1 My family page 10	**Family** brother, dad, mom, sister **Numbers 1** one, two, three, four, five, six	I'm six. Are you five? Yes./No. **Asking and answering about family** Who's this? This is my brother.	**A new friend** friend, happy, sad; Oh no!	**Self-awareness:** Identifying my emotions 1 happy, sad Are you happy? I'm sad.	**Science:** Shadows cloudy, shadows, sunny
2 My room page 20	**Room** bed, chair, desk, poster **Toys** ball, kite, puppet, scooter, teddy bear, yo-yo	It's a ball. It's small. **Asking and answering about toys** Is it a kite? Yes. It's a kite.	**The puppet show** Let's play!	**Self-awareness:** Identifying my emotions 2 grumpy I'm not grumpy. Let's play!	**Math:** Shapes circle, rectangle, triangle
3 My school page 30	**School items** backpack, book, crayon, marker, pencil, ruler **Numbers 2** seven, eight, nine, ten	I have two rulers. **Asking and answering about objects** How many books? I have one book.	**The surprise** surprise, tortoise; Wow!	**Self-awareness:** Identifying my emotions 3 nervous I'm not nervous. It's OK. Don't worry.	**Math:** Plus and minus is, minus, plus
4 My body page 40	**Body** arm, body, hand, head, leg, nose **Actions 1** clap, shake, stomp, touch	Stomp your feet. Don't move. **Asking and answering about the body** What's this? It's my nose.	**Fun with Shelly** I have an idea. I'm excited! Yippee!	**Self-awareness:** Expressing my emotions cry, excited, jump, smile I'm happy. I smile.	**Technology:** Coding up, down, left, right; Go left!
5 My clothes page 50	**Clothes 1** pants, shoes, skirt, socks **Clothes 2** coat, dress, hat, scarf, sweater, T-shirt	My coat is red. **Talking about clothes** I'm wearing my T-shirt.	**The yo-yo** Come and play!	**Self-management:** Persistence Good job! Keep trying!	**Technology:** Materials cotton, leather, wool

Welcome
page 6

Colors
black, blue, brown, green, orange, pink, purple, red, white, yellow

Hello / Hi / Welcome, class!; Goodbye
Hi, I'm (name).

Relationship skills
Welcoming new people to class

	Vocabulary	Grammar and communication	Story	Personal and Social Skills	Cross-curricular
6 Nature page 60	**Bugs** ant, beetle, butterfly, ladybug **Nature** flower, mushroom, pond, river, rock, tree	I can see a beetle. **Asking and answering about nature** What color is it? It's red.	**A good team** Help me! It's a team.	**Social awareness:** Teamwork Let's all help. Good idea!	**Math and art:** Symmetry spots, stripes
7 Food page 70	**Food 1** apples, cake, soup, tea **Food 2** cookies, ice cream, juice, noodles, pizza, sandwiches	I like pizza. **Talking about likes and dislikes** I like soup. I don't like noodles.	**Lunch for Cam** hungry, lunchbox; Thanks.	**Self-management:** Empathy nice I can help. Let's all share. Thank you.	**Art:** Food prints bell pepper, mushroom, onion; cut, paint
8 Animals page 80	**Animals** bird, elephant, lion, monkey, zebra **Actions 2** climb, fly, run, swim, walk	I can swim. **Describing animal abilities** Monkeys can climb.	**Sports day** glasses, hero, shoes; Now I can run. Here you are.	**Self-awareness:** Asking for help I can do it. I need help.	**Science:** Animal needs food, home, water
9 In the city page 90	**City** car, house, street, train **Adjectives** fast, long, new, old, short, slow	It's a fast car. **Describing things in the city** It's a train. It's very fast.	**A school trip** snake; Are you OK? Be nice!	**Self-awareness:** Being brave That's brave. I'm very brave.	**Social Science:** Road safety Go. Look left/right. Stop. Wait.

Picture dictionary pages 100–109   **Alphabet** pages 110–111   **Stickers and Cut outs**

Welcome to My Disney Stars and Heroes!

My Disney Stars and Heroes is a primary course for children aged 6 to 12 that brings together the engagement of Disney stories, a focus on Future Skills, the Global Scale of English, and classroom tools that make teaching easy.

We have based the course on the following principles:

* Engaged children will learn better.
* Future Skills are key to children's development.
* Students and teachers need to see pedagogical rigor and progress.
* Teachers need flexibility.

Engaged children will learn better

Disney characters

Working with Disney, we have created a course that will engage students and help them build a solid foundation for learning English.

Disney characters are instantly recognizable to young learners, making children feel at ease and motivated to learn. Engagement with the characters will help students enjoy their lessons and develop a positive attitude to language learning. It will also help them focus on the lesson, stay on task longer, and retain more of what they have learned. The context of Disney stories is often familiar to learners, which means they can relate the new language they are learning to the realities of the Disney universe.

Stories

Children of elementary school age love listening to stories. Stories and storytelling provide a natural and engaging context for language learning. They encourage young learners to use their imagination and explore the world. Listening to, watching, and acting out stories help develop a wide range of linguistic, cognitive, social, and emotional skills, while also promoting cultural understanding.

My Disney Stars and Heroes takes a dual approach to stories – a story to watch and a story to read. We believe that this will help students develop a love of reading and storytelling, with plenty of opportunities for the teacher to retell and easily exploit, and for the children to act out and even generate stories in class.

It also helps exploit themes related to Personal and Social Skills, which run across both types of stories in every unit.

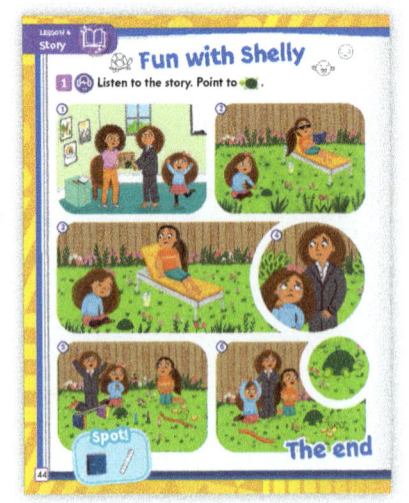

Each unit of the course has two stories at its core:

* A story to watch, with Disney characters, that runs through the whole unit. Each unit is dedicated to a different movie, so learners can meet their favorite Disney heroes as well as enjoy a variety of different movies.

  Unit openers introduce both the characters and the main topic of the unit, within a video clip. Another video clip follows later in the unit helping students focus on the new language and concepts they are learning.

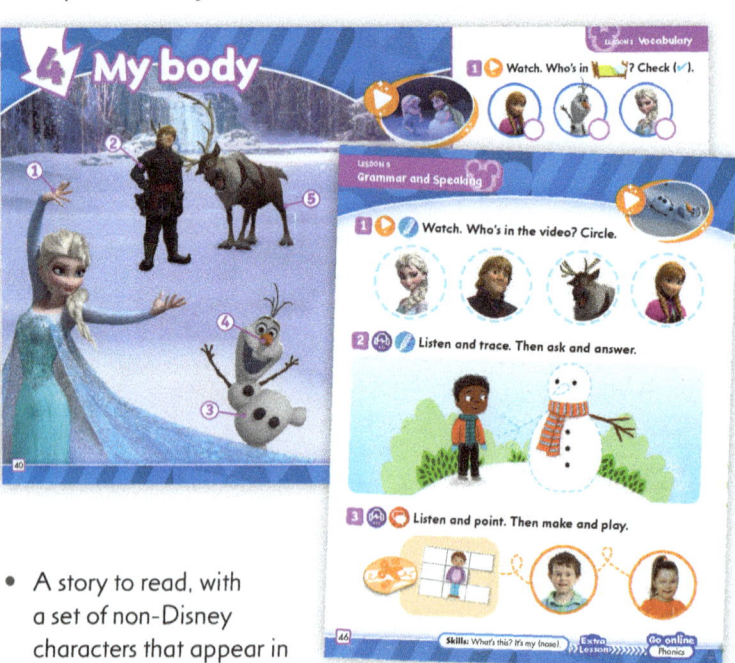

* A story to read, with a set of non-Disney characters that appear in every unit of the level. The characters are schoolchildren, like the students, and bring with them the usual everyday life experiences that learners can relate to. These stories help consolidate new language and the themes of the unit, and bring a variety of everyday experiences that students are familiar with.

Future Skills are key to children's development ★*

Future Skills in *My Disney Stars and Heroes*

My Disney Stars and Heroes helps develop Future Skills alongside language learning. These are skills that students will need to function well in the world, both individually and with others, and to become responsible citizens. They go beyond the classroom, and are essential for personal development, social inclusion, active citizenship, and in later life, successful employment.

The *My Disney Stars and Heroes* course methodology weaves Future Skills into the course activities throughout the unit: in the Disney videos, in the stories, in the dedicated *Myself and others* lessons, via project work, and in the Reviews. Clearly signposted sections in the teaching notes provide extra support to teachers through tips and ideas to further enhance Future Skills learning and practice.

In the *Myself and others* lesson

Drawing on Pearson's Framework for Personal and Social Capabilities, and other internationally-recognized frameworks, we have developed a Personal and Social Skills syllabus specific to *My Disney Stars and Heroes*. The syllabus comprises five overarching areas of competence, with the dedicated *Myself and others* lesson in each unit focusing on one skill area within each of the five umbrella competences.

Social awareness
The ability to understand the perspectives of and empathize with others, including those from diverse backgrounds, cultures, and contexts. This includes showing concern and respect for others, expressing thanks, and appreciating different viewpoints.

Self-management
Managing one's emotions, thoughts, and behaviors effectively in different situations, and using self-management tools to achieve goals and aspirations. Specific areas of focus include impulse control, stress-management, self-discipline and motivation, taking initiative, and setting goals.

Responsible decision-making
The ability to make good, safe, and ethical choices about personal behavior and social interactions across diverse situations. This includes learning to make reasoned judgements, evaluating the benefits and consequences of actions, and applying critical thinking to solve personal and social problems.

Relationship skills
The ability to establish and maintain healthy relationships and navigate friendships with diverse individuals and groups. This includes a focus on effective communication, social engagement, building relationships, working collaboratively and problem solving, and conflict resolution.

Self-awareness
The ability to identify and understand thoughts, values, and emotions, and link them to behaviors, as well as recognizing strengths and interests to develop a well-rounded sense of self.

Developing the Personal and Social Skills

Lessons and activities that explore Personal and Social Skills are clearly signposted with an icon and a green background.

Students build their skills as they work through the unit, gradually collecting a "piece" of their Personal and Social Skills badge in Lessons 1 and 4, before reaching Lesson 6 where it is complete!

Elsewhere in the unit

The course also includes **21st Century skills: communication** and **creativity**, as well as **critical thinking**. In addition, stories and songs provide students with opportunities to develop their creativity skills.

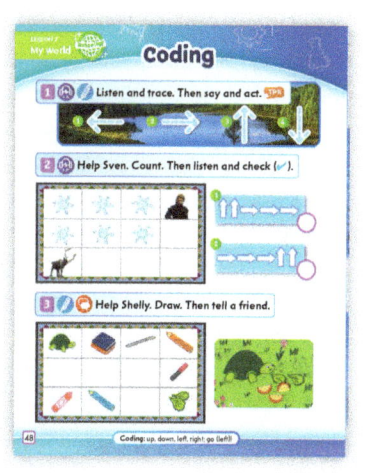

Welcome 7

Students and teachers need to see pedagogical rigor and progress ⭐*

The Global Scale of English

The Global Scale of English (GSE) is a numerical scale that measures English language proficiency. It is also a framework of learning objectives that describe what a learner can do at each level of proficiency on the scale for each of the four skills: listening, reading, speaking, and writing. The GSE enables teachers and students to answer the following questions accurately:

- How good is my English?
- What progress have I made towards my learning goal?
- What do I need to do next to improve?

The GSE is fully aligned to the Common European Framework of Reference for Languages (CEFR), but the numerical scale enables proficiency to be measured more accurately, more regularly, and within a CEFR level. This keeps learners motivated as they see regular evidence of progress.

The GSE helps teachers to find the right course materials for the exact level and learning goals of their students. The chart on the back of the Student's Book shows the range of objectives that are covered within the content. Knowing this range helps you select course materials with the right level of support and challenge for your students to help them make progress.

My Disney Stars and Heroes	
Level	GSE
Starter	10–20
Level 1	14–24
Level 2	18–28
Level 3	22–32
Level 4	26–36
Level 5	30–40
Level 6	34–45

My Disney Stars and Heroes has been created using the GSE Learning Objectives for Young Learners. These have been used to ensure that the content and activities are at the correct level and have informed the lesson goals given at the start of each unit.

In *My Disney Stars and Heroes*, the skills syllabus has been developed using the GSE Learning Objectives as well as the GSE Skill Development Framework for Young Learners, which provides structured scaffolding to support teachers and students. Within the four language skills, the sets of learning objectives are grouped into sub-skills relating to accuracy and appropriacy, complexity and organization, and interaction and strategies. The four skills are systematically developed within each level and across the course as a whole.

In addition to the GSE alignment, the vocabulary syllabus is mapped to Pearson International Certificate Young Learners and Cambridge Young Learners exams for those students taking international exams at the end of primary.

GSE Teacher Resources

You can find a full list of all the GSE Learning Objectives covered in this coursebook in the Global Scale of English Teacher Booklet, available online as part of the Teacher's Resources.

For more information about how the GSE can support your planning and teaching, your assessment of your learners, and the selection or creation of additional materials to supplement your core program, please go to www.pearsonenglish.com/gse.

For easy access to all the GSE Learning Objectives, GSE Grammar, GSE Vocabulary, and the GSE Text Analyzer (to estimate the GSE level of a written text), use the GSE Teacher Toolkit – freely available online at https://www.english.com/gse/teacher-toolkit/user/lo.

For more information about assessments that can be used to measure progress on the GSE proficiency scale, please go to https://www.pearson.com/english/assessment.html. We recommend using English Benchmark Young Learners for students studying with this course.

Global Scale of English in My Disney Stars and Heroes

Every unit of the Teacher's Book starts with an overview of the areas of skills development for reading, listening, speaking, and writing, so you can see what is expected of students.

Each lesson of the Teacher's Book lists the GSE Learning Objectives for that lesson.

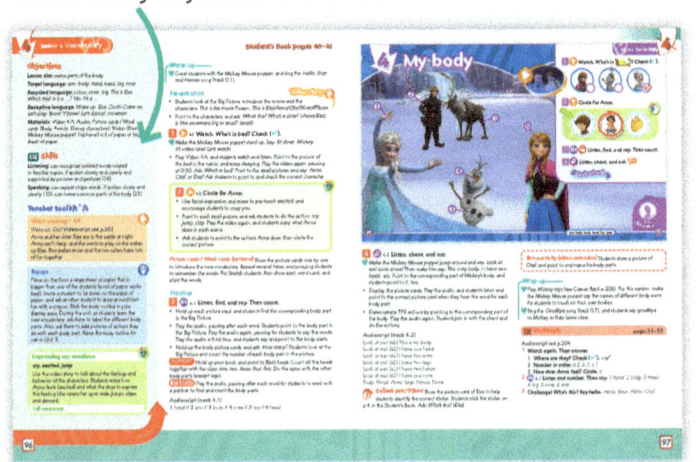

To see the full range of GSE Learning Objectives for the course, with their specific ratings, please refer to the GSE Teacher Mapping Books available online.

Measuring progress

In *My Disney Stars and Heroes*, we encourage both formal and informal assessment.

Assessment for learning

My Disney Stars and Heroes includes assessment for learning methodology, aiming to help students take responsibility for their own learning right from the beginning. Assessment for learning lets students understand where they are on their learning journey, identify gaps in their understanding, and plan how to seek the help they need. It also encourages continuous reflection and self-assessment. Elements of assessment for learning include:

Activating prior knowledge

At the start of the unit and lessons, students are encouraged to consider what they already know in relation to the topic. This activates prior knowledge and gives them focus and engagement with the topic.

> **Presentation** — Video story
> - Students look at the Big Picture. Introduce the movie and the characters: *This is the movie Frozen. This is Elsa/Anna/Olaf/Kristoff/Sven.*
> - Point to the characters, and ask: *Who's this? Who's a sister? (Anna/Elsa) Is (the snowman) big or small? (small)*

Clear goals for every lesson

Throughout the unit, students always have visibility of the lesson objectives on the page, so they can see their goals. At Starter level, these goals are worded in terms of the target language for the lesson.

> **Skills:** What's this? It's my (nose).

Self-assessment

At the end of the unit, students assess what they have learned, reflect on their progress, and are rewarded for their effort. This develops their understanding of the learning process.

Assessment pack

The assessment pack, available online, is designed for more formal in-course assessment. It includes:

- Diagnostic test
- Unit tests
- End-of-level test

The assessment pack evaluates students' mastery of the learning objectives presented in the Student's Book and Workbook.

The diagnostic test helps teachers evaluate students' language level at the start of the year. It will provide an overall picture of where the class is, but also provides awareness for teachers of where individual students or a whole class may need more support as they work through the course.

Unit tests correspond to the content material in each of the units and reflect the learning objectives of the unit. These tests provide feedback to teachers and students on the progress made against the unit learning objectives. The results of these tests can also help teachers to adjust plans for the next unit and identify any areas requiring additional practice.

The End-of-level test provides teachers with a tool to assess progress against all the key development indicators for the level and to assess class readiness for the next level.

English Benchmark Young Learners

The GSE underpins everything we create at Pearson English, including coursebooks and assessments. We recommend using English Benchmark Young Learners for students studying with *My Disney Stars and Heroes*.

By using our Benchmark assessments alongside *My Disney Stars and Heroes*, you will be able to see the progress being made by students during their course of study, and you will receive rich score reports that identify strengths and weaknesses along with recommendations on how to address any weaknesses using the course. We recommend English Benchmark Young Learners from Level 1 of *My Disney Stars and Heroes*. The Starter level should be considered as preparation and scaffolding towards this. Find out more about this test at https://www.pearson.com/english/assessment/english-benchmark-young-learners.html.

Your students may also want to take a test that gives them a proficiency certificate. For level 1 of *My Disney Stars and Heroes*, we recommend preparation for International Certificate Young Learners Level 1 Firstwords. Again, the Starter level provides scaffolding towards this. Find out more about this test at https://qualifications.pearson.com/en/qualifications/international-certificate/young-learners/test-levels.html.

Welcome 9

Teachers need flexibility ★*

My Disney Stars and Heroes provides a variety of options and pathways through the material, so you can tailor your approach to both your students' needs and your particular teaching context.

Different numbers of teaching hours

To help you plan, we estimate that teaching materials for the Student's Book and related practice in the Workbook may take around 40 minutes of classroom time per lesson. The actual time it may take you to complete a unit with your class depends on many factors, such as the makeup and needs of your class, as well as how well students cooperate as a group. You may also consider how much time is needed for review or for language presentation, as well as how many times features such as songs, stories, or games are revisited.

You can extend the core material by using additional extra activities in the Teacher's Book, digital activities, and using the Workbook in the class rather than for homework.

Every unit includes two additional lessons available online only so that you can choose the material your students really need. These are Phonics and Big Projects.

The Student's Book and Teacher's Book include an access code to digital resources, which means teaching can be done either using only paper components or using a blended approach. The digital resources include the Presentation Tool for the teacher, as well as eBooks for students.

In the table below, we suggest options for adjusting the material to suit different situations.

Possible pathways through material

Option 1 (3 lessons a week)	Option 2 (4 lessons a week)	Option 3 (5 lessons a week)
Student's Book core activities. Workbook activities done mostly at home	Student's Book and Workbook, with all activities done mostly in class, plus some online Phonics or Big Project lessons	Student's Book and Workbook, with all activities done in class, plus all online Phonics and Big Project lessons, and Extra reading
	Online modules »»»»»»	Online modules »»»»»»

Additional practice can be added by focusing more on the songs, chants, stories, videos, games, digital activities, and extra activities given in the teaching notes.

Example unit plan

There are nine units in the course, and we suggest the following approach to cover one unit every four weeks.

Week	Lesson	Focus
1	1	Vocabulary
	2	Vocabulary
	3	Grammar
2	4	Story
	5	Grammar and Speaking
		Phonics

Week	Lesson	Focus
3	6	Myself and others
	7	My world
4	8	Review
		Big Project
		Unit Test

Inclusion and differentiation

Another aspect in which teachers need flexibility is adjusting lessons to the needs of different students. Children make progress at different rates and vary widely in terms of their strengths and how they learn most effectively. *My Disney Stars and Heroes* aims to support teachers with managing inclusive classrooms and creating an environment in which all students can progress in the following ways:

Systematic review and recycling

Recycling of all core language and key GSE-aligned learning outcomes has been carefully built into the course material. Language is systematically developed and built up over the course of the unit leading to the final project task, and clear review opportunities are provided in the *Review* lessons. The recycling and review of language from previous units and levels is also prioritized in the Lesson 1s, the stories and videos, the *My world* texts, and in the cumulative review activities in the Workbook *My practice* lesson.

Variety of activities

Including a variety of different activities aiming at different skills and learning styles is key for young learners, who need a frequent change of focus within a lesson. This approach is also beneficial in inclusive teaching, where different learners might respond to some approaches better than others. *My Disney Stars and Heroes* recycles new language across different contexts, focusing on different modes of input as well as including songs, movement, artwork, games, and digital interactive activities.

Differentiated instruction

Naturally, in classes where there is a wide range of abilities, some students will require extra support and reinforcement, while others will benefit from extension and additional practice. Teaching notes include suggestions for Support and Stretch activities that help organize the lesson in such a way that students can work at the level that is right for their skills and abilities. Activities marked SUPPORT are designed for students who may need slightly simpler goals. Activities marked STRETCH are aimed at students who can try to perform above expectations for the class.

> **SUPPORT** Say an action word, and students do the corresponding action. Start slowly, giving students time to think and respond, then gradually say the words more quickly.
> **STRETCH** Students work in pairs, taking turns to point to a photo for their partner to name and do the action shown in the photo.

In mixed ability classes, it is vital that everyone can take part in activities whatever their abilities, and this can present challenges for teachers. Special attention is paid to differentiated instruction in the *Review* lesson, where teachers can also find suggestions for remediation activities. These focus students on the core language and skills they need to master in the unit.

> **ACHIEVE**
> Students name different parts of the body and emotions, and say and act out the actions they do to express their feelings.
>
> **SUPPORT**
> Play the game all together as a class against the Mickey Mouse puppet. Make Mickey make mistakes once or twice to help the class win the game. Allow students to use single words and short phrases.
>
> **STRETCH**
> Demonstrate the game, then students work in pairs to play the game, using the grid in one of their books. They take turns to choose a square, say the word or phrase, and do the TPR action. One student draws O and the other student draws X.

Extra tasks

Some students will benefit from having a little bit more time to complete activities, while others may be ready to move on. To keep the fast finishers active, extra activities in the Teacher's Book provide an extension of the lesson content so they can expand on what they have learned, while the rest of the class focuses on the core activities.

> **Extra activity (fast finishers)** Students draw things that make them feel happy or excited. They could also cut out pictures from old magazines. They could stick the pictures onto construction paper and make a classroom display.

Peer support

Working in mixed ability pairs or groups allows students not only to learn from each other, but also to appreciate one another's differences. It is also an important social skill for students to recognize and praise other children's work, highlight their achievements, and gently suggest ways for improvement. The collaborative speaking tasks throughout the Student's Book and Workbook naturally encourage this type of cooperation, and allow students to feel less pressure in participating. Peer support is often suggested in teaching notes, with ideas for pairing more confident and less confident children to complete tasks.

> **SUPPORT** As you name the two actions, hold up the corresponding picture cards for students to do the actions.
> **STRETCH** Students work in pairs, taking turns to say two actions for their partner to do.

Assessment for learning

Assessment for learning methodology is more than testing. It involves ongoing engagement with learners, focusing them on key outcomes for each lesson, and helping them reflect on how well they have achieved those goals. Having clear goals makes it easier for all students to follow what is happening in the lesson, and shows how what they know now helps to inform what they learn next. As students grow older, they will be able to increasingly see what gaps they might have and understand how they can take an active role in their education, seeking out the help they need to meet their goals.

Praise for effort

Praising for effort rather than ability is an important aspect of working with all young learners, but

> **Teaching star**
> **Growth mindset** At this age, students may find it difficult to play games in teams. In the game in activity 1, choose a different student to answer each time. Give the student time to think before they answer, and encourage the other team members to whisper the correct answer to the student so they can check their answers. Give a round of applause for each correct answer, and say *Good try!* for any incorrect answers.

is key with students with special educational needs. It encourages learners to keep trying despite difficulties, which is very important for their future educational success. It is also very motivating for all students.

Further tips

→ Tips for supporting inclusive classrooms can be found on p.29.

Component overview

1 Plan

Teacher's Book

In this Teacher's Book, you can find everything you need to teach with *My Disney Stars and Heroes*. It includes comprehensive and easy-to-follow teaching notes, answer keys, extra activities and ideas, suggestions and tips, audioscripts, and videoscripts, plus information on how to take full advantage of all the course material.

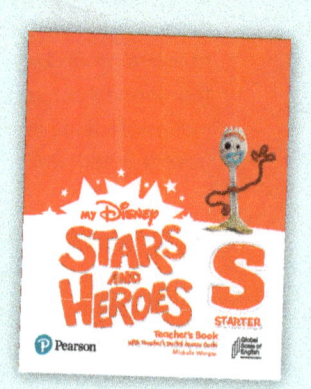

Teacher's Digital Resources

The digital resources that accompany the Teacher's Book provide you with all the tools you need to run a blended or hybrid lesson – all in one place.

2 Teach

Student's Book

The Student's Book is designed for use in class, with the teacher. It contains nine units of eight lessons each that present and practice the core learning material. It includes stickers, cut-outs, and an access code to the Student's Book eBook, Workbook ebook, and digital resources.

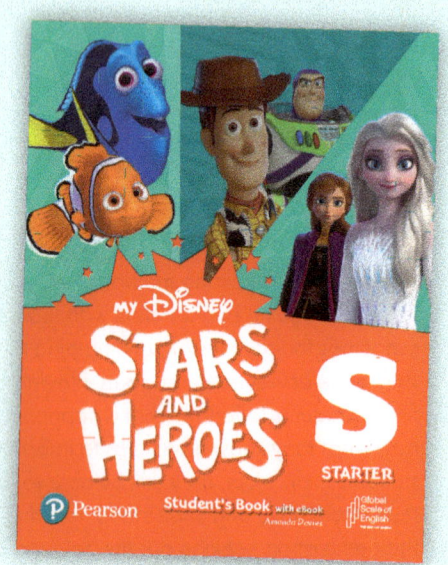

eBooks

Digital versions of the Student's Book and Workbook are available for all levels.

Presentation Tool

Using the Presentation tool, teachers can present the student's components on screen, access interactive games, audio, and video with a simple click of a button. Access to the Presentation Tool is provided with every Teacher's Book.

Class audio

The class audio contains all the recordings for the Student's Book and Workbook. All tracks are correspondingly numbered on the pages of both components, and the audio for the series can be found in the Teacher's Resources on the Pearson English Portal.

Teacher's Digital Resources

Additional resources are available through the Pearson English Portal to support your teaching, including class games and worksheets.

Picture cards / Word cards

The picture cards / word cards help present and practice all key vocabulary for each level. There are 110 picture cards at Starter level, illustrating the two vocabulary sets for each unit. The lesson notes, and the Games Bank on p.206, offer ideas and support for using picture cards to present, practice, and consolidate language through games and activities.

Disney video stories

My Disney Stars and Heroes offers two Disney video stories per unit at Levels Starter to 2. The *Teaching with the videos* section on p.15 provides ideas for getting the most out of the video material in class.

Posters

The posters designed for *My Disney Stars and Heroes* are a great visual aid for presenting or consolidating vocabulary, reviewing the Personal and Social Skills, and measuring progress through the level.

Mickey Mouse puppet

The course comes with a Mickey Mouse puppet to bring more engagement to the classroom. The teacher's notes suggest Mickey is used to introduce every new lesson.

3 Practice

Workbook

The Workbook provides additional practice for all the language and content introduced in the Student's Book. While it can be used in the classroom, teachers may ask students to complete certain activities at home, depending on the situation.

Student's Digital Resources

Students can access songs, videos, and additional practice materials to revisit the course material at home. Access to digital resources is provided via an access code included in every Student's Book.

Fun, auto-graded interactive exercises can be assigned as homework or extra practice, and accessed on the student site. Also included are *Speak and Record* activities to help monitor students' speaking skills.

4 Assess

Assessment

A comprehensive suite of assessment materials is included, with Diagnostic pre-tests, Practice tests, Unit tests, Progression tests, Final exams, and materials for oral assessment, all built on the GSE.

Teachers can use the English Benchmark Young Learners Test to measure students' progress. We suggest this test is taken once a year in Level 1 and twice a year in subsequent levels.

Teacher Gradebook

Teachers and students can view class progress at a glance online, to inform teaching and support students.

Component overview

Unit tour

LESSON 1 Vocabulary

Objectives
- Immersion into the world of Disney and familiarization with the Disney characters for the unit
- Introduction to the unit Personal and Social Skills focus via a Disney video
- Presentation and spoken practice of Vocabulary 1 with audio support

Student's Book

The magic of Disney is brought to life via a storytelling video that links to the unit topic and target vocabulary. The video also illustrates the Personal and Social Skills focus that students will explore throughout the unit.

A video gist activity draws attention to the themes and Disney characters, and lightly engages students with the new vocabulary.

The Personal and Social Skills activity draws students' attention to the unit focus for the first time, and supports them in recognizing the behaviors and strategies shown by the Disney characters in the video.

Vocabulary 1 is put into practice via a fun chant.

Linking back to the *Say hello!* spread at the start of the level, students collect their Disney friends and heroes as they work through the units.

Students engage with the vocabulary contextualized in the Big Picture, listening to and saying the words, before practicing. Word labels are introduced from Unit 5 onwards to support the development of reading skills.

Workbook

Students watch the video story again and engage with their new Disney friends and the Personal and Social Skills further through a fun mini-quiz.

Listening, and later reading practice of Vocabulary 1 at word level.

A *Challenge!* activity brings added engagement to learning.

Teaching with the videos ⭐*

Video is a great tool for conveying information to young learners. A combination of images, movement, colors, sounds, music, and language supports learning at all levels. At the same time, video provides an effective vehicle through which to explore Personal and Social Skills. *My Disney Stars and Heroes* offers two Disney video stories per unit at Levels Starter to 2.

Lesson 1 video story

Students first meet their Disney heroes for the unit through the Lesson 1 video story – a snippet of the original feature film that brings the recognizable characters on their Student's Book page to life! This video links to the topic for the unit, while also illustrating the unit Personal and Social Skills focus. As well as supporting the Lesson 1 vocabulary presentation, it also provides exposure to other target language for the unit receptively in context, so if time allows, the video can be revisited at the end of the unit to wrap up the topic and give students a chance to reflect on how much more they understand.

Lesson 5 grammar video

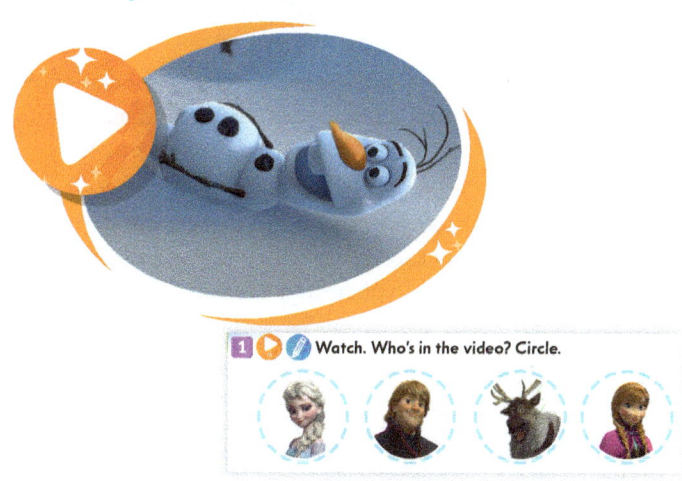

A second Disney video snippet from the original feature film for the unit presents the target grammar in context in a fun and relatable way for students. They see their favorite Disney friends on screen, and understand the meaning and use of the new structures through animated scenarios, before practicing the language through activities in their Student's Book and Workbook.

When to use the videos

- To present new material. Students will not understand the entire text presented in the recording, but they will get the meaning of the pictures, sounds, and the rhythm of the spoken language. They will remember some phrases, especially those that are often repeated.
- To review the material. Children have good short-term memories, but watching the same episodes again two months after new material was introduced will considerably stimulate their memorizing ability.
- To consolidate the covered material. The recordings include vocabulary and grammar structures introduced previously and practiced during lessons with the Student's Book.

Video activities

- Ask students to guess which items of vocabulary are in the videos. Place the corresponding picture cards on the board, then watch together to see if they were correct. Alternatively, give each student or small group a picture card of an item that appears in the video. Students stand up with their card when they see the item in the video.
- Watch the video with students from the beginning to the end. Encourage students to say aloud the English words that they remember from the recording.
- Watch the video again, stopping the recording after each scene so that you can ask students questions about the things they can see.
- Listen to the video with the screen covered (blind listening), and ask students about what they have heard, to support listening skills development.
- Watch the video with the sound muted (silent viewing), and ask students to name objects, describe the scenes, or imagine what is being said, to review key language and support critical thinking skills.
- After the video, place a selection of picture cards on the board. Ask students to remember which of the vocabulary items were in the video. Watch again and check their ideas.
- Pause the video at intervals for students to guess what happens next.

Unit tour 15

LESSON 2 Vocabulary

Objectives
- Presentation of Vocabulary 2 with audio support
- Identification of new vocabulary in context via listening
- Spoken practice of Vocabulary 2

Student's Book

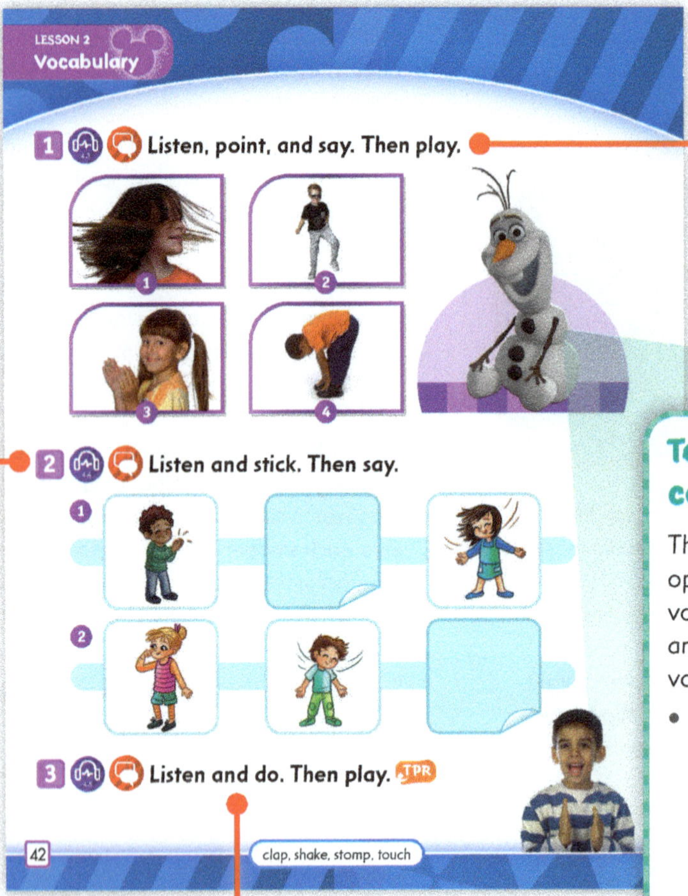

The new vocabulary items are introduced at word level through a photographic presentation. Word labels are introduced from Unit 5 onwards to support the development of reading skills.

Students identify the new vocabulary in the context of a listening. Audio can be played several times to support students' understanding of the words in context: play first for gist, a second time for specific details, and a final time to check answers.

Teaching with the picture cards / word cards ★*

The picture cards and word cards provide an optional way of presenting and practicing new vocabulary that helps students learn, remember, and review the target lexis. To introduce the new vocabulary in Lessons 1 and 2:

- Show students a picture card, and repeat the word it presents two or three times loudly and clearly. Students repeat the word three times. Do the same while teaching another word. Go back to the first word, and check if students remember it.
- Use the accompanying audio presentation in Lessons 1 and 2 for support on pronunciation for the presentation and practice stages.
- Once students are comfortable with the new vocabulary, encourage them to use the words in an example sentence. This will support with retention of the target lexis.

The final activity supports communicative speaking practice of Vocabulary 2 with TPR elements.

More ideas for using the picture cards and word cards can be found in the Games Bank on p.206.

Workbook

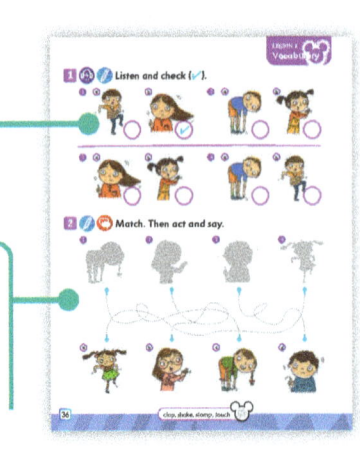

Activity 1 develops listening skills via a comprehension task.

The second activity focuses on pre-writing skills, which are developed through engaging mark-making tasks. By the end of the level students trace single words.

16 Unit tour

LESSON 3 Grammar

Student's Book

Objectives
- Presentation of Grammar 1 via song
- Identification of new grammar in context via listening
- Communicative spoken practice of the target language

An upbeat song provides examples of the new grammar in context. TPR elements help with vocabulary retention.

Students are provided with further identification of the target language via a listening activity.

The final activity facilitates controlled spoken practice of the new grammar through a communicative game, allowing students to internalize the meaning.

Teaching with songs and chants ★

Songs are immediately familiar to young learners, and provide a supportive and fun way of assimilating new language. They naturally include repetition and aid retention of vocabulary and structures through their use of rhythm. Students will be motivated to participate in singing or chanting and miming the actions, in turn promoting exposure to English in an active and enjoyable way.

The songs in Lesson 3 cover a variety of appealing musical genres that students are familiar with outside of the classroom, and each song is supported in the teaching notes by TPR (Total Physical Response) instructions to make the new vocabulary more meaningful.

- First, allow students to listen to the song/chant two or three times.
- Show students how they should clap to the rhythm of the song/chant (clapping with two fingers on the other hand will not be as loud as traditional clapping with both hands).
- Focus on the most important words that are repeated in the song/chant, as students will remember these first.
- Read aloud particular lines of the song/chant loudly and clearly (to the rhythm of the melody). Students repeat after you in the same rhythm.
- At the end of the class, encourage students to sing the song/chant.
- During the following lessons, establish the habit of singing a song/chant as a language warm-up or during breaks between tasks.
- Use songs/chants and the key words included within them to help students remember language from previous units.

Workbook

Activity 1 provides a review of the target structure presented in the Student's Book via a listening task.

Carefully-staged activities allow students to put the new vocabulary and grammar into productive practice.

Unit tour 17

LESSON 4 Story

Student's Book

Objectives
- Development of listening and pre-reading skills and strategies
- Re-engagement with the unit Personal and Social Skills focus via a course character story
- Internalization of unit language through acting out the story

Students engage with the course characters for the level, and explore different situations, events, and reactions with them.

More detailed questions focus on specifics of the story (characters, events) to check comprehension.

In activity 1, students listen to the story audio and follow the pictures in their book. A *While Listening* question develops students' listening skills in line with the GSE Learning Outcomes for the level. From Unit 5 onwards, useful language chunks are gradually introduced as text on the page to support the development of reading skills.

Students re-engage with the Personal and Social Skills focus for the unit introduced in Lesson 1. The tasks encourage them to recognize behaviors, skills, or strategies being expressed and notice aspects about how the characters deal with situations they are presented with. Here, students collect the second "piece" of their Personal and Social Skills badge!

A fun search-and-find activity further promotes the magic of storytelling, as well as aspects of critical thinking. Students look for details in the artwork to solve a visual puzzle.

Students act out the story, allowing them to internalize the language and reflect on the behaviors of the characters in a fun, memorable way.

Workbook

Activity 1 provides a review of the key points in the story and deepens students' understanding of what they have read. Further comprehension tasks develop listening and pre-reading sub-skills aligned to the GSE Learning Outcomes.

Students identify characters' actions and responses through a Personal and Social Skills practice task. They personalize the themes presented in the story through creative mark-making tasks and speaking.

Teaching with stories and story cards ★*

Stories are an essential part of language learning because they allow students to absorb information in a fun and stimulating way. Using stories in the classroom greatly enhances students' motivation, and encourages less confident students to contribute their ideas and opinions because they are not confined to the limits of a certain structure. Stories provide larger chunks of language in context as well as an opportunity for students to produce language, while also providing a springboard for the Personal and Social Skills focus.

Below is a four-stage method for using stories in the classroom that starts with anticipation and ends with language production.

Stage 1
Anticipating the story

Before listening to the audio, ask students questions or have a simple discussion in English or L1 to get them thinking about the story. This will enable students to begin forming an idea of the theme of the story and how the story might develop. It also provides an opportunity to introduce any new vocabulary or to review previously learned language. Teachers should not provide any answers at this stage, but rather allow students to think for themselves.

Stage 2
Hearing and seeing the story

At this stage, students listen to the story and work through it to find answers to your questions. Audio can be accessed in the online resources and played directly in the eBook. If you want to read the audioscript, you can find it in the lesson plans and on the story cards, but the story can be brought to life via the sound effects and professional actors used in the audio.

Stage 3
Checking the story

Some suggested questions to be asked after listening to the story are provided in the teaching notes and on the story cards. This gives teachers the possibility to further assess the depth of students' comprehension of the story and of the language used. It also sparks students' creativity and imagination by encouraging them to visualize how the story develops.

Stage 4
Acting out the story

After listening to the story several times, students are ready to act it out in groups, providing them with the opportunity to reproduce chunks of language. Props can be brought to class and used to make the experience even more stimulating. Teachers may play the audio or read the audioscript from the Teacher's Book, while students act it out, or recite the story from memory. Try to ensure that, as far as possible, every student has an opportunity to be involved in the role-play.

Below are some suggestions for extra work with the stories:

- While students listen to the story, they perform a specific action for target vocabulary (e.g., clap when they hear the word *purple* or stamp their feet when they hear the word *blue*).
- Students draw a new picture for any frame of the story.
- Students create a new ending for the story.
- Students draw or describe their favorite character.
- Students comment on how they would feel or behave if they were in a similar situation to one of the story characters.
- You might like to give students feedback, e.g., *Fantastic actions! Great teamwork! Talk a little louder next time.* This feedback could be given in L1.
- Select a story for which you can prepare simple costumes and props. Invite parents or caregivers to a mini-performance.

Story card activities

The story cards are greatly versatile and can be used in conjunction with the suggested activities below. On the back of each story card, teachers will find the audioscript for the corresponding part of the story, as well as comprehension questions to be asked after listening.

- Place the story cards in random order on the board, and students put them in the correct order.
- Place the story cards on the board in order. Students close their eyes while you remove one card, and then they guess which card is missing.
- Hide the story cards around the classroom. Students find the cards and place them on the board in the correct order.
- Students invent a new dialog for one or all of the cards.
- Read the audioscript printed on the back of the story cards, making deliberate mistakes (e.g., say *red* instead of *yellow*). Students correct your mistakes.
- Hand each story card to a different student. When you read the audioscript, the student with the appropriate story card stands up and shows it to the class.
- Without showing the story card, recite a line from the story. Students try to remember which character said the line and their name. Check answers by showing the correct story card.
- Describe a scene or character form the story. Ask the class to guess which story frame or character you are describing, either with books open or closed.

LESSON 5 Grammar and Speaking

Student's Book

Objectives
- Presentation of Grammar 2 via Disney video
- Identification of new grammar via listening
- Communicative spoken practice of the target language, supported by communication cut-outs

A Disney video clip provides examples of the new grammar in context.

Students are provided with further identification of the target language and pronunciation reinforcement via a listening activity.

Final activity encourages communicative practice of the target grammar in combination with the unit vocabulary. Students use the communication cut-outs to build their confidence and develop their speaking skills.

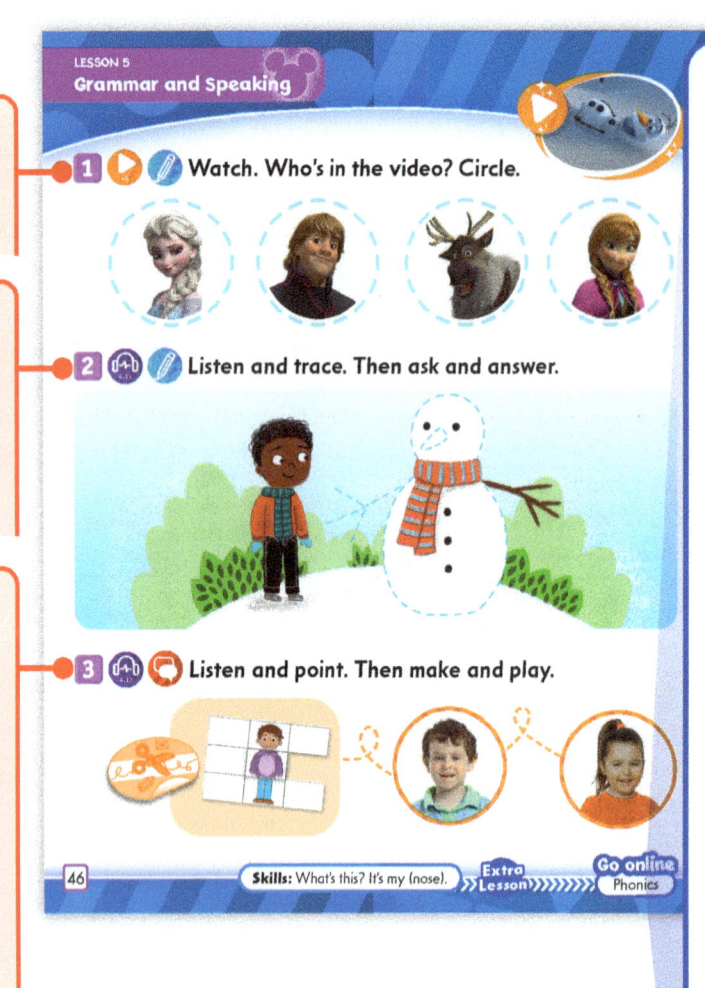

Online modules Phonics

Each Lesson 5 includes a jump off to an additional online Phonics module, for maximum flexibility depending on your teaching context. The *My Disney Stars and Heroes* Phonics lessons use a systematic phonics approach adapted for EFL students. The initial sounds of the 26 letters are introduced in order to familiarize students with the English alphabet.

Presentation and practice are focused on getting students to first identify the letters of the alphabet and the initial sounds they make, before recognizing them in the initial position of simple and familiar words.

The Phonics lessons take the following path:

Warm-up and review (optional)
The suggested warm-up activities in the lesson plans provide the following review sequence:
1. Review the sounds through a game
2. Review the letters through a game: connecting upper- to lower-case letters, recalling the alphabet sequence

Present new letter-sounds
Students see the letter, and hear the letter name and its initial sound.

Initial practice of new letter-sounds
Students identify the letters and try saying the letter-sounds themselves.

Identification of the letter-sound in the initial position
Students are introduced to key words starting with the specific letter-sounds for the lesson, then connect the letter-sounds with words.

Introduction to writing the letters
Students learn how to form the letters of the alphabet, then practice tracing and writing them themselves.

Workbook

Activity 1 reviews the target structure via a Disney-themed engaging task, accompanied by audio. The task provides scaffolding to support further practice of the new language.

The second activity is a creative mark-making task where students select or draw a prompt for communication. This final speaking practice allows students to put the language into productive practice.

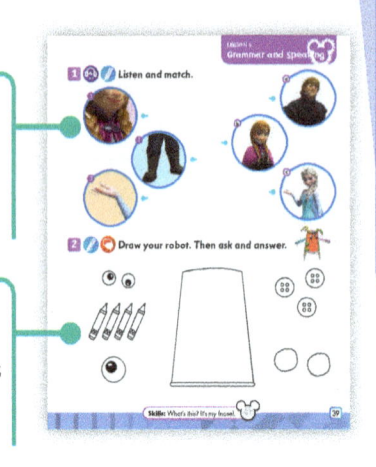

Facilitating communication and speaking ★*

Communication is a social process by which information is exchanged in order to convey meaning and achieve desired outcomes. The approach to verbal communication in *My Disney Stars and Heroes* provides students with opportunities to engage in confidence-building communicative activities and develop oracy and communication skills.

The stories, songs, and chants in the unit all provide students with opportunities to practice and improve on their communication. They give students the opportunity to listen, sing along, dance, and role-play, using their listening, speaking, and body language skills.

Speaking activities encourage students to work with a friend to practice and produce new and previously learned language.

While a wide range of motivating speaking activities appear throughout the units in *My Disney Stars and Heroes*, the final activity in Lesson 5s provides a special, supported opportunity for students to build up a short exchange in a safe environment. The cut-outs and speaking props are an engaging aid to facilitate meaningful practice of the target language. Students cut out, make, and personalize their props, developing their fine motor skills, before using them in a fun, communicative speaking task with friends. The cut-outs link thematically with the unit topic and vocabulary, and help make the language fun and meaningful for students.

GSE Learning Outcome	Key development indicator
Can repeat phrases and short sentences, if spoken slowly and clearly. (16)	Pronounce letters and individual sounds correctly, as well as repeat simple words or phrases.
Can say single words related to familiar topics, if supported by pictures or gestures. (18)	Use a few words to name, talk about or describe familiar situations.

Within the skill of Speaking, the first Learning Outcome is grouped under the sub-strand of *Pronunciation and Intonation*, and the second Learning Outcome is grouped under *Production*.

By achieving these outcomes, students are showing progress against two key development indicators for Starter level.

Tips for encouraging students to speak in the classroom

- Give your students a reason to speak. A conversation starter is a good way of doing this. Make sure that students are provided with the language and the scaffolding they need.
- Ensure students know what they need to do by demonstrating the activity with a volunteer.
- Provide plenty of opportunities for pairwork or small groupwork. While some students always volunteer to speak in front of the class, others may be nervous and speak more in the relaxed setting of a small group.
- When students work in pairs, monitor and praise them, offering support where needed.
- Allow enough time for students to complete the task, especially when working in small groups. Shy students especially may feel demotivated if they miss their opportunity to speak because of time constraints.
- Provide extension activities for the fast finishers so that they do not disrupt other students, and all students have the opportunity to finish the task. Ideas for these can be found within the lesson notes.
- Pair students strategically. Experiment with pairing stronger students with ones who need more support for some activities, while pairing students at a similar level for other activities.
- Speak as much English as possible in the classroom. Deliver instructions in English, even if they need to be repeated in L1 for younger students, to start to create a safe English space.
- Don't discourage young students from speaking in L1. Instead, praise their responses, and ask them if they can say any of the words in English. Ask the whole class to help.
- Encourage students to ask how to say things in English and praise them for doing so.

The focus on communication and speaking comes through clearly in this lesson through scaffolded steps. Prior to using the cut-outs, students are presented with an easy-to-follow listening model on the class audio to stimulate accurate recognition of the language before they are expected to produce it. Students then apply the core language within a clearly defined framework, building confidence in speaking ahead of their end-of-unit project.

How the GSE skills strands help develop speaking

Within each of the four language skills (Speaking, Listening, Reading, and Writing), sets of GSE Learning Objectives are aligned to key development indicators. This supports more focused development and assessment of the four skills. The development indicators capture each discrete skill that learners are aiming to acquire at that level.

We can look at how this works in practice through the final activity and cut-outs in this lesson.

This activity supports students developing the following GSE Speaking Learning Outcomes.

Unit tour

LESSON 6 Myself and others

Student's Book

Objectives
- Identification and exploration of the Personal and Social Skills focus for the unit
- Development and application of strategies
- Personal response to the Personal and Social Skills focus, and production of related functional language

The first activity brings together the elements of the Personal and Social Skills presented earlier in the unit, and allows students to re-engage with examples from Lessons 1 and 4 via the Disney and course characters. Students are reminded of the responses, behaviors, and emotions presented, and may compare contexts.

Students are encouraged to identify and describe the Personal and Social Skills focus in a new, real-life context. This activity models a strategy or behavior to be put into practice.

The Personal and Social Skills song summarizes the main themes explored through the level, and provides a supportive context for students to engage with the lesson before they move to their strategies work.

Students work on the Personal and Social Skills focus via a personalized task. They reflect on their own behaviors or ways they may support or understand others in hypothetical scenarios, with further opportunity to produce functional language.

In the *I'm a hero!* feature, students are rewarded with a sticker.

Workbook

Students show that they can identify, understand, and reflect upon the Personal and Social Skills focus from the Student's Book.

The second activity encourages students to work on the Personal and Social Skills in a way that relates to themselves and their lives. In each unit, they build up a "portfolio" of skills work that shows their ongoing development and allows them to reflect on their social and emotional growth through the level.

22 Unit tour

Teaching the Personal and Social Skills ★

Personal and Social Skills are the transversal skills that go beyond the classroom and are crucial for personal development, active citizenship, and future success. The *Myself and others* lesson in each unit focuses on a specific area under one of the following five overarching areas that comprise the *My Disney Stars and Heroes* syllabus:

★ Self-awareness ★ Social awareness ★ Relationship skills ★ Self-management ★ Responsible decision-making

Why teach the Personal and Social Skills?

From 6–12 years, children start to form stable friendships, engage with more complex emotions, and recognize they have choices. Teaching Personal and Social Skills in the classroom can help students become more self- and socially-aware, and equip them with the strategies they need to manage complex relationships with themselves, their peers, and their community. As a result, students are better able to develop healthy identities, resolve difficulties, create frameworks to achieve goals, build supportive and positive relationships, and make considerate and responsible decisions.

How can I teach these these skills?

A successful approach to the Personal and Social Skills is one that weaves them into all of students' educational experiences. As the classroom is at the heart of students' learning process, it is the ideal place to start! The *My Disney Stars and Heroes* methodology has been designed with the teacher in mind, to make it as easy and straightforward as possible to integrate Personal and Social Skills into their English lessons. Each unit targets an explicit area of the Personal and Social Skills through sequenced activities in Lessons 1, 4, and 6 that foster skills development:

The skill for the unit is first contextualized via the Disney video in Lesson 1. In this example, the focus is on expressing emotions (Self-awareness).

The Lesson 4 story links back to the Personal and Social Skills focus introduced in the unit opener.

Finally, the dedicated *Myself and others* lesson brings together the key themes introduced by both the video and the story, allowing students to explore the skill in greater detail and personalize it.

Alongside the *My Disney Stars and Heroes* focused program of instruction, a safe and supportive classroom environment will provide a strong foundation for students to explore the Personal and Social Skills themes.

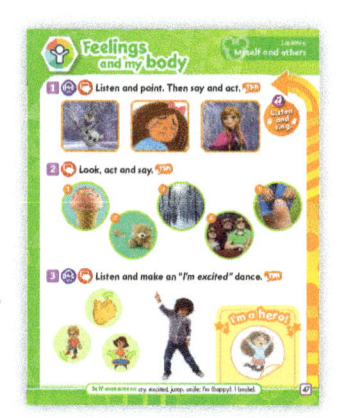

You can do it!

You do not need specialist knowledge to teach the Personal and Social Skills. As a teacher, you are already accustomed to working with values, understanding the different personalities of your students, and promoting a caring class culture. *My Disney Stars and Heroes* just provides a systematic framework to make social and emotional instruction most effective.

Throughout the teaching notes, you will find specific guidance on working with the Personal and Social Skills in each unit. In addition, you may find the following tips helpful.

Tip 1 Establish ground rules

Class ground rules are a great way to ensure a safe teaching and learning environment! Before teaching the *Myself and others* lessons, agree on respectful behaviors with your students in L1. Examples could be: *Everybody can join in and speak if they want to. We make sure everyone feels safe and OK. We listen to everyone equally.* Once agreed, display the rules in the classroom.

Tip 2 Be a role model

Students take their cue from you, so show them that this is a respectful, non-judgemental space in which everyone is listened to. Modeling the strategies explored in the *Myself and others* lessons will also help reinforce the good behaviors, tools, and techniques that your students can apply.

Tip 3 Celebrate difference and diversity

Your students will all come to the class with a wide range of different experiences, attitudes, and beliefs, not to mention personalities! Ensure that everyone knows that they have the equal right to express their opinion, and there may not be a "correct" answer. Celebrate differences to learn from one another.

Tip 4 Respect the "right to pass"

Some students may feel shy to contribute to certain topics or activities. If students are reluctant to speak, let them know that is OK, and that they can always come and speak to you individually.

Tip 5 Use a puppet or persona doll

A character such as the Mickey Mouse puppet is a great way to help students feel comfortable in the lessons. You could use this puppet or another character doll to demonstrate good behaviors such as empathy, bring scenarios to life, or facilitate class discussions.

Tip 6 Make space for reflection

Check in regularly on how students are feeling — this will encourage them to reflect on their own emotions and responses. Also, asking students to journal their work will help them see their development of Personal and Social Skills. They can draw their thoughts and feelings or write something in L1. They could share these portfolios with parents and caregivers to give a window into the classroom.

Unit tour

LESSON 7 My world

Student's Book

Objectives
- Content learning about another area of the curriculum
- Presentation and identification of cross-curricular vocabulary
- Understanding and application of content learning via thinking-skills activities

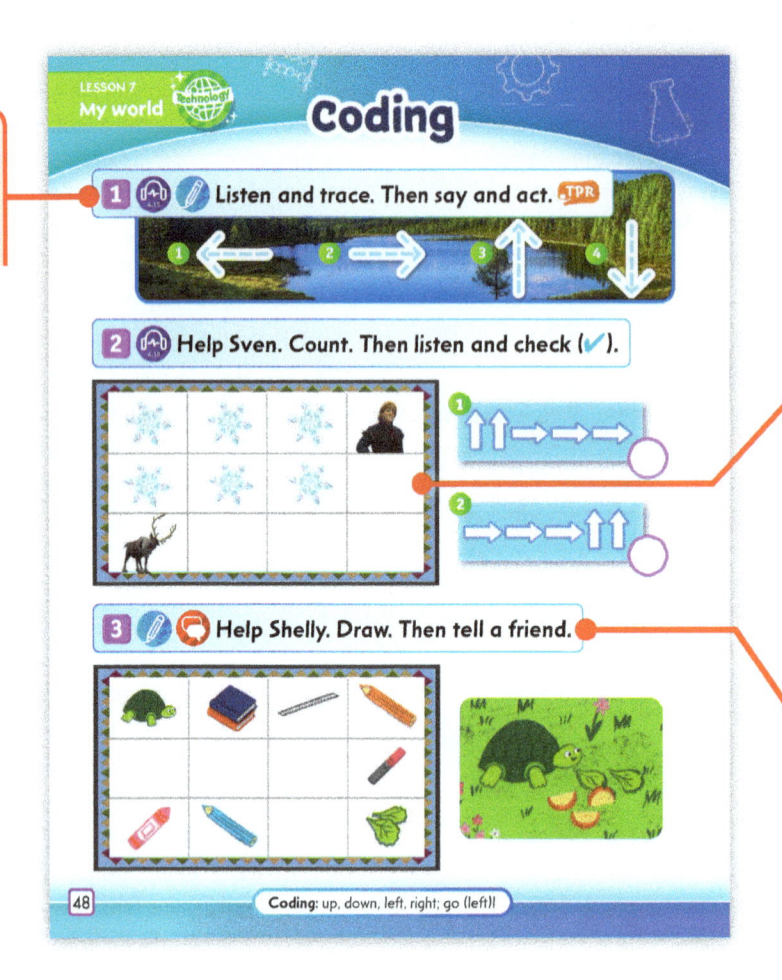

Students explore the content topic via a task that presents the cross-curricular vocabulary and develops listening skills.

Thinking skills are scaffolded from lower- to higher-order as students work through an activity that allows them to demonstrate understanding of the concept and start to apply critical thinking.

The final activity supports students in further developing their thinking skills through a variety of different tasks, encouraging practical application, synthesizing information, and creative response.

Workbook

Activity 1 checks comprehension of the concepts and provides practice of the cross-curricular vocabulary.

Activity 2 supports further application of the content learning and allows students to relate the cross-curricular subject to their own worlds.

24 Unit tour

Teaching cross-curricular content ★*

The Content Language Integrated Learning (CLIL) approach encourages students to learn English through other subjects: science, technology, engineering, art and design, or math (STEAM). The *My world* lessons are thematically linked to each unit, but provide an opportunity to develop a deeper understanding, through the medium of English, of curriculum material. Learning English through STEAM subjects is motivating for students because it gives them a reason to learn, to understand, and to discuss the subject matter. Language learning through STEAM subjects will support students' development of important skills for their future studies.

Engaging

Students benefit from prior knowledge of the subject for understanding, engagement, and to enable them to develop their knowledge of English. They bring a lot of prior knowledge into the language-learning classroom. You can start the *My world* lesson by inviting students to look at a picture relating to the lesson topic and asking some warm-up questions to introduce the topic (e.g., *What can you see in the picture? Where …? Who …? What …? How …?*). At this stage, you can use L1 if necessary. Throughout the lesson notes in the Teacher's Book, you will find ideas and suggestions for engaging students with the cross-curricular content.

> **Cross-curricular**
> Physical movement can really help students internalize language and concepts. If possible, use masking tape to design a grid on the classroom floor or in the playground, and students move around the grid, following instructions: *go left, go right, go up, go down*.

Exploring

Content that students listen to or read can provide a context for related speaking and writing activities. As students progress through the lesson's activities, check that they understand key content-related vocabulary. Write the words in a list on the board, and encourage them to use these words during the speaking and writing activities. Students can create their own running dictionaries by copying the list into their notebooks and drawing pictures, or by adding notes to help them remember the meaning of each word.

Extending

Cross-curricular lessons can instigate motivating project work, which can be done either individually, in pairs, or in small groups. Jump-off projects could take the form of a mini-book, a poster, a presentation, or even further research opportunities. Throughout the lesson notes in the Teacher's Book, you will find ideas and suggestions for extending the lesson material.

> **Extend**
> Set up a treasure hunt in the classroom or in a small area in the school yard. Make clues with arrow sequences, e.g., three left arrows means three steps to the left. Place the clues in different places to show students where to go next. Students can play in teams. The "treasure" students find at the end of the hunt could be a fun activity that they enjoy.

💡 Developing HOTS

Following Bloom's taxonomy, the activities in the *My world* lessons are structured from lower-order thinking skills (remembering, understanding, applying) to higher-order thinking skills (analyzing, evaluating, creating).

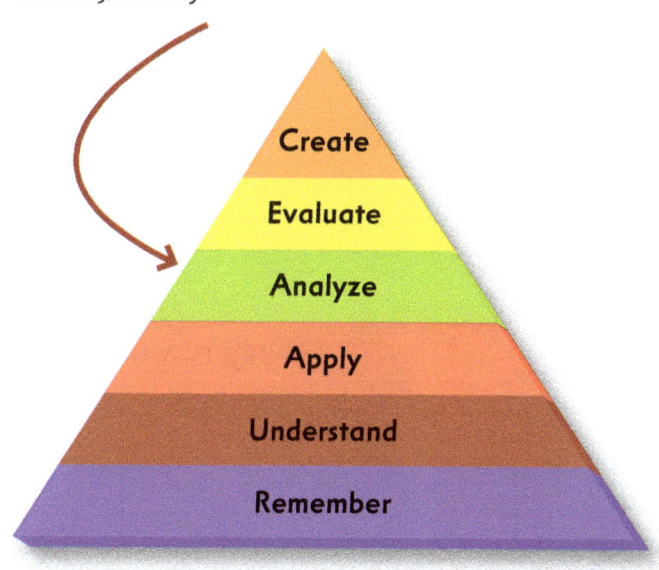

Pyramid levels (top to bottom): Create, Evaluate, Analyze, Apply, Understand, Remember.

In the teaching notes, the *Thinking skills* boxes show the progression from the lower- to higher-order thinking skills happening within the *My world* lessons, ensuring that students are provided with the support for developing their critical thinking skills through a variety of contexts.

> **Thinking skills**
> **Understand** In activity 2, students follow a series of visual directions in a maze in order to identify the correct path.
> **Apply** In activity 3, students apply their understanding of how simple directions show how to reach an objective by drawing arrows in a partially completed maze. They give directions orally as they "read" their maze.

Unit tour 25

LESSON 8 Review

Student's Book

Objectives
- Review of the vocabulary and language learned through the unit
- Development of listening, speaking, and early writing (mark-making and tracing) skills
- Evaluation against the unit outcomes

Activities review and practice grammar and vocabulary from the unit, and provide a tool for teachers to evaluate against the GSE-aligned learning outcomes for the level.

In the *I can …* section, students reflect on the unit and what they have learned. They can say which activities they liked best and evaluate their performance in these activities.

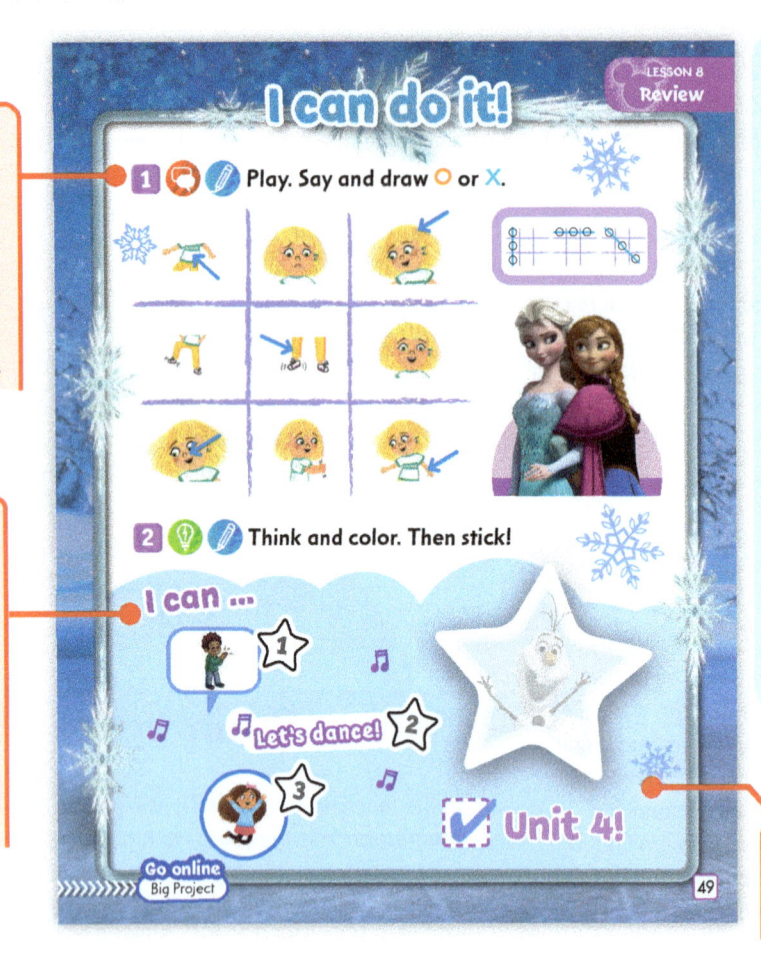

The Picture Dictionary

After learning the new vocabulary in Lessons 1 and 2, students can be directed to the Picture Dictionary at the back of their Student's Books for a full overview of the unit vocabulary by completing the words by tracing. The Picture Dictionary also supports learner autonomy and makes vocabulary more memorable, with the added focus on developing literacy skills suitable for this level.

At the end of the unit, students enjoy a fun and motivating Disney stickering activity to reward them for their progress.

Workbook

The *My progress* and *My practice* pages in the Workbook includes GSE-aligned activities that allow students to demonstrate their progress in English. As with the Student's Book, the activities serve as a tool for the teacher to measure progress against the learning outcomes for the unit and level.

The first activity focuses on students' understanding of the unit language.

The second activity allows students to apply their new knowledge of English.

Activity 1 of *My practice* checks the understanding of the level language cumulatively via large composite artwork. The first activity focuses the target language for the unit. The floating task encourages students to recall what they already know.

At the end of the unit, students reflect on and personalize their learning via self-assessment tasks.

Reviewing material and measuring progress ★*

The activities within the Student's Book *Review* lesson and the Workbook *My progress journal* and *My practice* lessons are designed to consolidate the vocabulary and grammar introduced and informally assess students' understanding and retention of the language from the unit. Each of the activities in Lesson 8 of the Student's Book and Workbook focus on objectives relating to the key GSE Learning Outcomes for the unit and level. These can be used by the teacher as formative and summative tools throughout the year to provide a clear picture of the progress students are making.

In the Teacher's Book, for each of the activities within the *Review* lessons, you will find guidance on the expected performance against the learning outcome, plus recommendations for how to adjust expectations, which in turn can be used to identify areas where students may need additional practice or support:

> **SUPPORT** Ask the question, then hold up a picture card, and say: *It's my … .* Students repeat and complete the sentence.
> **STRETCH** Students work in pairs, taking turns to ask and answer questions about the picture, following the model in the audio. They can also ask and answer using the Big Picture in Lesson 1.

The Remediation ideas in the Teacher toolkit section also provide support for language points and skills that may need further review:

> **Remediation**
> You can provide additional practice of target language for those who need it and also involve students who are comfortable with the language. Play a TPR game to review the names of body parts and actions, inviting students who know the vocabulary to give the instructions. This will help create an atmosphere of support and cohesion within the class, as well as leading to higher levels of confidence and the feeling of *I can do it!*

Self-assessment
The *I can …* box in the Student's Book and the final activity in the *My practice* Workbook lesson at the end of each unit enable students to reflect on their learning from the unit. Students are asked to evaluate the key learning points they feel comfortable with before they can add a sticker to reward their completion of the unit. This systematic and conscious review of learning objectives and assessment of learning progression helps develop in students an ability to self-assess and a sense of responsibility for their own learning. It is important to check how confident students feel before moving on to the next unit, and to provide plenty of positive reinforcement in focusing them on the skills they have successfully acquired.

Encouraging a growth mindset
My Disney Stars and Heroes promotes persistence and a growth mindset in the classroom, which helps students to view ability as something that is changeable rather than fixed. Activities encourage students to relish challenges, embrace their mistakes as part of the learning process, value the importance of effort, respond carefully to feedback, and take inspiration from others. This will help them to achieve, not only in the English classroom, but also in their future lives as adults.

Online modules Big Projects

Each Lesson 8 includes a jump off to an additional Big Project module, delivered online, for maximum flexibility. The *My Disney Stars and Heroes* Big Projects apply elements of project-based learning to extend the course material and allow students to put the new language and themes from the unit into practice via fun, hands-on project work. Each optional Big Project is structured in a systematic way to support students with the tools they need to bring their learning together.

The Big Project lessons take the following path:

Context and objective-setting
At the start of the Big Project, students are presented with a challenge to work on, along with clear objectives for their project work. The context for the project is established, and students can relate their learning from the unit to learning outcomes for the Big Project.

Thinking and research
Students think back to the language and topics learned in the unit. They can look back through their Student's Book to review the information needed for their project, and make personalized decisions about what to include. As well as building the core knowledge and skills for their project, students also have the to further explore the My World / STEAM topics for the unit with opportunities to tinker and experiment during this stage.

Application
Students apply their learning and put creativity into action through scaffolded steps that support them in designing, creating, and refining their final project. They are encouraged to use original thinking and imagination, and can create the project either in class or in their own time with access to the tools and materials they need.

Review and reflection
Students reflect on their completed project output and what they have included in their project. Their competed plans and notes at this stage can be used as support or as a reminder ahead of showcasing their work.

Showcasing
The final stage allows students to present their work, share their findings, or use their project outputs as part of a real-world communicative task.

Depending on your teaching context, the Big Projects can also be used as a framework for instruction from the start of the unit, so that students do project tasks alongside the main lessons.

Teaching with the posters ★*

Posters can play a key role in the English language lesson as they are such a powerful visual tool. They can be a valuable way to focus students' attention, allowing them to really engage with the topic and also consolidate and extend the language already learned. There are 12 posters provided in the *My Disney Stars and Heroes Poster Pack* for use alongside Levels Starter to 3 of the course. These are intended to be hung in a visible place in the classroom and referred to when you want to review the material covered, or as general support for the class.

Tips for working with posters

Predicting In order to create an atmosphere of anticipation and to invoke curiosity, give students the title of the poster before you show it to them. Tell students that in a moment they will see a poster with, e.g., weather. Ask them to think about the vocabulary that may be presented in the poster. Encourage them to provide examples of particular words related to this thematic group (e.g., *sunny, cloudy, rainy, windy*). Then hang the poster, and check together how many words students predicted correctly.

Asking questions Point to the objects, characters, colors, etc., presented in the poster, and ask questions: *What's this? What color is it? How many (balls) can you see? Is it a (doll)?*

Finding and pointing Ask individual students to come to the poster, find and point to appropriate objects, e.g., *Point to the (red car)*. You can also divide students into two teams and change finding particular elements into an exciting competition. Ask one student from the team to come to the poster and find a particular object. If he/she does it correctly, the team scores a point. If he/she makes a mistake, another team takes a turn. Students can replace the teacher and give the commands.

Memory game Set a specific time limit, e.g., 30 seconds. Tell students to look at the poster carefully and remember as much as they can. Then cover the poster or take it off the wall, and ask students one by one about the objects presented in the poster. You can also ask about the features of these objects, e.g., *Is the (ball) (big)? What color is the (kite)?* Students answer from memory. You can also do this activity as a team competition, with a time limit. The team who provides the biggest number of names of objects from the poster wins.

True or false? Point to various objects in the poster, and make true or false sentences related to these objects. For example, point to a lion and say: *It's a horse.* Students answer: *No. It's a lion!*

Quiz Tell students that you are thinking about a certain picture from the poster. Students guess which picture you are thinking about. You can describe the object you have in mind for more advanced students, e.g., *It's gray. It's small. It has a tail. What is it?* Students answer: *It's a rabbit.*

Peeping through a keyhole Cut out a hole (2 inches wide) resembling a keyhole in the middle of a large sheet of paper. Place the sheet on the poster, and ask students what they can see. Move the sheet around the poster so that each time, students guess the name of a different object.

Placing words on the poster If students can recognize written words, you can ask them to place appropriate word cards below the pictures in the poster. One by one, students come to the poster and place a word card next to a corresponding picture. Then you can ask all students to read the words aloud together.

Poster 1 My Progress

The *My Progress* poster features all students' favorite Disney heroes that appear in the level. It can be used frequently throughout the year to highlight student progress through the course learning objectives.

Poster 2 Vocabulary

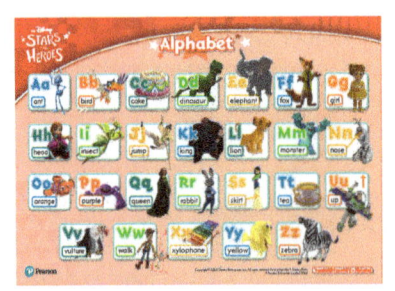

The *Vocabulary* posters offer supporting information that can be useful throughout the year. There are four vocabulary posters provided, covering:

- shapes, colors, and numbers
- the alphabet
- weather, seasons, months of the year, and physical feelings
- telling the time, days of the week, daily routine, and activities

Poster 3 Myself and others

The *Myself and others* (Personal and Social Skills) poster can be used in conjunction with the *Myself and others* lessons. Place the poster at the front of the classroom where everyone can see it, and refer to it during these classes. At the start of the year, look at the poster as a class. As you work through the course material and the Personal and Social Skills for each unit, encourage students to refer to the poster and use the language and strategies.

Classroom management

Dividing students into pairs and groups

When working in pairs, groups, or in a whole-class setting, students engage in cooperative learning — learning with and from each other. The following suggestions focus on different ways of grouping or pairing students. All the activities presented here are suited to any group size, age, or interest.

Grouping by order Organize students in a specific order, then divide them up. Ask students to get in line in alphabetical order (according to their first name or last name), by the number of letters in their name, order of birthdays (grouped either by month or by their date of birth), or height.

Animal sounds This is a loud but fun way to divide up students. Write names of animals on slips of paper. Distribute the slips of paper and ask students not to show them to each other. When they are ready, ask them to start making the sound of the animal that is written on their slip of paper. They have to find the other members of their animal family.

Pick and mix Students can be divided into groups or pairs by asking them to pick objects from a bag. Then you can ask them to find teammates who have the same objects. Some examples of objects you can use are colored counters, colored pencils, or numbered lollipop sticks. Students find their group or pair with the same color or sequential number.

Signaling that the activity has finished

When assigning speaking activities and playing games in large classes, it can often be hard to get students' attention. With this in mind, here are some suggestions to help you deal with this situation.

Can you hear me? Start talking to students in a very low voice and say: *If you can hear me, raise your hand.* Students who hear you raise their hands, which will get the attention of other students, who will do the same.

Clapping Clap your hands in different rhythms and at different speeds. Students have to join you in clapping. Say: *Clap once if you can hear me.* Some students join you. Then say: *Clap twice if you can hear me.* And finally, say: *Clap three times if you can hear me.* At this point, students will notice that the activity has finished.

Eyes on me Count to three, saying: *One, two, three … eyes on me!* Students stop the activity and say: *One, two, three … eyes on you!* This way, if the other students have not heard you, they will hear the students and then notice that the activity has finished.

Give me five Raise one hand, and say: *Give me five.* Students raise their hands and say: *Five.* Then they start to count from one to five. If this does not get everyone's attention, say: *Give me five again.* Students repeat the count.

Raising hands Raise both hands. Wait until students notice your hands are raised and gradually stop talking.

Ring a bell Set a timer for the amount of time you would like the activity to last, or ring a bell. When students hear the sound, they stop the activity.

Silent request Create a signal for silence. Then practice the signal with your students until they know that every time you make that signal it's time to stop the activity.

Singing Play or sing the *My Disney Stars and Heroes* Welcome song (*Hello, Stars and Heroes*, track 0.2). Ask students to join in.

Managing inclusive classrooms

Set clear objectives Sharing the lesson objective with students at the beginning of the lesson and making sure they know what to expect (and what is expected of them) decreases students' anxiety and allows them to prepare themselves for the tasks they find more difficult, and to look forward to the tasks they enjoy more.

Diagnose before presenting new language By taking the time to ascertain what students already know on a topic, teachers gain instant feedback on what to focus on in the lesson. This is particularly useful in inclusive classrooms where there may be a very wide range of knowledge among students.

Group strategically Depending on the activity, you may want to group students using one of these combinations: more confident and less confident students together, confident students together, less confident students together, talkers and listeners together. Whatever you choose, do not let students know what your strategy is so that all feel confident and included equally.

Take a multisensory approach Students all learn in different ways and encountering language in multiple modes is very beneficial. *My Disney Stars and Heroes* presents language through text, images, audio, song, and video. Ensuring a balance between different modes holds the class's attention and sets up all learners to achieve.

Give more space to activities Allowing students the time and flexibility to do activities in a way that suits their needs will ensure that all students can participate in the same activity, increasing their confidence and motivation. Students who struggle with written tasks, for example, may benefit from doing only one or two task items in written form and completing the rest of the activity orally.

Adjust expectations rather than materials Expecting all learners to achieve at the same level is often unrealistic and puts undue pressure on less confident students, students with special educational needs, as well as teachers. Plan to adapt your lessons, using the differentiation support in the lesson notes so that all students can complete at least some of the activity. Some may complete only the first few task items, but being set the same activity as the rest of the class avoids students feeling singled out and increases confidence.

Work with your students' strengths Find out what your students' strengths are, and see how you can include them in your lessons. Some students may not be confident with speaking, or are particularly shy, but may be very good at drawing or crafts. A student who struggles with attention or has difficulty with more traditional classwork may be very good at acting or group tasks, or be very caring and eager to help others.

Teacher's Book tour

Unit overviews

The unit objectives are clearly outlined for the teacher, showing what outcomes students will achieve by the end of the unit. There is a summary of the key GSE learning outcomes for all four skills, linked to the unit objectives, showing how key competences have been integrated into the course material.

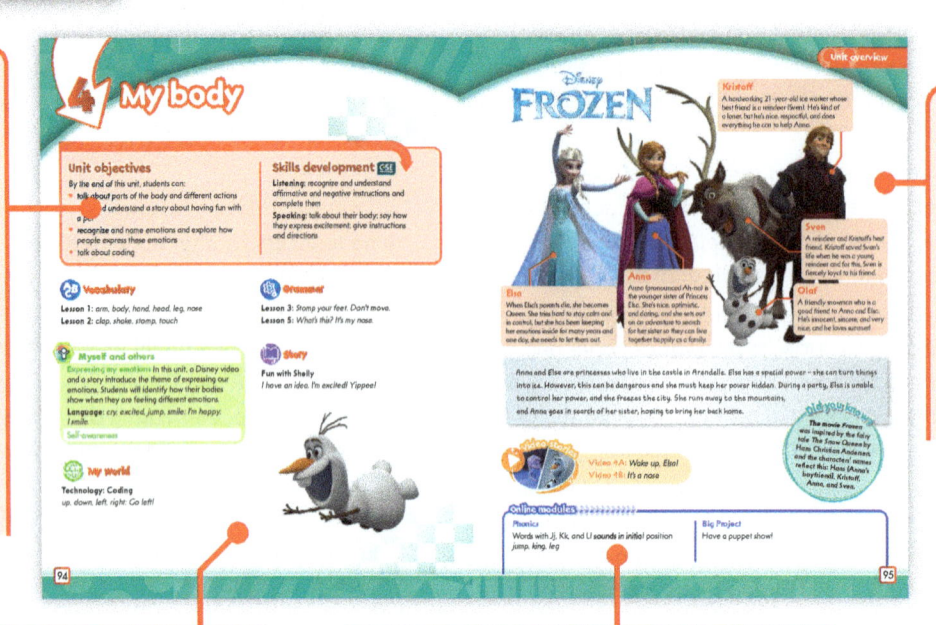

A brief synopsis of the Disney movie for the unit is provided for reference, along with an introduction to the main characters that appear in the unit. There is also a fun *Did you know?* fact for further background context.

A summary map highlights the linguistic content of the unit, and also lists the Personal and Social Skills and cross-curricular content.

There is an at-a-glance overview of the additional online modules and supporting components that can be used either in conjunction with the lessons or for extension.

Teacher toolkit

The Teacher toolkit sections in each of the lesson overviews provide key background information for feature lessons, as well as additional suggestions for how to enrich students' learning experience and extend the lesson content. The Teacher toolkit can be considered your "one-stop shop" for contextual support and creative, yet easy-to-implement ideas, for taking the lesson content beyond the book.

KEY

Engage Creative ideas that help students engage with and understand the lesson or unit aim. In Lesson 1, this takes the form of an idea that students can work on progressively across the unit, utilizing the unit language as they learn it.

Extend Practical and imaginative suggestions that expand the lesson focus, going beyond the book material or the board. In many cases, these ideas may be realia-based or real-world focused.

Home-school link Simple, take-home ideas for students to showcase English to their parents or caregivers, along with any preparation students can do for the following lessons.

Video/Story summaries (Lessons 1, 4, and 5) Concise summaries of the lesson video or story, reflecting Personal and Social Skills as relevant.

Teaching vocabulary/grammar (Lessons 2, 3, and 5) Support for presenting and practicing the new language, helping students make sense of and contextualize it, and addressing common errors.

Personal and Social Skills (Lessons 1, 4, and 6) Summaries of the Personal and Social Skills developed in the lessons, with ideas for how to explore and personalize the topics.

Cross-curricular (Lesson 7) Summaries, background information, and ideas for how to explore the cross-curricular content.

Remediation (Lesson 8) Ideal for extra practice of unit vocabulary or structures, for any students needing it.

Lesson notes

Why not make a note of the Teacher toolkit ideas and Teaching star tips that work best for you?

The lesson overviews include the objectives and GSE learning outcomes for the skills covered.

Lesson plans are clearly structured into stages, and include comprehensive instructions for delivering the Student's Book material, along with Warm-up, Wrap-up, and Extra activity ideas.

→ **My teacher progress journal**
Reflect on what worked best for you on p.208.

Presentation: This is the stage where the key focus of the lesson is introduced, for example, the new vocabulary or grammar structures.

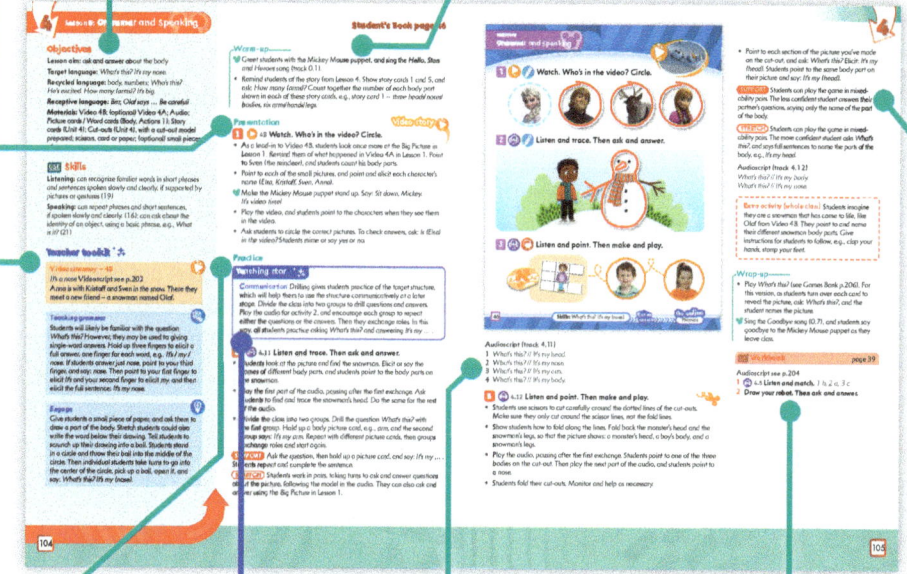

The *Support* and *Stretch* ideas help less confident students achieve a suitable activity output and provide more confident students with additional challenge.

Practice: This stage signals activities that practice elements relating to the lesson focus such as receptive listening, speaking with a partner, reading, and writing the answers to comprehension questions. Students may also be guided to produce language through various forms, for example, writing, speaking, acting, drawing, or making. Lesson 8 follows a different organization, providing consolidated skillswork practice of the unit content.

The class audioscript is provided for all listening activities, while the Workbook audioscripts can be found on p.204.

Answers to Student's Book activities are overlaid on the reduced Student's Book pages (or within the teaching notes). The Workbook answer key can be found in the Workbook section at the end of each lesson.

Teaching star

An activity-focused teaching tip, or a tip focused on a particular stage in the lesson flow, provides a concrete idea with an accompanying pedagogical reason. These helpful tips provide support in the following areas:

- Communication
- Classroom management
- Linguistic competence
- Diversity and inclusion
- Application
- Creativity
- Support understanding
- Social-emotional learning
- Growth mindset
- Learning to learn

Teacher's Book tour 31

Say hello!

Student's Book pages 4–5

Objectives

Lesson aim: say hello

Target language: Hello, (Nemo). Goodbye.

Receptive language: teacher, friends; It's …

Materials: Picture cards (Disney characters); Audio; Mickey Mouse puppet; (optional) students' teddy bears or toys; soft beanbag or small ball

GSE Skills

Listening: can understand short, simple classroom instructions (with pictures/gestures to help) (13); can sing a simple song, if supported by pictures (22)

Speaking: can use basic informal expressions for greeting and leave-taking, e.g., hello, hi, bye (10); can say a short, simple rhyme or chant from memory (16)

Teacher toolkit

Welcoming new people to class

In the first lesson, it's important to create a positive learning environment and to help students get to know each other. Say hello to each student individually, both as yourself and using the Mickey Mouse puppet. Encourage them to say hello back, or to smile or wave.

Relationship skills

Engage

Invite students to bring in their favorite teddy bear or toy. Invite them to use their toy to say hello or wave to the Mickey Mouse puppet. Sometimes shyer students can feel more comfortable communicating through a toy.

Some students may be very shy during the first few lessons, and may be reluctant to speak or interact with you or each other. Try to make students feel comfortable by providing a warm, friendly atmosphere, and avoid trying to make students speak or join in before they are ready to do so.

Home-school link

Encourage students to say hello to different people in their families and to tell them about the Mickey Mouse puppet.

Warm-up

- Greet students by saying: *Hello!* Tell students your name, if you haven't already done so.
- Show students your Student's Book, and say the title: *My Disney Stars and Heroes*. Students look at the pictures on the cover and say if they know any of the Disney characters, using the book and the picture cards.
- Introduce the Mickey Mouse puppet. Make Mickey say hello to students, and encourage students to say hello to Mickey.

Presentation

1 0.1 **Listen, sing, and act.**

- Say: *teacher*, and point to yourself.
- Play the song while students listen. If they wish to, they can clap their hands to the rhythm. As you sing, hold up the Mickey Mouse puppet, and make him wave to the class (*Hello, Friends.*), then to you (*Hello, Teacher.*). Then make Mickey wave to the Disney characters in the book or in the picture cards (*Hello, Heroes.*). Play the song again. Students wave to each other, to you, and to the Disney characters in their books or in the picture cards.
- Play the song again, and encourage students to join in with the words *Hello, hello*, and to wave to each other and to you as they sing. This song will be played at the beginning of each lesson. Bring out Mickey before you play the song each lesson, and ask him to say hello to the class.

Audioscript (track 0.1)

Hello, hello, hello, Friends. // Hello, hello, hello, Friends. // Hello, hello, hello, Teacher. // Hello, hello, hello, Heroes. // Hello, hello, hello, Teacher.

Practice

2 0.2 **Listen, point, and say.**

- Give students time to look at the characters on the page.
- Play the audio, pausing after each name for students to point to the character.
- Play the audio again. This time, when you pause, say: *Hello, (Nemo)!*, and encourage students to do the same. They can point to (Nemo) or wave to him.
- Say: *It's (Nemo)*, and ask the class to say: *Hello, (Nemo)!* all together.

Audioscript (track 0.2)

It's Nemo. … It's Merida. … It's Mike. … It's Forky. … It's Elsa. … It's Mulan. … It's Flick. … It's Belle. … It's Simba. … It's Judy.

Extra activity (whole class) Make the Mickey Mouse puppet say hello to each student. Encourage the student to say their own name, and make Mickey say: *Hello, (Akiko)*.

Say hello!

1. 🎵 Listen, sing, and act. TPR 🎵 Hello, Stars and Heroes
2. 🎧 Listen, point, and say.

- Nemo (W)
- Merida (1)
- Mike (2)
- Forky (3)
- Elsa (4)
- Mulan (5)
- Flik (6)
- Belle (7)
- Simba (8)
- Judy (9)

3 ✏️ Be a hero. Draw.

Name: _____

4 Collect your friends!

Teaching star

Communication Encourage students to learn each other's names during the first lesson. You can play a game like *Throw the ball* (see Games Bank p.206). Students sit in a circle and throw or roll a ball to each other. Each time they get the ball, they say their name. The other students say: *Hello, (name)*.

3 Be a hero. Draw.

- Using L1, explain that the Disney characters are our course heroes. Tell students that they can be heroes as they learn English, too!
- Model the activity by drawing a box on the board, then drawing a picture of yourself inside the box. Choose one or more of the Disney characters from the page, and draw them with you inside the box. Don't worry if your drawings aren't very accurate – this is an excellent way to show students that it doesn't matter if our drawings aren't very good and to promote a growth mindset.
- Ask students to draw a picture of themselves in their books.

SUPPORT Students at this age may still be learning to write their name. Write each student's name on a slip of paper for them to copy, if necessary. Students with large handwriting may have difficulty writing their name in the space provided. Allow them to use the white space next to the picture.

4 Collect your friends!

- Explain that students are to collect the Disney characters stickers as they progress through the course.

Wrap-up

- Place all ten picture cards on the board and elicit the names of each of the Disney characters. Then point to individual characters and elicit the names.
- Sing the *Goodbye* song (track 0.7). As you sing, hold the Mickey Mouse puppet, and make him wave to the class (*Goodbye, Friends*), then to you (*Goodbye, Teacher*), then to the different movie characters in the book (*Goodbye, Heroes*). At the end of the song, students wave to you and then line up ready to leave the classroom.
- Make Mickey say goodbye to each student individually as they leave class.

Audioscript (track 0.7)

Goodbye, goodbye, goodbye, Friends.
Goodbye, goodbye, goodbye, Teacher.
Goodbye, goodbye, goodbye, Heroes.
Goodbye, goodbye, goodbye, Teacher.

Welcome!

Unit objectives

By the end of this unit, students can:
- identify and name colors
- say greetings: *hello* and *goodbye*
- understand introductions and introduce themselves, using *I'm (name)*
- read and understand a story about the first day of school
- act out a story

Skills development

Listening: recognize and understand colors, greetings and introductions, and understand a short, simple cartoon story

Speaking: name colors; say *hello* and *goodbye*; introduce themselves

Vocabulary

Lesson 1: *black, blue, brown, green, orange, pink, purple, red, white, yellow*
Lesson 2: *class, welcome*

Grammar

Hello. / Hi. / Welcome, class!
Goodbye.
Hi, I'm (name).

Myself and others

Welcoming new people to class In this unit, a Disney video and a story introduce the theme of greeting new friends and introducing ourselves. Students will learn how to say their name and say hello to their new friends.
Language: *Hello/Hi, I'm …*

Relationship skills

Story

Hello, Class!
Hello. I'm (Maya).
Welcome, (Maya)!

Disney · PIXAR FINDING NEMO

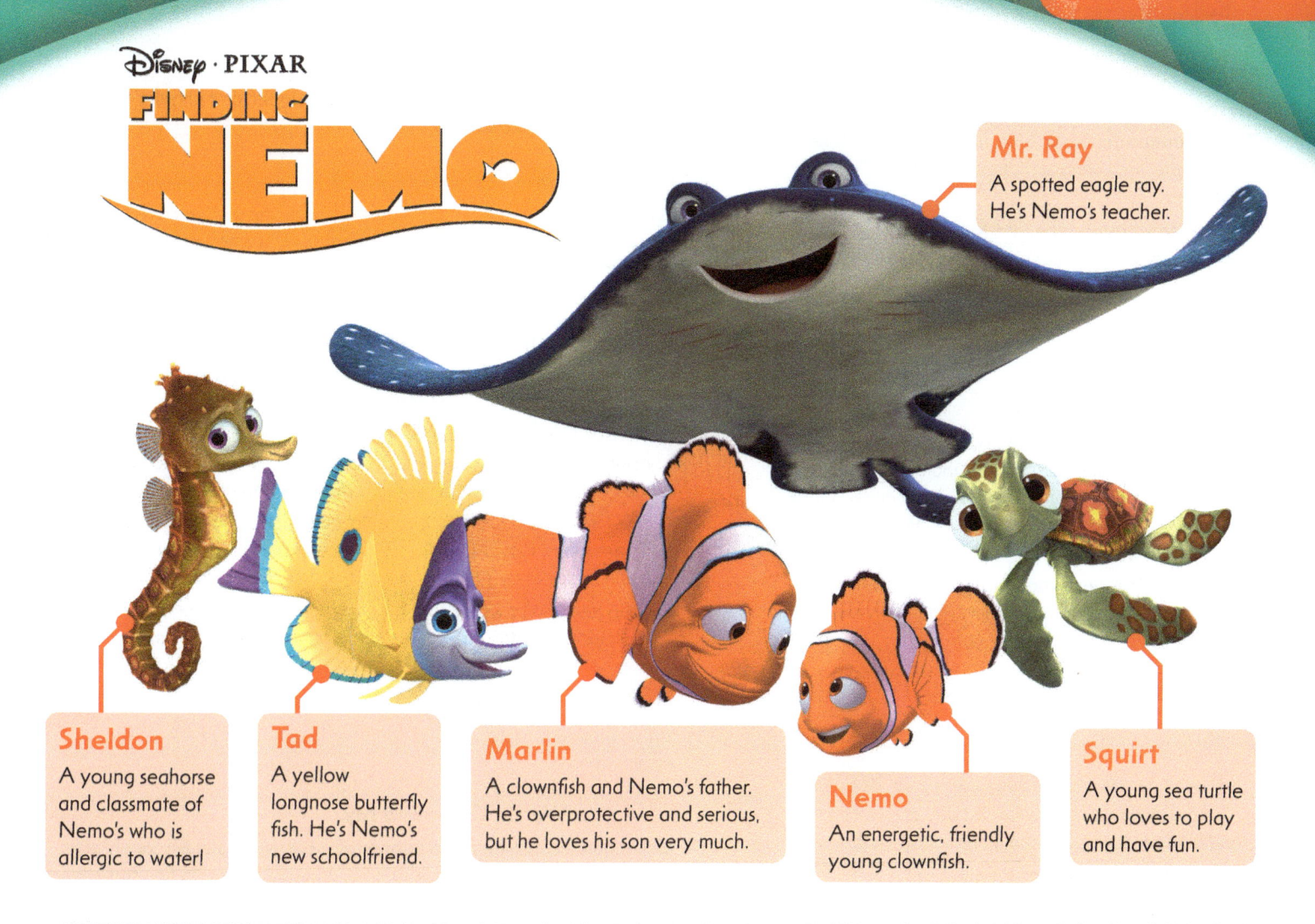

Unit overview

Mr. Ray
A spotted eagle ray. He's Nemo's teacher.

Sheldon
A young seahorse and classmate of Nemo's who is allergic to water!

Tad
A yellow longnose butterfly fish. He's Nemo's new schoolfriend.

Marlin
A clownfish and Nemo's father. He's overprotective and serious, but he loves his son very much.

Nemo
An energetic, friendly young clownfish.

Squirt
A young sea turtle who loves to play and have fun.

Nemo lives with his dad, Marlin, in the Great Barrier Reef off the coast of Australia. When Nemo goes to school, he shows off to his friends. He swims by himself beyond the reef, and he is captured in a net by a scuba diver. The scuba diver is a dentist, and he puts Nemo in an aquarium in his office in Sydney, Australia. Nemo makes friends with the fish and other sea creatures in the aquarium. Meanwhile, Marlin sets out to look for his son. Joined by a fish named Dory, Marlin travels a long way through the ocean and has many adventures. In the end, Nemo's friends in the fish tank help Nemo escape, and he is reunited with his dad in the ocean.

Video stories
Video 0A: Say hello with Nemo!

Did you know?
Nemo has a very small right fin. In the movie, he calls it his "lucky fin."

Lesson 1: Colors and greetings

Student's Book pages 6–7

Objectives

Lesson aim: name colors and introduce yourself

Target language: *black, blue, brown, green, orange, pink, purple, red, white, yellow; Goodbye, Hello/Hi; I'm (name).*

Receptive language: *It's time for school. Wow! Look at the fish. Wow! Ha, ha.*

Materials: Video 0A; Audio; Picture cards / Word cards (Colors, Disney characters); Sticker (Nemo); Mickey Mouse puppet

GSE Skills

Listening: can recognize isolated words related to familiar topics, if spoken slowly and clearly and supported by pictures and gestures (16); can recognize familiar words and phrases in short, simple songs or chants (18)

Speaking: can repeat single words, if spoken slowly and clearly (10); can recite a short, simple rhyme or chant (16)

Teacher toolkit

Video summary – 0A
Say hello *with Nemo!* **Videoscript see p.202**
Nemo wakes up early for his first day at school. He and his dad leave their home and set off on their way to school. They see lots of different-colored fish on the way. In the school playground, Nemo makes lots of new and interesting friends.

Engage
Create a display where you can stick pictures, students' work, and other visuals throughout the school year. To start with, you could ask students to think about their favorite movie or TV characters and draw pictures. At the end of this lesson, stick the picture cards on the display. In each unit you can change the picture cards, reviewing the words from the previous unit before you remove them.

Home-school link
Encourage students to point to and name the colors of different items they see at home.

Warm-up
- Greet students with the Mickey Mouse puppet, and sing the *Hello, Stars and Heroes* song (track 0.1).

Presentation

Picture cards / Word cards (optional) Show the picture cards one by one to introduce the new vocabulary. Repeat several times, encouraging students to remember the words. For Stretch students, show each word card, and elicit the words.

1 0.3 **Listen, point, and say. Then play.**
- Students look at the Big Picture. Introduce the movie and the characters: *This is the movie* Finding Nemo. *This is Nemo and Marlin. This is Sheldon* (the seahorse) / *Tad* (the yellow fish).
- Point to the colored stars on the page. Hold up a color picture card, say the color word, and students point to the corresponding colored star.
- Say: *Listen and point.* Play the audio, and students point to the corresponding colored stars. Play the audio again, pausing after each word. Students point again to the corresponding colored star and repeat the word.
- Then say a color word, and students repeat it and point to the corresponding star. Repeat with different colors several times, getting faster and faster each time.

Audioscript (track 0.3)
red … orange … blue … pink … green … purple … yellow … black … white … brown

2 0A **Watch. Color and say.** *Video story*
- Students look at the Big Picture once more. Make the Mickey Mouse puppet say each of the color words, and students try to find something in the picture for each color.
- Make Mickey stand up. Say: *Sit down, Mickey. It's video time!*
- Play Video 0A, and students watch and listen. Point to the picture of Pearl (the octopus), and ask: *What color?*, pointing to the color picture cards. Play the video again, pausing when Pearl appears [0:55]. Elicit the answer (*pink*).
- Students color the picture of Pearl in their books.

3 0A **Find and stick. Then circle who's in the video.**
- Demonstrate a TPR action for each character in the pictures: the seahorse – stand up with your arms by your sides and then wave your arms back and forth as if moving your tail; the manta ray – hold out both arms to the side as if gliding through the water; the turtle – flap your arms one after the other, alternately.
- Students look at the stickers and place them in the correct positions.
- Play the video again, and students do each character's TPR action when they see the character in the video. Then point to each sticker picture, and students do the mime if the character is in the video.

Welcome!

LESSON 1 Colors and greetings

1 Listen, point, and say. Then play. TPR

2 Watch. Color and say.

6   black, blue, brown, green, orange, pink, purple, red, white, yellow

3 Find and stick. Then circle who's in the video.

4 Listen and say.

5 Listen, chant, and act. TPR

♪ Hi, hello! ♪

Go to page 4

goodbye, hello, hi; I'm (name).   7

4 🎧 0.4 Listen and say.

- Point to Nemo in the Big Picture, and play the first sentence in the audio. Then point to the picture of Pearl in activity 2, and play the second sentence in the audio. Alternatively, play video 0A from 0:55 to 1:07 again.
- Play the audio again, pausing after the first sentence. Say: *Hello. I'm Nemo.*, and students repeat. They can mime swimming like Nemo. Then play the audio of the second sentence, and say: *Hello. I'm Pearl.* Students can mime moving their arms like an octopus's tentacles.
- Invite two confident students to act out the role-play. Then invite students to choose Nemo or Pearl and to say: *Hello, I'm (Nemo)*.

Audioscript (track 0.4)
Nemo says, "Hello. I'm Nemo."
Pearl says, "Hello. I'm Pearl."

5 🎵 0.5 Listen, chant, and act.

- Make the Mickey Mouse puppet say: *Hi, I'm Mickey.* Encourage students to respond *Hi*.
- Play the audio, and students listen and clap to the rhythm.
- Demonstrate the TPR actions. Play the audio again, and students join in with the chant and do the actions.

TPR chant
Hello – wave with your right hand
Hi – wave with your left hand
I'm … – point to yourself

Audioscript (track 0.5)
Hello. Hello. // Hi. Hi. Hi.
I'm … . // Goodbye. Goodbye.

❓ **Collect your friend** Show the picture card of Nemo to help students identify the correct sticker. Students stick the sticker on p.4 in the Student's Book. Ask: *Who's this?* (Nemo).

Wrap-up

- Play *Color hunt* (see Games Bank p.206). Say the name of a color, and students look for items of that color in the classroom.
- Sing the *Goodbye* song (track 0.7), and students say goodbye to the Mickey Mouse puppet as they leave class.

📖 **Workbook**   page 2

1 Look and color. Then say.
2 Draw and color your own fish. Say *Hello! I'm …*

Lesson 2: Greetings

Student's Book pages 8–9

Objectives

Lesson aim: listen to and understand a story about the first day of school

Target language: *Goodbye, Hello/Hi; I'm (name).; class, welcome*

Recycled language: colors

Receptive language: *I'm your teacher.*

Materials: Audio; Story cards (Welcome); (optional) paper; *My progress* poster

GSE Skills

Listening: can recognize a few familiar everyday nouns and adjectives (e.g., colors, numbers, classroom objects), if spoken slowly and clearly (10); can understand a few basic words and phrases in a story that is read aloud (18)

Speaking: can use basic informal expressions for greeting and leave-taking (e.g., *hello*, *hi*, *bye*) (10); can repeat phrases and short sentences, if spoken slowly and clearly (16)

Teacher toolkit

Story summary
It is the first day of school, and Maya, Leyla, Peter, and Cam meet each other and their teacher, Ms. Smart.

Engage
Students draw a picture of themselves for the class display. Depending on whether or not they are confident writers, they could write their name. Stick the pictures on the display, and invite students to introduce themselves.

Welcoming new people to class
In the story, it's the children's first day at school. Their teacher, Ms. Smart, invites everyone to introduce themselves and say hello. Encourage the students to say their names and say hello to each other and to the Mickey Mouse puppet.

Relationship skills

Warm-up

- Greet students with the Mickey Mouse puppet, and sing the *Hello, Stars and Heroes* song (track 0.1).
- Make Mickey act a little shy, e.g., hide Mickey behind a desk. Say: *Hello, Mickey. Say hello to the class.* Then invite the class to say *Hello, Mickey!*, and make Mickey slowly come out from his hiding place and wave happily to the class.
- Play *Where is …?* (see Games Bank p.206), using the color picture cards.

Presentation

1 Find and say.

- Point to the orange splotch, and elicit the color word. Then students look at the story pictures and try to find something orange. Repeat with the other splotches.

2 0.6 Listen and point.

- Introduce students to the four main characters before reading the story. Maya, Cam, Leyla, and Peter appear in the story in every unit. Students will get to know these characters during the course, but you can ask students to predict information about the characters now, and ask them to choose their favorite character (students' favorite character may change from unit to unit).
- Make the Mickey Mouse puppet stand up. Say: *Sit down, Mickey. It's story time!*
- Play the audio. Students listen to the story and follow in their books. As they listen to the exchange for each story frame, students point to each character as they speak. Pause as necessary to give students time to locate and point to the correct character in each of the story frames.
- Use the story cards to tell the story again, with or without the audio. Say each character's name, and students find him or her in the story cards.

Practice

3 Match and say the names.

- Point to the picture of Leyla. Say: *Hello, Leyla.* Students find Leyla in the story frames (frame 3). Point to the pictures of the backpack, the notepad, the paper plane, and the skirt. Then students look at story frame 3 again and find what Leyla has (the skirt). Ask: *What color?* (*pink*). Demonstrate how to use a pencil to draw a line to match the dot next to Leyla with the dot next to the skirt.
- Do the same with Cam, Maya, and Peter. Students match each of the characters with their belongings in the story. Encourage students to say the characters' names.

Teaching star

Linguistic competence Help students pronounce the characters' names by drilling as many times as necessary. Say each name slowly, and exaggerate the sounds, if necessary. Encourage students to copy you.

LESSON 2
Greetings

1 Find and say.

2 Listen and point.

Hello, Class!

Maya: Hello. I'm Maya.
Ms. Smart: Welcome, Maya!
Everyone: Hello, Maya.

Cam: Hello. I'm Cam.
Ms. Smart: Welcome, Cam!
Everyone: Hello, Cam.

Leyla: Hello. I'm Leyla.
Ms. Smart: Welcome, Leyla!
Everyone: Hello, Leyla.

Peter: Hello. I'm Peter.
Ms. Smart: Welcome, Peter!
Everyone: Hello, Peter.

Ms. Smart: Hello, class. I'm Ms. Smart. I'm your teacher.
Everyone: Hello, Teacher!

Say hello.

3 Match and say the names.

4 Act out the story.

5 Listen, sing, and act. **TPR** 🎵 Goodbye, goodbye 🎵

Hello, goodbye, I'm (name); class, welcome

---

4 Act out the story.
- Students look at the photos of the boy and the girl. Point to the girl, then point to the story, and elicit who she is role-playing (Leyla).
- Give each student a role: Maya, Cam, Leyla, or Peter, or let them choose which character they wish to role-play.
- Play the story audio, and students act out their character. Encourage them to say: Hello, I'm (Peter).

5 🎵 0.7 Listen, sing, and act.
Play the song, and students wave goodbye to the Mickey Mouse puppet, each other, and to you. (Play the Goodbye song at the end of every lesson, then put Mickey away.)

Audioscript (track 0.7)

Goodbye, goodbye, goodbye, Friends.
Goodbye, goodbye, goodbye, Teacher.
Goodbye, goodbye, goodbye, Heroes.
Goodbye, goodbye, goodbye, Teacher.

> **Extra activity (story extension)** Students choose and do one of the activities the children do in the story: draw a picture or make a paper plane. Then they say hello to another student and show them what they've made.

Wrap-up
- Play *Pass Mickey!* (see Games Bank p.206). Students sit in a circle and pass the Mickey Mouse puppet around the circle. Play music as they pass him around. Then pause the music, and students stop passing Mickey around. Hold up a picture card, and the student holding Mickey says the word. Then continue with the music, and students pass Mickey around the circle once more.
- Draw students' attention to the *My progress* poster, and ask them to identify the picture that reflects this unit. Read aloud with students the *I can …* statements (I can name colors. I can say hello).
- Sing the *Goodbye* song again (track 0.7), and students say goodbye to Mickey as they leave class.

Workbook   page 3

Audioscript see p.203

1 Match and color. Then say. *1 c, 2 b, 3 d, 4 a*
2 🎧 0.1 Listen and circle. Then say. *2 Maya*

> **Picture Dictionary**
> Students look at the Picture Dictionary on p.100 in the Student's Book and complete the activities. (**Answers:** 1 red, 2 blue, 3 black, 4 red, 5 yellow)

1 My family

Unit objectives
By the end of this unit, students can:
- talk about their family and ask and answer about their age
- read and understand a story about feeling different emotions
- recognize and name emotions and explore how to make other people happy
- talk about shadows

Skills development
Listening: recognize and understand family words and numbers, and simple questions and statements

Speaking: introduce their family, say their age, name emotions, talk about the weather and shadows

ABC Vocabulary
Lesson 1: brother, dad, mom, sister
Lesson 2: one, two, three, four, five, six

Grammar
Lesson 3: I'm six. Are you five? Yes./No.
Lesson 5: Who's this? This is my brother.

Myself and others
Identifying my emotions 1 In this unit, a Disney video and a story introduce the theme of identifying emotions. Students will learn how to recognize the basic emotions they feel in different situations.
Language: happy, sad; Are you happy? I'm sad.

Self-awareness

Story
A new friend
friend, happy, sad; Oh, no!

My world
Science: Shadows
cloudy, shadows, sunny

Disney · PIXAR
BRAVE

Unit overview

King Fergus
Merida's father, the king. He's a big, strong warrior who hates bears!

Queen Elinor
Merida's mother, the queen. She's wise, measured, and diplomatic, and is the real leader of the land.

Merida
The intrepid, adventurous daughter of the king and queen. She's independent, feisty, and courageous.

Angus
Merida's beloved horse.

The triplets
Merida's younger brothers. They're always up to mischief, and they love cake!

Merida is the brave daughter of the king and queen, and she loves spending time outdoors, shooting arrows, and climbing mountains. However, Merida's future has already been planned out: she's expected to marry a lord, and Merida isn't happy with this plan. But things don't turn out as expected.

Did you know?
Disney designed a new tartan pattern for the Dunbroch clan and registered it with the Scottish Register of Tartans.

Video stories
Video 1A: *Merida's family*
Video 1B: *Who's this?*

Online modules

Phonics
Words with Aa, Bb, and Cc sounds in initial position
apple, bear, cake

Big Project
Make a family portrait

41

1 Lesson 1: Vocabulary

Student's Book pages 10–11

Objectives

Lesson aim: name family members
Target language: *brother, dad, mom, sister*
Recycled language: colors, greetings; *Hello, I'm …*
Receptive language: *cake, bear, happy; They love stories. This is (mom). Here's …*
Materials: Video 1A; Audio; Picture cards / Word cards (Family, Disney characters); Sticker (Merida); Mickey Mouse puppet; (optional) students' family photos

GSE Skills

Listening: can recognize isolated words related to familiar topics, if spoken slowly and clearly and supported by pictures and gestures (16); can understand simple language related to naming and describing family members (21)

Speaking: can say single words related to familiar topics, if supported by pictures or gestures (18)

Teacher toolkit

Video summary – 1A

Merida's family **Videoscript see p.202**
Merida lives happily with her mom, dad, and three younger brothers in a castle. One day, Merida's mom turns into a bear. Merida and her mom go fishing in the river and have lots of fun.

Engage

Students bring in photos of their family members or draw pictures of them. Create a display of students' pictures, and use this display to practice new vocabulary and structures during the unit.

Identifying my emotions 1

happy, sad
Talk about Merida's feelings and behavior in the video story. Say: *Imagine you're Merida. You're happy!* Students mime what Merida does when she's happy in the video story, e.g., tell stories, eat cake, play games. Then students point to other things in the video that make them feel happy. This will develop students' empathy with the characters, and will help them understand their own feelings and behavior.

Self-awareness

Warm-up

Greet students with the Mickey Mouse puppet, and sing the *Hello, Stars and Heroes* song (track 0.1).

Presentation

- Students look at the Big Picture. Introduce the movie and the characters: *This is the movie Brave. This is Merida. This is King Fergus / Queen Elinor.*
- Point to different items in the picture, e.g., grass, castle, and ask: *What color?* (*green, brown,* etc.).

1 **1A Watch. Who's in the video? Check (✓).**

- Make the Mickey Mouse puppet stand up. Say: *Sit down, Mickey. It's video time! Let's watch!*
- Play Video 1A, and students watch and listen.
- Play the video again, pausing when you see Merida's dad [0:34] and Merida's mom [0:54]. Point to the picture of the character in the book, then point to the screen, and elicit *yes* or *no* with a TPR response (*yes* – nod head, *no* – shake head from left to right). Then point to the picture of the horse in the book, and elicit *no*.
- Students check the correct pictures.

2 **1A Circle for Merida.**

- Use facial expression and mime to pre-teach *happy* and *sad*, and students copy you.
- Point to each small picture, and ask: *happy or sad?* Use the accompanying mime to support understanding. Students point to and say the correct word for each picture.
- Ask: *Is Merida happy or sad?* Play the video again, pausing at 1:47 to elicit the answer (*happy*).
- Ask students to circle the correct picture.

Picture cards / Word cards (optional) Show the picture cards one by one to introduce the new vocabulary. Repeat several times, encouraging students to remember the words. For Stretch students, then show each word card, and elicit the words.

Practice

3 **1.1 Listen, find, and say. Then play.**

- Students explore the Big Picture. Point to and say the family words: *sister, dad, mom,* and *brother*.
- Play the audio, pausing after each word. Students point to the family member in the Big Picture. Check that they are pointing to the correct person. Play the audio again, pausing for students to say the words. Play the audio a third time, and students say and point to the family members.
- Point to different people in the Big Picture, and students say the correct words.

1 My family

LESSON 1 Vocabulary

1 ▶ Watch. Who's in the video? Check (✓).

2 Circle for Merida.

3 🎧 Listen, find, and say. Then play.

4 🎵 Listen, chant, and act. **TPR**

🎵 Hello, Mom! 🎵

brother, dad, mom, sister

Go to page 4

SUPPORT Point to different people in the Big Picture, and say the words. Students repeat the words.

STRETCH Students work in pairs, taking turns to point to a family member for their partner to name.

Audioscript (track 1.1)
1 sister // 2 dad // 3 mom // 4 brother

4 🎵 **1.2 Listen, chant, and act.**

- Place the family picture cards around the classroom. Say: *Hello, (Mom)!*, and wave to the *mom* picture card. Repeat with the other picture cards.
- Play the audio, demonstrate the TPR action (*hello* – wave your hand), and students listen to the chant, waving when they hear *hello*.
- Play the audio again. Students join in with the chant and wave to the corresponding picture cards around the classroom. For the last line, students wave to the whole class.

Audioscript (track 1.2)
Hello, Mom! Hello, hello. *(x2)*
Hello, Dad! Hello, hello. *(x2)*
Hello, Sister! Hello, Sister!
Hello, Brother! Hello, Brother!
Hello, hello, everyone!

Collect your friend Show the picture card of Merida to help students identify the correct sticker. Students stick the sticker on p.4 in the Student's Book. Ask: *Who's this?* (Merida).

Wrap-up

- Play *Talk to Mickey* (see Games Bank p.206) with the Mickey Mouse puppet and the family picture cards. Make Mickey say: *Hello, (brother)!*, and the student with the *brother* picture card responds: *Hello, Mickey!*
- Sing the *Goodbye* song (track 0.7), and students say goodbye to Mickey as they leave class.

Workbook pages 4–5

Audioscript see p.203

1 **Watch again. Then circle.**
   1 Find the cake in the video. *a*
   2 Who is a bear? *a*
   3 Merida's brothers are … *a*
2 🎧 **1.1 Listen, find, and color. Then say.** *mom – blue, brother – green, sister – red, dad – black*
3 **Challenge! Color and say.**

43

Lesson 2: Vocabulary

Student's Book page 12

Objectives

Lesson aim: say numbers 1–6
Target language: *one, two, three, four, five, six*
Recycled language: colors, family
Materials: Audio; Picture cards / Word cards (Family, Numbers 1); Stickers; Mickey Mouse puppet; (optional) number blocks or number lines, a photo of a cake

GSE Skills

Listening: can recognize cardinal numbers up to ten in short phrases and sentences spoken slowly and clearly (10)
Speaking: can use cardinal numbers up to ten (10); can say how many things there are up to ten (13)

Teacher toolkit

Teaching vocabulary
Make a game out of vocabulary practice. Hide a number of fingers behind your back, and students guess how many. Play the game, either all together as a class, or students play in pairs.

Extend
Help students make connections to the CLIL subject math. If you have number blocks, number lines, or other realia used in math class, use these to elicit and practice the numbers. You could also set up a scavenger hunt: students find and count the number of a specified item, e.g., ball, in the classroom.

Home-school link
Encourage students to count different items in their home or things they see when they are out and about, e.g., the number of dogs in the park. They count and say how many to their families.

Warm-up

- Greet students with the Mickey Mouse puppet, and sing the *Hello, Stars and Heroes* song (track 0.1).
- Make Mickey hold up each of the family picture cards, and students wave and say hello to each of the family members, e.g., *Hello, sister!*
- Say: *Listen and chant!*, and play the chant from Lesson 1 (track 1.2). Students join in with the chant and do the actions.

Presentation

Picture cards / Word cards (optional) Show the number picture cards one by one to introduce the new vocabulary. Repeat several times, encouraging students to remember the words. For Stretch students, then show each word card, and elicit the words.

> **Teaching star**
>
> **Support understanding** After showing the cake to the Mickey Mouse puppet (see activity 1), pretend to take the cake from the picture and eat it. Say: *Mmm … one cake!* Then pretend to take more cakes from the picture, and hand these invisible cakes to students, counting up to six: *one cake, two cakes, three cakes*, etc.

1 1.3 **Listen, point, and stick. Then play.**

- Show students a photo of a cake. Put the cake photo near the Mickey Mouse puppet, and make him act enthusiastically. Ask: *Is Mickey happy?* (yes) *Why?* Encourage students to point to the photo of the cake.
- Say: *How many cakes? Listen and point.* Play the audio, and students point to the corresponding pictures. After number two, say: *one, two*, then point to the sticker space. Play the rest of the audio, and do the same after *four*.
- Play the audio again, and students stick the cake stickers in the spaces. Play the audio a third time, pausing after each number. Students point to the corresponding pictures and repeat the words.

SUPPORT Say a number from one to six, e.g., *four*. Students find the corresponding picture and then count the cakes all together as a class, e.g., *one–two–three–four*.

STRETCH Students play a game in pairs. One student says a number from one to six, e.g., *four*, and the other student points to the corresponding picture and counts, e.g., *one–two–three–four*.

Audioscript (track 1.3)

one … two … three … four … five … six

Practice

2 1.4 **Listen and show. Then play.**

- Point to the photo, and ask: *How many?* (four). Show students how to use their fingers to count from one to six.
- Play the audio, and pause for students to hold up the correct number of fingers.

44

LESSON 2
Vocabulary

1 🎧 💬 **Listen, point, and stick. Then play.**

2 🎧 💬 **Listen and show. Then play.**

3 💬 **Count, clap, and say.** TPR

one, two, three, four, five, six

- Play the game all together as a class. Make the Mickey Mouse puppet choose a number picture card. Make Mickey say the number, and students hold up the correct number of fingers. Then invite one or more students to hold Mickey and choose a number.

SUPPORT Say a number, then count with students from one up to this number, e.g., *Four! One–two–three–four.* Students hold up each finger in turn until they have (four).

STRETCH Students play the game in pairs, taking turns to say a number for their partner to show using their fingers.

Audioscript (track 1.4)
four … six … three … five … two … one

3 **Count, clap, and say.**
- Hold up one finger, then clap once. Say: *one*. Repeat with *two, three, four, five, six*.
- Point to the first picture, and count the arrows all together as a class (*one, two, three, four, five*). Then clap five times, and say: *five*.
- Point to the second picture, and students work on their own to count the items (*two*). Then students clap twice and say *two*. Do the same with the third picture (*three*).

SUPPORT Do the whole activity all together as a class. Count the items in each picture, then clap the same number of times, and say the number.

STRETCH Students work in pairs to count the items in each picture, clap the same number of times, and say the number.

> **Extra activity (class game)** Play *Color hunt!* (see Games Bank p.206). Say the name of a color, and students look for items of that color in the classroom and count them. Repeat with other colors.

Wrap-up
- Play *Mickey says …* (see Games Bank p.206). Make the Mickey Mouse puppet say a number from one to six, and students clap the same number of times.
- Sing the *Goodbye* song (track 0.7), and students say goodbye to Mickey as they leave class.

Workbook page 6

Audioscript see p.203
1 **Follow and count cakes. Then say.** Students count as they follow the cupcakes.
2 🎧 **1.2 Match and color. Then listen and say.**
1 purple, 2 blue, 3 red, 4 green, 5 yellow, 6 orange

> **Picture Dictionary**
> Students look at the Picture Dictionary on p.101 in the Student's Book and complete the activities. (*Answer:* 3)

Lesson 3: Grammar

Student's Book page 13

Objectives

Lesson aim: talk about how old you are
Target language: *I'm six. Are you five? Yes./No.*
Recycled language: numbers
Materials: Audio; Picture cards / Word cards (Family, Numbers 1); Mickey Mouse puppet

GSE Skills

Listening: can understand the main information when people introduce themselves, e.g., name, age, where they are from (19); can understand simple questions about personal information, e.g., name or age, if spoken slowly and clearly (20)

Speaking: can say how old they are using a basic phrase (12); can recite a short, simple rhyme or chant (16)

Teacher toolkit

Teaching grammar
Show students a TPR action to help them identify questions and answers. Question: hold up your index finger, then bend it down twice quickly (ASL). Answer: hold up both index fingers in front of you, and point towards the class. Once students know these signs, you can use them to prompt questions and answers from the class or from individual students.

Engage
Students draw a picture of themselves with the same number of balloons as their age. If students already drew pictures of themselves for the class display (see Welcome unit), they could just draw the balloons and stick these above their picture.

Differentiation
Some students may not yet be ready to ask questions or to answer orally. Try not to pressure students into speaking if they don't feel comfortable. Instead, allow them to demonstrate receptive understanding of the structures by holding up a specified number of fingers.

Warm-up
- Greet students with the Mickey Mouse puppet, and sing the *Hello, Stars and Heroes* song (track 0.1).
- Review numbers one to six from Lesson 2. Hold up a series of random number picture cards, and students jump the correct number of times on the spot.

Presentation

1 Sing-along   1.5 Listen and point. Then sing and act.

- Point to the picture, and ask: *Who's this?* (Cam and Maya).
- Students look at the picture more closely. Point to Cam's hands, and ask: *How many fingers?* Demonstrate by counting with your fingers: *one–two–three … four–five.* Then point to Maya's hands, and do the same, counting with your fingers: *one–two–three … four–five–six.*
- Play the song audio. Pause after each verse, and students point to the correct character.
- Demonstrate the TPR actions. Then play the song again, and students do the TPR actions and clap to the beat of the song.
- Play the song a third time, and encourage students to join in with some of the words as they do the TPR actions and dance. When students are confident with the words, play the karaoke version (track 1.5_karaoke), and students sing along.

TPR song
numbers – hold up the correct number of fingers
Oh, yeah! – jump / pump your fist

Audioscript (track 1.5)

Sing with me. *(x3)* // One, two, three.
I'm five, I'm five. // Are you five? // Yes, I'm five!
Sing with me. *(x3)* // Four, five, six.
I'm six, I'm six. // Are you six? // Yes, I'm six!
Sing with me. *(x3)* // One, two, three.
Sing with me. *(x3)* // Four, five, six.
Oh, yeah!

Teaching star
Linguistic competence Help students use an appropriate intonation in questions by using an exaggerated, sing-song voice. Use your hand to show how the tone moves up and down.

Practice

2   1.6 Listen and find. Then ask and answer.

- Students look again at Cam and Maya in the picture in activity 1. Ask: *Who is five?* (show five fingers) *Cam or Maya?* (Cam) *Who is six?* (show six fingers) *Cam or Maya?* (Maya).

Sing-along

1 🎵 **Listen and point. Then sing and act.** TPR

Sing with me

2 🎧 💬 **Listen and find. Then ask and answer.**

3 🎧 💬 **Listen and color. Then play.**

Song: I'm (six). Are you (five)? Yes./No.

13

- Play the audio, pausing after each exchange. Students point to the correct child in the picture (1 – Cam, 2 – Maya). Play the first part of the audio again, and pause after the question. Point to Cam and ask: *Are you six?* Elicit yes/no or a TPR response, then play the answer. Do the same with the second exchange. Play each line of the audio again. Students say yes/no or answer with a TPR response, and say: *I'm (five/six)*.

SUPPORT Students answer each question with yes/no or a TPR response, and they hold up the correct number of fingers.

STRETCH Students role-play the dialog. Play the audio, and students work in pairs to repeat the questions and the answers.

Audioscript (track 1.6)

1 **Maya:** *Are you six?*
   Cam: *No, I'm five.*
2 **Cam:** *Are you six?*
   Maya: *Yes, I'm six.*

LESSON 3
Grammar

3 🎧 **1.7 Listen and color. Then play.**

- Play the audio, and pause after the first exchange. Demonstrate by coloring four balloons. Play the rest of the audio, pausing after each exchange for students to color the correct number of balloons in each picture.
- Play the audio again, pausing after each question and each sentence for students to repeat it. Drill the question *Are you (four)?* as many times as necessary, until students can repeat this confidently.
- Play the game. Silently, choose one of the pictures. Invite different students to ask *Are you …?* questions to find out which picture you have chosen. Continue until a student guesses correctly.

SUPPORT If students have difficulty using the full question form *Are you …?*, encourage them to say only the number.

STRETCH Students play the game in pairs, taking turns to choose a picture silently and to ask questions to guess the picture.

Audioscript (track 1.7)

1 Are you four? // Yes, I'm four.
2 Are you three? // Yes, I'm three.
3 Are you six? // No, I'm five.

Extra activity (class survey) Do a class survey. Ask each student questions with *Are you …?* to find out how old they are. Invite confident students to ask questions for you. Draw a chart on the board to show the age range of your students, then add a check mark next to each number for each answer.

Wrap-up

- Play *Mickey's card* (see Games Bank p.206) with the number picture cards and the Mickey Mouse puppet. Students take turns to guess how old Mickey is, e.g., *Are you (five)?*
- Sing the *Goodbye* song (track 0.7), and students say goodbye to Mickey as they leave class.

📝 **Workbook** page 7

Audioscript see p.203

1 🎧 **1.3 Listen and color.** *1 five, 2 three, 3 six*
2 **Trace, color, and match. Then say.** *1 b, I'm six.; 2 a, I'm two.; 3 c, I'm five.*

47

Lesson 4: Story

Student's Book pages 14–15

Objectives

Lesson aim: listen to and understand a story about feeling different emotions

Story language: *friend, happy, sad; Oh, no!*

Recycled language: *numbers; I'm (six).*

Receptive language: *This is my friend. Look. Come here.*

Materials: Audio; Picture cards (Characters); Story cards (Unit 1); Mickey Mouse puppet; (optional) a cap, a teddy bear

GSE Skills

Listening: can understand a few basic words and phrases in a story that is read aloud (18)

Speaking: can repeat phrases and short sentences, if spoken slowly and clearly (16)

Teacher toolkit

Story summary

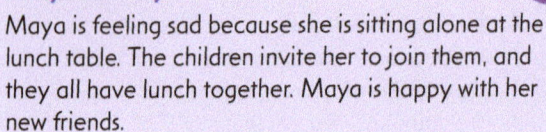

Maya is feeling sad because she is sitting alone at the lunch table. The children invite her to join them, and they all have lunch together. Maya is happy with her new friends.

Engage

Students draw a picture of a friend. This could be a real person or a teddy bear, like Ted in the story. Invite students to show their picture and say how they feel with their friend.

Identifying my emotions 1

In the story, Maya feels both happy and sad. Students show you their happy and sad faces. Say: *You're (happy)!*, and students smile. Do the same for *sad*. Use the Mickey Mouse puppet to model corresponding body language, e.g., *happy*: head raised, arms out to the sides, bouncing or clapping; *sad*: head down, arms down or folded.

Self-awareness

Warm-up

- Greet students with the Mickey Mouse puppet, and sing the *Hello, Stars and Heroes* song (track 0.1). If you have a cap, put it on Mickey's head.
- Show the character picture cards and elicit the characters' names. Alternatively, say their names, and students point to the correct characters (Maya, Leyla, Cam, and Peter).

Presentation

1 🎧 **1.8 Listen to the story. Point to Maya.**

- Make the Mickey Mouse puppet stand up. Say: *Sit down, Mickey. It's story time!*
- Point to the small picture of Maya and elicit her name and her age (*six*). Students find Maya in the story frames.
- Play the audio. Students listen to the story and follow in their books. As they listen to the exchange for each story frame, they point to Maya in the picture.
- Use the story cards to tell the story again, with or without the audio. Pause after each story frame to ask a comprehension question, e.g., *How many children are here?* (four) *Where's the teacher?* (students point) *Where's Maya?* (students point) *Is Maya happy?* (no) *Who's Ted?* (students point) *Is Maya happy now?* (yes).

Spot! Students find the apple juice in the story. (**Answer:** story frames 1, 4, and 6)

Teaching star

Diversity and inclusion Students may not have much experience reading comic stories, and some students may have specific learning differences like dyslexia or AD(H)D, which can make following a story challenging. Point to and say the number in each frame, and show students how we move from one story frame to the next. Ask them to move their finger through the frames as you play the audio.

Practice

2 🎧 **1.9 Who says it? Listen, circle, and say.**

- Stick the picture cards for Maya and Cam on the board. Play the first part of the audio, then pause, and students point to Maya. Students circle the picture of Maya in their books.
- Do the same for the second and third parts of the audio, with Leyla and Cam, then Ms. Smart and Peter.
- Give each student a role: Maya, Cam, Peter, or Ms. Smart. Play the audio, and students act out the scene.

STRETCH Students repeat the lines from the story as they act out the scene.

Audioscript (track 1.9)

1 **Maya:** *One, two, three, four. Oh, no.*
2 **Cam:** *Ted's one.*
3 **Ms. Smart:** *Are you happy, Maya?*

48

LESSON 4
Story

A new friend

1 Listen to the story. Point to 😊.

① **Maya:** One, two, three, four. Oh, no!
② **Ms. Smart:** Maya! Are you sad?
Maya: Yes, I'm sad.
③ **Ms. Smart:** Look, Maya's sad.
Cam: Oh, no!
④ **Cam:** Maya! Come here.
⑤ **Cam:** This is my friend, Ted. Ted's one.
Maya: And I'm six. Hello, Ted.
⑥ **Ms. Smart:** Are you happy, Maya?
Maya: Yes! I'm happy!

The end

2 Who says it? Listen, circle, and say.

3 Look and draw 😊 or 🙁.

4 Act out the story.

Story: friend, happy, sad; Oh, no!

---

3 Look and draw 😊 or 🙁.
- Point to each picture of Maya, and ask: *Is she happy or sad?*, miming each emotion. Then draw a happy face and a sad face on the board.
- Students draw a happy mouth or a sad mouth to complete each emoji.

4 Act out the story.
- Students look at the photos of children. Ask: *Is he/she happy or sad?* Then students find a story frame where Maya feels happy and a story frame where she feels sad.
- Students stand up to act out the story. Show the first story card, and students copy Maya's posture, holding the lunch tray. Then they copy her worried/sad expression.
- Play the story audio (track 1.8), and hold up the corresponding story cards. Students act out Maya's role as they listen. Point to Maya on each story card for support.

SUPPORT Allow students to act out the story silently.
STRETCH Pause the audio after each line for students to repeat the lines together.

Extra activity (story extension) Give each group of students a story card. Each group acts out the scene on their story card, and the other students point in their books to the correct story frame.

Wrap-up
- Place the story cards on the board. Make the Mickey Mouse puppet say a line from one of the story frames, e.g., *Maya! Come here!* Invite a student to come up and touch the correct story card. Repeat with other lines and different students.
- Sing the *Goodbye* song (track 0.7), and students say goodbye to Mickey as they leave class.

📝 Workbook page 8

Audioscript see p.203
1. 1.4 **Listen and circle.** *1 a, 2 b*
2. **Match. Then say for Cam.** *1 b, 2 a*

Lesson 5: Grammar and Speaking

Student's Book page 16

Objectives

Lesson aim: talk about families
Target language: *Who's this? This is my brother.*
Recycled language: *family; numbers*
Receptive language: *bow, forest, fun, present*
Materials: Video 1B; Audio; Picture cards / Word cards (Family, Characters); Story cards (Unit 1); Cut-outs (Unit 1), with a cut-out model prepared; Mickey Mouse puppet; scissors, tape, (optional) photos of your family

GSE Skills

Listening: can understand simple language related to naming and describing family members (21)
Speaking: can name everyday objects, animals, or people around them or in pictures, using single words (18)

Teacher toolkit

Video summary – 1B
Who's this? **Videoscript see p.202**
We meet a young Merida and her family outside the castle. Merida's dad gives her a bow, and she practices shooting arrows. Merida misses the target and goes to search for her arrow in the forest.

Teaching grammar
Bring in photos of people in your family, and use the target language to introduce them: *Who's this? This is my … .* Then ask students to imagine they are you. Ask: *Who's this?*, and encourage them to say *This is my …* and the corresponding family word.

Extend
Make a class family tree display. Create a tree background, and then give students small pieces of paper cut out in the shape of apples (or circles). On each shape, they draw one person from their family. Stick on the tree all of students' completed shapes. Then ask the class questions about the people on the tree: *Who's this?*, and encourage the corresponding student to answer: *This is my … .*

Warm-up

- Greet students with the Mickey Mouse puppet, and sing the *Hello, Stars and Heroes* song (track 0.1).
- Remind students of the story from Lesson 4. Make Mickey show one of the story cards, point at different characters, and ask: *Who's this?* Demonstrate meaning by doing a TPR action: shrug your shoulders and put your hands facing upwards. Invite different students to say the names of the characters.

Presentation

1 ▶ **1B Watch. Who gives a bow? Circle.**

- As a lead-in to Video 1B, ask students to look once more at the Big Picture in Lesson 1, and remind them of the movie *Brave*. Point to Merida, mom, dad, and the brothers, do the TPR action, and ask: *Who's this?* Invite different students to answer.
- Ask students to look at each of the small pictures, and ask again: *Who's this?* Students answer *Merida, mom, dad*.
- Point to the small picture of the bow, and mime giving it to the Mickey Mouse puppet. Ask: *Who gives a bow?*, and do the TPR action again.
- Make Mickey stand up. Say: *Sit down, Mickey. It's video time!*
- Play the video, pausing after Merida's dad gives her the bow [1:06]. Ask again: *Who gives a bow?*, and point to the small pictures. Students answer *dad*, then they circle the correct picture.

Practice

2 🎧 **1.10 Listen and find. Then ask and answer.**

- Show students the picture card for Cam. Ask: *Who's this?* (*Cam*). Point to the picture and say: *This is Cam's family.*
- Play the audio, and students point to each person in the picture.
- Play the audio again, pausing after each exchange for students to repeat the last word: *sister, mom, dad, brother*.
- Play the audio a third time, pausing after *This is my …*, for students to say the correct family word, e.g., *sister*. If your students are familiar with the language, encourage them to say the full sentence.
- Point to a person in the picture, and ask: *Who's this?* Students say the answer to the student sitting next to them.

SUPPORT Students answer your questions all together as a class. Prompt as needed by saying *This is my … .* (*sister*).

STRETCH Students work in pairs to ask and answer questions about the picture, following the model in the audio.

Audioscript (track 1.10)
1 **Peter:** *Who's this?*
 Cam: *This is my sister.*
2 **Peter:** *Who's this?*
 Cam: *This is my mom.*
3 **Peter:** *Who's this?*
 Cam: *This is my dad.*
4 **Peter:** *Who's this?*
 Cam: *This is my brother.*

LESSON 5
Grammar and Speaking

1 ▶ ✏️ Watch. Who gives a ✂️? Circle.

2 🎧 💬 Listen and find. Then ask and answer.

3 🎧 💬 Listen and say. Then make and play.

Skills: Who's this? This is my (brother).

>> Extra Lesson >>>>> Go online Phonics

16

Teaching star

Communication Making communication real and relevant to students' lives is more likely to motivate them to talk. Ask students to bring in family photos like Cam's, then ask them to present their families to the class. Encourage students to share information, such as their family members' names and ages.

3 🎧 1.11 **Listen and say. Then make and play.**

- Show students the finger puppets you have made. For each finger puppet, ask: Who's this? Students say which family members they think they are.
- Play the audio, and students listen and repeat the sentences.
- Students use scissors to cut carefully around the dotted lines of the cut-outs. Tell students to draw any family member they like, then cut out their puppets. As they work, monitor and help as necessary.
- Help students stick the puppets together with tape, and then place them on their fingers.

- Students work in pairs, taking turns to ask and answer about their puppets: Who's this? This is my (mom).
- **SUPPORT** Students can play the game in mixed-ability pairs, with the less confident student saying only the family name of each of the puppets, e.g., sister.
- **STRETCH** Students can play the game in mixed-ability pairs. The more confident student asks What's this?, and says full sentences about each of the puppets, e.g., This is my sister.

Audioscript (track 1.11)
Who's this? // This is my dad.
Who's this? // This is my sister.

> **Extra activity (video extension)** Tell students to choose a character from Video 1B in activity 1 (Merida, mom, dad). Play the video again, and students role-play their character.

Wrap-up

- Play What's this? (see Games Bank p.206). Place all the family picture cards face-down. Say a word and invite a student to find the corresponding picture card. As the students turns over each card to reveal the picture, ask him/her to say the word. Ask the class to say yes or no. Repeat with different students.
- 🎵 Sing the Goodbye song (track 0.7), and students say goodbye to the Mickey Mouse puppet as they leave class.

📝 Workbook   page 9

Audioscript see p.203

1 🎧 **1.5 Look and match. Then listen and check.**
1 c, 2 d, 3 b, 4 a

2 Draw your family. Then ask and answer.

Lesson 6: Myself and others

Happy and sad Student's Book page 17

Objectives

Lesson aim: recognize and name emotions
Target language: *Are you happy? I'm sad.*
Recycled language: *no, yes; happy, sad*
Materials: Audio; (optional) Video 1A; *Myself and others* poster; Stickers; Mickey Mouse puppet; (optional) cards for Teacher toolkit

GSE Skills

Listening: can recognize isolated words related to familiar topics, if spoken slowly and clearly and supported by pictures or gestures (16); can get the gist of a simple song, if supported by gestures (21)

Speaking: can sing a simple song, if supported by pictures (22); can ask people how they are using a basic phrase (14)

Teacher toolkit

Identifying my emotions 1

In this lesson, students explore how to cheer each other up when they feel sad. At this age, students can understand basic emotional expressions and situations. Use the Mickey Mouse puppet to help students connect the lesson to real life actions. Make Mickey look sad. Invite individual students to help Mickey feel happy again. They can give him a hug, sing, and dance for him, etc.

Self-awareness

Extend

Set up a system where students can express how they feel during a lesson. You could give each student a "feelings card," with a happy face on one side of the card and a sad face on the other side of the card. Ask students to keep the card on their desk. When they are having trouble doing an activity or feeling sad, they place the card with the sad face facing up. As you monitor the class, pay attention to the "feelings cards," and check in with any students who need it, encouraging them to name their emotion, e.g., *I feel sad.*

Home-school link

Tell students to find something that makes them feel happy at home. This could be a toy, a place, some food, or even a person. When they find it, they say to their families: *I'm happy!*

Warm-up

- Greet students with the Mickey Mouse puppet, and say the *Hi, hello!* chant (track 0.5).
- Review *happy* and *sad*, using Mickey. Make Mickey act sad and ask: *Is Mickey happy?* (no) *Is Mickey sad?* (yes). Use mime to tell students that Mickey likes singing and dancing.
- Show the *Myself and others* poster and point to the Unit 1 picture. Say *I'm happy!*, and invite students to identify the happy girl in the picture. Then say *I'm sad!*, and invite students to identify the sad girl in the picture.

🎵 **1.12 Listen and sing.**

- Choose an action to represent *happy*, e.g., cheering or a fist pump, and *sad*. Play the audio. Students listen and mime happy and sad as they listen.
- Play the audio again, pausing after each line. Students repeat the words.
- Play the audio one more time, and students join in with *Hello. Hello.* Encourage students to clap to the rhythm as they sing.
- Ask several students: *Are you happy today?* They say *yes/no*.
- Make Mickey act happy, and ask: *Is Mickey happy now?* (yes).

Audioscript (track 1.12)

Hello. Hello. // I'm happy today. *(x2)*
Hello. Hello. // Are you happy today? *(x3)*
Hello. Hello. // Are you sad today?
Hello. Hello. // Are you nervous today?
Hello. Hello. // Are you excited today?

Presentation

1 🔊 **1.13 Listen and point. Then say.**

- Remind students of the situations and the characters in Video 1A in Lesson 1 and the story. If required, play Video 1A and look at the story again.
- Students look at the pictures. Say the names of each of the characters (*Merida, Cam, Maya*), and ask students to find their picture.
- Point to the first picture, and ask: *Is she happy or sad?* (happy). Do the same for the other pictures.
- Play the audio, and ask students to point to the pictures, pausing after each one to elicit the correct emotion.
- Point to each picture again, and students say and act out *happy* or *sad*.

Audioscript (track 1.13)

1 Are you happy, Merida? // Merida says, "Yes, I'm happy."
2 Are you happy, Merida? // Merida says, "No, I'm sad."
3 Are you happy, Cam? // Cam says, "Yes, I'm happy."
4 Are you happy, Maya? // Maya says, "No, I'm sad."

Practice

2 Draw ☺ or ☹ for you. Then ask and answer.

- Students look at the first photo. Mime eating ice cream, and say: *I'm happy.* Ask: *Are you happy?*, and elicit answers. Draw a happy emoji on the board.

Happy and sad

**LESSON 6
Myself and others**

1 🎧 💬 Listen and point. Then say.

🎵 Listen and sing.

2 ✏️ 💬 Draw 🙂 or ☹️ for you. Then ask and answer.

3 💬 Make your friend happy. Act and say. *TPR*

⭐ **I'm a hero!** ⭐

Self-awareness: Are you (happy)? I'm (sad).

17

- Students look at the fourth photo. Mime being outside in the rain, and say: *I'm sad.* Ask: *Are you sad?*, and elicit answers. Draw a sad emoji on the board.
- Point again to each of the photos, and ask: *Are you happy or sad?* Give students time to complete the emojis.
- Then point to each photo again, and ask: *Are you (happy)?* Students say either: *I'm happy* or *I'm sad.*

SUPPORT Ask and answer all together as a class. Point to each picture, and ask: *Are you happy/sad?* Students respond *yes* or *no*.

STRETCH Students work in pairs, taking turns to point to a picture and ask: *Are you happy or sad?* for their partner to answer.

Teaching star ✦✨

Growth mindset Praise students for effort and attitude rather than for their abilities. This kind of "process praise" motivates students and helps build resilience. Say: *Good job! I can see you worked hard today. I'm proud of you.*

3 Make your friend happy. Act and say.

- Students look at the first photo. Ask: *Are you happy?* (yes). Students mime hugging someone. Do the same for the second photo, and students mime giving someone a gift.
- Say: *I'm sad*, and mime the emotion. Encourage students to try to make you happy by miming one of the strategies in the photos. Then mime and say: *I'm happy! Thank you!*
- Students work in pairs, taking turns to role-play feeling sad and to role-play doing something to make their partner feel happy, saying *I'm sad! I'm happy!* as appropriate.

⭐ **I'm a hero!** ⭐ Point to the sticker picture, and elicit that Maya is making Leyla happy. Ask the class to act feeling sad, and invite a student to try to make them happy. Repeat with other students. Then students stick the sticker in their books.

> **Extra activity (class game)** Play *Let's dance!* (see Games Bank p.206). For this version, use the song *I'm happy today!* (track 1.12).

Wrap-up

- Invite four students to stand near the *Myself and others* poster. Say: *I'm (happy)*, and students find the happy girl in the Unit 1 picture as quickly as they can on the poster. Do the same with *I'm sad!*
- Play *Behind the doors* (see Games Bank p.206). Hold your hands in front of your face like two closed doors. Make a face showing an emotion, behind your hands. Ask students to guess the emotion. Then open the two doors and show students your expression. Then invite students to play the game. For this version, students make a happy or a sad face.
- Sing the *Goodbye* song (track 0.7), and students say goodbye to the Mickey Mouse puppet as they leave class.

📝 Workbook page 10

1 Circle 🙂 green. Circle ☹️ blue. *Cam and Leyla (the boy and the girl with the ball) – green. Maya (the girl on the bench) and Peter (the boy who has fallen over) – blue.*

2 Draw yourself 🙂 and ☹️. Then say.

Lesson 7: My world

Objectives

Lesson aims: learn about shadows
Target language: cloudy, shadows, sunny
Recycled language: family, colors
Receptive language: toys
Materials: Audio; Picture cards (Colors); Mickey Mouse puppet; (optional) a flashlight or flex lamp, a pair of sunglasses, lots of magazine pictures of outdoor places

GSE Skills

Listening: can recognize isolated words related to familiar topics, if spoken slowly and clearly and supported by pictures or gestures (16)
Speaking: can repeat single words if spoken slowly and clearly (10); can say single words related to familiar topics, if supported by pictures or gestures (18)

Teacher toolkit

Cross-curricular
Bringing the real world into cross-curricular lessons will make learning more memorable. Take the class outside, or ask students to look through a window to see if they can see any shadows. Ask: *Sunny or cloudy?*, and students respond. If it's sunny or bright, help students look for shadows, e.g., a shadow made by the school building, trees, benches, street lights, cars.

Engage
Use a flashlight or a flex lamp to make shadows. Students can hold their hand in front of the light and see where the shadow is, or they can place objects, e.g., the Mickey Mouse puppet, in front of the light. Experiment by moving the light closer or further away from the object, and see how this affects the size and shape of the shadow.

Home-school link
Students make a shape with their body on a sunny day and ask a family member to draw around their shadow with chalk. You could also ask students to do their own shadow drawings with their toys, as in activity 2 in the Workbook.

Science: Shadows Student's Book page 18

Warm-up

- Greet students with the Mickey Mouse puppet, and say the *Hi, hello!* chant (track 0.5). Make Mickey wear sunglasses.
- Play *Yes or no?* (see Games Bank p.206). For this version, use the Mickey Mouse puppet and the color picture cards to review colors. Give Mickey a color picture card, and say the name of the color. Make Mickey sometimes say the wrong word, e.g., Mickey holds a blue picture card and says *orange*. Students say *yes* for the correct color word and *no* for the incorrect color word. They then say the correct name of the color.

Presentation

1 1.14 **Listen and point. Then say.**

- Students look at the pictures. Ask: *What colors?* Students name and point to different colors in the pictures. For support, say the name of a color for students to find in the pictures.
- Point to the shadows in the first picture, and say: *Look, shadows.* If possible, make a shadow by placing a lamp or flashlight in front of an object to help students understand the concept of shadows. Then point to the second and third pictures, and say: *Look, it's sunny. It's cloudy.*
- Show students a TPR action for each word. If possible, show students the ASL sign for *sunny* (hold your hand open but slightly curved, to make a lamp shape above one side of your head) and *cloudy* (hold one hand over the other, palms facing each other, slightly curved, then make circular motions alternately).
- Play the audio, pausing after each word for students to point to the correct picture.
- Play the audio again, and students repeat the words.
- Play the audio a third time, and students say the words and do the TPR actions or ASL signs.

Audioscript (track 1.14)
1 shadows // 2 sunny // 3 cloudy

Practice

2 **Say *sunny* or *cloudy*. Then circle the shadows.**

- Point to each photo, and ask: *Sunny or cloudy?* Students answer and do the corresponding TPR action or sign (*sunny, cloudy*).
- Ask: *Where are the shadows?* Students point the correct photo (*photo 1*) and to the shadows in the photo.
- Then students circle the shadows in the photo.

SUPPORT Point to the second photo, and ask: *Shadow?* (no) *Is it sunny?* (no) *Is it cloudy?* (yes).

STRETCH Students work in pairs, taking turns to point to different pictures in activities 1 and 2 and say *shadows, sunny, cloudy*.

LESSON 7
My world

Shadows

1 🎧 Listen and point. Then say.

2 💬 ✏️ Say *sunny* or *cloudy*. Then circle the shadows.

3 ✏️ Look and match.

Shadows: cloudy, shadows, sunny

Thinking skills

Understand In activity 2, students identify the shadows in the pictures of different types of weather to show their understanding of when shadows occur.

Apply In activity 3, students apply their understanding of how shadows form shapes on the ground by matching shadows to the objects that create them.

Extra activity (extension) Do a class survey to find out if students prefer sunny or cloudy weather. Say: *It's sunny. Are you happy or sad?*, and students do a TPR action. Do the same for *It's cloudy*. For each, count the number of happy students and sad students. Then draw a bar chart on the board to display the results.

Wrap-up

- Play *Follow the leader* (see Games Bank p. 206). Ask the "leader" to say: *It's sunny/cloudy.*, and do an action they do in that weather, e.g., play soccer, ride a bike, for the other students to copy.
- Sing the *Goodbye* song (track 0.7), and students say goodbye to the Mickey Mouse puppet as they leave class.

📖 Workbook   page 11

1 **Look and circle. Then count shadows.** *1 a, three shadows; 2 b*
2 **Trace and color the shadows.**

Teaching star ✨

Creativity Use the pictures in activity 3 to help students notice how the shape of shadows can look different, depending on where the sun is. Then draw some objects on the board, e.g., a tree, a banana, a pencil, a book, and ask students to draw what they think these objects' shadows look like.

3 Look and match.

- Students look at the picture. Point to each item in the picture, and say: *Look, a (house). Where's the shadow?* Students find the shadow for each item in the picture.
- Give students time to draw lines to match the shadows to the objects.
- Ask: *What color are shadows?* Students look at the pictures in activities 1 and 2 to help them answer (*black* or *brown*).
- Students color the shadows in a dark color of their choice.

1 Lesson 8: Review

Objectives

Lesson aim: review target language from Unit 1
Target language: family, numbers; *I'm (happy).*
Recycled language: colors
Materials: Audio; (optional) Video 1A, Video 1B; Picture cards / Word cards (Family, Numbers 1); Stickers; Mickey Mouse puppet; small cards and counters (e.g., erasers, pencil sharpeners); *My progress* poster

GSE Skills

Listening: can recognize isolated words related to familiar topics, if spoken slowly and clearly and supported by pictures and gestures (16); can understand simple language related to naming and describing family members (21)

Speaking: can say single words related to familiar topics, if supported by pictures or gestures (18); can say how many things there are up to ten (13)

Teacher toolkit

Video review
You can return to Video 1A and Video 1B at the end of the unit for a "second play." Review the target structures, and students wave their hands when they hear one of these structures in the video.

Remediation
Put students who need further support in a group, and review the family vocabulary and numbers using the picture cards. Students count the balloons on page 13, activity 3. Use your classroom display to review the questions: *How many?* and *Who's this?*

Home-school link
Ask students to use at home the language they've learned in the unit. Encourage them to say *Hello, (mom)!* to their family members, and to count items at home or on their way to or from school.

I can do it! Student's Book page 19

Warm-up
- Greet students with the Mickey Mouse puppet, and say the *Hi, hello!* chant (track 0.5).
- Play *Pass Mickey!* (see Games Bank p.206). For this version, use the family picture cards, and ask students to count to six as they pass the Mickey Mouse puppet around.
- Play the song audio from Lesson 3 (track 1.5), and students join in with the words and the actions. If students are confident with the words, play the karaoke version (track 1.5_karaoke).

I can do it!

1 Play and say.
- To play the game, each student will need two small cards and a counter. They draw and color one circle on one card (*one*), and two circles on the other card (*two*). Then they place these dice cards face down on their desks.
- Play the game all together as a class. A student turns over a card and says the number of circles on the card, *one* or *two*. Move your counter the same number of squares on the game board. Then ask a question about the picture on the square, e.g., *Who's this? Is she/he happy/sad? How many cakes?* Students whisper the answer to their partner, then the whole class yells out the answer all together, on the count of three (*one, two, three!*). Repeat until your counter reaches the *Finish* square, and students clap to show that the game has ended.

ACHIEVE
Students name family members in pictures, say if someone is happy or sad, and can count the number of items in a picture.

SUPPORT
Play the game all together as a class, but ask questions that only require the answers *yes* or *no*, e.g., *Is this Merida? Does she feel happy? Six?* After students answer, model the target answer, either *yes* or *no*, and students repeat it.

STRETCH
Students play the game in pairs. They mix their cards together and place them face-down in a pile on their desk. Then they take turns to turn over a card, say *one* or *two*, and move their counter the same number of squares on the board. When they land on a square, they look at the picture and say the word or count the number of items.

Teaching star

Classroom management It can be tricky to assess individual students when you have a large class. To check whether students understand the target vocabulary, call out a word and ask students to find a corresponding picture in their books. Check to see if they are pointing correctly, and make a note of any words that some students may need to review.

LESSON 8 Review

I can do it!

1 🗨 **Play and say.**

2 💡 ✏️ **Think and color. Then stick!**

I can …
1.
2. Sing with me
3.

✓ Unit 1!

Go online – Big Project

19

2 💡 **Think and color. Then stick!**

- Point to each picture, and say *I can …* statements: *I can say family words. I can sing a song. I can say when I'm happy and sad.* For each statement, give an example, and then ask: *Can you do this?* If necessary, explain in L1.
- Students demonstrate what they can do. They work in pairs to say family words. Sing the song again all together as a class. They work in pairs to say and act out *happy* and *sad*. Monitor and assess students' performance.
- Students color the stars next to what they can do. Then they stick the reward sticker to show they have completed Unit 1.

My Star and Hero! Students look at the picture of Merida on p.4 in the Student's Book. They describe Merida, e.g., *She's a sister. She's happy.* They can also point to her hair, eyes, and clothing, and name the colors.

Extra activity (fast finishers) Students play *Miming* (see Games Bank p.206) using the unit picture cards.

Wrap-up

- Students reflect on which lesson they most enjoyed in Unit 1. Have a class vote, and choose one activity to do again as a class, e.g., watch the video, sing the song or chant, listen to the story, or play a game.
- Draw students' attention to the *My progress* poster, and ask them to identify the picture that reflects this unit. Read aloud with students the *I can …* statements (*I can ask and answer about my family, I can say I'm happy/sad*).
- 🎵 Sing the *Goodbye* song (track 0.7), then students say goodbye to the Mickey Mouse puppet and tell him their favorite word from Unit 1.

📓 Workbook pages 12–13

My progress
Audioscript see p.203

1. 🎧 **1.6 Listen, match, and say.** 1 dad, 2 mom, 3 sister, 4 brother
2. **How old are they? Color. Then ask and answer.**

Units W–1 My practice
1. **Color the bear family. Then say.** 1 blue, 2 green, 3 red, 4 yellow, 5 orange, 6 purple
   Count flowers. Find something brown and red. brown – cat, bear, book; red – ball
2. **How old are you? Draw and say.**

Unit 1! My favorite activity: Students stick the small star sticker next to their favorite activity.

2 My room

Unit objectives

By the end of this unit, students can:
- talk about their bedroom and toys
- read and understand a story about feeling different emotions
- recognize and name emotions and explore how their behavior can affect their feelings
- talk about shapes

Skills development

Listening: recognize and understand bedroom objects and toys, and simple descriptions of these

Speaking: describe toys; ask and answer about toys and bedroom objects

Vocabulary

Lesson 1: bed, chair, desk, poster
Lesson 2: ball, kite, puppet, scooter, teddy bear, yo-yo

Grammar

Lesson 3: It's a ball. It's small.
Lesson 5: Is it a kite? Yes. It's a kite.

Myself and others

Identifying my emotions 2 In this unit, a Disney video and a story develop the theme of identifying emotions. Students will learn to recognize their emotions in different situations, and that their actions can affect their feelings.

Language: grumpy; I'm not grumpy.

Self-awareness

Story

The puppet show
Let's play!

My world

Math: Shapes
circle, rectangle, triangle

Unit overview

Disney · PIXAR
MONSTERS UNIVERSITY

Randall
A purple lizard-like monster and Mike's roommate. He's a good student, and he can become invisible.

Mike Wazowski
A small, round green monster who dreams of becoming a professional Scarer.

Sulley (James P. Sullivan)
A huge monster with blue fur and purple spots. He's great at scaring children, but he's really a kind-hearted guy.

Mike has always wanted to be a Scarer. He starts university, and he's excited to learn all the skills and techniques of becoming a Scarer. However, he does something wrong, and he gets suspended. Mike has only one chance to return to his university studies – he needs to win the Scare Games.

Did you know?
There are 500 different monsters in the movie, and each one was designed and animated individually!

Video stories
Video 2A: *At school with Mike*
Video 2B: *Is it a bed?*

Online modules

Phonics
Words with Dd, Ee, and Ff sounds in initial position
desk, elephant, family

Big Project
Make a "My things" jigsaw

2 Lesson 1: Vocabulary

Student's Book pages 20–21

Objectives

Lesson aim: name things in my room
Target language: *bed, chair, desk, poster*
Recycled language: colors; *friend, happy; This is my …*
Receptive language: *Let's play. Here's Mike's room. Mike is grumpy.*
Materials: Video 2A; Audio; Picture cards / Word cards (Room, Disney characters); Sticker (Mike); (optional) students' toys or objects

GSE Skills

Listening: can recognize isolated words related to familiar topics, if spoken slowly and clearly and supported by pictures and gestures (16)
Speaking: can name a few everyday objects (10)

Teacher toolkit

Video summary – 2A
At school with Mike **Videoscript see p.202**
It's Mike's first day at the Monsters University. He meets his new roommate and moves into his room. But then Sulley suddenly comes in through the window and starts to create chaos. Mike isn't happy!

Engage
Set up a table in the classroom, and ask students to bring in to class a toy or another object from their bedroom. As students learn new words and structures during the unit, they name (Lesson 2), describe (Lesson 3), and ask and answer (Lesson 5) about these personal possessions.

Identifying my emotions 2
grumpy
Use the video story to talk about the feelings and behavior of the characters: *Is Mike happy/sad?* Elicit how Mike feels when Sulley comes in (*grumpy*). Students mime Mike's actions when he's grumpy in the video story (Mike frowns, stands up, walks over to Sulley, and points at him). This develops students' empathy with the characters and will help them better understand their own feelings and behavior.
Self-awareness

Warm-up
- Greet students with the Mickey Mouse puppet, and sing the *Hello, Stars and Heroes* song (track 0.1).

Presentation *Video story*
- Students look at the Big Picture. Introduce the movie and the characters: *This is the movie Monsters University. This is (Mike).*
- Point to items and characters in the picture, and ask: *What color is it?* (green, blue, purple) *How many monsters?* (five, including the picture from the video).

1 ▶ **2A Watch. Who has a backpack? Point.**
- Make the Mickey Mouse puppet stand up. Say: *Sit down, Mickey. It's video time! Let's watch!*
- Play Video 2A, and students watch and listen. Point to the picture of the backpack in the rubric, and mime putting it on.
- Play the video again, and students mime putting on a backpack when they see it. Pause the video, and point to Mike and Sulley in the Big Picture. Ask: *Who has a backpack?*, and students point to the character (*Mike*).

2 ▶ **2A Circle for Mike.**
- Use facial expression, and mime to review *happy* and *sad*, and to pre-teach *grumpy*. Point to the three small pictures. Call out each emotion word (*grumpy, happy, sad*), and students point to each corresponding picture.
- Point to Mike in the Big Picture. Play the video again, pausing at 2:35. Then point to each small picture, and ask: *Is Mike (happy)?* Elicit *yes* or *no* answers with a TPR response (*yes* – nod head, *no* – shake head). Students circle the correct picture.

Picture cards / Word cards (optional) Show the picture cards one by one to introduce the new vocabulary. Repeat several times.

Practice

3 **2.1 Listen, find, and say. Then play.**
- Students explore the Big Picture. Point to and say the room words: *bed, chair, desk,* and *poster*.
- Play the audio, pausing after each word. Students point to the items in the Big Picture. Play the audio again, pausing for students to say the words. Play the audio a third time, and students say and point to the objects.
- Say a number (1–4) for students to find the number in the Big Picture and say the correct word.

SUPPORT Demonstrate TPR actions for each word (see TPR: chant). Say a word, and students do the corresponding action.
STRETCH Students play the game in pairs, taking turns to point to an object in the Big Picture for their partner to name.

Audioscript (track 2.1)
1 desk // 2 bed // 3 poster // 4 chair

2 My room

LESSON 1 Vocabulary

1. Watch. Who has a 🦷? Point. *Mike*
2. Circle for Mike.
3. Listen, find, and say. Then play.
4. Listen, chant, and act. **TPR**
   🎵 *This is my bed* 🎵

bed, chair, desk, poster

4 🎵 2.2 Listen, chant, and act.

- Place the picture cards around the classroom. Say: *This is my (bed)*, pointing to the bed picture card.
- Play the audio, demonstrate the TPR actions, and students do the actions as they listen. Play the audio again. Students join in with the chant and do the TPR actions.

TPR chant

bed – mime sleeping	desk – mime drawing in a book
chair – sit down	poster – point

Audioscript (track 2.2)

This is my bed. My bed, my bed.
This is my bed. Oh, yeah! Oh, yeah!
This is my poster. My poster, my poster.
This is my poster. Oh, yeah! Oh, yeah!
This is my desk. My desk, my desk.
This is my desk. Oh, yeah! Oh, yeah!
This is my chair. My chair, my chair.
This is my chair. Oh, yeah! Oh, yeah!

Collect your friend Show the picture card of Mike to help students identify the correct sticker. Students stick the sticker on p.4 in the Student's Book. Ask: *Who's this?* (Mike).

Wrap-up

- Play *Draw it!* (see Games Bank p.206), using the picture cards from the lesson.
- Sing the *Goodbye* song (track 0.7), and students say goodbye to the Mickey Mouse puppet as they leave class.

📝 Workbook   pages 14–15

Audioscript see p.203

1. **Watch again. Then check (✓).**
   1. Who is in Mike's room? *a ✓, b ✓*
   2. What do you see in the video? *a ✓, c ✓, d ✓*
   3. Who is grumpy? *a ✓*
2. 2.1 **Listen, find, and color. Then say.** *poster – green, chair – yellow, bed – white, desk – brown*
3. **Challenge! Who's this? Ask and answer.** *Sulley, Mike, Randall*

Lesson 2: Vocabulary

Student's Book page 22

Objectives

Lesson aim: name toys
Target language: ball, kite, puppet, scooter, teddy bear, yo-yo
Recycled language: colors, numbers
Materials: Audio; Picture cards / Word cards (Toys); Stickers; Mickey Mouse puppet; (optional) small toys

GSE Skills

Listening: can recognize a few familiar everyday nouns and adjectives, e.g., colors, numbers, classroom objects, if spoken slowly and clearly (10); can recognize isolated words related to familiar topics, if spoken slowly and clearly and supported by pictures or gestures (16)
Speaking: can name a few everyday objects (10)

Teacher toolkit ✦✧

Teaching vocabulary
Create interest by showing students a picture of a toy box. Ask them what toys they think are inside the toy box. Use the picture card to pre-teach each of the vocabulary items, then ask students to choose three toys they think are in the toy box.

Engage
Bring in a few small toys for the toy table that was set up in Lesson 1, e.g., a small teddy bear, a small ball, a yo-yo, a toy car. Encourage students to name the toys and say: *This is my (ball)*. Then set aside a few minutes each lesson for free play, encouraging students to name and share their toys with each other.

Home-school link
Ask students to see how many of this lesson's toys they have at home. Encourage them to tell their families the names of the toys in English.

Warm-up

- Greet students with the Mickey Mouse puppet, and sing the *Hello, Stars and Heroes* song (track 0.1).
- Make Mickey whisper a word from Lesson 1 into your ear, e.g., *poster*. Invite students to guess what word Mickey said. Then say the word, and students find and point to a real example in the classroom.
- Say: *Listen and chant!*, and play the chant from Lesson 1 (track 2.2). Students join in with the chant and do the actions.

Presentation

Picture cards / Word cards (optional) Show the picture cards one by one to introduce the new vocabulary. Repeat several times, encouraging students to remember the words. For Stretch students, then show each word card, and they say the words.

1 🎧 **2.3 Listen, point, and say. Then play.**

- Show students the teddy bear picture card. Make the Mickey Mouse puppet act happy. Say: *It's a teddy bear. Mickey is happy!*
- Students look at the pictures and find the picture of a teddy bear.
- Say: *Listen and point*. Play the audio, and students point to the corresponding pictures.
- Demonstrate suitable TPR actions for the words, e.g., throw a ball and ride a scooter. Play the audio again, pausing after each vocabulary item. Students repeat the word and do the TPR action.
- Say a word, e.g., *puppet*, ask students to point to the corresponding picture, and then elicit the number. Repeat with the other words.

SUPPORT Say a word, and students do the corresponding TPR action.
STRETCH Students play the game in pairs, taking turns to do a TPR action for their partner to name the toy.

Audioscript (track 2.3)
1 yo-yo // 2 teddy bear // 3 ball // 4 scooter // 5 puppet // 6 kite

Practice

Teaching star ✦✧

Application Help students apply the lesson content to the math skill of recognizing patterns. Draw five circles on the board, and color the first four circles: *red, yellow, red, yellow*. Then point to the fifth circle and ask: *Red or yellow?* Color the circle according to the students' answer. Then guide students through the sequence to check their answer, and correct it, if necessary.

2 🎧 **2.4 Look, stick, and say. Then listen and check.**

- Point to the first picture sequence, and elicit the words: *ball, yo-yo, ball, yo-yo*. Say the sequence of words again, and students repeat.
- Then point to the empty sticker frame in the first sequence, and elicit the word *ball*. Students place the correct sticker in the empty frame. Do the same with the second picture sequence.

LESSON 2
Vocabulary

1 🎧 💬 Listen, point, and say. Then play.

2 💬 🎧 Look, stick, and say. Then listen and check.

3 ✏️ 💬 Draw. Then say and act. TPR

ball, kite, puppet, scooter, teddy bear, yo-yo

- Play the audio for students to listen and check their answers. Point to each picture as you hear the corresponding word, and students do the same. Then students stick the stickers in the correct places.
- Say each sequence of toys all together as a class.

Audioscript (track 2.4)
1 ball, yo-yo, ball, yo-yo … ball
2 scooter, kite, scooter, kite … scooter

3 Draw. Then say and act.
- Draw five boxes on the board. Elicit the names of two toys, and draw one toy, e.g., *kite*, in the first box and one toy, e.g., *puppet*, in the second box. Then repeat the sequence in the remaining boxes, e.g., *kite, puppet, kite, puppet, kite*.
- Students draw their own toy picture sequence in their books. Set a short time limit for the drawing activity, e.g., two to three minutes.
- Use the picture sequence you have drawn on the board to demonstrate the speaking activity. Say the sequence of toys, and students do the corresponding TPR action.

- Invite confident students to say their sequence of toys to the class. Students do the corresponding TPR actions.

SUPPORT Invite individual students to mime their toy sequence. Ask the rest of the class to copy the TPR actions and, if they know the word, say the name of the toy.

STRETCH Students work in pairs, taking turns to say their toy sequence for their partner to do the corresponding TPR actions.

> **Extra activity (class game)** Play a memory game. Place the picture cards around the classroom. Call out a simple sequence of toys, e.g., *teddy bear, ball, teddy bear, ball*. Students go and touch the picture cards in order. With large classes, play in groups.

Wrap-up
- Play *Faster and faster* (see Games Bank p.206), using the Mickey Mouse puppet and the picture card. Make Mickey point to each picture card.
- Sing the *Goodbye* song (track 0.7), and students say goodbye to Mickey as they leave class.

📝 Workbook   page 16

Audioscript see p.203
1 🎧 **2.2 Listen and match.** 1 d, 2 b, 3 a, 4 f, 5 e, 6 c
2 **Complete, color, and say.** ball, kite, teddy bear, scooter, yo-yo, puppet

> **Picture Dictionary**
> Students look at the Picture Dictionary on p.102 in the Student's Book and complete the activities. (**Answer:** *teddy bear*)

Lesson 3: Grammar

Objectives

Lesson aim: describe toys
Target language: *It's a ball. It's small.*
Recycled language: toys, colors
Materials: Audio; Picture cards / Word cards (Room, Toys, Colors); Mickey Mouse puppet; (optional) an old toy

GSE Skills

Listening: can identify everyday objects, people, or animals in their immediate surroundings or in pictures from short, basic descriptions, e.g., color, size, if spoken slowly and clearly (19)
Speaking: can use a few simple words to describe objects, e.g., color, number, if supported by pictures (19)

Teacher toolkit

Teaching grammar
Include the indefinite article *a* as you review the names of toys, e.g., *a ball, a yo-yo.* Help students to notice that *a* collocates with the noun (*a + ball*) rather than collocating with *It's* … . This will be helpful in this lesson as you teach the structure *It's …* with nouns (*It's a ball*) and with adjectives (*It's small*).

Engage
Bring to class an old toy you played with as a child, or, if you have children, bring in their favorite toys. Show the toy(s) to the class, and demonstrate how to play with it. Ask students to describe the toys, e.g., *It's (a kite). It's (big). It's (green).* Encourage students to say whether or not they like your toy.

Differentiation
Some students won't yet be ready to produce sentences, only the names of individual vocabulary items. However, you can ensure they have a receptive understanding of the structures by using sentence prompts: *It's a …* or *It's …*, getting students to complete the sentence with the correct vocabulary item.

Student's Book page 23

Warm-up
- Greet students with the Mickey Mouse puppet, and sing the *Hello, Stars and Heroes* song (track 0.1).
- Place the room picture cards, spaced out, on the floor or on a desk in front of the class. Say: *This is Mickey's bedroom.* Put Mickey on top of the chair picture card, and elicit *chair.* Then do the same with Mickey's toys, inviting students to place them in Mickey's bedroom.

Presentation

1 Sing-along 🎵 **2.5 Listen and point. Then sing and act.**

- Point to the picture, and ask: *Who's this?* (*Leyla, Maya,* and *Peter*).
- Ask: *What toys?*, and elicit *ball, puppet,* and *scooter.* Use the TPR actions to pre-teach the adjectives *big* and *small.* Point to each toy, and ask: *Is it big or small? What color?*
- Play the song audio. Pause after each verse, and students point in the picture to the ball, the puppet, and the scooter as they hear each item described.
- Demonstrate the TPR actions. Play the whole song, and students do the TPR actions. Play the song a third time, and encourage students to join in with some of the words as they do the TPR actions and dance. When students are confident with the words, play the karaoke version (track 2.5_karaoke), and they sing along.

> **TPR song**
> *ball, puppet, scooter* – use the TPR actions from Lesson 2
> *toys* – mime using any toy
> *Woo hoo!* – hold both arms up in the air
> *big* – spread arms wide
> *small* – cup hands together

Audioscript (track 2.5)

Toys, toys, toys! Toys for me. // Toys, toys, toys! Toys for you.
Toys, toys, toys! Woo hoo!
It's a ball. It's a ball. It's small. It's blue. *(x2)*
It's a puppet. It's a puppet. It's big. It's brown. *(x2)*
It's a scooter. It's a scooter. It's big. It's green. *(x2)*
Toys, toys, toys! Toys for me. // Toys, toys, toys! Toys for you.
Toys, toys, toys! Woo hoo!

Practice

2 2.6 Listen and find. Then say.

- Students look again at the song picture in activity 1. Ask, using TPR actions to reinforce meaning: *What color is the (scooter)? Is it big or small?*
- Play the audio, pausing after each set of sentences for students to point to the correct toy in the picture.
- Play the beginning of the audio again, and pause after the second sentence. Say: *It's a …*, and elicit *puppet.* Then play the third sentence (*It's a puppet*). Do the same with the second and third sets of sentences.

Sing-along

1 🎵 **Listen and point. Then sing and act.** TPR

Toys, toys, toys

2 🎧 **Listen and find. Then say.**

3 ✏️ **Color. Then point and say.**

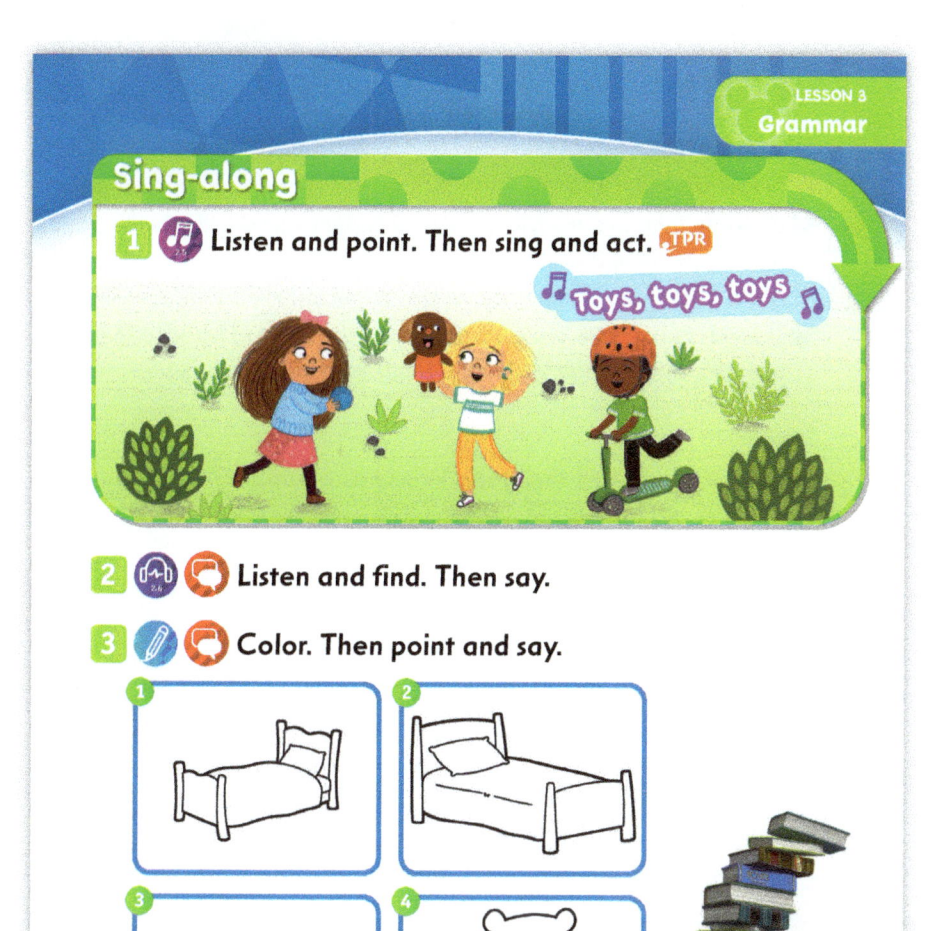

Song: It's a (ball). It's (small/red).

LESSON 3
Grammar

3 **Color. Then point and say.**

- Point to each of the pictures, and ask: *What's this?* (bed, teddy bear).
- Students color the pictures, using any color(s) they like.
- Demonstrate the activity, using a picture card. Say: *It's (small). It's (purple and green). It's a (teddy bear).*
- Invite a confident student to bring their Student's Book to the front of the class. Ask them to describe one of their pictures. Prompt by pointing to the visual instructions on the board. The other students look at their pictures and say if/how they are different.

SUPPORT Use a student's completed pictures, and say: *It's a …* to elicit the name of the toy, and *It's …* to elicit the toy's size and its color.

STRETCH Students work in pairs, taking turns to point to one of their pictures and describe it using full sentences.

> **Extra activity (fast finishers)** Students draw a picture of a simple bedroom with a bed, a desk, and a chair. Then they draw three toys. Ask students to work in pairs, taking turns to say the names of the objects in their picture.

Wrap-up

- Play *Circle it!* (see Games Bank p.206). For this version, describe one of the bedroom objects or toys.
- 🎵 Sing the *Goodbye* song (track 0.7), and students say goodbye to the Mickey Mouse puppet as they leave class.

📋 **Workbook**   page 17

Audioscript see p.203

1 🎧 **2.3 Listen, choose, and color. Then say.**
1 a big yellow ball, 2 a small pink kite, 3 a big brown teddy bear, 4 a small blue bed

2 Find and color. Then say. *a green teddy bear, a blue scooter, a pink ball, an orange kite*

SUPPORT Point to a toy from the picture, and ask: *Is it big/small? Is it red/blue/yellow/brown?* Elicit yes/no answers from the class.

STRETCH Students work in pairs, taking turns to describe a toy from the picture, e.g., *It's green. It's big.*, for their partner to say the word (scooter).

Audioscript (track 2.6)
1 It's big. It's brown. … It's a puppet.
2 It's small. It's blue. … It's a ball.
3 It's big. It's green. … It's a scooter.

Teaching star ✨

Support understanding Show students a gesture to accompany *It's*, e.g., raising your right arm in the air. Every time you raise your arm, students say *It's*. Raise your arm, then point to a picture card to elicit *It's (a kite). It's (yellow).* Repeat with other picture cards. This will help students use the target structure correctly in the oral activity below.

Lesson 4: Story

Student's Book pages 24–25

Objectives

Lesson aim: listen to and understand a story about playing together

Story language: *Let's play!*

Recycled language: toys; colors; *It's a (puppet). It's (pink). It's (small).*

Receptive language: *Come here. Bring Ted the teddy bear.*

Materials: Audio; Picture card (*yo-yo*); Story cards (Unit 2); Mickey Mouse puppet; (optional) a teddy bear, a shoebox, scissors, popsicle sticks, paper or card

GSE Skills

Listening: can understand a few basic words and phrases in a story that is read aloud (18)

Speaking: can repeat phrases and short sentences, if spoken slowly and clearly (16)

Teacher toolkit

Story summary
The children are making puppets at school. Cam arrives later and doesn't have a puppet. He feels left out because he can't join in with his friends. Then Leyla has an idea – she gives Cam Ted the teddy bear, and Cam joins in with the puppet show.

Engage
Set up a puppet theater (either a full-size or a shoebox theater), and students create a puppet show. To make a shoebox theatre, place a shoebox on its side so that the theater has a floor, a roof, and two walls. Cut a rectangular space in the roof for the puppets to drop down into the stage area. Stick puppets on popsicle sticks. Students stand behind the theater, holding the popsicle sticks in place and moving them around the stage.

Identifying my emotions 2
In the story, Cam feels different emotions (*grumpy, happy*). Ask students to look at Cam's face and body, and to identify his feelings in each scene. Encourage them to copy Cam's body language. Students act out themselves feeling *grumpy* and *happy*.

Self-awareness

Warm-up
- Before the lesson, stick the *yo-yo* picture card somewhere in the classroom.
- Greet students with the Mickey Mouse puppet, and sing the *Hello, Stars and Heroes* song (track 0.1).
- Make Mickey act grumpy. Say: *Mickey is grumpy. Where's Mickey's yo-yo?*
- Students look for the *yo-yo* picture card and bring it to Mickey. Then make Mickey act happy, and say: *Thank you!*

Presentation

1 2.7 **Listen to the story. Who has a puppet?**

- Make the Mickey Mouse puppet stand up. Say: *Sit down, Mickey. It's story time!*
- Point to the small picture of the puppet, and elicit the word *puppet*. Students look in the story pictures to find the puppets.
- Play the audio. Students listen to the story and follow in their books.
- Use the story cards to tell the story again, with or without the audio. Pause after each story frame to ask a comprehension question, e.g., *Who's this?* (point to Cam) *Is Cam happy?* (no) *Who is Cam's puppet?* (Ted – the teddy bear).
- Ask: *Who has a puppet?*

Spot! Students find the yo-yo. (**Answer:** frame 4)

SUPPORT Point to each character, and ask: *Does (Maya) have a puppet?* Elicit a *yes/no* or TPR response.

Teaching star

Diversity and inclusion Some students might have difficulty seeing some of the details in the story frames. Invite students to sit in a circle, and show them each of the story cards in turn, allowing enough time for students to look carefully at each of the pictures. Support their understanding by pointing out different details.

Practice

2 2.8 **Who says it? Listen and point. Then say.**

- Point to the small pictures and ask: *Who's this?* (*Cam, Leyla, Maya*) Play the first part of the audio, then pause for students to point to the corresponding character (*Maya*). Do the same with the second part of the audio (*Cam*) and the third part of the audio (*Leyla*).
- Play the audio again, and students repeat the lines.
- Give each student a role: Maya, Cam, or Leyla. Play the audio, and students role-play their character in the scene, saying the lines if they wish to.

Audioscript (track 2.8)
1 **Maya:** *It's a puppet.*
2 **Cam:** *Hello, everyone.*
3 **Leyla:** *Cam! Come here.*

66

LESSON 4
Story

The puppet show

1 Listen to the story. Who has a 🖍️? Maya, Leyla, and Peter

① Maya: It's a puppet. It's pink and purple.
Peter: Wow!

② Peter: Hello, Cam!
Cam: Hello, Peter. Hello, everyone.

③ Cam: Oh! It's a puppet!
Maya: Yes!

④ Boy: Cam. It's a yo-yo. Let's play!
Cam: No. It's small.

⑤ Leyla: Cam! Come here. Bring Ted the teddy bear.

⑥ Leyla: Hello, Ted!
Cam: Grrrr!

The end

2 Who says it? Listen and point. Then say.

3 Look and match. Then listen and say.

4 Act out the story.

Story: Let's play!

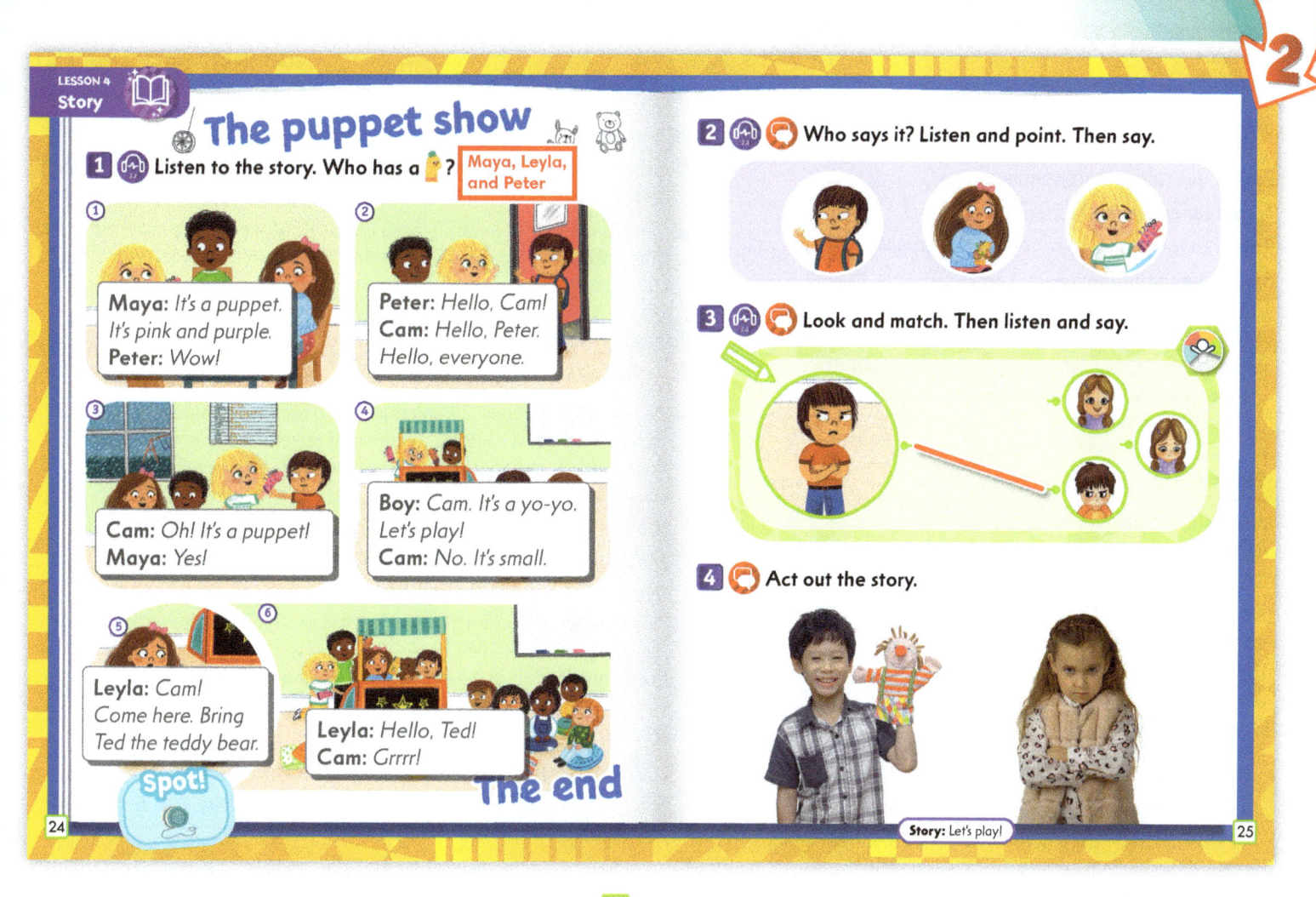

3 2.9 Look and match. Then listen and say.

- Students look at the picture of Cam and then find the same picture in the story (frame 4).
- Elicit the emotion shown in each smaller picture (happy, sad, grumpy). Ask: Is Cam happy/sad/grumpy? Students draw a line to match the picture of Cam to the grumpy picture.
- Play the audio, and students repeat the phrase and act out grumpy behavior.

Audioscript (track 2.9)
I'm grumpy!

4 Act out the story.

- Point to each photo, and elicit happy/grumpy. Then students find the story frames where Cam shows these emotions (happy – frames 2 and 6, grumpy – frames 4 and 5).
- Students act out different parts of the story and say some of the words, with or without the audio as a prompt. Walk around the class, praising students' acting efforts. Watch individual students, and say: Wow! You're very grumpy.

SUPPORT Students act out the whole story all together as a class with the audio. They can choose to repeat the lines or just do actions.

STRETCH Students act out the story in groups of five (Cam, Maya, Peter, Leyla, and Boy). Confident students can say some of the words.

Extra activity (story extension) Students make a simple puppet using a ruler. They use the puppets to say: Hello! I'm (name). Goodbye!

Wrap-up

- Place the story cards on the board in random order. Students come up to the board and place the story cards in the correct order. Make the Mickey Mouse puppet nod for the correct order or shake his head for the incorrect order and they try again.
- Sing the Goodbye song (track 0.7).

Workbook page 18

Audioscript see p.203

1 2.4 Listen and put a ✔ or ✘. Then point and say.
1 ✘, 2 ✘, 3 ✘

2 How does Cam feel? Match and say. 1 b, 2 a

Lesson 5: Grammar and Speaking

Student's Book page 26

Objectives

Lesson aim: ask and answer about toys
Target language: *Is it a kite? Yes. It's a kite.*
Recycled language: toys; colors; *It's big/small.*
Receptive language: *new house; oops, mmm, thanks, Ouch!, uh-oh, goodnight*
Materials: Video 2B; Audio; Picture cards / Word cards (Room, Toys); Story cards (Unit 2); Cut-outs (Unit 2), with a cut-out model prepared; scissors; (optional) small toys and a cloth bag

GSE Skills

Listening: can identify everyday objects, people, or animals in their immediate surroundings or in pictures from short, basic descriptions (e.g., color, size), if spoken slowly and clearly (19)
Speaking: can ask about the identity of an object, using a basic phrase (21)

Teacher toolkit

Video summary – 2B
Is it a bed? **Videoscript see p.202**
Mike and Sulley move into a new house. Their new landlord shows them around the house, and he shows them to their room, which is very small!

Teaching grammar
Provide a context for students to ask questions by making a mystery box or a mystery bag. Place a picture card or an item inside the box. Model the question: *Is it a (kite)?* Then invite individual students to use the questions to guess what item is inside the box or bag.

Extend
Take close-up photos of vocabulary items from the unit. You could also take photos of the toys from the toy table you set up in Lesson 1. Show students the photos, and invite them to guess the items, using the target structure *Is it a …?*

Warm-up

- Greet students with the Mickey Mouse puppet, and sing the *Hello, Stars and Heroes* song (track 0.1).
- Remind students of the story from Lesson 4. Make Mickey show different story cards, point to different toys and room items, and ask: *What's this?* Elicit: *It's a … .*

Presentation

1 2B **Watch. Check (✓) the bed.**

- As a lead-in to Video 2B, ask students to look once more at the Big Picture in Lesson 1, and remind them of the movie *Monsters University*. Point to Mike and Sulley, and elicit their names. Review the Lesson 1 vocabulary, pointing to room items and eliciting the words.
- Point to the pictures of the beds, and ask: *How many beds?* (three).
- Make the Mickey Mouse puppet stand up. Say: *Sit down, Mickey. It's video time!*
- Play the video, pausing after we see the bed [1:05]. Students look at the small pictures in their books and point to the bed from the video. Elicit answers, and students check the picture of the bunk beds.

Practice

2 2.10 **Listen and circle. Then ask and answer.**

- Point to the close-up pictures on the left of the activity. Ask: *Is it a (kite)? Is it a (chair)?*, etc.
- Point to each of the pictures on the right, and elicit the words (*puppet, poster, desk, chair, ball, yo-yo*).
- Play the first exchange in the audio, and ask: *Is it a puppet?* (No.) *Is it a poster?* (Yes.). Students circle the picture of the poster.
- Play the second and third exchanges, pausing after each exchange for students to think and circle the correct picture.
- Play the audio again, this time pausing after each question for students to answer *No. / Yes. It's a … .* Then play the answer for students to check their answers.

SUPPORT Use picture cards to drill the questions and answers chorally with the class as many times as necessary.

STRETCH Students work in pairs, taking turns to ask and answer questions about the pictures, following the model in the audio. They can also point to other pictures in the unit.

Audioscript (track 2.10)

1 Is it a puppet? // No.
  Is it a poster? // Yes. It's a poster.
2 Is it a chair? // No.
  Is it a desk? // Yes. It's a desk.
3 Is it a ball? // No.
  Is it a yo-yo? // Yes. It's a yo-yo.

LESSON 5
Grammar and Speaking

1 Watch. Check (✓) the bed.

2 Listen and circle. Then ask and answer.

3 Listen and point. Then make and play.

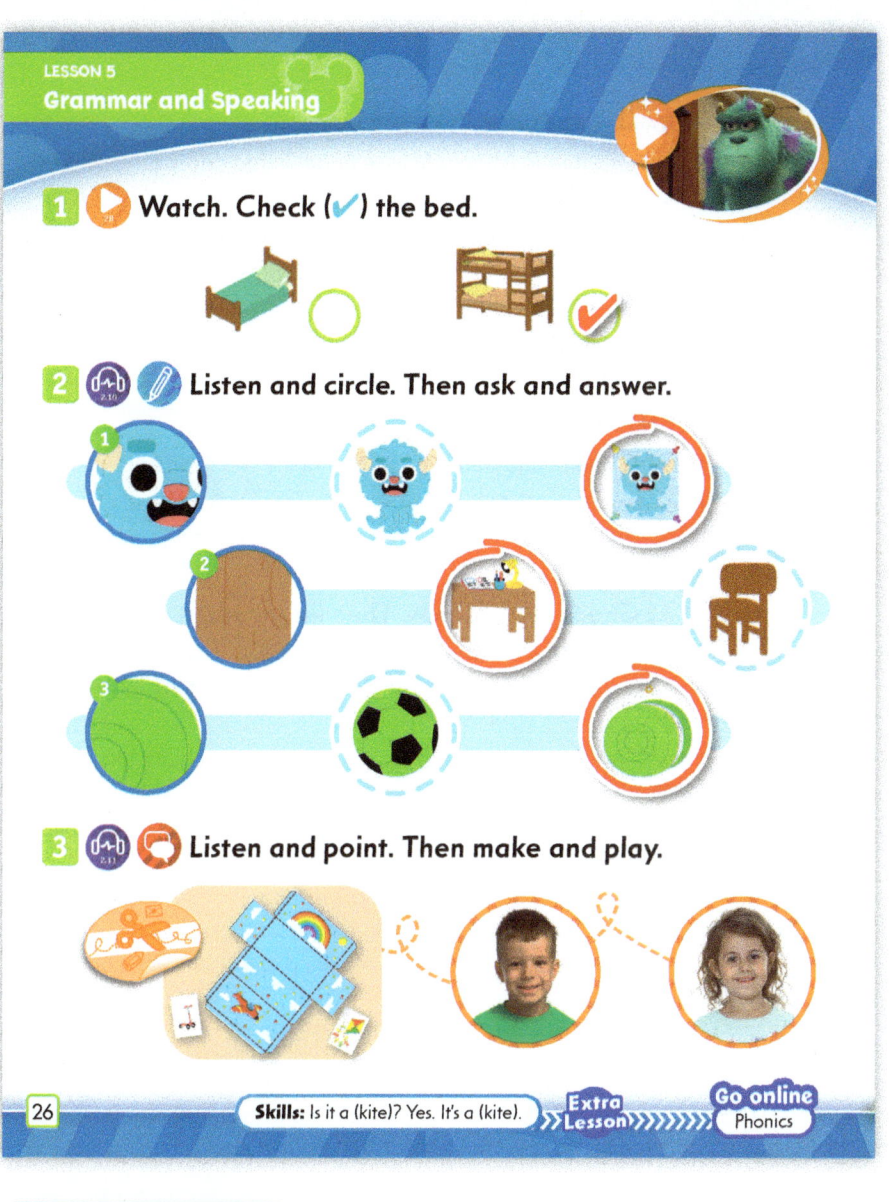

Skills: Is it a (kite)? Yes. It's a (kite).

Extra Lesson >>>>>>>> Go online Phonics

Teaching star

Learning to learn Show students some simple card games they can play with the cards from activity 3, in order to practice the structures and vocabulary, e.g., guessing games or matching games. They can play these games with pictures or cards in any unit.

3 🎧 **2.11 Listen and point. Then make and play.**

- Hand out the cut-outs, and students look at the small pictures of toys. Play the audio, pausing for students to find the picture of the kite and the picture of the scooter.
- Show students the model toy box and cut out toy cards you have prepared.
- Students use scissors to cut carefully around the dotted lines of the toy box and the toy cards. Help them fold and stick together the sides of the box.
- Place two toy cards inside your model toy box, and close the box's lid. Students guess which toys are inside, e.g., *Is it a (ball)?*, until they have correctly identified both toys.

- Play the game as a class. Invite a student to put a toy inside their toy box. Show a toy picture card and elicit from the class the question *Is it a ...?*, for the student to answer.

SUPPORT Students can play the game in mixed-ability pairs. The less confident student answers their partner's questions using *yes* or *no*.

STRETCH Students can play the game in mixed-ability pairs. The more confident student asks *Is it a ... ?*, and says full sentences to name the toys, e.g., *It's a ball.*

Audioscript (track 2.11)
A: *Is it a kite?*
B: *Yes. It's a kite. It's yellow, green, and red. It's big.*
A: *Is it a ball?*
B: *No.*
A: *Is it a scooter?*
B: *Yes. It's a scooter. It's pink. It's small.*

> **Extra activity (class game)** 🐭 Make the Mickey Mouse puppet hold a picture card from Unit 1 or 2 so that students can't see it. Invite them to take turns to guess what it is.

Wrap-up

- Play *It's in the bag* (see Games Bank p.206). For this version, bring in a selection of small toys. Invite students to guess what it is, asking: *Is it a ...?* Students say: *No. / Yes. It's a ... .*
- 🐭 Sing the *Goodbye* song (track 0.7), and students say goodbye to the Mickey Mouse puppet as they leave class.

📝 Workbook   page 19

Audioscript see p.203
1 🎧 **2.5 Listen and circle.** *1 a, 2 a, 3 b*
2 **Draw a toy. Then ask and answer.**

Lesson 6: Myself and others

I'm not grumpy Student's Book page 27

Objectives

Lesson aim: recognize and name emotions
Target language: *grumpy; I'm not grumpy. Let's play.*
Recycled language: *I'm happy/sad.*
Materials: Audio; (optional) Video 2A, Video 2B; *Myself and others* poster; Stickers; Mickey Mouse puppet; (optional) cards for Teacher toolkit, poster paper, glue

Skills

Listening: can recognize isolated words related to familiar topics, if spoken slowly and clearly and supported by pictures or gestures (16)
Speaking: can say how they feel, using a limited range of common adjectives, e.g., *happy, cold* (22)

Teacher toolkit

Identifying my emotions 2

In this lesson, students build upon the basic emotions of *happy* and *sad*, and explore how their emotions can change in different situations. At this age, students are starting to develop behavioral strategies to manage their emotions. Using L1, discuss when Mike is grumpy in the video (when Sulley makes a mess in his room), and when Cam is grumpy in the story (when he doesn't have a puppet).

Self-awareness

Extend

Make a poster with strategies for dealing with negative emotions, e.g., *sad, grumpy*. Students draw or cut out pictures for the poster, using ideas for strategies developed through this lesson. When you notice a student expressing one of the negative emotions, point out the strategies, and encourage them to choose and practice one.

Home-school link

Ask students to notice when they feel grumpy at home, and to choose an activity or strategy from this lesson that helps them feel better. Encourage them to teach one of these strategies to a family member.

Warm-up

- Greet students with the Mickey Mouse puppet, and sing the *Hello, Stars and Heroes* song (track 0.1).
- Show the *Myself and others* poster and review *happy* and *sad*. Point to the happy girl in the Unit 1 picture and elicit *I'm happy!* Then point to the sad girl in the Unit 1 picture and elicit *I'm sad!*
- Make Mickey act out sad/happy/grumpy behavior, and ask: *Is Mickey happy? Is he sad? Is he grumpy?*

🎵 **1.12 Listen and sing.**
- Play the song audio, and students join in with the words and the actions.
- Ask: *How do you feel? Are you happy?*, and students respond.

Presentation

1 🎧 **2.12 Check (✓) grumpy. Then listen, point, and say.**

- Remind students of the situations and the characters in Video 2A in Lesson 1 and the story. If required, play Video 2A and look at the story again.
- Students look at the pictures and say the names of the characters (*Mike and Cam*).
- Point to the first picture, and ask: *Is Mike happy? Is he sad? Is he grumpy?* Mime each emotion as you say the word. Do the same for each of the pictures.
- Say: *I'm grumpy.*, and mime the emotion. Ask: *Who is grumpy?*, and point to the four pictures. Students check the pictures showing characters expressing the grumpy emotion.
- Play the audio, and students point to the pictures.
- Play the audio again, pausing after each sentence for students to repeat and act out *I'm grumpy* or *I'm not grumpy*.

Audioscript (track 2.12)
1 Mike says, "I'm not grumpy."
2 Mike says, "I'm grumpy."
3 Cam says, "I'm not grumpy."
4 Cam says, "I'm grumpy."

Teaching star

Social and emotional learning Make use of Videos 2A and 2B to help students remember the stories and to lead a discussion of the emotions that are shown. Students act out and name the emotions as they watch. Pause the video as suitable, to discuss why the characters are feeling these emotions, using L1 as necessary.

Practice

2 🎧 **2.13 Listen and circle. Then act and say for you.**

- Students look at the first photo. Ask: *Is he grumpy?*, and elicit answers, getting students to do a grumpy or not grumpy face. Then play the audio, and students circle the correct picture. Do the same with the second photo.

I'm not grumpy

LESSON 6 — Myself and others

1 Check (✓). Then listen, point, and say.

Listen and sing.

2 Listen and circle. Then act and say for you.

3 Listen and check (✓). Then say.

I'm a hero!

Self-awareness: I'm (not) grumpy. Let's play!

27

- Using L1, ask students how they feel when they eat vegetables. Then ask how they feel when they're having fun and they have to go home. Elicit *grumpy* or *not grumpy*.
- Elicit in L1 more situations when students feel grumpy, e.g., when they don't want to do something or when their favorite toy breaks. Invite students to act out each situation, and ask the class to say how they feel: *grumpy* or *not grumpy*.

Audioscript (track 2.13)
1 Mmm. I'm not grumpy.
2 Mom! I'm grumpy.

3 🎧 **2.14 Listen and check (✓). Then say.**

- Students look at the photos. Play the audio, and students point to the correct photo.
- Play the audio again, and students check the correct photo.
- Ask: *Is he/she grumpy?* (yes). Ask (using L1 if necessary): *What does he do?* (plays a game with a friend). Then elicit more ideas about what you can do when you're grumpy, e.g., do something funny with a friend, dance, and sing.

SUPPORT Demonstrate a few strategies to help yourself or other people stop feeling grumpy, e.g., take deep breaths, stomp around like a monster, pull funny faces to make students laugh, put your hand on the Mickey Mouse puppet's shoulder and ask: *Are you OK?* After each strategy, students say or act: *I'm grumpy. / I'm not grumpy*.

STRETCH Students work in groups to choose three strategies. They act them out for the class, then ask *grumpy or not grumpy?*, and elicit responses from the class.

Audioscript (track 2.14)
I'm grumpy. // Let's play! // I'm not grumpy now!

⭐ **I'm a hero!** ⭐ Point to the sticker picture, and elicit that Leyla is trying to help Cam stop feeling grumpy. Encourage the class to act grumpy, and invite one student to try to make them feel better. Repeat with other students. Then students stick the sticker in their books.

> **Extra activity (fast finishers)** Students work in pairs, taking turns to act grumpy for their partner to try out different strategies to make their friend feel better, e.g., singing a song, dancing, reading a story, taking deep breaths, counting to six, doing something funny.

Wrap-up
- Play *Behind the doors* (see Games Bank p. 206). For this version, students make a happy or a grumpy face.
- Draw students' attention once more to the *Myself and others* poster, and ask them to identify the picture that reflects the lesson aim. Point to the boy in the picture and elicit *I'm grumpy!* Then point to the girl in the picture and elicit *I'm not grumpy!*
- Sing the *Goodbye* song (track 0.7), and students say goodbye to the Mickey Mouse puppet as they leave class.

📝 Workbook — page 20

1 When are you grumpy? Color and say.
2 What makes you not grumpy? Draw and tell a friend.

2 Lesson 7: My world

Math: Shapes Student's Book page 28

Objectives

Lesson aims: identify shapes
Target language: *circle, rectangle, triangle*
Recycled language: colors; *monster*
Receptive language: *body*
Materials: Audio; Mickey Mouse puppet; (optional) pictures of objects with different shapes, lots of different sized shapes cut out of colored card, glue

GSE Skills

Listening: can recognize isolated words related to familiar topics, if spoken slowly and clearly and supported by pictures or gestures (16)

Speaking: can repeat single words if spoken slowly and clearly (10); can use a few simple words to describe objects, e.g., color, number, if supported by pictures (19)

Teacher toolkit

Cross-curricular
Recognizing and comparing shapes helps develop students' visual-spatial awareness. Help students connect their learning with the real world by asking them to look around the classroom for things with each shape, e.g., *circle:* clock, *rectangle:* window, board. If possible, bring in some pictures of real objects showing each shape, and ask students to classify them according to shape.

Extend
Students make different-shaped monsters out of colored shapes. These could be cut from old cereal boxes or other recycling materials. Put students in groups, and give each group a set of colored shapes of different sizes. Students work together in their group to choose a large shape for the monster's body, then add smaller shapes for the monster's arms, legs, and facial features. When students are happy with their design, they glue their monster together.

Home-school link
Students find more examples of shapes at home, in their toys, or in things around the home. They can show and name the shapes to their families.

Warm-up
- Greet students with the Mickey Mouse puppet, and sing the *Hello, Stars and Heroes* song (track 0.1).
- Play *Color hunt* (see Games Bank p.206) to review the names of colors.

Presentation

1 🎧 **2.15 Listen and point. Then say.**

- Students look at the pictures and say what color the shapes are.
- Point to the first picture, and say: *It's blue. It's a …*, and see if any students know the word *circle*. Do the same with the triangle and the rectangle.
- Play the audio, pausing after each word for students to point to the correct shape.
- Show students a TPR action for each shape: curve two hands together to make a circle; place your hands up together with your palms facing out, and join your thumbs to create a triangle; make L-shapes with your index fingers and thumbs, then turn one hand and join it to the other hand to make a rectangle.
- Play the audio again, and students repeat the shape words, then do the TPR action.

SUPPORT Say the name of each shape, and students do the TPR action.

STRETCH Students work in pairs, taking turns to point to a shape for their partner to name.

Audioscript (track 2.15)
1 circle // 2 triangle // 3 rectangle

Teaching star
Linguistic competence Students may need support in pronouncing *triangle* and *rectangle*. Break up the words into syllables, and drill each one, e.g., *tri – an – gle*, showing students how to make the correct shapes with their mouths.

Practice

2 Find and say. Then trace and circle.

- Students look at the photo of a bedroom. Ask: *What shapes can you see? Can you see a (circle)?* Point to an item in the photo and say: *Look, it's a (circle).* Give students time to look and point to different shapes they see.
- Ask: *How many circles?* Count the circles all together as a class (*four*). Then point to the circle icon and the two number options. Demonstrate how to trace the numbers. Then demonstrate how to circle the number 4.
- Do the same with triangles and rectangles.

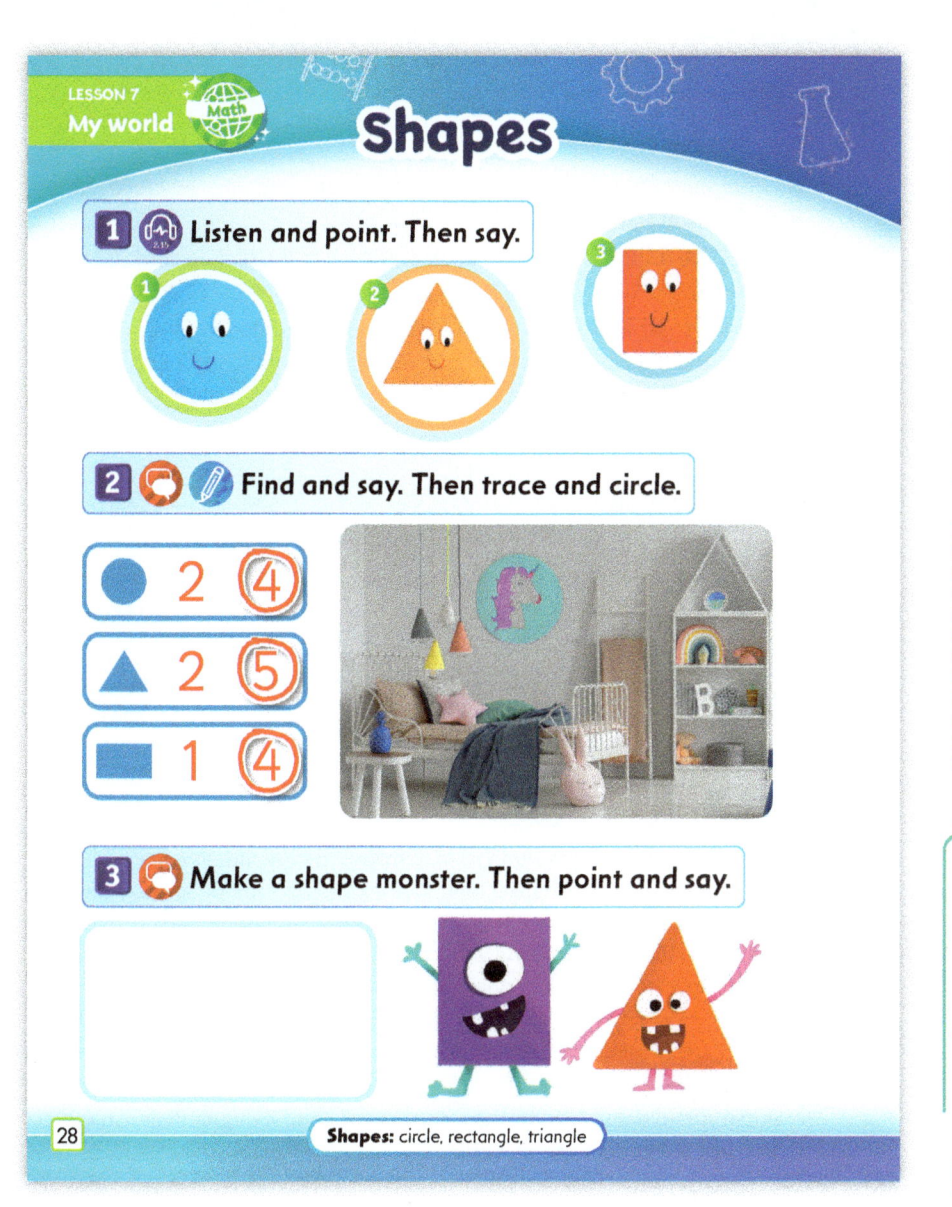

LESSON 7
My world Math

Shapes

1 🎧 Listen and point. Then say.

2 💬 ✏️ Find and say. Then trace and circle.

3 💬 Make a shape monster. Then point and say.

Shapes: circle, rectangle, triangle

28

Thinking skills

Apply In activity 2, students apply their knowledge of the forms of each shape by locating them in a picture from a real-world context.

Create In activity 3, students design a monster using a shape as the basis for the monster's body. They describe the monster and identify its shape.

Extra activity (extension) Students sit in pairs, one behind the other. Tell the student sitting at the back to think of a shape and to use their finger to draw it on their partner's back. The student sitting at the front guesses the shape. Then they both turn around and repeat. They can do this a few times.

Wrap-up

- Play *Monster munch* (see Games Bank p.206). Tell students that today the monster can only eat rectangles. Invite them to come to the front of the class and feed the monster anything of a rectangular shape, e.g., their book, a ruler.
- Sing the *Goodbye* song (track 0.7), and students say goodbye to the Mickey Mouse puppet as they leave class.

📖 Workbook   page 21

1 **Draw and color. Then say.** *1 It's a triangle. It's big. It's yellow. 2 It's a circle. It's small. It's red. 3 It's a triangle. It's small. It's green.*

2 **Look and color. Then say and count.** *5 squares, 3 triangles, 6 circles*

---

3 Make a shape monster. Then point and say.

- Draw a shape monster on the board, using either a circle, or a triangle, or a rectangle for its body. Say: *Look at my monster! What shape is it?*
- Students look at the two shape monsters in the picture, and they name the shapes (*rectangle, triangle*).
- Students choose a shape and draw it in the space next to the shape monsters. Then they draw arms, legs, and a face on their shape, to turn it into a monster.
- Describe the shape monster on the board: *It's a triangle. It's blue. It's grumpy.*
- Ask students questions about their shape monster, e.g., *What shape? Is it a circle? What color? Is it big or small? Is it happy?* Invite individual students to answer the questions about their monster.

SUPPORT Invite one student to hold up their picture. Ask the class questions about the student's shape monster, allowing the class to answer all together.

STRETCH Students work in pairs or small groups, taking turns to present their monsters to each other.

73

2 Lesson 8: Review

I can do it! Student's Book page 29

Objectives

Lesson aim: review target language from Unit 2
Target language: toys, objects; *It's (big). I'm grumpy.*
Recycled language: colors
Materials: Audio; (optional) Video 2A, Video 2B; Picture cards / Word cards (Room, Toys); Stickers; Mickey Mouse puppet; *My progress* poster

GSE Skills

Listening: can recognize isolated words related to familiar topics, if spoken slowly and clearly and supported by pictures and gestures (16)
Speaking: can say single words related to familiar topics, if supported by pictures or gestures (18)

Teacher toolkit

Video review
You can return to Video 2A and Video 2B at the end of the unit for a "second play." Ask students to stand up as they watch. They jump when they hear one of the words from the unit.

Remediation
Some students may need more consolidation and support with the unit language than others. Games allow you to provide additional language practice while students are having fun! Play a variety of games to provide sufficient practice of both the unit vocabulary and target structures, for example *Find it!*, *Throw the ball*, or *Draw it!* (see Games Bank p.206).

Home-school link
Students use the language they've learned in the unit to describe their toys at home, e.g., *It's a puppet. It's red.*

Warm-up
- Greet students with the Mickey Mouse puppet, and sing the *Hello, Stars and Heroes* song (track 0.1).
- Play *What's this?* (see Games Bank p.206) with the picture cards from the unit.
- Play the song audio from Lesson 3 (track 2.5) and students join in with the words and the actions. If students are confident with the words, play the karaoke version (track 2.5_karaoke).

I can do it!

1 Play and say.
- Show students how to do the maze activity. Point to Sulley at the beginning of the maze, and then point to Mike at the end of the maze.
- Demonstrate with your finger how to move through the maze. Move your finger to the first picture, and say: *It's a …* . Elicit *chair*.
- Students work in pairs, taking turns to travel through the maze. When they reach each picture, they say a sentence, e.g., *It's a poster*. Monitor as students play, and provide support as necessary.

Teaching star

Growth mindset Some students might want to play the game in a different way or use different language to describe the pictures. Allow students to be creative, as this will help build their independence, even if it means they are not reviewing the target language. Then you can encourage them to reflect on what they learned in the game.

ACHIEVE
Students make simple sentences, naming toys and things in their room, and describing their size and color.

SUPPORT
Do the whole maze all together as a class. Follow the maze with your finger. When you reach a picture say: *It's a …*, and students name the object in the picture.

STRETCH
Students play the game in pairs, taking turns to make a statement or ask their partner a question about the picture, e.g., *Is it a (chair)? Is it (red)?*

2 Think and color. Then stick!
- Point to each picture, and say *I can …* statements: *I can name toys. I can sing a song. I can say, "I'm grumpy."* For each statement, give an example, and then ask: *Can you do this?* If necessary, explain in L1.
- Students demonstrate what they can do. They work in pairs, taking turns to say the names of different toys and bedroom objects. Sing the song all together as a class. Students work in pairs, taking turns to say and act out feeling grumpy and not grumpy. Monitor and assess students' performance.

LESSON 8 Review

I can do it!

1 🗣 **Play and say.**

2 💡 ✏️ **Think and color. Then stick!**

I can ...
1
2 Toys, toys, toys
3

✓ Unit 2!

Go online — Big Project

29

- Students color the stars next to what they can do. Then stick the reward sticker to show they have completed Unit 2.

My Star and Hero! Students look at the picture of Mike on p.4 of the Student's Book. They describe Sulley, e.g., *He's a monster. He's green. He's small. He's grumpy.*

Extra activity (whole class) Set up the classroom as a market. Set up several desks as stalls, and place several toy and room picture cards on each one. Put students in groups around the "stalls." Invite one student in each group to role-play a shopkeeper, and ask the other students to role-play people who are window shopping. Demonstrate a simple dialog, and encourage students to have similar conversations, e.g., *Hello. / Hello. Look! It's a (scooter). / It's (blue).*

Wrap-up

- Students reflect on which lesson or activity they most enjoyed in Unit 2. Have a class vote and choose one activity to do again as a class, e.g., watch the video, sing the song or chant, listen to the story, or play a game.
- Draw students' attention to the *My progress* poster, and ask them to identify the picture that reflects this unit. Read aloud with students the *I can ...* statements (*I can talk about my things, I can say I'm (not) grumpy*).
- Sing the *Goodbye* song (track 0.7). Then students say goodbye to the Mickey Mouse puppet and tell him their favorite word from Unit 2.

📝 **Workbook** pages 22–23

My progress
Audioscript see pp. 203–204

1 **Find and match. Then say.** 1 teddy bear, 2 poster, 3 chair, 4 ball, 5 kite, 6 bed

2 🎧 2.6 **Listen and check (✓). Then ask and answer.** 1 c ✓, 2 a ✓, 3 b ✓

Units W–2 My practice

1 **Trace and color. Then say.** Students trace and color the chair, poster, kite, and ball.
   Find the toys. Then count and say. *five: a teddy bear, a yo-yo, a kite, a ball, a scooter*

2 **What's in your room? Circle.**

Unit 2! My favorite activity: Students stick the small star sticker next to their favorite activity.

3 My school

Unit objectives

By the end of this unit, students can:
- talk about their school things and talk about how many things they have
- read and understand a story about feeling nervous on your first day at school
- recognize and name emotions and explore what makes people feel nervous
- talk about equations

Skills development

Listening: recognize and understand school items and numbers, and simple statements about quantity

Speaking: talk about their school things; help people when they're nervous; talk about math problems

Reading: recognize and decode single number and letter symbols and their corresponding sounds

Vocabulary

Lesson 1: backpack, book, crayon, marker, pencil, ruler
Lesson 2: seven, eight, nine, ten

Grammar

Lesson 3: I have two rulers.
Lesson 5: How many books? I have one book.

Myself and others

Identifying my emotions 3 In this unit, a Disney video and story develop the theme of identifying emotions. Students will identify the feeling of being nervous, and will recognize situations when they may feel nervous.

Language: nervous; I'm not nervous. It's OK. Don't worry.

Self-awareness

Story

The surprise
surprise, tortoise; Wow!

My world

Math: Plus and minus
is, minus, plus

Unit overview

Disney · PIXAR TOY STORY 4

Bonnie
A little girl who is now the owner of Andy's toys from the earlier *Toy Story* movies, including Woody. Bonnie is just starting kindergarten and is nervous. Bonnie feels comforted by her toys.

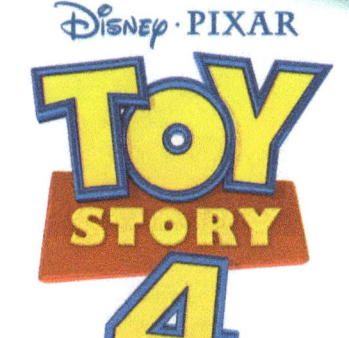

Buzz Lightyear
A space ranger action figure, who stars in all the *Toy Story* movies. He's strong, brave, and is a natural leader.

Woody
A cowboy sheriff toy, who stars in all the *Toy Story* movies. He's loyal and will do anything to protect his human friends.

Forky
A toy that Bonnie made from a recycled fork and craft materials. Forky doesn't feel at home with the toys and prefers to live in the trash bin!

Bo Peep
A shepherdess toy that was once part of a lamp, Bo is a tough, brave, funny girl who always tries to help others.

Bonnie has a new toy that she has made at school: Forky. Bonnie and her family go on a trip, and she takes all her favorite toys, including Woody. Unfortunately, Forky doesn't think he's a toy, and he keeps trying to escape. Woody and the other toys have lots of adventures trying to rescue Forky and bring him back to Bonnie.

Did you know?
The antiques store in *Toy Story 4* contains lots of hidden references to other Pixar movies, including objects from *A Bug's Life* and *Finding Nemo*.

Video stories
Video 3A: *Bonnie's toys*
Video 3B: *How many?*

Online modules

Phonics
Words with Gg, Hh, and Ii sounds in initial position
girl, hat, in

Big Project
Make a stationery store

3 Lesson 1: Vocabulary

Student's Book pages 30–31

Objectives

Lesson aim: name school items
Target language: *backpack, book, crayon, marker, pencil, ruler*
Recycled language: *room; toy, mom, dad; This is (the teacher). It's big.*
Receptive language: *Let's make a toy. Who's this?*
Materials: Video 3A; Audio; Picture cards / Word cards (School items, Disney characters); Sticker (Forky); Mickey Mouse puppet; (optional) boxes or trays, classroom materials

GSE Skills

Listening: can recognize isolated words related to familiar topics, if spoken slowly and clearly and supported by pictures and gestures (16); can recognize familiar words and phrases in short, simple songs or chants (18)
Speaking: can name a few everyday objects (10); can say single words related to familiar topics, if supported by pictures or gestures (18)

Teacher toolkit

Video summary – 3A
Bonnie's toys **Videoscript see p.202**
It's Bonnie's first day at school. Bonnie doesn't know any of the children, and she sits at a desk on her own. But Woody, Bonnie's toy friend, helps her make a new friend.

Engage
Students work in groups to create boxes of school items. Bring to class a box or tray for each group. As you progress through the unit, invite each group to collect different school items for their box, as they learn the new vocabulary, e.g., crayons, markers, pencils, rulers. Encourage them to count the number of each item. Groups can also decorate their materials box, using recycled materials.

Identifying my emotions 3
nervous
Use the video story to talk about Bonnie's feelings and behavior in different situations. Students demonstrate Bonnie's feelings, using facial expression and body language.
Self-awareness

Warm-up
- Greet students with the Mickey Mouse puppet, and sing the *Hello, Stars and Heroes* song (track 0.1).

Presentation
- Students look at the Big Picture. Introduce the movie and the characters: *This is the movie Toy Story 4. This is Bonnie / Woody / Buzz Lightyear / Bo Peep.*
- Point to a desk and chair in the Big Picture, and ask: *What's this?* (a desk) *What color is it?* (brown) *Is it big or small?* (big)

1 3A Watch. Who's in school? Check (✓).
- Demonstrate a TPR action for each toy: strong arms (Buzz), put on hat (Woody), hold a staff (Bo).
- Make the Mickey Mouse puppet stand up. Say: *Sit down, Mickey. It's video time! Let's watch!*
- Play Video 3A, and students do the corresponding TPR action when they see each toy in the video.
- Point to each small toy picture, and ask: *Is he/she in school?* Students answer *yes* or *no*. Then ask students to check the toy from the video.

2 3A Circle for Bonnie.
- Make the Mickey Mouse puppet act out *happy, sad,* and *grumpy,* and elicit the words.
- Use facial expression and mime to pre-teach *nervous.*
- Play the video again, pausing at 0:28 (*sad*), 1:43 (*nervous*), and 3:39 (*happy*). and students point to the small pictures.
- Ask students to circle the correct pictures.

Picture cards / Word cards (optional) Show the picture cards one by one to introduce the new vocabulary. Repeat several times, encouraging students to remember the words. For Stretch students, then show each word card, and elicit the words.

Practice

3 3.1 Listen, point, and say. Then play.
- Students explore the Big Picture and find the school items on the picture cards.
- Play the audio, pausing after each word. Students point to the school items in the Big Picture. Play the audio again, pausing for students to say the words. Play the audio a third time, and students say and point to the school items.
- Point to different school items in the small pictures, and students say the correct words.

SUPPORT Demonstrate TPR actions for each word (see the TPR box below). Say a word, and students do the corresponding TPR action.
STRETCH Students work in pairs to play the game, taking turns to say a word for their partner to find in the Big Picture.

78

Audioscript (track 3.1)
1 backpack // 2 book // 3 ruler // 4 marker // 5 pencil // 6 crayon

4 🎵 3.2 Listen, chant, and act.
- Place the *book* picture card on a desk at the front of the classroom. Say: *Look! My (book) on my desk.* Do the same with the other picture card, one by one. Play the audio, and demonstrate the TPR actions while students listen to the chant.
- Students work in groups. They place the school items on a desk and point to each one when they hear it in the chant. Play the audio a third time, and students join in and do the TPR actions.

> **TPR chant**
> *backpack* – mime putting on a backpack
> *book* – mime opening a book
> *ruler* – mime drawing a line with a ruler
> *marker* – mime writing on the board with a marker
> *pencil* – mime drawing a house
> *crayon* – mime coloring with a crayon

Audioscript (track 3.2)
Look! Look! My backpack / book / ruler / marker / pencil / crayon on my desk.

Collect your friend Show the picture card of Forky to help students identify the correct sticker. Students stick the sticker on p.4 in the Student's Book. Ask: *Who's this?* (Forky).

Wrap-up
- Play *What's this?* (see Games Bank p.206). For this version, use the school items picture cards.
- Sing the *Goodbye* song (track 0.7), and students say goodbye to the Mickey Mouse puppet as they leave class.

📖 Workbook   pages 24–25

Audioscript see p.204

1 **Watch again. Then circle.**
  1 Where does Bonnie go? *b*
  2 What do you see in the video? *a, e, f*
  3 How does Bonnie feel? *b*
2 🎧 **3.1 Listen and color. Then say.** *1 backpack – orange, 2 book – red, 3 ruler – yellow, 4 marker – blue, 5 pencil – purple, 6 crayon – green*
3 **Challenge! Draw and color. Then say.** *1 ruler, 2 crayons*

3 Lesson 2: Vocabulary

Student's Book page 32

Objectives

Lesson aim: say numbers 7–10
Target language: seven, eight, nine, ten
Recycled language: numbers 1–6, things at school
Materials: Audio; Picture cards / Word cards (Numbers 2); Mickey Mouse puppet

GSE Skills

Listening: can recognize cardinal numbers up to ten in short phrases and sentences, if spoken slowly and clearly (10)

Speaking: can use cardinal numbers up to ten (10); can say how many things there are up to ten (13)

Teacher toolkit

Teaching vocabulary

Place seven to ten varied school items on the desk, e.g., pencils, crayons, rulers, markers, all of them together adding up to a maximum of ten. Count each of the items, e.g., pencils, with students, and ask: *How many (pencils)?* Do the same for each of the items. Then count all the items together, and elicit the total number of items (should be no more than ten items in total). Repeat a few times with different numbers of school items.

Engage

Take students on a walk around the school, and they count different items they see, e.g., posters, doors, windows (students don't need to know these words – just point them out). You could also take students outside and ask them to count trees and clouds.

Home-school link

Students count for their families different items in their home, e.g., the number of chairs in the house or the number of flowers on a plant.

Warm-up

- Greet students with the Mickey Mouse puppet, and sing the *Hello, Stars and Heroes* song (track 0.1).
- Make Mickey hold different school objects, e.g., *pencil, book, crayon, ruler*, and ask: *What's this?*
- Say: *Listen and chant!*, and play the chant from Lesson 1 (track 3.2). Students join in with the chant and do the actions.

Presentation

Picture cards / Word cards (optional) Show the picture cards one by one to introduce the new vocabulary. Repeat several times, encouraging students to remember the words. For Stretch students, then show each word card, and elicit the words.

1 3.3 **Listen, point, and say. Then play.**

- Place crayons one by one on a desk. Count with the class: *one, two, three, four, five, six*. Then place one more crayon, and elicit or prompt: *seven*. Do the same with *eight, nine,* and *ten*. Then ask: *How many crayons?* Count all the crayons with the class, from *one* to *ten*.
- Say: *How many? Listen and point.* Play the audio, and students point to the corresponding photos.
- Play the audio again, pausing after each number. Students point to the corresponding photos and repeat the words.
- Point to different photos, and students count from *one* to the number shown in the photo.

SUPPORT Say a number from seven to ten, and students point to the correct photo. Then count all together as a class, from *one* to that number. Repeat with different numbers.

STRETCH Students work in pairs to play a game, taking turns to point to a photo for their partner to count the number of crayons.

Audioscript (track 3.3)

seven … eight … nine … ten

Practice

Teaching star

Classroom management Some students will be faster at coloring, and other students will want to take their time to color carefully. Tell students that the aim of this activity is to practice counting numbers, and it isn't a test of their coloring skills. Ask them to use the same color for all the items in a set, and tell them to not worry about being neat.

2 3.4 **Listen and color. Then count and say.**

- Point to the first picture, and ask: *How many books?* Count the books with students. Then play the first exchange, and ask again: *How many books?* (*eight*). Demonstrate coloring eight books, then students color the books.
- Play the remaining exchanges, and students color the correct number of school items.

LESSON 2
Vocabulary

1 🎧 👂 Listen, point, and say. Then play.

2 🎧 🖍 Listen and color. Then count and say.

a   b   c

3 💬 Find 📗, 🎒, and ✏️. Count and say.

seven, eight, nine, ten

- Then ask: *How many (books)?* (eight) *How many backpacks?* (seven) *How many pencils?* (ten). Students count from one to the correct number for each school item.

STRETCH Students work in pairs, taking turns to name a school object from the scene for their partner to find and count.

> **Extra activity (fast finishers)** Students count different objects in the classroom, up to ten, e.g., posters, chairs, backpacks, windows.

Wrap-up

- Play *Color hunt* (see Games Bank p. 206). For this version, name school items of different colors. Ask students to look for them in the classroom, e.g., *Find a red marker*.
- 🐭 Sing the *Goodbye* song (track 0.7), and students say goodbye to the Mickey Mouse puppet as they leave class.

📝 Workbook   page 26

Audioscript see p. 204

1 🎧 **3.2 Count and color. Then listen and say.**
1 seven, 2 eight, 3 nine, 4 ten

2 Join the dots. Then say. backpack

> **Picture Dictionary**
> Students look at the Picture Dictionary on p. 103 in the Student's Book and complete the activities. (**Answers:** backpacks – nine, chairs – five)

- Say: *books*, and students count the books they colored. Do the same with *markers* and *rulers*, encouraging students to say, e.g., *eight books*.

SUPPORT Pause after each exchange for students to color each set of items.

STRETCH Students work in pairs, taking turns to point to a picture and ask: *How many (books)?*, for their partner to answer.

Audioscript (track 3.4)
a Books. // One, two, three, four, five, six, seven, eight. Eight books.
b Markers. // One, two, three, four, five, six, seven, eight, nine. Nine markers.
c Rulers. // One, two, three, four, five, six, seven. Seven rulers.

3 Find a book, a backpack, and a pencil. Count and say.

- Point to the three small pictures, and elicit the words (*book*, *backpack*, and *pencil*). Point to the scene, and say: *Where are the books?* Point to each book, and count them all together as a class (*eight books*).
- Do the same to find and count the backpacks and the pencils. Count each item all together as a class.

Lesson 3: Grammar

Student's Book page 33

Objectives

Lesson aim: say what things I have
Target language: *I have two rulers.*
Recycled language: school items, numbers 1–10
Materials: Audio Picture cards / Word cards (School items; Numbers 1, 2); Mickey Mouse puppet; (optional) home-made jigsaw puzzles, backpack, or bag

GSE Skills

Listening: can get the gist of a simple song, if supported by gestures (21); can recognize familiar words and phrases in short, simple songs or chants (18)

Speaking: can use cardinal numbers up to ten (10); can name a few everyday objects (10); can recite a short, simple rhyme or chant (16)

Teacher toolkit

Teaching grammar
Bring to class a real backpack or bag, and put some pencils, crayons, rulers, and markers inside. Use the Mickey Mouse puppet to model guessing what is inside, e.g., *two crayons?* Put your hand inside, and take out the crayons one by one, counting them as you do so. Say: *I have one, (two, three, four) crayons!*

Engage
Make some simple jigsaw puzzles by printing a picture of a toy, sticking it onto card, then cutting it up into five or six pieces. Give a puzzle to each student or pair of students. When they complete it, they say what they have, e.g., *I have a (kite).*

Differentiation
Show students gestures for each word in the target structure, e.g., the ASL signs: *I* (point to yourself), *have* (curved hands, thumbs sticking up, bring your hands towards your chest), *two* (hold up two fingers), then use the TPR action for the school item, e.g., *pencil.*

Warm-up

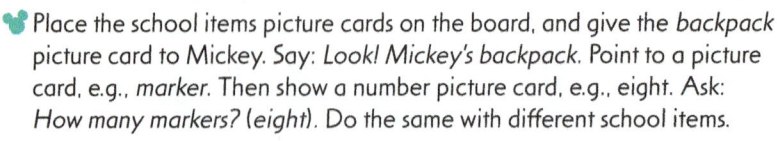

- Greet students with the Mickey Mouse puppet, and sing the *Hello, Stars and Heroes* song (track 0.1).
- Place the school items picture cards on the board, and give the *backpack* picture card to Mickey. Say: *Look! Mickey's backpack.* Point to a picture card, e.g., *marker.* Then show a number picture card, e.g., *eight.* Ask: *How many markers?* (*eight*). Do the same with different school items.

Presentation

1 Sing-along 3.5 **Listen and point. Then sing and act.**

- Name different characters and school items, and students find them in the picture.
- Play the song audio. Students point to each of the school items in the picture as they hear them. Pause after each verse, and ask: *How many (books)?*
- Demonstrate the TPR actions. Then play the whole song, and students do the TPR actions.
- Play the song a third time, and encourage students to join in with some of the words as they do the TPR actions. When students are confident with the words, play the karaoke version (track 3.5_karaoke), and they sing along.

> **TPR song**
>
> *Look!* – put hand over eyes and look around
> *backpack* – mime putting on a backpack
> *book* – mime opening a book
> *ruler* – mime drawing a line with a ruler
> *marker* – mime writing on the board with a marker
> *pencil* – mime drawing a house

Audioscript (track 3.5)

This is my backpack. One, two, three.
This is my backpack. Look with me!
I have a book. // Look! Look! // I have a book in my backpack.
I have two rulers. // Look! Look! // I have two rulers in my backpack.
This is my backpack. One, two, three.
This is my backpack. Look with me!
I have four markers. // Look! Look! // I have four markers in my backpack.
I have three pencils. // Look! Look! // I have three pencils in my backpack.
This is my backpack. One, two, three.
This is my backpack. Look with me!

Practice

2 3.6 **Listen and find. Then say.**

- Students look once more at the picture in activity 1. Ask, using TPR actions to reinforce meaning: *Who has markers?* Students find the markers in the picture and answer (*Peter*).
- Play the audio, pausing after each sentence, and students point to the correct child in the picture.

LESSON 3
Grammar

Sing-along

1 🎵 Listen and point. Then sing and act. **TPR**

🎵 This is my backpack 🎵

2 🎧 💬 Listen and find. Then say.

3 ✏️ 💬 Draw. Then ask and answer.

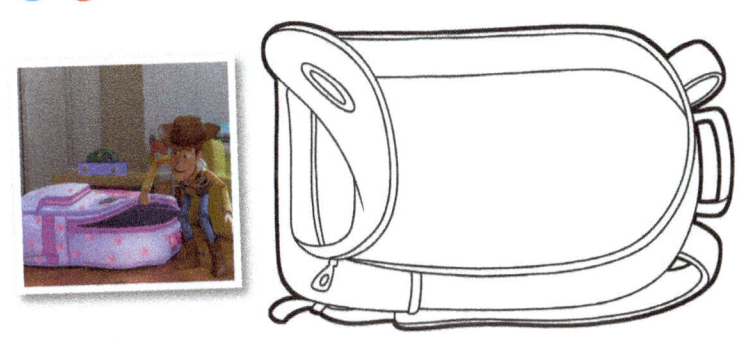

Song: I have (two) (rulers).

33

- Point to Peter and say: *I have …* . Students look at the picture and count Peter's markers. Play the first sentence again, and pause for students to finish your sentence (*four markers*). Do the same with the rest of the sentences.
- Say: *I'm (Maya). I have …* . Students complete the sentence (*two rulers*). Do the same for the other children.

SUPPORT Play the audio, and students say the number and do the TPR action for each sentence.

STRETCH Students play a game. One student silently chooses one character: Cam, Maya, Leyla, or Peter. They say what they have, e.g., *I have (four markers)*, and the other students say which character it is.

Audioscript (track 3.6)
1 **Peter:** *I have four markers.*
2 **Cam:** *I have a book.*
3 **Leyla:** *I have two rulers.*
4 **Maya:** *I have three pencils.*

Teaching star ✨

Growth mindset Praise students when they attempt to say something in English, even if they don't say it correctly or don't use a full sentence. Say: *Good job! Good try!* Then help them say it correctly, e.g., *I have three pencils.*, and encourage them to try again. In the Stretch activity, praise students for attempting to ask and answer questions, and for good communication and collaboration during pairwork.

3 Draw. Then ask and answer.

- Draw an empty backpack outline on the board. Elicit items in a backpack, e.g., *markers, a pencil, a ruler, a book*. Draw some of these items inside the backpack.
- Students draw different school items inside the backpack in their books. They can draw several of the same object, e.g., *four pencils*.
- Point to the backpack you drew on the board, and say: *I have (two) (pencils). And you?*
- Invite a confident student to look at their own picture and say, e.g., *I have three pencils.* Repeat with different students and different school items.

SUPPORT Say: *I have (two) (pencils). And you? How many pencils?* Students look at their pictures and answer by saying the number or by holding up the correct number of fingers.

STRETCH Students work in pairs, taking turns to say what school items are in their picture, comparing answers with their partner.

Extra activity (fast finishers) Students show each other what is in their backpacks, e.g., *I have (six pencils). Look! My (pencil).*

Wrap-up

- Play *Whispers* (see Games Bank p.206). For this version, use the structure: *I have (a crayon).*
- Sing the *Goodbye* song (track 0.7), and students say goodbye to the Mickey Mouse puppet as they leave class.

📓 **Workbook**   page 27

Audioscript see p.204

1 🎧 **3.3 Listen and match.** *1 b, 2 c, 3 a*
2 **Find and circle. Then say.** *1 two rulers/markers, 2 four pencils, 3 rulers*

83

3 Lesson 4: Story

Student's Book pages 34–35

Objectives

Lesson aim: listen to and understand a story about a class pet

Story language: surprise, tortoise; Wow!

Recycled language: school items; puppet; This is Sara. Is it a (book)? I have (crayons).

Receptive language: I have a surprise.

Materials: Audio; Story cards (Unit 3); Mickey Mouse puppet; (optional) a toy, a cardboard box, a few treats

GSE Skills

Listening: can understand a few basic words and phrases in a story that is read aloud (18)

Speaking: can repeat phrases and short sentences, if spoken slowly and clearly (16); can say how they feel, using a limited range of common adjectives, e.g., happy, cold (22)

Teacher toolkit

Story summary

It's Sara's first day at the school, and she's feeling nervous. The teacher brings a nice surprise – a class tortoise named Shelly. Sara loves tortoises, and she shows the other children how to take care of it. Sara makes Shelly a beautiful home.

Engage

A mystery box can be a great way to engage learners with the unit topic and to practice new vocabulary and structures. Decorate a small cardboard box. Put a treat inside the box, then ask the class guess what's inside. Say: *I have a surprise!* Whoever guesses the treat item correctly, wins it.

Identifying my emotions 3

In the story, Sara feels nervous on her first day at school. Students look at Sara's face and body, and identify her feelings in different story scenes. Tell students to imagine they are Sara at the beginning of the story, and ask them to act out how they feel. Then say: *You have Shelly.*, and ask them to act out how they feel now.

Self-awareness

Warm-up

- Before the lesson, put a toy inside a cardboard box.
- Greet students with the Mickey Mouse puppet, and sing the *Hello, Stars and Heroes* song (track 0.1).
- Point at the box, and ask: *What's in the box?* Have students suggest ideas, e.g., *Is it a (ball)?* After most students have guessed, open the box and show them what is inside. Say: *Wow! It's a (ball)!*

Presentation

1 🎧 **3.7 Listen to the story. Is Shelly 6, 7, or 8?**

- Make the Mickey Mouse puppet stand up. Say: *Sit down, Mickey. It's story time!*
- Point to the small picture of the tortoise, and say: *It's a tortoise. Its name is Shelly.* Students look at the story frames to find the tortoise.
- Play the audio. Students listen to the story and follow in their books. They point to each frame as they listen to the story.
- Use the story cards to tell the story again, with or without the audio. Pause after each story frame to ask a comprehension question, e.g., *Is Sara happy?* (no) *What's in the box?* (a tortoise) *Sara says: I have ….* (crayons and pencils).
- Ask: *Is Shelly six, seven, or eight?*, holding up each number of fingers (seven).

Spot! Students find the pencil. (**Answers:** frames 5 and 6) Ask: *What color is the pencil?* (green).

Teaching star

Application Making connections between different characters develops students' thinking skills. Use a Venn diagram to help students make connections between Bonnie from Video 3A in Lesson 1 and Sara from the story in this lesson, using the English they know. Elicit what students know about both girls, writing words or drawing pictures in the diagram.

Practice

2 🎧 **3.8 Listen and point. Then say.**

- Point to each picture, and students name the characters (*Shelly, Sara, Cam, Leyla, Mrs. Smart*).
- Play the first part of the audio, then pause for students to point to the corresponding picture (picture 3). Do the same with the second part of the audio (picture 1) and the third part of the audio (picture 2).
- Give each student a role, either Peter, Layla, Maya, or Ms. Smart. Play the audio, and students act out their role in the story.

Audioscript (track 3.8)

1 **Ms. Smart:** *I have a surprise.*
   Peter: *Is it a book?*
   Leyla: *Is it a puppet?*
2 **Ms. Smart:** *This is Shelly. Shelly's seven.*
3 **Maya:** *Look! He's happy!*
   Peter: *Wow, Sara.*

LESSON 4 Story

The surprise

1 🎧 Listen to the story. Is 🐢 6, 7, or 8? **7**

①
Ms. Smart: *Maya. This is Sara.*
Maya: *Hello, Sara! Nice backpack!*
Sara: *Thanks.*

②
Ms. Smart: *Hello, everyone. I have a surprise.*
Peter: *Is it a book?*
Leyla: *Is it a puppet?*

③
Ms. Smart: *This is Shelly. Shelly's seven.*

④
Maya: *Wow!*
Cam: *It's a tortoise!*
Sara: *Shhh!*

⑤
Sara: *It's OK, Shelly. Don't worry. I have crayons and pencils.*

⑥
Maya: *Look! He's happy!*
Peter: *Wow, Sara!*

The end

2 🎧 Listen and point. Then say.

3 Who's nervous? Circle.

4 💬 Act out the story.

Story: surprise, tortoise; Wow!

---

3 Who's nervous? Circle.
- Students look at the two pictures and then find them in the story (frame 1 and frame 4).
- Point to the first picture, and elicit Sara's emotion *(nervous)*. Do the same with Maya in the second picture *(happy)*. Students circle the correct picture.

4 Act out the story.
- Students look at the photos of a girl and a boy. Ask: *Is she/he nervous? Is she/he happy?*
- Students stand up to act out the story. Show the first story card, and students copy Sara's posture and facial expression *(nervous)*.
- Play the story audio (track 3.7), and hold up the corresponding story cards. Students act out Sara's behavior.

SUPPORT Allow students to choose whether they want to repeat some of the words or just do actions.

STRETCH More confident students role-play different characters, joining in with their words.

Extra activity (story extension) Say: *Shelly is a tortoise. What animals do you like?*, using gesture to reinforce meaning. Students draw a picture of a class pet they would like to have.

Wrap-up
- Place the story cards around the classroom. Say a line from the story, and students go to the corresponding story card. Repeat with other lines. With large classes, groups of students take turns.
- 🐭 Sing the *Goodbye* song (track 0.7), and students say goodbye to the Mickey Mouse puppet as they leave class.

📝 **Workbook** page 28

Audioscript see p.204

1 🎧 **3.4 Listen and circle.** *1 b, 2 b, 3 a*
2 **How does Shelly feel? Match and say.** *1 a, 2 b*

3 Lesson 5: Grammar and Speaking

Student's Book page 36

Objectives

Lesson aim: ask and answer about objects
Target language: *How many books? I have one book.*
Recycled language: numbers 1–10; school items
Receptive language: *Forky says … Bingo!*
Materials: Video 3B; Audio; Picture cards / Word cards (School items; Numbers 1, 2); Stickers; Mickey Mouse puppet; Story cards (Unit 3); Cut-outs (Unit 3), with a cut-out model prepared; scissors; (optional) small objects, e.g., bottle tops, feathers, pompoms, buttons, small pebbles

GSE Skills

Listening: can recognize familiar words in short phrases and sentences spoken slowly and clearly, if supported by pictures or gestures (19)
Speaking: can use cardinal numbers up to ten (10); can name a few everyday objects (10)

Teacher toolkit

Video summary – 3B
How many? **Videoscript see p.202**
Bonnie comes home from school and takes her toys out of her backpack. She wants to sleep with her favorite toys, but Forky has other ideas!

Teaching grammar
Place lots of pencils, crayons, rulers, books, and markers on a desk at the front of the classroom (no more than ten of each item). Ask: *How many (pencils)?* Invite a student to come and count the (pencils), and ask the class to join in with the counting. Say: *I have …*, and elicit, e.g., *nine pencils*.

Engage
Bring to class a selection of small objects, e.g., bottle tops, feathers, pompoms, buttons, small pebbles. Give a pile of objects to each group of students, and from this pile, give a different item to each individual student. Then collect from the pile more of the same item, e.g., more buttons. Students take turns to ask: *How many?*, and answer: *I have (four).*

Warm-up

- Greet students with the Mickey Mouse puppet, and sing the *Hello, Stars and Heroes* song (track 0.1).
- Invite six students to stand at the front of the class, and give each student a school item picture card. Show each story card from Lesson 4, and students say which school items they can see. Ask the students holding the corresponding picture cards to raise them above their heads.

Presentation

Video story

1 ▶ **3B Watch and check (✔).**

- As a lead-in to Video 3B, students look once more at the Big Picture in Lesson 1 to remind them of the video story. Review the Lesson 1 vocabulary, pointing to school items and eliciting the words.
- Ask students to look at the first pair of pictures, and ask: *How many backpacks?* Do the same with the second pair of pictures.
- Make the Mickey Mouse puppet stand up. Say: *Sit down, Mickey. It's video time!*
- Play the video, pausing after we see the backpack [0:15]. Ask: *How many backpacks: one or two?*, pointing to the first pair of pictures on the page. Elicit answers, and students check the correct picture. Do the same with the second pair of pictures.

Practice

2 🎧 **3.9 Listen and stick. Then ask and answer.**

- Point to the school items in the pictures and stickers, and elicit the words.
- Play the audio, pausing after each exchange for students to find and point to the corresponding school items.
- Play the audio again, pausing after each exchange, for students to name the missing school item (*1 crayons, 2 pencils*). Then students stick the stickers in the correct places.
- Play the audio a third time, pausing after each question or answer for students to repeat.
- Divide the class into two groups. Drill the question: *How many (pencils)?* with the first group, using the picture cards. Point to the first picture and encourage the second group to answer, e.g., *I have (three) (pencils)*. Repeat with different school items across the two pictures.

SUPPORT Use number picture cards to elicit answers to the question *How many …?*

STRETCH Students work in pairs, taking turns to ask and answer questions about the school items in pictures 1 and 2, following the model in the audio.

Audioscript (track 3.9)

1 **A:** *How many books?*
   B: *One. I have one book.*
   A: *How many pencils?*
   B: *Three. I have three pencils.*
   A: *How many crayons?*
   B: *Two. I have two crayons.*

LESSON 5
Grammar and Speaking

1 Watch and check (✓).

2 Listen and stick. Then ask and answer.

3 3.10 Listen and point. Then make and play.

Skills: How many (books)? I have (one) (book).

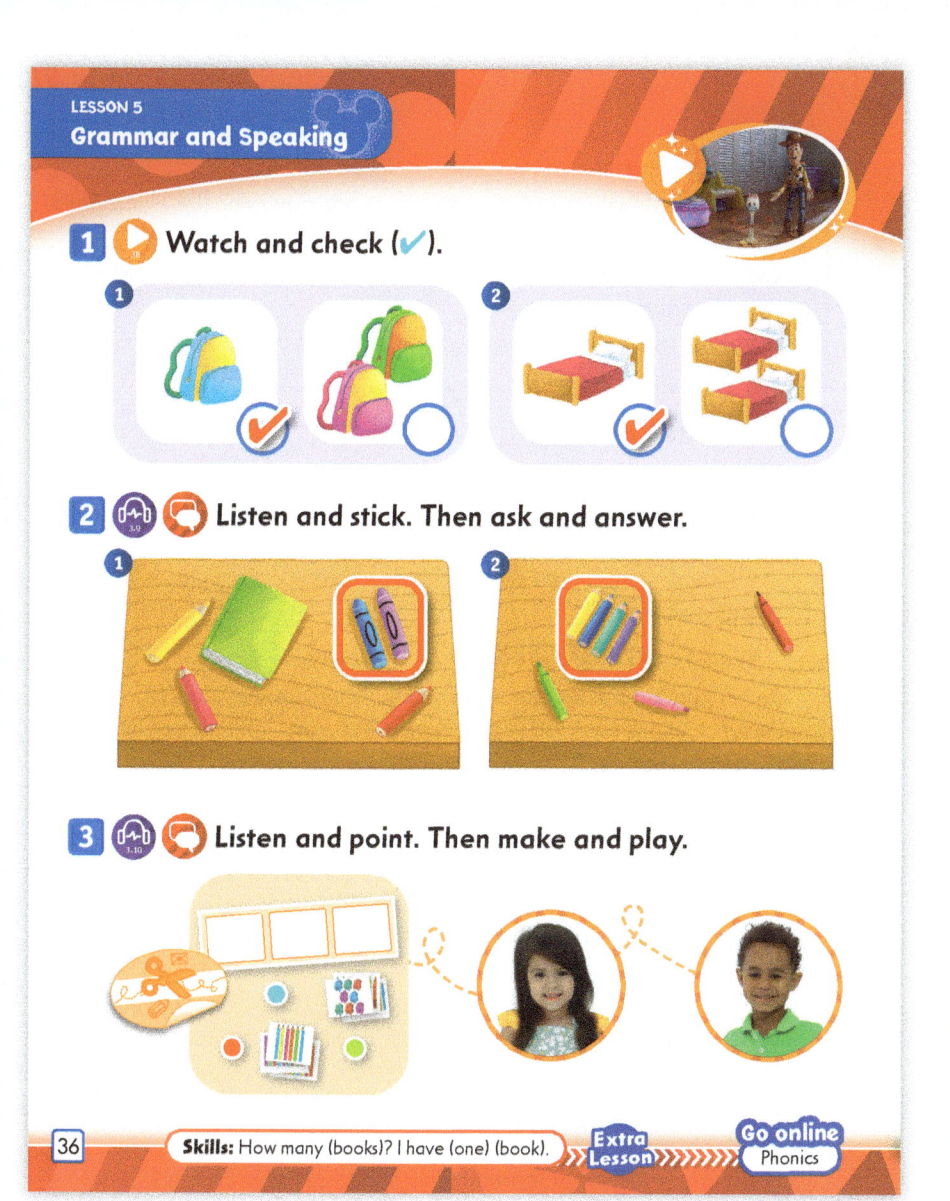

2 **A:** How many markers?
B: Three. I have three markers.
A: How many pencils?
B: Four. I have four pencils.

Teaching star

Diversity and inclusion Some students may find small counters fiddly and difficult to manipulate. Ask students to turn over the cards when playing Bingo instead of using the counters.

3 3.10 **Listen and point. Then make and play.**
- Students cut carefully around the dotted lines of the cut-outs and the counters on.
- Demonstrate the game. Put the game board on a desk, and put the following cards face-up on the board: *six pencils, seven rulers, nine markers*. Play the audio, and pause after the first part. Point to the corresponding card on the game board, and place a counter on top. Then play the rest of the audio, and repeat. Say: *Bingo! I have six pencils, seven rulers, nine markers!*

- Tell students to choose three cards and place them on their game board. Have your cards in a pile on your desk. Take the first card, and say how many of an item are on the card, e.g., *six books*. Give students time to look at the game cards on their board. If they have (six books), they place a counter on the picture. Repeat until a student has a counter on all three pictures. Say: *Bingo!* all together as a class, then invite the student to say *I have ...* and name the items in the pictures.

SUPPORT Students can play the game in mixed-ability pairs. The less confident student says only the number and the name of the classroom object.

STRETCH Students can play the game in mixed-ability pairs. The more confident student says full sentences, using *I have ...*, the number, and the name of the classroom object.

Audioscript (track 3.10)
A: *Eight backpacks. ... Six pencils.*
B: *Bingo! I have six pencils. I have seven rulers. I have nine markers!*

Extra activity (whole class) Ask students to place any number of school items on their desk, as they choose. Invite a confident student to ask questions, e.g., *How many (crayons)?* Students count their items. Invite a student to answer, e.g., *I have (two) (crayons)*. Then other students say if they have a different number of that school item.

Wrap-up
- Play *Which is different?* (see Games Bank p.206). For this version, draw five pencils, five rulers, six books, and five markers.
- Sing the *Goodbye* song (track 0.7), and students say goodbye to the Mickey Mouse puppet as they leave class.

Workbook   page 29

Audioscript see p.204

1. 3.5 Listen and check (✓). Then say.
1 a ✓, 2 a ✓, 3 b ✓
2. **Count and circle. Then ask and answer.**
8 pencils, 2 backpacks, 6 rulers, 4 markers

3 Lesson 6: Myself and others

I'm nervous Student's Book page 37

Objectives

Lesson aim: recognize and name emotions
Target language: nervous; I'm not nervous. It's OK. Don't worry.
Recycled language: I'm (not) happy/sad/grumpy.
Materials: Audio; (optional) Video 3A; Myself and others poster; Stickers; Mickey Mouse puppet; a "mood-o-meter" (see Teacher toolkit); (optional) cards for Teacher toolkit, the cardboard box from Lesson 4

GSE Skills

Listening: can recognize isolated words related to familiar topics, if spoken slowly and clearly and supported by pictures or gestures (16); can recognize familiar words in short phrases and sentences spoken slowly and clearly, if supported by pictures or gestures (19)

Speaking: can say how they feel, using a limited range of common adjectives, e.g., happy, cold (22)

Teacher toolkit

Identifying my emotions 3

In this lesson, students explore different situations where they may feel nervous. At this age, students can start to link their feelings with personal experiences. Ask students to mime situations when they feel nervous, e.g., when they try something for the first time, or when they can't find their parents in a busy place. They say: *I'm nervous!* Then ask the class to say: *It's OK. Don't worry.*

Self-awareness

Engage

Make a "mood-o-meter" for the display area in your classroom, with an arrow that can be moved along the mood-o-meter. Stick a photo of the corresponding emotion for the lesson above the mood-o-meter (in this lesson: nervous), and invite students to go and move the arrow as you discuss the different situations mentioned in the lesson.

Home-school link

Ask students to tell their families when they feel nervous, saying *I'm nervous*. Also, encourage them to use the phrases: *It's OK. / Don't worry.*, when they see someone at home looking nervous or sad.

Warm-up

- Greet students with the Mickey Mouse puppet, and sing the *Hello, Stars and Heroes* song (track 0.1).
- Show the *Myself and others* poster and review *I'm happy!*, *I'm sad!* and *I'm (not) grumpy!*.
- Make Mickey act sad/happy/grumpy, and ask: *Is Mickey happy? Is he sad? Is he grumpy?*

🎵 **1.12 Listen and sing.**

- Play the song audio, and students join in with the words and the actions.
- Ask: *How do you feel? Are you (happy)?*, and students respond *yes/no / I'm (happy)!*

Presentation

1 **Who's nervous? Check (✓). Then say.**

- Remind students of the situations and the characters in Video 3A in Lesson 1 and the story. If required, play Video 3A and look at the story again.
- Students look at the pictures and say the names of the characters (Sara, Shelly, Bonnie, Woody).
- Point to each picture, and ask and mime: *Is (Sara) happy? Is she sad? Is she grumpy? Is she nervous?* If necessary, use L1 to remind students of each character's story. (Sara and Bonnie are nervous because it is their first day at school. Shelly might be nervous because children are making a noise.)
- Then say and mime: *I'm nervous*. Point to the pictures, and ask and mime: *Who is nervous?* Students check the *nervous* pictures and say *I'm (nervous)*.

Teaching star

Social and emotional learning Play Video 3A from Lesson 1, and students mime to copy Bonnie's emotions at each point in the story. Ask students what makes Bonnie feel better when she's nervous or sad (*her toys*). Encourage students to empathize with Bonnie, and ask if their toys help them to feel better, too.

Practice

2 **3.11 Listen and point. Then act and say.**

- Students look at each of the photos. Ask: *Is she/he nervous?*, and elicit *yes* or *no* answers.
- Play the audio, and students point to the correct photos.
- Using L1, discuss what students think is happening in the photos. Ask students how they feel when they go to the dentist and the hair salon. Ask: *Are you nervous?*, and elicit *yes* or *no* answers.
- Say: *You're at the dentist.*, and point to pictures 1 and 2. Students act out being at the dentist, e.g., tilting their head back and opening their mouth wide. Say: *I'm nervous or I'm not nervous?* Students say and mime their answer. Do the same with the hair salon. If some students say they're nervous, say: *Don't worry. It's OK.*

88

I'm nervous

LESSON 6
Myself and others

1 Who's nervous? Check (✓). Then say.

2 Listen and point. Then act and say. TPR

3 Look and colour for you. Then say.

Self-awareness: I'm (not) nervous. It's OK. Don't worry.

SUPPORT Students act out how they feel in each situation and say only *nervous* or *not nervous*.

STRETCH Students work in pairs, taking turns to respond to each situation. They say how they feel, e.g., *I'm nervous / not nervous.*, for their partner to respond, if appropriate, e.g., *It's OK. Don't worry.*

⭐ **I'm a hero!** ⭐ Point to the sticker picture, and elicit that Peter is nervous. Ask students what Maya is saying. (*It's OK. Don't worry!*). Then students stick the sticker in their books.

> **Extra activity (whole class)** Tell students to imagine they are at the dentist. Students decide whether they are nervous or not nervous, and say: *I'm (not) nervous.* Invite one student to role-play being the dentist and say, e.g., *It's OK. / Don't worry.* You could play the audio for support.

Wrap-up

- Look at the *Myself and others* poster all together. Point to different emotions, and students act them out. Encourage them to use the target language, e.g., *It's OK. Don't worry.*
- Sing the *Goodbye* song (track 0.7), and students say goodbye to the Mickey Mouse puppet as they leave class.

📖 **Workbook**   page 30

1 **Who's nervous? Circle. Then say for you.** *Cam*
2 **Where in your body do you feel nervous? Color.**

Audioscript (track 3.11)
1 I'm nervous. // It's OK. Don't worry.
2 I'm not nervous.
3 I'm not nervous.
4 I'm nervous. // Don't worry. It's OK.

3 Look and color for you. Then say.

- Draw on the board two arrows, each with five bars, similar to the arrows under the photos. Point to the first photo, and ask: *Is Mickey nervous?* Make the Mickey Mouse puppet act not nervous (happy), and color one bar. Do the same for the second photo, but this time make Mickey act very nervous. Color five bars. To reinforce this, count from *one* to *five*, miming five stages from not nervous to very nervous.
- Point to each photo, and ask: *Are you nervous?* Students color the bars for how they feel about each photo, from one bar (not nervous) to five bars (very nervous).
- Point to each photo again, and ask: *Are you nervous?* Students count the number of bars they colored, then hold up the same number of fingers, saying: *I'm nervous / I'm not nervous.*

Lesson 7: My world

Objectives

Lesson aims: understand equations
Target language: *is, minus, plus*
Recycled language: numbers 1–10, school items
Receptive language: *equations*
Materials: Audio; Picture cards (Numbers 1, 2); Mickey Mouse puppet; paper, scissors, school items; (optional) bottle tops, zip-lock bags

GSE Skills

Listening: can recognize cardinal numbers up to ten in short phrases and sentences spoken slowly and clearly (10)
Speaking: can use cardinal numbers up to ten (10); can say how many things there are up to ten (13)

Teacher toolkit

Cross-curricular
Using objects and realia can help students understand abstract concepts such as addition and subtraction. Give students counting cubes or other objects that they can manipulate to provide a multi-sensory approach to math.

Engage
Ask students to bring to class bottle tops from water and juice bottles. Give students markers, and ask them to draw different numbers on the bottle tops and also math symbols. Then put all the bottle tops in zip-lock bags. In any lesson, fast finishers can take a bag of numbered bottle tops and use them to make equations, e.g., $3 + 3 = 6$.

Home-school link
Students use school items or toys to make and say an equation for their families to solve, e.g., *Seven minus three is ….* (*four*).

Math: Plus and minus Student's Book page 38

Warm-up
- Greet students with the Mickey Mouse puppet, and sing the *Hello, Stars and Heroes* song (track 0.1).
- Play *What's missing?* (see Games Bank p.206) to review numbers.

Presentation

1 🎧 **3.12 Listen and point. Then show and say.**

- Write a simple math equation on the board: $2 + 2 = ?$. Say: *Two plus two is …* . Students answer: *four*.
- Play the audio, pausing after each word for students to point to the symbols.
- Play the audio again, and students repeat the words.
- Point to each part of the equation in the model on the board, and say: *two plus two is …* . Again, students say *four*, then write in the answer. Write another equation on the board, this time using *minus*, e.g., $3 - 1 = ?$. Say: *Three minus one is …* . (*two*), and write *2*.
- Show students a TPR action for each math symbol: *plus* – hold left arm horizontally and cross with right arm vertically, *minus* – hold left arm horizontally, *is* – hold both arms parallel horizontally.
- Say each word, and students repeat it and do the corresponding TPR action. Then do a TPR action, and students say the corresponding word.

SUPPORT Say each word, and students do the corresponding TPR action.

STRETCH Students work in pairs, taking turns to do a TPR action for their partner to say the word.

Audioscript (track 3.12)
1 plus // 2 minus // 3 is

Teaching star

Support understanding To help students complete the equations, draw a number line on the board. Show students how to move their finger to jump from one number to the next, e.g., *one, two* (move your finger from one to two); *one, two, three* (move your finger three more spaces from *two*, to reach *five*). Say: *Two plus three is five*.

0 1 2 3 4 5 6 7 8 9 10

Practice

2 🎧 **3.13 Listen and draw. Then point and say.**

- Students look at the pictures in the first equation. Ask: *How many pencils? Two, three, five.* Do the same with the other equations.
- Draw on the board the three math symbols (+, -, =). Then point to the white circle in each equation and ask: *Plus, minus, or is?* Play the first part of the audio, and students point to the correct symbol on the board. Then they draw this symbol to complete the equation. Do the same for the other two equations.
- Point to each part of the first equation, and read it all together as a class: *Two plus three is five.* Do the same for the other two equations.

LESSON 7
My world

Plus and minus

1 Listen and point. Then show and say. TPR

① + ② − ③ =

2 Listen and draw. Then point and say.

① 2 + 3 = 5
② 5 + 4 = 9
③ 7 − 1 = 6

3 Make equations. Then test your friend.

Math: is, minus, plus

SUPPORT Go around the class, and choose individual students' equations. Help the student say their equation for the class to solve.

STRETCH Students work in pairs, taking turns to make an equation for their partner to solve.

Thinking skills
Understand In activity 2, students recognize the format of simple addition and subtraction equations, in both numerical and pictorial form. They complete the equations, using the pictures for support.

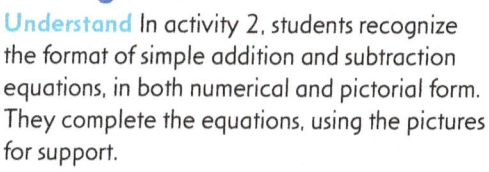

Create In activity 3, students use their knowledge to create their own equations, forming the corresponding math symbols, and using real world items to represent the numbers.

Extra activity (extension) Use the Mickey Mouse puppet to make incorrect equations, using the number picture cards and the paper symbols from activity 3. Make Mickey say the equation. Then ask the class to say: *No, Mickey!* Invite a student to say the correct answer.

Wrap-up
- Play *Monster munch* (see Games Bank p.206). For this version, students feed the monster equations. Tell them that today, the monster can only eat equations that make *five*.
- Sing the *Goodbye* song (track 0.7), and students say goodbye to the Mickey Mouse puppet as they leave class.

Workbook — page 31
Audioscript see p.205
1 **Trace and color. Then say.** *1 plus, 2 minus, 3 is*
2 3.6 **Look and draw. Then listen and check.**
1 eight balls, 2 two kites

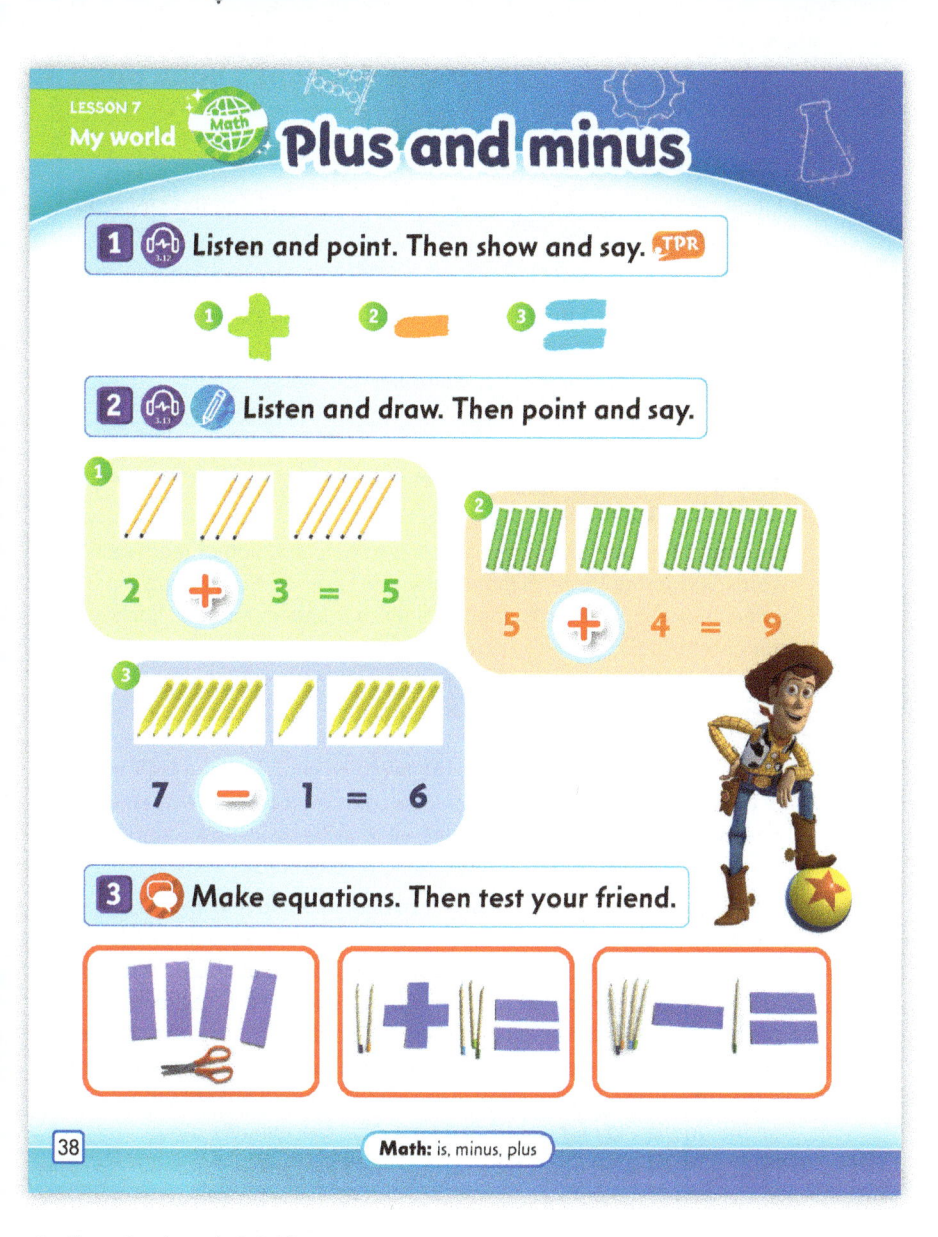

Audioscript (track 3.13)
1 Two plus three is five.
2 Five plus four is nine.
3 Seven minus one is six.

3 Make equations. Then test your friend.
- Show students how to cut out four rectangles from a piece of paper. Alternatively, hand out four small rectangles of paper to each student. Show students how to make the four symbols by turning and placing the rectangles on the desk, as in the photos.
- Recreate on a desk the equation from the second photo, using pencils and the paper symbols you have prepared. Say: *Two plus three is …*, and elicit *five*. Then place five more pencils at the end to complete the equation.
- Students make their own equations, using their own school items and their cut-out symbols.
- Invite individual students to recreate their equation on a desk at the front of the class. They say their equation, e.g., *Four minus one is …*, and ask the class to solve it (*three*).

3 Lesson 8: Review

Objectives

Lesson aim: review target language from Unit 3

Target language: school items; *How many (backpacks)? I have (two) (crayons).*

Recycled language: colors

Materials: Audio; (optional) Video 3A, Video 3B; Picture cards / Word cards (School items; Numbers 1, 2); Stickers; Mickey Mouse puppet; *My progress* poster

GSE Skills

Listening: can recognize isolated words related to familiar topics, if spoken slowly and clearly and supported by pictures and gestures (16)

Speaking: can say single words related to familiar topics, if supported by pictures or gestures (18)

Teacher toolkit

Video review
You can return to Video 3A and Video 3B at the end of the unit for a "second play." Review the target structures, and students wave their hands when they hear one of these structures in the video.

Remediation
With students who need more support, give the Mickey Mouse puppet two crayons and review the structure *I have (two) (crayons).* Make Mickey say *I have …*, and elicit the correct number and word. Then ask students to repeat the sentence.

Home-school link
Students share with their families the language they've learned in the unit, naming and counting school items in their backpacks or at home.

I can do it! Student's Book page 39

Warm-up
- Greet students with the Mickey Mouse puppet, and sing the *Hello, Stars and Heroes* song (track 0.1).
- Play *Where is …?* (see Games Bank p.206) with picture cards from the unit.
- Play the song audio from Lesson 3 (track 3.5), and students join in with the words and the actions. If students are confident with the words, play the karaoke version (track 3.5_karaoke).

I can do it!

> **Teaching star**
>
> **Learning to learn** Encourage students to help each other learn new words. Suggest to students that if they don't know a word during the game, they should listen to their partner or ask them for help. Encourage students to realize that we can learn from each other.

1 Play and say.

- To play the game, you will need the two dice cards and the counter made in Unit 1. Stick the school item picture cards on the board in a column, one below the other. Play the game all together as a class, keeping a tally on the board next to the corresponding picture cards.
- Start in any square on the board. A student picks up a dice card and says the number of circles on the card, *one* or *two*. Follow the arrows to move the counter the same number of squares on the game board. When you land on a square, elicit, e.g., *I have a book*, and write *1* on the board next to the *book* picture card. If you land on the pictures of Bonnie, elicit *I'm nervous!* or *I'm not nervous!* Continue in the same way, moving onto different squares, eliciting sentences, and keeping a tally of school items on the board. Play for a specified time, e.g., five minutes.
- Point on the board to each school item picture card and its tally. Ask: *How many (crayons)?* Count with students or say, e.g., *One plus one plus one is three.* Then say: *I have (three) (crayons).* Do the same for all school items.

> **ACHIEVE**
> Students say what school items they have, count and add up different items, and say whether someone is nervous or not nervous.
>
> **SUPPORT**
> Provide sentence prompts to help students make sentences: *I have a … . I'm … .* Students will show their receptive understanding of the structures as they complete them.
>
> **STRETCH**
> After playing the game as a class, students work in pairs to ask and answer questions about the number of items in the tally, e.g., *How many backpacks? I have four backpacks.*

LESSON 8 Review

I can do it!

1 🗨 Play and say.

Throw again

2 💡 ✏️ Think and color. Then stick!

I can ...

Unit 3!

Go online Big Project

39

2 💡 Think and color. Then stick!

- Point to each picture, and say *I can ...* statements: *I can name school items. I can sing a song. I can say, "I'm nervous."* For each statement, give an example, and then ask: *Can you do this?* If necessary, explain in L1.
- Students demonstrate what they can do. They work in pairs, taking turns to say the names of different school items. Sing the song all together as a class. Students work in pairs, taking turns to say and act out feeling nervous and not nervous. Monitor and assess their performance.
- Students color the stars next to what they can do. Then they stick the reward sticker to show they have completed Unit 3.

My Star and Hero! Students look at the picture of Forky on p.4 of the Student's Book. They say how they think he feels.

Extra activity (class game) Play *Draw it!* (see Games Bank p.206), using the unit picture cards.

Wrap-up

- Students reflect on which lesson or activity they most enjoyed in Unit 3. Have a class vote, and choose one activity to do again as a class, e.g., watch the video, sing the song or chant, listen to the story, or play a game.
- Draw students' attention to the *My progress* poster, and ask them to identify the picture that reflects this unit. Read aloud with students the *I can ...* statements (*I can ask and answer about school things, I can say I'm (not) nervous*).
- Sing the *Goodbye* song (track 0.7), then students say goodbye to the Mickey Mouse puppet and tell him their favorite word from Unit 3.

📝 Workbook   pages 32–33

Audioscript see p.204

My progress

1 🎧 3.7 **Listen and circle. Then act and say.**
1 six pencils, 2 eight crayons, 3 two markers, 4 one backpack

2 **Follow and count. Then ask and answer.**
five pencils, three rulers, two backpacks

Units W–3 My practice

1 **Color and count. Then ask and answer.**
seven books, three markers, four pencils, one ruler, six crayons, one backpack
Circle the toys. Find the family.

2 **Draw your backpack. Then say.** five pencils, three rulers, two backpacks

Unit 3! My favorite activity: Students stick the small star sticker next to their favorite activity.

4 My body

Unit objectives

By the end of this unit, students can:
- talk about parts of the body and different actions
- read and understand a story about having fun with a pet
- recognize and name emotions and explore how people express these emotions
- talk about coding

Skills development GSE

Listening: recognize and understand affirmative and negative instructions and complete them

Speaking: talk about their body; say how they express excitement; give instructions and directions

Vocabulary

Lesson 1: arm, body, hand, head, leg, nose
Lesson 2: clap, shake, stomp, touch

Grammar

Lesson 3: Stomp your feet. Don't move.
Lesson 5: What's this? It's my nose.

Myself and others

Expressing my emotions In this unit, a Disney video and a story introduce the theme of expressing our emotions. Students will identify how their bodies show when they are feeling different emotions.

Language: cry, excited, jump, smile; I'm happy. I smile.

Self-awareness

Story

Fun with Shelly
I have an idea. I'm excited! Yippee!

My world

Technology: Coding
up, down, left, right; Go left!

Unit overview

Disney Frozen

Elsa
When Elsa's parents die, she becomes Queen. She tries hard to stay calm and in control, but she has been keeping her emotions inside for many years and one day, she needs to let them out.

Anna
Anna (pronounced Ah-na) is the younger sister of Princess Elsa. She's nice, optimistic, and daring, and she sets out on an adventure to search for her sister so they can live together happily as a family.

Kristoff
A hardworking 21-year-old ice worker whose best friend is a reindeer (Sven). He's kind of a loner, but he's nice, respectful, and does everything he can to help Anna.

Sven
A reindeer and Kristoff's best friend. Kristoff saved Sven's life when he was a young reindeer and for this, Sven is fiercely loyal to his friend.

Olaf
A friendly snowman who is a good friend to Anna and Elsa. He's innocent, sincere, and very nice, and he loves summer!

Anna and Elsa are princesses who live in the castle in Arendelle. Elsa has a special power – she can turn things into ice. However, this can be dangerous and she must keep her power hidden. During a party, Elsa is unable to control her power, and she freezes the city. She runs away to the mountains, and Anna goes in search of her sister, hoping to bring her back home.

Did you know?
The movie Frozen was inspired by the fairy tale *The Snow Queen* by Hans Christian Andersen, and the characters' names reflect this: Hans (Anna's boyfriend), Kristoff, Anna, and Sven.

Video stories
Video 4A: *Wake up, Elsa!*
Video 4B: *It's a nose*

Online modules

Phonics
Words with Jj, Kk, and Ll sounds in initial position
jump, king, leg

Big Project
Have a puppet show!

4 Lesson 1: Vocabulary

Student's Book pages 40–41

Objectives

Lesson aim: name parts of the body
Target language: arm, body, hand, head, leg, nose
Recycled language: colors; sister, big; This is Elsa. Who's this? Is it a …? No. It's a …
Receptive language: Wake up, Elsa. Ouch! Come on. Let's play. Snow! Yippee! Let's dance!; snowman
Materials: Video 4A; Audio; Picture cards / Word cards (Body, Family, Disney characters); Sticker (Elsa); Mickey Mouse puppet; (optional) roll of paper or large sheet of paper

GSE Skills

Listening: can recognize isolated words related to familiar topics, if spoken slowly and clearly and supported by pictures and gestures (16)
Speaking: can repeat single words, if spoken slowly and clearly (10); can name common parts of the body (23)

Teacher toolkit

Video summary – 4A
Wake up, Elsa! **Videoscript see p.202**
Anna and her sister Elsa are in the castle at night. Anna can't sleep, and she wants to play, so she wakes up Elsa. Elsa makes snow, and the two sisters have lots of fun together.

Engage
Place on the floor a large sheet of paper that is bigger than one of the students (a roll of paper works best). Invite a student to lie down on the piece of paper, and ask another student to draw around him/her with a crayon. Stick the body outline in your display area. During the unit, as students learn the new vocabulary, ask them to label the different body parts. Also, ask them to add pictures of actions they do with each body part. Keep the body outline for use in Unit 5.

Expressing my emotions
cry, excited, jump
Use the video story to talk about the feelings and behavior of the characters. Students mime how Anna feels (excited) and what she does to express this feeling (she opens her eyes wide, jumps, claps, and dances).
Self-awareness

Warm-up
- Greet students with the Mickey Mouse puppet, and sing the *Hello, Stars and Heroes* song (track 0.1).

Presentation — Video story
- Students look at the Big Picture. Introduce the movie and the characters: *This is the movie* Frozen. *This is Elsa/Anna/Olaf/Kristoff/Sven.*
- Point to the characters, and ask: *Who's this? Who's a sister? (Anna/Elsa) Is (the snowman) big or small? (small)*

1 4A **Watch. Who's in bed? Check (✓).**
- Make the Mickey Mouse puppet stand up. Say: *Sit down, Mickey. It's video time! Let's watch!*
- Play Video 4A, and students watch and listen. Point to the picture of the bed in the rubric, and mime sleeping. Play the video again, pausing at 0:30. Ask: *Who's in bed?* Point to the small pictures and say: *Anna, Olaf, or Elsa?* Ask students to point to and check the correct character.

2 4A **Circle for Anna.**
- Use facial expression and mime to pre-teach *excited*, and encourage students to copy you.
- Point to each small picture, and ask students to do the action: *cry, jump, clap*. Play the video again, and students copy what Anna does in each scene.
- Ask students to point to the actions Anna does, then circle the correct picture.

Picture cards / Word cards (optional) Show the picture cards one by one to introduce the new vocabulary. Repeat several times, encouraging students to remember the words. For Stretch students, then show each word card, and elicit the words.

Practice

3 4.1 **Listen, find, and say. Then count.**
- Hold up each picture card, and students find the corresponding body part in the Big Picture.
- Play the audio, pausing after each word. Students point to the body part in the Big Picture. Play the audio again, pausing for students to say the words. Play the audio a third time, and students say and point to the body parts.
- Hold up the body picture cards, and ask: *How many?* Students look at the Big Picture and count the number of each body part in the picture.

SUPPORT Hold up your book, and point to Elsa's head. Count all the heads together with the class: *one, two, three, four, five.* Do the same with the other body parts (except legs).

STRETCH Play the audio, pausing after each word for students to work with a partner to find and count the body parts.

Audioscript (track 4.1)
1 hand // 2 arm // 3 body // 4 nose // 5 leg // 6 head

4 My body

LESSON 1 Vocabulary

1 ▶ Watch. Who's in 🛏? Check (✓).

2 ▶ Circle for Anna.

3 🎧 Listen, find, and say. Then count.

4 🎵 Listen, chant, and act. TPR

🎵 Look at me!

arm, body, hand, head, leg, nose

4 🎵 **4.2 Listen, chant, and act.**

🐭 Make the Mickey Mouse puppet jump around and say: *Look at me! Look at me!* Then make him say: *This is my body. / I have one head.*, etc. Point to the corresponding part of Mickey's body, and students point to it, too.

- Display the picture cards. Play the audio, and students listen and point to the correct picture card when they hear the word for each body part.
- Demonstrate TPR actions by pointing to the corresponding part of the body. Play the audio again. Students join in with the chant and do the actions.

Audioscript (track 4.2)
Look at me! *(x2)* This is my body.
Look at me! *(x2)* I have one head.
Look at me! *(x2)* I have two arms.
Look at me! *(x2)* I have two legs.
Look at me! *(x2)* I have two hands.
Look at me! *(x2)* I have one nose.
Body. Head. Arms. Legs. Hands. Nose.

❓ **Collect your friend** Show the picture card of Elsa to help students identify the correct sticker. Students stick the sticker on p.4 in the Student's Book. Ask: *Who's this?* (Elsa).

Extra activity (video extension) Students draw a picture of Olaf, and point to and name his body parts.

Wrap-up
🐭 Play *Mickey says* (see Games Bank p.206). For this version, make the Mickey Mouse puppet say the names of different body parts for students to touch on their own bodies.
🐭 Sing the *Goodbye* song (track 0.7), and students say goodbye to Mickey as they leave class.

📝 **Workbook** pages 34–35

Audioscript see p.204

1 **Watch again. Then answer.**
  1 Where are they? Check (✓). *a ✓*
  2 Number in order. *a 2, b 3, c 1*
  3 How does Anna feel? Circle. *a*
2 🎧 **4.1 Listen and number. Then say.** *1 hand, 2 body, 3 head, 4 leg, 5 nose, 6 arm*
3 **Challenge! Who's this? Say hello.** *Hello, Sven. Hello, Olaf.*

4 Lesson 2: Vocabulary

Student's Book page 42

Objectives

Lesson aim: name actions
Target language: clap, shake, stomp, touch
Recycled language: body
Materials: Audio; Picture cards / Word cards (Body, Actions 1); Stickers; Mickey Mouse puppet; (optional) music

GSE Skills

Listening: can understand basic action words, e.g., *clap, stamp, jump, walk* (15); can understand simple spoken commands as part of a game (18)

Speaking: can repeat single words, if spoken slowly and clearly (10); can use language related to basic actions, e.g., *clap, stamp, jump, walk* (21); can name common parts of the body (23)

Teacher toolkit

Teaching vocabulary

Play a game to practice the verbs after presenting them with the picture cards. Invite two students to the front, and ask them to stand with one student in front of the other. Tell the student in front that she/he is a puppet. The student behind is the "puppeteer." He/She holds the "puppet's" arms and moves them around. Give instructions to the "puppeteer." e.g., *Touch your head. Touch the desk. Clap your hands. Shake your arms.*

Engage

Play some music, and students use different body parts to make percussion sounds to accompany the beat. First, they clap their hands. Then, they stomp their feet. Elicit other ways in which students can make sounds with their bodies and the objects around them, e.g., tapping fingers on a desk, shaking a box of crayons, clicking your tongue. Then each student chooses one way of making a sound, and working together, the class provides the percussion section as you play the piece of music.

Home-school link

Students teach a family member the different actions they've learned.

Warm-up

- Greet students with the Mickey Mouse puppet, and sing the *Hello, Stars and Heroes* song (track 0.1).
- Make Mickey hold up the body picture cards from Lesson 1, and students say the words and point to their own body parts.
- Say: *Listen and chant!*, and play the chant from Lesson 1 (track 4.2). Students join in with the chant and do the actions.

Presentation

Picture cards / Word cards (optional) Show the picture cards one by one to introduce the new vocabulary. Repeat several times, encouraging students to remember the words. For Stretch students, then show each word card, and elicit the words.

1 4.3 Listen, point, and say. Then play.

- Make the Mickey Mouse puppet demonstrate each of the actions: *shake* (head), *clap* (hands), *stomp* (feet), *touch* (toes). Students look at the photos and point to the one showing the same action that Mickey is doing.
- Say: *Listen and point.* Play the audio, and students point to the corresponding photos. Play the audio again, pausing after each action. Students point to the corresponding photo and repeat the word.
- Point to a photo, and students do the action shown in the photo and say the word. Repeat with different photos.

SUPPORT Say an action word, and students do the corresponding action. Start slowly, giving students time to think and respond, then gradually say the words more quickly.

STRETCH Students work in pairs, taking turns to point to a photo for their partner to name and do the action shown in the photo.

> **TPR**
>
> clap – clap your hands   touch – touch your feet
> stomp – stomp your feet   shake – shake your head

Audioscript (track 4.3)
1 shake // 2 stomp // 3 clap // 4 touch

Practice

Teaching star

Classroom management TPR games can be a fun way to give all students additional language practice, but they can easily get out of hand. Use non-verbal signals, e.g., hold up your hand to get students to stand still and listen, then bring your hand down when you want students to move.

2 4.4 Listen and stick. Then say.

- Point to the first picture sequence, and elicit the actions (*clap, shake*).
- Then point to the empty sticker frame, and students say which action they think is missing (either *stomp* or *touch*). Play the first part of the audio, then pause for students to do the action they hear. Do the same with the second picture sequence.

LESSON 2
Vocabulary

1 🎧 💬 **Listen, point, and say. Then play.**

2 🎧 💬 **Listen and stick. Then say.**

3 🎧 💬 **Listen and do. Then play.** TPR

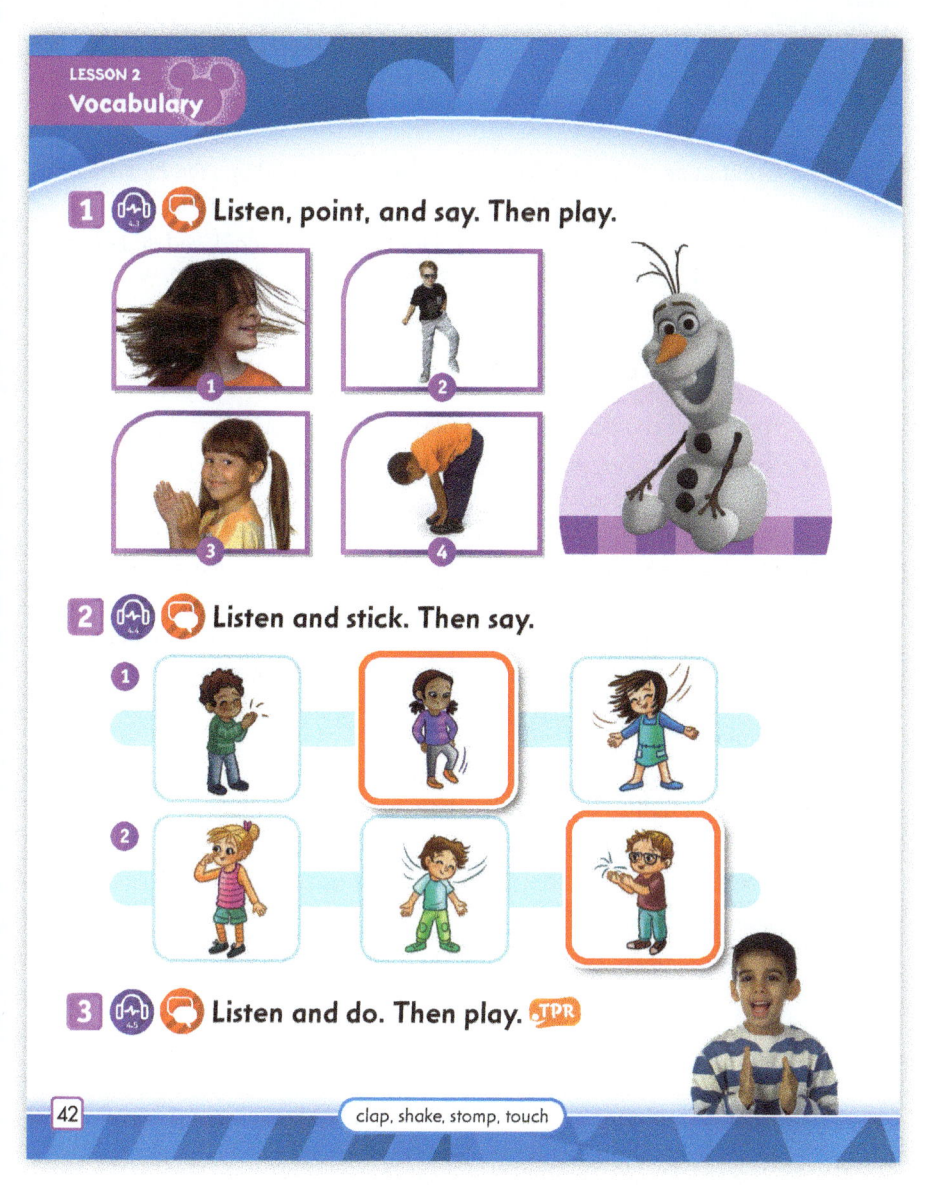

42   clap, shake, stomp, touch

- Play the audio again for students to listen and stick the correct stickers in the empty frames.
- Play the audio a third time, pausing for students to point and repeat the words.
- Say any three action words in sequence, e.g., *shake, touch, clap*. Students repeat the words and do the three actions in the correct order. Repeat with different action word sequences, changing the order of the actions each time.

Audioscript (track 4.4)
1 clap … stomp … shake
2 touch … shake … clap

3 🎧 **4.5 Listen and do. Then play.**
- Clap your hands and stomp your feet at the same time. Students copy you and say the words (*clap, stomp*). Then shake your head and touch your nose (*shake, touch*).
- Play the audio, pausing after each instruction for students to do the actions.
- Name and demonstrate two actions, and students do these actions. Then name two different actions, without demonstrating, and students do these new actions. Repeat a few times.

- Invite two confident students to name actions for the class to do. Repeat with different students and actions.

SUPPORT As you name the two actions, hold up the corresponding picture cards for students to do the actions.

STRETCH Students work in pairs, taking turns to say two actions for their partner to do.

Audioscript (track 4.5)
Clap and shake. … Stomp and touch. … Touch and shake. … Clap and stomp.

> **Extra activity (whole class)** Play the chant from Lesson 1 (track 4.2), and students do the actions they have learned in this lesson, e.g., *touch your body / shake your head / shake your arms / stomp your feet/legs / clap your hands / touch your nose*.

Wrap-up
- Play *Pass Mickey* (see Games Bank p. 206). For this version, students count to ten as they pass the Mickey Mouse puppet around. When they reach *ten*, they stop passing Mickey around. Show an action picture card, and the student holding Mickey stands up, says the word, and does the action.
- Sing the *Goodbye* song (track 0.7), and students say goodbye to Mickey as they leave class.

Workbook   page 36

Audioscript see p. 204
1 🎧 4.2 **Listen and check (✓).** 1 b ✓, 2 a ✓, 3 b ✓, 4 b ✓
2 **Match. Then act and say.** 1 c, touch; 2 b, clap; 3 d, shake; 4 a, stomp

> **Picture Dictionary**
> Students look at the Picture Dictionary on p. 104 in the Student's Book and complete the activities. (*Answer:* 6)

4 Lesson 3: Grammar

Student's Book page 43

Objectives

Lesson aim: give instructions
Target language: *Stomp your feet. Don't move.*
Recycled language: body, actions
Materials: Audio; Picture cards / Word cards (Body, Actions 1); Mickey Mouse puppet; (optional) pictures of places

GSE Skills

Listening: can understand basic action words, e.g., *clap, stamp, jump, walk* (15); can understand simple negative instructions related to everyday situations, e.g., *Don't run!*, if supported by gestures (16)

Speaking: can recite a short, simple rhyme or chant (16); can use language related to basic actions, e.g., *clap, stamp, jump, walk* (21); can name common parts of the body (23)

Teacher toolkit

Teaching grammar

Stand still in front of the class, and elicit from a confident student the name of an action from Lesson 2, e.g., *stomp*. Say: *Stomp. Hands?* (mime "stomping" your hands). Then elicit *feet*, and say: *Stomp your feet.*, and do the action. Students repeat *stomp your feet* and copy the action. Do the same with *shake (your head), clap (your hands), touch (your head)*.

Engage

Think of some places where you can and can't do the actions from the lesson, e.g., the library, the playground, a hospital, the school corridor, a theater. Show a picture of each place, and students say, e.g., *Clap your hands. / Don't clap your hands.*, depending on whether or not the action is appropriate in that place.

Differentiation

Some students may not be able to do the actions or may not wish to do them. Allow these students to remain seated during activities 2 and 3, if they prefer. Invite them to give instructions to their classmates, but only if they feel comfortable and ready to use the new language.

Warm-up

- Greet students with the Mickey Mouse puppet, and sing the *Hello, Stars and Heroes* song (track 0.1).
- Review the actions from Lesson 2. Hold up a picture card, and students say the word. Then make Mickey do the action. Repeat for all four actions.

Presentation

1 Sing-along ▶ **4.6 Listen and point. Then sing and act.**

- Point to the characters, and ask: *Who's this?* (Cam, Maya, Peter, and Leyla).
- Say: *Look at Cam.* Hold up each action picture card, and ask: *Stomp? Clap? Shake? Touch?* Students say or mime *yes* or *no* to answer about the action Cam is doing (*shake*). Do the same for the other characters.
- Play the song audio. For each action, students point in the picture to the corresponding character.
- Play the song again, and students do the actions and dance during the chorus. Pause after *Don't move*, and demonstrate freezing. Students stop dancing and freeze. Then continue the song, and students continue moving.
- Play the song a third time, and encourage students to join in with some of the words as they do the TPR actions and dance. If students are confident with the words, play the karaoke version (track 4.6_karaoke), and students sing along.

Audioscript (track 4.6)

Shake, shake, shake your head. // Shake your head. *(x2)*
Shake, shake, shake your head. // Shake your head with me.
Let's dance! // Don't move! // Let's dance! // Don't move!
Stomp, stomp, stomp your feet. // Stomp your feet. *(x2)*
Stomp, stomp, stomp your feet. // Stomp your feet with me.
Let's dance! // Don't move! // Let's dance! // Don't move!
Clap, clap, clap your hands. // Clap your hands. *(x2)*
Clap, clap, clap your hands. // Clap your hands with me.
Let's dance! // Don't move! // Let's dance! // Don't move!
Touch, touch, touch your head. // Touch your head. *(x2)*
Touch, touch, touch your head. // Touch your head with me.
Let's dance! // Don't move! // Let's dance! // Don't move!

Practice

2 4.7 **Listen and do. Then say.**

- Play the first line of the audio, and pause for students to shake their heads. Then play the next line of the audio, and pause again. Mime *don't*, e.g., shaking your finger from side to side, and students stop shaking their heads.
- Play the first part of the audio again, and students do the action and then stop when they hear *don't*. Do the same with the rest of the action instructions.
- Play the audio, pausing after each sentence. Students repeat the sentence and follow the instruction.

Sing-along

LESSON 3 Grammar

1 🎵 Listen and point. Then sing and act. (TPR)

Let's dance!

2 🎧 💬 Listen and do. Then say.

3 🎧 💬 Listen and do. Then play. (TPR)

Elsa says ...

Song: Stomp your feet. Don't (move).

43

SUPPORT Play a game all together as a class. Name an action, e.g., *Touch your head.*, and students do the action. Then say: *Don't (touch your head).*, and students stop doing the action. Encourage them to repeat the words.

STRETCH Students work in pairs, taking turns to give an action instruction for their partner to do or not do.

Audioscript (track 4.7)

Shake your head.
Don't shake your head.
Stomp your feet.
Don't stomp your feet.
Clap your hands.
Don't clap your hands.
Touch your head.
Don't touch your head.

Teaching star ✨

Social and emotional learning Students of this age can find competitive games upsetting when they don't win. Avoid eliminating students in games like the one below. The game can still be fun without a competitive element.

3 🎧 **4.8 Listen and do. Then play.**

- Use the picture cards to review the names of parts of the body.
- Say: *Touch your ...*, and hold up a picture card. Students touch the corresponding body part on their own body. Do the same with *shake*, and ask students to see if they can shake that part of their body, e.g., they might find it difficult to shake their nose!
- Play the audio, and play the game all together as a class. When Elsa gives an instruction, students do the action and repeat the words. When she says *Don't ...*, they don't do any action, but they repeat the words.

Audioscript (track 4.8)

Elsa says, "Touch your nose."
Elsa says, "Don't stomp your feet."
Elsa says, "Don't clap your hands."
Elsa says, "Shake your leg."
Elsa says, "Clap your hands."
Elsa says, "Touch your head."

Extra activity (fast finishers) Students play the game in pairs, giving action instructions to their partner, with or without *Don't ...* .

Wrap-up

- Play *Whispers!* (see Games Bank p.206). For this version, use the actions.
- Sing the *Goodbye* song (track 0.7), and students say goodbye to the Mickey Mouse puppet as they leave class.

📝 **Workbook** page 37

Audioscript see p.204

1 🎧 **4.3 Listen and put a ✓ or ✗.** *girl* ✗, *boy* ✓

2 Put a ✓ or ✗. Then say and do. Students check the actions they want to do and put an ✗ on those they don't want to do.

101

Lesson 4: Story

Student's Book pages 44–45

Objectives

Lesson aim: listen to and understand a story about having fun with a pet

Story language: *I have an idea. I'm excited! Yippee!*

Recycled language: body, school items, actions; *small; Don't jump. This is Shelly. He's brown. He's happy. Let's play. Don't worry.*

Receptive language: *Have fun! Sorry.*

Materials: Audio; Story cards (Unit 4); Mickey Mouse puppet; (optional) modelling clay, a picture of a tortoise or a toy tortoise

GSE Skills

Listening: can understand a few basic words and phrases in a story that is read aloud (18)

Speaking: can repeat phrases and short sentences, if spoken slowly and clearly (16); can say how they feel, using a limited range of common adjectives, e.g., *happy, cold* (22)

Teacher toolkit

Story summary
Leyla takes Shelly the tortoise home. However, Shelly doesn't come out of his shell, and Leyla feels sad. Leyla's mom has an idea. She makes an obstacle course for Shelly, and this makes both Shelley and Layla happy.

Engage
Students make an obstacle course for an imaginary class pet, using different classroom objects. If you have modelling clay, students could make a toy pet and make it complete the obstacle course.

Expressing my emotions
In the story, Leyla is excited to take home the tortoise Shelly. Hold up the tortoise picture or a tortoise toy, and tell students to imagine they can take him home. Ask: *Are you happy/sad/grumpy/excited/nervous?* Students say or mime yes or no.

Self-awareness

Warm-up

- Greet students with the Mickey Mouse puppet, and sing the *Hello, Stars and Heroes* song (track 0.1).
- Show students the tortoise picture or toy. Hold up the different body picture cards. Elicit the word for each body part, and students find it on the tortoise.

Presentation

Teaching star

Diversity and inclusion It is important for students to sit still during story time, but some students might have difficulty sitting still. Make sure that students have a comfortable space to sit in, and allow them to hold a teddy bear or small toy, if this helps them to sit still. Discuss the rules for story time, e.g., sit cross-legged, keep your hands to yourself, look and listen to the teacher and the story cards.

1 4.9 **Listen to the story. Point to Shelly.**

- Make the Mickey Mouse puppet stand up. Say: *Sit down, Mickey. It's story time!*
- Point to the small picture of the tortoise in the rubric, and ask: *What's his name?* (Shelly).
- Play the audio. Students listen to the story and follow in their books, pointing to Shelly when they see the tortoise in the story frames.
- Use the story cards to tell the story again, with or without the audio. Pause after each story frame to ask a comprehension question, e.g., *What's this?* (point to the box) (*a tortoise / Shelly*) *Who's this?* (*Leyla's sister*) *Is Leyla happy or sad?* (*sad*) *Leyla says, "I have … ."* (*books, a marker, a pencil, a ruler*) *Is Leyla happy now?* (*yes*).

Spot! Students find the blue book and the white ruler in the story. (**Answers:** book – frames 2 and 5; ruler – frame 5)

Practice

2 4.10 **Who says it? Listen and point. Then say.**

- Point to the small pictures, and ask: *Who's this?* (*Leyla, mom, sister*). Play the first part of the audio, then pause for students to point to the picture of the corresponding character (*mom*). Do the same with the second part of the audio (*Leyla*) and the third part of the audio (*sister*).
- Give each student a role: either Leyla, Leyla's mom, or Leyla's sister. Play the audio, and students act out their role, repeating the phrases.

Audioscript (track 4.10)

1 **Leyla's mom:** *Don't worry, Leyla. I have an idea.*
2 **Leyla:** *Wow! He's happy!*
3 **Leyla's sister:** *Clap your hands for Shelly!*

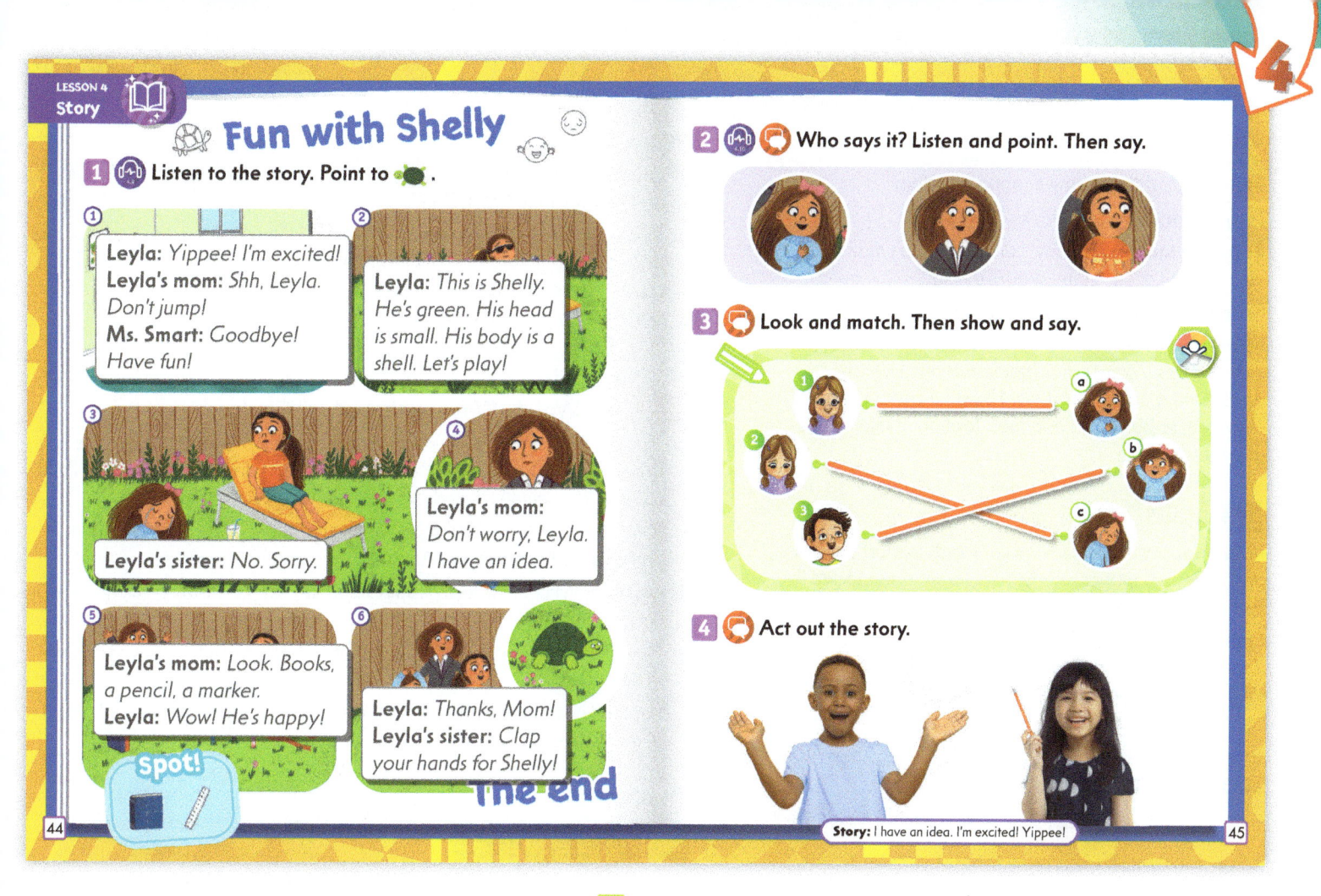

LESSON 4 Story

Fun with Shelly

1 Listen to the story. Point to 🐢.

① **Leyla:** Yippee! I'm excited!
Leyla's mom: Shh, Leyla. Don't jump!
Ms. Smart: Goodbye! Have fun!

② **Leyla:** This is Shelly. He's green. His head is small. His body is a shell. Let's play!

③ **Leyla's sister:** No. Sorry.

④ **Leyla's mom:** Don't worry, Leyla. I have an idea.

⑤ **Leyla's mom:** Look. Books, a pencil, a marker.
Leyla: Wow! He's happy!

⑥ **Leyla:** Thanks, Mom!
Leyla's sister: Clap your hands for Shelly!

The end

2 Who says it? Listen and point. Then say.

3 Look and match. Then show and say.

4 Act out the story.

Story: I have an idea. I'm excited! Yippee!

---

3 Look and match. Then show and say.

- Point to picture 3, and ask: *Is he happy/sad/excited?* (*excited*). Ask students to find the picture of Leyla when she's excited, then use your finger to draw a line to match the two pictures.
- Point to each of the small pictures, and elicit the emotion shown in each picture (*1 happy, 2 sad, 3 excited, a happy, b excited, c sad*). Students draw lines to match pictures showing the same emotions.
- Point to picture 1, and say: *I'm happy.* Students point to picture a of Leyla and repeat after you (*I'm happy*). Do the same with *sad* and *excited*.

SUPPORT Say: *I'm happy.*, and students say the words and mime the emotion. Do the same with *I'm sad/excited*.

STRETCH Students work in pairs, taking turns to point to different pictures and say: *I'm (happy)*.

4 Act out the story.

- Students look at the photos of the boy and girl. Ask: *Is she/he happy/nervous/excited?* Play the story audio, and students act out Leyla's role.

Extra activity (story extension) Display the picture of a tortoise or a toy tortoise, and students think about what actions a tortoise can do. Hold up each action picture card, and say: *(Jump.) Yes or no?*, and point to the tortoise. Students mime the action if they think a tortoise can do it.

Wrap-up

- Hold up a story card. Say: *I'm (Leyla). I'm (excited).*, and students mime *yes* or *no*. Then do the same with the other story cards and with different emotions.
- Sing the *Goodbye* song (track 0.7), and students say goodbye to the Mickey Mouse puppet as they leave class.

Workbook page 38

Audioscript see p.204

1. 4.4 Listen and number in order. *a 2, b 3, c 1, d 4*
2. Who's excited? Draw. *Leyla*

Lesson 5: Grammar and Speaking

Student's Book page 46

Objectives

Lesson aim: ask and answer about the body
Target language: *What's this? It's my nose.*
Recycled language: body, numbers; *Who's this? He's excited. How many (arms)? It's big.*
Receptive language: *Brrr, Olaf says … Be careful!*
Materials: Video 4B; (optional) Video 4A; Audio; Picture cards / Word cards (Body, Actions 1); Story cards (Unit 4); Cut-outs (Unit 4), with a cut-out model prepared; scissors, card or paper; (optional) small pieces of paper

GSE Skills

Listening: can recognize familiar words in short phrases and sentences spoken slowly and clearly, if supported by pictures or gestures (19)

Speaking: can repeat phrases and short sentences, if spoken slowly and clearly. (16); can ask about the identity of an object, using a basic phrase, e.g., *What is it?* (21)

Teacher toolkit

Video summary – 4B
It's a nose Videoscript see p.202
Anna is with Kristoff and Sven in the snow. There they meet a new friend – a snowman named Olaf.

Teaching grammar
Students will likely be familiar with the question *What's this?* However, they may be used to giving single-word answers. Hold up three fingers to elicit a full answer, one finger for each word, e.g., *It's / my / nose*. If students answer just *nose*, point to your third finger, and say: *nose*. Then point to your first finger to elicit *It's* and your second finger to elicit *my*, and then elicit the full sentence: *It's my nose*.

Engage
Give students a small piece of paper, and ask them to draw a part of the body. Stretch students could also write the word below their drawing. Tell students to scrunch up their drawing into a ball. Students stand in a circle and throw their ball into the middle of the circle. Then individual students take turns to go into the center of the circle, pick up a ball, open it, and say: *What's this? It's my (nose)*.

Warm-up
- Greet students with the Mickey Mouse puppet, and sing the *Hello, Stars and Heroes* song (track 0.1).
- Remind students of the story from Lesson 4. Show story cards 1 and 5, and ask: *How many (arms)?* Count together the number of each body part shown in each of these story cards, e.g., story card 1 – *three heads/noses/bodies, six arms/hands/legs*.

Presentation

1 ▶ **4B Watch. Who's in the video? Circle.** *Video story*

- As a lead-in to Video 4B, students look once more at the Big Picture in Lesson 1. Remind them of what happened in Video 4A in Lesson 1. Point to Sven (the reindeer), and students count his body parts.
- Point to each of the small pictures, and point and elicit each character's name (*Elsa, Kristoff, Sven, Anna*).
- Make the Mickey Mouse puppet stand up. Say: *Sit down, Mickey. It's video time!*
- Play the video, and students point to the characters when they see them in the video.
- Ask students to circle the correct pictures. To check answers, ask: *Is (Elsa) in the video?* Students mime or say *yes* or *no*.

Practice

Teaching star

Communication Drilling gives students practice of the target structure, which will help them to use the structure communicatively at a later stage. Divide the class into two groups to drill questions and answers. Play the audio for activity 2, and encourage each group to repeat either the questions or the answers. Then they exchange roles. In this way, all students practice asking *What's this?* and answering *It's my …*.

2 🎧 **4.11 Listen and trace. Then ask and answer.**

- Students look at the picture and find the snowman. Elicit or say the names of different body parts, and students point to the body parts on the snowman.
- Play the first part of the audio, pausing after the first exchange. Ask students to find and trace the snowman's head. Do the same for the rest of the audio.
- Divide the class into two groups. Drill the question *What's this?* with the first group. Hold up a body picture card, e.g., *arm*, and the second group says: *It's my arm*. Repeat with different picture cards, then groups exchange roles and start again.

SUPPORT Ask the question, then hold up a picture card, and say: *It's my …*. Students repeat and complete the sentence.

STRETCH Students work in pairs, taking turns to ask and answer questions about the picture, following the model in the audio. They can also ask and answer using the Big Picture in Lesson 1.

LESSON 5
Grammar and Speaking

1 Watch. Who's in the video? Circle.

2 Listen and trace. Then ask and answer.

3 Listen and point. Then make and play.

Skills: What's this? It's my (nose).

- Point to each section of the picture you've made on the cut-out, and ask: *What's this?* Elicit: *It's my (head).* Students point to the same body part on their picture and say: *It's my (head).*

SUPPORT Students can play the game in mixed-ability pairs. The less confident student answers their partner's questions, saying only the name of the part of the body.

STRETCH Students can play the game in mixed-ability pairs. The more confident student asks *What's this?*, and says full sentences to name the parts of the body, e.g., *It's my head.*

Audioscript (track 4.12)
What's this? // It's my body.
What's this? // It's my nose.

> **Extra activity (whole class)** Students imagine they are a snowman that has come to life, like Olaf from Video 4B. They point to and name their different snowman body parts. Give instructions for students to follow, e.g., *clap your hands, stomp your feet.*

Wrap-up

- Play *What's this?* (see Games Bank p.206). For this version, as students turn over each card to reveal the picture, ask: *What's this?*, and the student names the picture.
- Sing the *Goodbye* song (0.7), and students say goodbye to the Mickey Mouse puppet as they leave class.

Workbook   page 39

Audioscript see p.204
1. 4.5 **Listen and match.** 1 b, 2 a, 3 c
2. **Draw your robot. Then ask and answer.**

Audioscript (track 4.11)
1. What's this? // It's my head.
2. What's this? // It's my nose.
3. What's this? // It's my arm.
4. What's this? // It's my body.

3 4.12 **Listen and point. Then make and play.**

- Students use scissors to cut carefully around the dotted lines of the cut-outs. Make sure they only cut around the scissor lines, not the fold lines.
- Show students how to fold along the lines. Fold back the monster's head and the snowman's legs, so that the picture shows: a monster's head, a boy's body, and a snowman's legs.
- Play the audio, pausing after the first exchange. Students point to one of the three bodies on the cut-out. Then play the next part of the audio, and students point to a nose.
- Students fold their cut-outs. Monitor and help as necessary.

Lesson 6: Myself and others

Feelings and my body Student's Book page 47

Objectives

Lesson aim: recognize and name emotions and actions
Target language: *cry, excited, jump, smile; I'm happy. I smile.*
Recycled language: *happy, sad, excited*
Materials: Audio; (optional) Video 4A; *Myself and others* poster; Stickers; Mickey Mouse puppet; (optional) cards for Teacher toolkit; cut out pictures from old magazines, construction paper

GSE Skills

Listening: can recognize familiar words in short phrases and sentences spoken slowly and clearly, if supported by pictures or gestures (19); can understand basic action words, e.g., *clap, stomp, jump, walk* (15)
Speaking: can say how they feel, using a limited range of common adjectives, e.g., *happy, cold* (22); can use language related to basic actions, e.g., *clap, stamp, jump, walk* (21)

Teacher toolkit

Expressing my emotions

In this lesson, students start to think about how they express different emotions. At this age, students are starting to be aware that strong feelings such as anger and excitement can have physical effects. Use the Mickey Mouse puppet to elicit actions we do when we feel different emotions. Make Mickey stomp his feet angrily, and say: *Mickey is grumpy. He stomps his feet.* Then make Mickey jump happily, and say: *Mickey is excited.* Ask students to demonstrate how they show different emotions: *happy, sad, grumpy, excited*.

Self-awareness

Engage

Make a digital emotions poster with the class. Invite students to act out different emotions, making sure they use appropriate body language and actions, and take photos or video them. Use presentation software or an online tool to create a simple poster, and insert or embed the photos or video. You could also create audio files, recording students saying what emotion they are feeling, e.g., *I'm happy!*

Home-school link

Ask students to show and tell their families what they do when they are happy, sad, or excited, e.g., *I'm happy. I clap my hands.* Encourage them to recognize when someone at home is happy, sad, or excited.

Warm-up

- Greet students with the Mickey Mouse puppet, and sing the *Hello, Stars and Heroes* song (track 0.1).
- Show the *Myself and others* poster and review different emotions. Make Mickey act out the following emotions: *happy, sad, nervous, grumpy, excited.* Ask: *Is Mickey excited? Is he nervous? Is he grumpy?* Students find each emotion on the *Myself and others* poster.

🎵 **1.12 Listen and sing.**

- Play the song audio, and students join in with the words and the actions.
- Ask: *How do you feel? Are you happy?*, and students respond *yes/no* or *I'm (happy)!*

Presentation

1 🎧 **4.13 Listen and point. Then say and act.**

- Remind students of the situations and the characters in Video 4A in Lesson 1 and the story. If required, play Video 4A and look at the story again.
- Students look at the pictures and say the names of the characters (*Olaf, Leyla, Anna*).
- Point to the first picture, and ask and mime: *Is Olaf happy? Is he excited? Is he grumpy?* Do the same for each of the pictures.
- Play the audio, and students point to the pictures.
- Play the audio again, pausing after each sentence for students to do or mime the corresponding actions: *jump, cry, smile*.
- Point to each picture again, and students copy the character's facial expression and action and say: *I'm (excited)*.

Audioscript (track 4.13)
1 Olaf says, "I'm excited. I jump."
2 Leyla says, "I'm sad. I cry."
3 Anna says, "I'm happy. I smile."

Practice

2 Look, act, and say.

- Point to the first photo. Mime eating ice cream, and say: *I'm happy!* Students do the same mime. Ask: *Are you happy? Are you excited? Are you sad?* Students say how they feel: *I'm … .*
- Do the same for the rest of the photos. Use the photos as prompts for your mimes. Say how you feel, using different emotion adjectives that students know, e.g., *I'm sad*. Ask students to mime and say how they feel, too. Allow a range of different emotion responses.

SUPPORT As students act, they can say single words for the emotions: *happy, sad, excited*.

STRETCH As students act, they can say the corresponding actions, too, e.g., *I'm excited. I jump! / I'm happy. I smile. / I'm sad. I cry.*

Feelings and my body

LESSON 6
Myself and others

1 Listen and point. Then say and act. TPR

Listen and sing.

2 Look, act and say. TPR

3 Listen and make an "I'm excited" dance. TPR

I'm a hero!

Self-awareness: cry, excited, jump, smile; I'm (happy). I (smile).

47

- Make a new dance all together as a class, doing different sequences of actions. Invite students to choose the actions. Then play the music, and do the dance together.

Audioscript (track 4.14)
[instrumental – rhythmic music]

⭐ **I'm a hero!** ⭐ Point to the sticker picture, and elicit that Leyla is jumping because she's excited. Ask students to think of something that makes them feel excited, then they jump (or dance or clap) and say: *I'm excited!* Students stick the sticker in their books.

> **Extra activity (fast finishers)** Students draw things that make them feel happy or excited. They could also cut out pictures from old magazines. They could stick the pictures onto construction paper and make a classroom display.

Wrap-up

- Invite two students to stand with their backs to the *Myself and others* poster. Point to an emotion on the poster, then ask the rest of the class to act it out for the two students to guess.
- Sing the *Goodbye* song (track 0.7), and students say goodbye to the Mickey Mouse puppet as they leave class.

Workbook page 40

1 **Match. Then point and say.** *1 I'm happy. I smile. 2 I'm excited. I jump. 3 I'm nervous. 4 I'm sad. I cry.*
2 **What do you do when you're excited? Circle.**

Teaching star ✨

Creativity Allowing students the freedom to be creative and imaginative can help them feel that they are a valued member of the class. Encourage students to devise their own actions for the dance in activity 3, even if these actions don't fit with the target vocabulary. You can give each move a name, or students can make up names for their new actions, e.g., turn around, floss, moonwalk.

3 🎧 4.14 **Listen and make an *I'm excited* dance.**

- Point to the small pictures showing actions, and elicit the words and phrases (*clap your hands, stomp your feet, jump*).
- Play the music and dance, doing different actions for four beats, e.g., clap your hands for four beats, then stomp your feet for four beats, then jump for four beats. Encourage students to join in with the dance.
- Say: *I'm excited! I clap my hands. I stomp my feet. I jump!*

Lesson 7: My world

Technology: Coding Student's Book page 48

Objectives

Lesson aims: understand coding
Target language: up, down, left, right; Go left!
Recycled language: colors
Receptive language: snowflakes
Materials: Audio; Mickey Mouse puppet; (optional) a large arrow cut out of card, masking tape, arrows and clues

GSE Skills

Listening: can recognize isolated words related to familiar topics, if spoken slowly and clearly and supported by pictures or gestures (16)
Speaking: can repeat single words, if spoken slowly and clearly (10); can repeat phrases and short sentences, if spoken slowly and clearly (16)

Teacher toolkit

Cross-curricular
Physical movement can really help students internalize language and concepts. If possible, use masking tape to design a grid on the classroom floor or in the playground, and students move around the grid, following instructions: *go left, go right, go up, go down*.

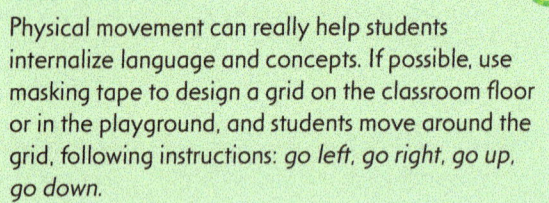

Extend
Set up a treasure hunt in the classroom or in a small area in the school yard. Make clues with arrow sequences, e.g., three left arrows means three steps to the left. Place the clues in different places to show students where to go next. Students can play in teams. The "treasure" students find at the end of the hunt could be a fun activity that they enjoy.

Home-school link
Students can play a directions game with their family. They can use chalk to draw a grid on the floor and demonstrate different directions, saying *go up, go right*, etc.

Warm-up

- Greet students with the Mickey Mouse puppet, and sing the *Hello, Stars and Heroes* song (track 0.1).
- Play *Follow the leader* (see Games Bank p. 206). For this version, students do a sequence of actions, e.g., *stomp my feet, clap my hands, jump*.

Presentation

1 🎧 **4.15 Listen and trace. Then say and act.**

- Demonstrate the TPR actions, and say the direction phrases. Students copy the actions.
- Ask students to look at the picture with different arrows. Play the audio, and students point to each arrow. Draw on the board a left-facing dotted arrow. Play the first part of the audio again, then pause and trace the arrow on the board. Students trace the first arrow in their books. Then play the rest of the audio, pausing after each phrase for students to trace the arrows. Play the whole audio again, and students do the corresponding TPR actions.
- If you have prepared a card arrow, use this to point up/down/left/right. Alternatively, point to the arrows on the page. Ask students to say the correct phrase, then do the TPR action.

SUPPORT Say a direction phrase, and students repeat it, then do the TPR action.

STRETCH Students work in pairs, taking turns to say a direction phrase and do the TPR action.

TPR
go left – step/jump to the left
go right – step/jump to the right
go up – stand on tiptoes, reaching up with arms
go down – crouch down

Audioscript (track 4.15)
1 go left // 2 go right // 3 go up // 4 go down

Practice

2 🎧 **4.16 Help Sven. Count. Then listen and check (✓).**

- Point to the picture of Sven (the reindeer), and say: *This is Sven*. Then point to Kristoff, and say: *This is Kristoff*. In L1, ask students to help Sven find Kristoff, pointing to Sven then Kristoff. Point to the pictures of snowflakes in the grid, and explain that they need to avoid these.
- Ask: *How many squares?* Follow the path from Sven to Kristoff, avoiding the snowflakes, counting the squares as a class: *one, two three, four, five*. Then point to the first sequence of arrows, and say: *go up, go up, go right, go right, go right*. Do the same with the second sequence of arrows.
- Ask students to compare the sequences of arrows with the squares in the grid, avoiding the snowflakes, and check the correct sequence.
- Play the audio, and students follow the direction phrases, moving their fingers along the grid.

LESSON 7
My world — Technology
Coding

1 🎧 ✏️ Listen and trace. Then say and act. **TPR**

2 🎧 Help Sven. Count. Then listen and check (✓).

3 ✏️ 💬 Help Shelly. Draw. Then tell a friend.

Coding: up, down, left, right; go (left)!

48

Audioscript (track 4.16)
go right … go right … go right … go up … go up

3 Help Shelly. Draw. Then tell a friend.

- Ask students to look at the grid, and ask: *Where's Shelly?* Students point to the picture of the tortoise. Say and mime: *Shelly is hungry.* Point to the picture of lettuce, and say and mime: *Mmm! Shelly likes lettuce!* Point to one or two school objects, and say: *Oh no, a (marker)!* In L1, explain that Shelly can't pass where there are school objects.
- Copy or display the grid on the board. Demonstrate how to draw a path from Shelly to the lettuce. Say: *go down, go right, go right, go down, go right.*
- Students draw the corresponding arrows in their own grids, to draw the path from Shelly to the lettuce.
- Elicit the direction phrases for Shelly's path (*go down, go right, go right, go down, go right*).

SUPPORT Students do the corresponding TPR action for each direction phrase.
STRETCH Students work in pairs, taking turns to say the direction phrases for Shelly's path.

Teaching star ✨

Application Use the floor grid to create a dance, to provide additional practice of the direction phrases. Invite a pair of students to stand in the grid. Say a pattern of direction phrases for the students to follow, e.g., *go left, go left, go right, go down, go right, go right, go left, go up.* Do the same with different pairs of students. Then invite individual confident students to say the direction phrases, to create the dance for pairs of students to follow.

Thinking skills 💡

Understand In activity 2, students follow a series of visual directions in a maze in order to identify the correct path.

Apply In activity 3, students apply their understanding of how simple directions show how to reach an objective by drawing arrows in a partially completed maze. They give directions orally as they "read" their maze.

Extra activity (extension) Students sit in pairs, one student behind the other so that they can use their finger to draw on their partner's back. The student at the front says directions, e.g., *go up, go right, go down, go left.* The student at the back draws the path through an imaginary grid on their partner's back. Then they both turn around and exchange roles.

Wrap-up

- Play *Mickey says* (see Games Bank p.206). Make the Mickey Mouse puppet say direction phrases for students to follow. If necessary, demonstrate each TPR action as Mickey says it.
- Sing the *Goodbye* song (track 0.7), and students say goodbye to Mickey as they leave class.

📝 Workbook   page 41

1. **Draw and color. Then say.** *1 right (yellow), 2 down (pink), 3 up (purple)*
2. **Help Anna. Draw and circle. Then say.** Students help Anna find Elsa and Sven. *1 Elsa, 2 Sven*

4 Lesson 8: Review

Objectives

Lesson aim: review target language from Unit 4
Target language: body, actions; *What's this? It's my (nose).*
Recycled language: colors
Materials: Audio; (optional) Video 4A, Video 4B; Picture cards / Word cards (Body, Actions 1); Stickers; Mickey Mouse puppet; *My progress* poster

GSE Skills

Listening: can recognize isolated words related to familiar topics, if spoken slowly and clearly and supported by pictures and gestures (16)
Speaking: can say single words related to familiar topics, if supported by pictures or gestures (18)

Teacher toolkit

Video review
You can return to Video 4A and Video 4B at the end of the unit for a "second play." Play on mute, and students say any words or phrases they know as they watch.

Remediation
You can provide additional practice of target language for those who need it and also involve students who are comfortable with the language. Play a TPR game to review the names of body parts and actions, inviting students who know the vocabulary to give the instructions. This will help create an atmosphere of support and cohesion within the class, as well as leading to higher levels of confidence and the feeling of *I can do it!*

Home-school link
Students share the language they've learned in the unit with a family member, e.g., *What's this? It's my leg.* Encourage students' families to ask the question *What's this?* to elicit answers in English in different situations at home.

I can do it! Student's Book page 49

Warm-up
- Greet students with the Mickey Mouse puppet, and sing the *Hello, Stars and Heroes* song (track 0.1).
- Play *Yes or no?* (see Games Bank p.206), using the unit picture cards.
- Play the song audio from Lesson 3 (track 4.6), and students join in with the words and the actions. If students are confident with the words, play the karaoke version (track 4.6_karaoke).

I can do it!

> **Teaching star**
>
> **Growth mindset** At this age, students may find it difficult to play games in teams. In the game in activity 1, choose a different student to answer each time. Give the student time to think before they answer, and encourage the other team members to whisper the correct answer to the student so they can check their answers. Give a round of applause for each correct answer, and say *Good try!* for any incorrect answers.

1 Play. Say and draw O or X.

- Students look at the pictures in the grid. Elicit or say the corresponding words and phrases (top line: *body, sad, head*; middle line: *stomp feet, leg, happy*; bottom line: *nose, clap hands, hand*).
- Copy the grid onto the board, and play all together as a class in two teams: Team O and Team X.
- A student from Team O chooses a picture from the grid. The student says the corresponding word or phrase and does the TPR action.
- If the word or phrase is correct, draw an O in the corresponding square in the grid on the board.
- Then Team X takes their turn in the same way. Teams continue to take turns. The team that wins three squares in a row (left to right, up down, or diagonally) wins the game.
- Play the game again, this time allowing Team X to go first.

ACHIEVE
Students name different parts of the body and emotions, and say and act out the actions they do to express their feelings.

SUPPORT
Play the game all together as a class against the Mickey Mouse puppet. Make Mickey make mistakes once or twice to help the class win the game. Allow students to use single words and short phrases.

STRETCH
Demonstrate the game, then students work in pairs to play the game, using the grid in one of their books. They take turns to choose a square, say the word or phrase, and do the TPR action. One student draws O and the other student draws X.

I can do it!

LESSON 8
Review

1 💬 ✏️ Play. Say and draw O or X.

2 💡 ✏️ Think and color. Then stick!

I can ...

Let's dance!

Unit 4!

Go online
Big Project

49

---

2 💡 **Think and color. Then stick!**
- Point to each picture and say the *I can ...* statements: *I can name parts of the body and actions. I can sing a song. I can say what I do when I'm excited, happy, and sad.* For each statement, give an example, and then ask: *Can you do this?* If necessary, explain in L1.
- Students demonstrate what they can do. They work in pairs, taking turns to point to or touch and say the names of different body parts, and to give each other instructions to follow. Sing the song all together as a class. Students work in pairs, taking turns to say and act out the emotions: *happy, sad,* and *excited.* Monitor and assess students' performance.
- Students color the stars next to what they can do. Then they stick the reward sticker to show they have completed Unit 4.

My Star and Hero! Students look at the picture of Elsa on p.4 of the Student's Book. They point to and name different parts of Elsa's body.
Extra activity (class game) Play *Draw it!* (see Games Bank p.206). Show a student a picture card from the unit, and they draw it on the board for other students to guess the word.

Wrap-up
- Students reflect on which lesson or activity they most enjoyed in Unit 4. Have a class vote and choose one activity to do again as a class, e.g., watch the video, sing the song or chant, listen to the story, or play a game.
- Draw students' attention to the *My progress* poster, and ask them to identify the picture that reflects this unit. Read aloud with students the *I can ...* statements (*I can talk about the body, I can express feelings*).
- 🎵 Sing the *Goodbye* song (track 0.7), and students say *goodbye* to Mickey and tell him their favorite word from Unit 4.

📝 **Workbook** pages 42–43

My progress
Audioscript see p.204
1. 🎧 4.6 Listen and check (✔). *1 b ✔, 2 a ✔, 3 b ✔*
2. **Match. Then ask and answer.** *a – nose, b – hand, c – leg, d – head, e – arm*

Units W–4 My practice
1. **Match. Then point and say.** Students match the puzzle pieces with the jigsaw, then point and name the body parts.
   Find 3 noses. Students look at the puzzle and find three noses. *snowman, polar bear, reindeer*
2. **Choose and circle. Then say and do.**
Unit 4! My favorite activity: Students stick the small star sticker next to their favorite activity.

5 My clothes

Unit objectives
By the end of this unit, students can:
- describe their clothes and say what they're wearing
- read and understand a story about a party
- identify and talk about the importance of persistence
- talk about different materials

Skills development
Listening: recognize and identify clothes from descriptions

Speaking: talk about their clothes; give others encouragement; describe what they are wearing

ABC Vocabulary
Lesson 1: *pants, shoes, skirt, socks*
Lesson 2: *coat, dress, hat, scarf, sweater, T-shirt*

Grammar
Lesson 3: *My coat is red.*
Lesson 5: *I'm wearing my T-shirt.*

Myself and others
Persistence In this unit, a Disney video and a story introduce the theme of persistence. Students will learn that when they are learning new skills, they will improve if they keep trying.

Language: *Good job! Keep trying!*

Self-management

Story
The yo-yo
Come and play!

My world
Technology: Materials
cotton, leather, wool

Disney MULAN

Unit overview

Mulan
A strong, independent 16-year-old girl who doesn't fit in with the traditional ideas of the people in her village. She's smart, creative, and resourceful.

Mushu
A tiny dragon who takes on the role of Mulan's guardian and advisor when she goes to join the army.

Fa Zhou
Mulan's father and a retired war hero who is ordered to return to battle. Fa Zhou has traditional ideas but welcomes and respects his daughter when she returns home.

Fa Li
Mulan's mother who is an elderly woman.

Yao, Ling, and Chien-Po
Three very different soldiers who are best friends. Although at first they don't like Mulan, they later become her friends.

Mulan's father is ordered to go and fight in the army. Because he is old and unwell, Mulan decides to go instead. She disguises herself as a man and joins the training camp. Mulan is a hard-worker, who does her best to improve and become the best soldier, with the help of her friend Mushu the dragon.

Did you know?
The movie Mulan is based on the story of Hua Mulan, a legendary female warrior from Chinese folk tales.

Video stories 
Video 5A: Keep trying, Mulan!
Video 5B: I'm wearing my pants

Online modules

Phonics
Words with Mm, Nn, and Oo sounds in initial position
mom, nose, orange

Big Project
Make a doll

5 Lesson 1: Vocabulary

Student's Book pages 50–51

Objectives

Lesson aim: name clothes

Target language: *pants, shoes, skirt, socks*

Recycled language: colors; *dad, big; This is Mulan. Who's this? Is it a …? No. It's a …*

Receptive language: *father, soldier, breakfast; Good morning! Let's go! Keep trying! Ouch! Good job!*

Materials: Video 5A; Audio; Picture cards / Word cards (Clothes 1, Body, Family, Disney characters); Sticker (Mulan); Mickey Mouse puppet; (optional) tissue paper in different colors

GSE Skills

Listening: can recognize isolated words related to familiar topics, if spoken slowly and clearly and supported by pictures and gestures (16)

Reading: can recognize single, familiar everyday words, if supported by pictures (21)

Speaking: can repeat single words, if spoken slowly and clearly (10); can name items of clothing if supported by pictures (22)

Writing (WB): can copy some short familiar words presented in standard printed form (10)

Teacher toolkit

Video summary – 5A
Keep trying, Mulan! **Videoscript see p.202**
Mulan lives with her family and pet dog. One day, she becomes a soldier. At first, Mulan thinks being a soldier is hard. However, Mulan keeps trying, and eventually she succeeds.

Extend
Use the life-size body outline you made in Unit 4 as a class doll. During this unit, students make clothes for the doll collaboratively. Elicit the names of the clothes items the doll is wearing, their colors, and encourage students to talk about the doll's clothes, using the target structures once they have learned them.

Persistence
Keep trying!
Use the video story to talk about how Mulan keeps trying. Students act out climbing the pole and falling down several times. Say: *Keep trying!*
Self-awareness

Warm-up
- Greet students with the Mickey Mouse puppet, and sing the *Hello, Stars and Heroes* song (track 0.1).

Presentation
Video story

- Students look at the Big Picture. Introduce the movie and the characters: *This is the movie Mulan. This is Mulan / Fa Zhou / Mushu.*
- Hold up the different body picture cards, and students point to and name the body parts in the Big Picture.

1 ▶ **5A Watch. Who's in the video? Check (✓).**

- Make the Mickey Mouse puppet stand up. Say: *Sit down, Mickey. It's video time! Let's watch!*
- Play Video 5A, and students watch and listen.
- Point to the small pictures of the characters, and say their names: *Mushu, Fa Zhou* (father), *Fa Li* (mother). Hold up the *dad* and *mom* picture cards as you name Mulan's father and mother.
- Play the video again. Then point to each of the small pictures, and students mime or say *yes* or *no* if they saw the character in the video. Then ask students to check the corresponding pictures.

2 ▶ **5A Who keeps trying? Circle.**

- Use mime to pre-teach *soldier*. Stand up straight, march like a soldier, and students copy you.
- Ask: *Who keeps trying?*, and point to the three small pictures. Play the video again, and students put their thumbs up when they see someone who keeps trying. When Mulan finally manages to climb the pole [2:41], give her a round of applause all together as a class. Then ask students to circle the correct picture.

Picture cards / Word cards (optional) Show the picture cards one by one to introduce the new vocabulary. Repeat several times, encouraging students to remember the words. Then show each word card, and elicit the words.

Practice

3 🎧 **5.1 Listen, find, and say. Then play.**

- Play the audio, pausing after each word. Students point to the clothes items in the Big Picture. Play the audio again, pausing for students to say the words. Play the audio a third time, and students read, say, and point to the clothes words.
- Point to clothes items in the Big Picture, in varied order, and students say the words.

SUPPORT Say each word in turn, and students point to the clothes item in the Big Picture. Start slowly, giving students time to think and respond, then gradually say the words more quickly.

STRETCH Students work in pairs, taking turns to say a word for their partner to find in the Big Picture.

Audioscript (track 5.1)
1 skirt // 2 shoes // 3 socks // 4 pants

5 My clothes

LESSON 1 Vocabulary

1. Watch. Who's in the video? Check (✓).

2. Who keeps trying? Circle.

3. Listen, find, and say. Then play.

4. Listen, chant, and act. TPR

♪ Pants, pants ♪

1. skirt
2. shoes
3. socks
4. pants

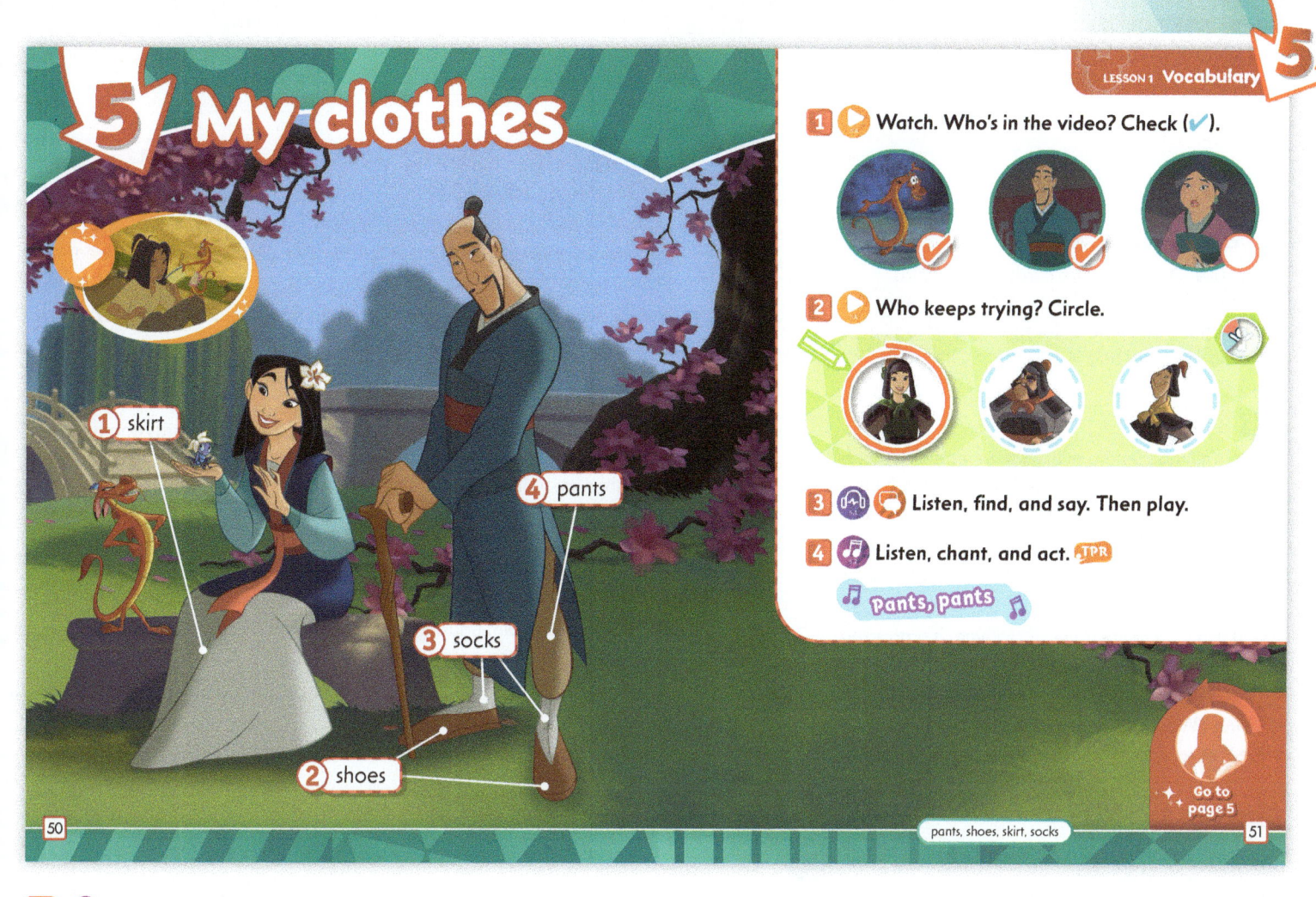

pants, shoes, skirt, socks

Go to page 5

---

4 🎵 **5.2 Listen, chant, and act.**

- Make the Mickey Mouse puppet say: *Pants, pants. I have pants. Pants, pants. On my legs.* Students point to Mickey's red pants.
- Play the audio, and students listen and point to the correct clothes item in the Big Picture when they hear the corresponding word.
- Demonstrate TPR actions for each word. Say a word, and students do the corresponding TPR action. Then play the audio again, and students do the TPR actions.

TPR chant

pants – step into pants and pull them up
socks – pull on a pair of socks
shoes – tie shoe laces

Audioscript (track 5.2)

Pants, pants. I have pants. // Pants, pants. On my legs.
Socks, socks. I have socks. // Socks, socks. On my feet.
Shoes, shoes. I have shoes. // Shoes, shoes. On my feet.

❓ **Collect your friend** Show the picture card of Mulan to help students identify the correct sticker. Students stick the sticker on p.4 in the Student's Book. Ask: *Who's this?* (Mulan).

Extra activity (video extension) Say: *Mushu has pants. Yes or no?* Students say or mime *yes* or *no*. Repeat with *socks* and *shoes*.

Wrap-up

- Play *Color hunt!* with clothes items (see Games Bank p.206). For this version, students look for colors on clothes.
- Sing the *Goodbye* song (track 0.7), and students say goodbye to the Mickey Mouse puppet as they leave class.

📘 **Workbook**   pages 44–45

1. **Watch again. Then check (✓).**
   1. *Who's Mushu?* a ✓
   2. *Which are Mulan's clothes?* a ✓
   3. *Keep trying, Mulan!* a ✓

2. **Trace and match. Then point and say.** *1 shoes, 2 pants, 3 skirt, 4 socks*

3. **Challenge!** 💡 **Find 3 kites. What color are they?** *pink (fish kite) on p.44, yellow on p.47, green (butterfly kites) on p.49*

115

5 Lesson 2: Vocabulary

Student's Book page 52

Objectives

Lesson aim: name clothes
Target language: *coat, dress, hat, scarf, sweater, T-shirt*
Recycled language: *clothes*
Materials: Audio; Picture cards / Word cards (Clothes 1, 2); Stickers; Mickey Mouse puppet; (optional) a washing line (for the Teacher toolkit), real clothes, a real bag

GSE Skills

Listening: can identify everyday objects, people, or animals in their immediate surroundings or in pictures from short, basic descriptions, e.g., color, size, if spoken slowly and clearly (19)

Reading: can recognize single, familiar everyday words, if supported by pictures (21)

Speaking: can name items of clothing, if supported by pictures (22); can answer simple questions about objects, e.g., color, size (22)

Writing (WB): can copy some short familiar words presented in standard printed form (10)

Teacher toolkit

Teaching vocabulary
Help students make connections between the new vocabulary items and their knowledge about and experience of the real world. Bring in a few items of clothing, e.g., a scarf, a T-shirt, a hat, and students name each item. You can also encourage multisensory learning by allowing students to touch the clothes and feel their texture.

Engage
Hang a washing line in the classroom at a suitable height for students to reach, and bring in pegs and clothes cut out of card (or real clothes). Students hang different clothes items on the washing line and name them.

Home-school link
Tell students to look inside their wardrobes at home and name their clothes. They could also teach the names of the clothes to a family member.

Warm-up

- 🐭 Greet students with the Mickey Mouse puppet, and sing the *Hello, Stars and Heroes* song (track 0.1).
- 🐭 Make Mickey hold up the clothes picture cards from Lesson 1, and students say the words and point to their own clothes, if they are wearing the same item.
- Say: *Listen and chant!*, and play the chant from Lesson 1 (track 5.2). Students join in with the chant and do the actions.

Presentation

Picture cards / Word cards (optional) Show the picture cards one by one to introduce the new vocabulary. Repeat several times, encouraging students to remember the words. Then show each word card, and elicit the words.

1 🎧 **5.3 Listen, point, and say. Then play.**

- Say: *Listen and point*. Play the audio, and students point to the corresponding photos.
- Play the audio again, pausing after each word. Students point to the corresponding photo and repeat each word.
- Say the words, and demonstrate TPR actions, putting on each clothes item, then students copy.
- Point to different photos, and students mime putting on each clothes item and say the word.

SUPPORT Say each word, and students point to the corresponding photo. Start slowly, giving students time to think and respond, then gradually say the words more quickly.

STRETCH Students work in pairs, taking turns to point to a photo, for their partner to say the corresponding word and do the action.

Practice

2 🎧 **5.4 Listen and stick. Then say.**

- Point to the picture of the washing line, and say: *Look! A scarf.* Then elicit the names of the remaining clothes items.
- Point to the two empty sticker frames, and students say which clothes items they think are missing. Play the audio, and students point to the clothes items as they hear them and place the stickers in the correct positions.
- Play the audio again, pausing for students to stick the stickers in the empty frames. Play the audio a third time, pausing for students to point and repeat the sentences.
- Point to the pictures, and students say: *It's a (scarf)*.

SUPPORT Point to the pictures, and students name the clothes items.

STRETCH Students work in pairs, taking turns to point to a picture for their partner to describe, using the audio as a model.

LESSON 2
Vocabulary

1 🎧 💬 **Listen, point, and say. Then play.**

1. T-shirt
2. sweater
3. dress
4. hat
5. scarf
6. coat

2 🎧 💬 **Listen and stick. Then say.**

3 💬 🎧 **Look and guess. Then listen and check.**

coat, dress, hat, scarf, sweater, T-shirt

52

Audioscript (track 5.4)
It's a scarf. It's orange.
It's a T-shirt. It's green.
It's a coat. It's red.
It's a dress. It's purple.
It's a hat. It's yellow.
It's a sweater. It's pink.

Teaching star ✦

Linguistic competence Some students may have difficulty pronouncing the consonant clusters *sk* in *scarf* and *skirt*, and *sw* in *sweater*. Drill the individual sounds (*s*, *k*), then blend them together (*sk*), drilling lots of times before asking students to attempt saying the full words.

---

3 🎧 **5.5 Look and guess. Then listen and check.**

- Point to the first photo, and ask: *What's this?* Hold up each picture card in turn, and ask: *Is it a (sweater)?* Students say or mime *yes* or *no*. Then say: *I think it's a (dress). And you?* Invite different students to say what they think it is, using *It's a …* .
- Do the same with the other photos.
- Display the picture cards. Play the audio, pausing after each exchange. Students point to the correct picture card, then check their answer from earlier in this activity.

Audioscript (track 5.5)
1 What's this? // It's a coat.
2 What's this? // It's a scarf.
3 What's this? // It's a hat.
4 What's this? // It's a sweater.

> **Extra activity (whole class)** Put some clothes items inside a bag. Invite students to put their hand in the bag and pull out a clothes item. Keep the neck of the bag closed so they aren't able to pull the clothes item all the way out of the bag. Ask students to look at what they can see of the clothes item and guess what it is.

Wrap-up

- Play *Miming* (see Games Bank p.206). Show a student a clothes picture card, and they mime putting on the item for the other students to guess.
- 💠 Sing the *Goodbye* song (track 0.7), and students say goodbye to the Mickey Mouse puppet as they leave class.

📘 Workbook   page 46

Audioscript see p.204
1 **Follow. Then say.** sweater, T-shirt, coat, dress, hat, scarf
2 🎧 **5.1 Listen and check (✓). Then trace and say.** 1 a ✓, 2 a ✓, 3 b ✓, 4 b ✓

> **Picture Dictionary**
> Students look at the Picture Dictionary on p.105 in the Student's Book and complete the activities. (**Answers:** pants, shoes)

5 Lesson 3: Grammar

Student's Book page 53

Objectives

Lesson aim: describe clothes
Target language: *My coat is red.*
Recycled language: clothes, colors
Materials: Audio; Picture cards / Word cards (Clothes 1, 2; Colors; Body); Mickey Mouse puppet

GSE Skills

Listening: can get the gist of a simple song, if supported by gestures (21)
Speaking: can recite a short, simple rhyme or chant (16); can name items of clothing, if supported by pictures (22)

Teacher toolkit

Teaching grammar
Teach the difference between the singular and plural forms. Place the picture cards on the board in two groups: singular (*skirt, T-shirt, sweater, dress, hat, scarf, coat*) and plural (*shoes, socks, pants*). Point and say: *My (coat) is (blue). My (pants) are (yellow)*, emphasizing the words *is* and *are*.

Extend
Make an aisle in the middle of the classroom, or set up a space at the front as a runway. Invite a few students to role-play fashion models, and ask them to walk down the runway, if they feel comfortable doing so. Alternatively, you could ask them to stand at the front. The other students can role-play photographers and journalists. Students say what each model is wearing. Encourage them to say, e.g., *My (dress) is (blue)*.

Differentiation
Some students may have a color vision deficiency, or they may have difficulty in identifying and naming similar colors, e.g., distinguishing between dark blue and black. Avoid correcting any visual processing errors. If you are unsure, check to see if the student can identify the color correctly in L1. If they can, review the names of colors in English to make sure the student knows them.

Warm-up

- Greet students with the Mickey Mouse puppet, and sing the *Hello, Stars and Heroes* song (track 0.1).
- Hold up each clothes picture card, and elicit the word. Then ask: *What color is it?*, and students answer.

Presentation

1 Sing-along 5.6 **Listen and point. Then sing and act.**

- Say: *I'm Maya. I have a … .* Hold up each clothes picture card, and say: *(T-shirt).* Students say or mime *yes* or *no*. Do the same for Peter.
- Play the song audio. Students point to each clothes item in the picture as they hear the corresponding word in the song.
- Demonstrate the TPR actions. Then play the song again, and students do the TPR actions.
- Play the song a third time, and encourage students to join in with some of the words as they do the TPR actions and dance. If students are confident with the words, play the karaoke version (track 5.6_karaoke), and students sing along.

> **TPR song**
> *clothes* – put your thumbs and forefingers together to hold up your top, next to your shoulders
> *coat* – mime putting on a coat
> *shoes* – tie shoe laces
> *sweater* – mime putting on a sweater

Audioscript (track 5.6)
Clothes! Clothes! Colorful clothes! *(x2)*
My coat is red. *(x2)* // Your coat is blue. *(x2)*
Let's play today!
My shoes are black. *(x2)* // Your shoes are brown. *(x2)*
Let's play today!
Clothes! Clothes! Colorful clothes! *(x2)*
My sweater is green. *(x2)* // Your sweater is pink. *(x2)*
Let's play today!
Clothes! Clothes! Colorful clothes! *(x2)*

Practice

Teaching star

Learning to learn Answer cards can help students focus on comprehension without having to worry about producing language. Ask students to make different colored answer cards, e.g., a red card and a green card. When you ask a question to the class, tell them which color card signals each answer option, e.g., *green for yes, red for no / green for Maya, red for Peter*. Students can use these cards to answer in activity 2 if they wish.

Sing-along

1 🎵 Listen and point. Then sing and act. TPR

🎵 Clothes! Clothes! 🎵

2 🎧 Listen and say *Peter* or *Maya*. Then play.

3 ✏️ 💬 Draw. Then compare with a friend.

Song: My (coat) is (red).

53

**LESSON 3
Grammar**

Audioscript (track 5.7)
1 My coat is blue.
2 My pants are yellow.
3 My sweater is green.
4 My shoes are black.
5 My hat is purple.

3 Draw. Then compare with a friend.

- Draw a stick figure on the board, like the one in the book. Elicit different clothes words, and draw these clothes items on your stick figure.
- Students work on their own to draw and color clothes items on the stick figure in their books.
- Invite a student to hold up their book. Compare their picture with your picture on the board, e.g., *My pants are brown. Your pants are green.* Encourage the student to spot any other differences.
- Do the same with other students, asking them to hold up their book to compare with your picture on the board. Invite the class to spot and say any differences, e.g., *My sweater is yellow.*

SUPPORT Students compare using single words, e.g., *sweater, yellow.*

STRETCH Students work in pairs to compare their pictures, taking turns to say sentences about them.

> **Extra activity (fast finishers)** Students make and perform a new verse for the song about the clothes in the picture they drew in activity 3.

Wrap-up
- Play *Which is different?* (see Games Bank p.206). For this version, use clothes and body picture cards.
- 🎵 Sing the *Goodbye* song (track 0.7), and students say goodbye to the Mickey Mouse puppet as they leave class.

📝 **Workbook** page 47

Audioscript see p.204
1 🎧 **5.2 Listen and match.** *1 b, 2 c, 3 d, 4 a*
2 **Choose and color. Then say with a friend.**

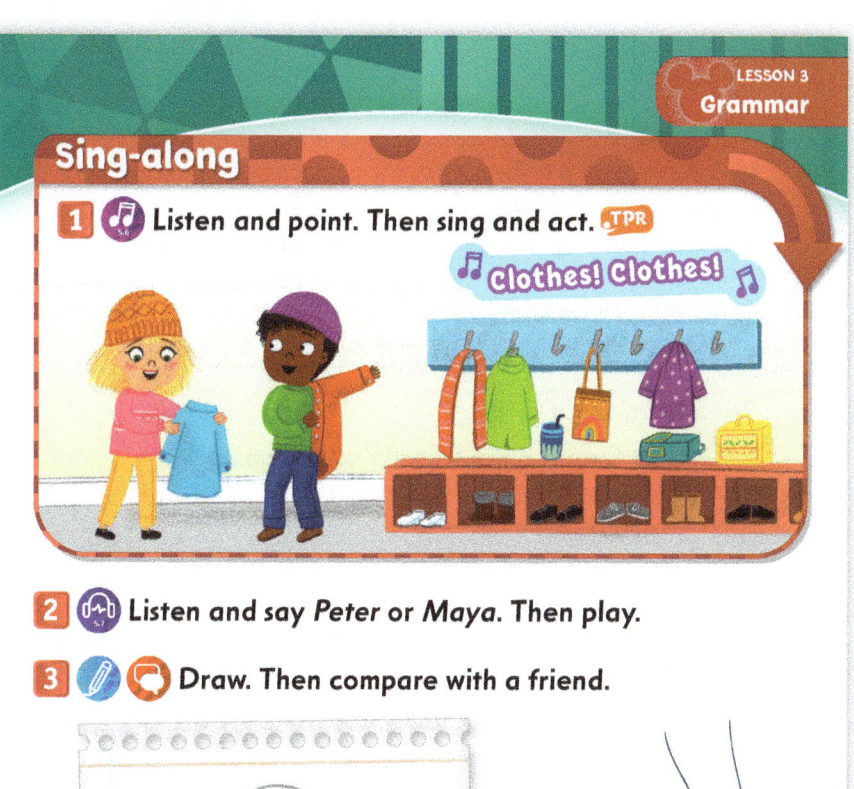

2 🎧 **5.7 Listen and say *Peter* or *Maya*. Then play.**

- Point to Maya in the picture in activity 1, and elicit what clothes items she has and what color they are. Do the same with Peter.
- Play the first line of the audio and pause. Point to the blue coat in the picture, and ask: *Maya or Peter?* (Maya).
- Play the audio, pausing after each sentence for students to find the clothing in the picture and say who it belongs to, Maya or Peter. Play the audio again, and students repeat the sentence, then point to the correct person in the picture. (**Answers:** *1 Maya, 2 Maya, 3 Peter, 4 Maya, 5 Peter*)
- Tell students to choose to be Peter or Maya. Say a sentence about the picture, e.g., *My shoes are black.* The students who have chosen the corresponding character, repeat the sentence.

SUPPORT Students respond using their Peter and Maya cards if they have them, or just point to Peter and Maya in the picture.

STRETCH Students work in pairs, taking turns to say a sentence for their partner to say if it is Peter or Maya. To provide scaffolding, write a rebus sentence on the board using the picture cards, e.g., *My (hat picture card) is (blue picture card).*

5 Lesson 4: Story

Student's Book pages 54–55

Objectives

Lesson aim: listen to and understand a story about the importance of persistence

Story language: *Come and play!*

Recycled language: clothes, colors; *My hat's blue. Your pants are yellow.*

Receptive language: *Let's play. No, thanks.*

Materials: Audio; Story cards (Unit 5); (optional) Video 5A; Picture cards / Word cards (Toys); Mickey Mouse puppet; (optional) a cap or hat, yo-yos, jump ropes, a ball

GSE Skills

Listening: can understand a few basic words and phrases in a story that is read aloud (18)

Reading: can recognize single, familiar everyday words, if supported by pictures (21)

Speaking: can repeat phrases and short sentences, if spoken slowly and clearly (16); can produce very short fixed expressions, using gestures and asking for help when necessary (21)

Teacher toolkit

Story summary

Peter and Maya are at a party. Maya finds it easy to play with the yo-yo, but Peter is having trouble. When Cam asks Peter to play with them, Peter decides to keep practicing. In the end, Peter learns to do lots of different tricks with his yo-yo.

Extend

Bring in a few yo-yos or another toy that students might have difficulty using. If you have an outdoor space, a jump rope would also work well. Put students in groups, and they take turns trying to play with the yo-yo (or jump rope). The other students in the group say *Keep trying!* as they practice, then *Good job!* if they show improvement.

Persistence

In the story, Peter finds out that practice makes perfect. Ask students in L1 if it's easy or difficult for Peter to play with the yo-yo (difficult). Point to Peter in story card 4 and then to Peter in story card 6, and ask: *Is Peter happy/sad/nervous/grumpy/excited?* Elicit answers (*sad/grumpy* in story card 4, *happy* in story card 6). Then ask students how they feel when they try something difficult and then succeed.

Self-awareness

Warm-up

- Greet students with the Mickey Mouse puppet, and sing the *Hello, Stars and Heroes* song (track 0.1).
- If you have a cap or hat, put it on Mickey's head. Say: *Look, Mickey has a (blue) hat.*
- Make Mickey show the toys picture cards, and elicit the words. Then mime playing with a yo-yo, and students say the word (*yo-yo*).

Presentation

1 🔊 **5.8 Listen to the story. Who's clapping?**

- Make the Mickey Mouse puppet stand up. Say: *Sit down, Mickey. It's story time!*
- Show students the first story card, and say: *Look! It's a party.* Point to Maya and Peter, and elicit their names.
- Play the audio. Students listen to the story and follow in their books.
- Use the story cards to tell the story again, with or without the audio. Pause after each story frame to ask a comprehension question, e.g., *Who has a (blue) hat?* (Maya) *Who has a yellow yo-yo?* (Peter) *Who wants to play?* (Cam) *Does Peter keep trying?* (yes).
- Point to the small picture in the rubric, and ask: *Who's clapping?* Show story card 6, and elicit the answer.

Count! Students find and count balloons in the story. (**Answer:** four balloons in frame 2)

Practice

2 🔊 **5.9 Who says it? Listen and point. Then say.**

- Point to the small pictures, and ask: *Who's this?* (Maya, Cam, Peter). Play the first part of the audio, then pause for students to point to the picture of the corresponding character (*Cam*). Then do the same with the second part of the audio (*Maya*) and the third part of the audio (*Peter*).
- Play the audio again, and students repeat the lines.
- Give each student a role: Maya, Cam, or Peter. Play the audio, and students act out their role, saying the lines if they wish to.

Audioscript (track 5.9)

1 **Cam:** *Come and play.*
2 **Maya:** *My pants are blue. And my yo-yo's blue.*
3 **Peter:** *Hey! Look at me!*

3 Who keeps trying? Look and circle.

- Show story card 4, and ask: *Is Peter happy?* Students say or mime *yes* or *no*. In L1, try to elicit that Peter isn't happy because he can't do tricks with his yo-yo. Then point to Maya in the same story card, and elicit that she can already do tricks.
- Show story card 5, and ask: *Who keeps trying with the yo-yo? Maya or Peter?* (Peter).
- Students look at the pictures, point to each picture and ask: *Who keeps trying?* Students point to the correct picture, then circle it.

LESSON 4
Story

The yo-yo

1 🎧 Listen to the story. Who's 🧤? **Maya**

1. **Maya:** Hi, Peter. My hat's blue. And your hat's yellow!
2. **Peter:** Wow!
   Maya: Let's play!
3. **Maya:** My pants are blue. And my yo-yo's blue. Your pants are yellow, Peter. And your yo-yo's yellow!
4. **Maya:** Keep trying, Peter.
5. **Cam:** Come and play, Peter!
   Peter: No, thanks.
6. **Peter:** Hey! Look at me!
   Maya: Good job, Peter.

The end

2 🎧 Who says it? Listen and point. Then say.

3 Who keeps trying? Look and circle.

4 Act out the story.

Story: Come and play!

Teaching star

Application To apply the concept of persistence to concrete examples, show Video 5A again, and ask students to notice how Mulan, like Peter, keeps trying. Say: *Mulan keeps trying.*, and students mime climbing. Then say: *Peter keeps trying.*, and students mime doing yo-yo tricks.

4 Act out the story.

- Point to the photos of the boy and the girl, and say: *My hat's red.* Students repeat.
- Put students in groups of three, and assign each student a role: Maya, Peter, or Cam.
- Play the story audio, and hold up the corresponding story cards as a prompt. Students act out the story as they listen.

Extra activity (story extension) Students imagine they are at a party. Tell them they can either play any game or they can play with any toy. Students mime playing, on their own, in pairs, or in groups. Go around the classroom, inviting students to say what they are playing with, if they know the word, e.g., *ball*.

Wrap-up

- Play *Throw the ball* (see Games Bank, p.206). For this version, students throw the ball to one another. If they can't catch the ball, encourage them to say *Keep trying!*, and let them try again.
- Sing the *Goodbye* song (track 0.7), and students say goodbye to the Mickey Mouse puppet as they leave class.

📖 Workbook   page 48

Audioscript see p.204

1. 🎧 **5.3 Listen and color.** *Maya's hat and yo-yo are blue. Peter's hat and yo-yo are yellow.*
2. **Check (✓) Keep trying. Then point and say.** *1* ✓

Lesson 5: Grammar and Speaking

Student's Book page 56

Objectives

Lesson aim: talk about clothes

Target language: *I'm wearing my T-shirt.*

Recycled language: clothes, numbers; *Who's this? It's … My skirt is white. She's nervous.*

Receptive language: *soldier; Come on! Let's play.*

Materials: Video 5B; Audio; Picture cards / Word cards (Clothes 1, 2); Mickey Mouse puppet; Story cards (Unit 5); Cut-outs (Unit 5), with a cut-out model prepared; card or paper, scissors, paper clip; (optional) real clothes

GSE Skills

Listening: can recognize familiar words in short phrases and sentences spoken slowly and clearly, if supported by pictures or gestures (19)

Speaking: can name items of clothing if supported by pictures (22); can use a few simple words to describe objects, e.g., color, number, if supported by pictures (19)

Teacher toolkit

Video summary – 5B
I'm wearing my pants Videoscript see p.202
Mulan lives in a village with her family. One day, news of war comes to the village. Mulan decides to dress like a soldier and join the army.

Teaching grammar
As you present the grammar structure *I'm wearing …,* emphasize the *m* in *I'm* so that students hear it clearly. Drill the word *I'm* several times, showing students how to close their lips to form the bilabial *m*. Then drill *I'm wearing my …,* and point to your own clothes, eliciting the name of the clothes item.

Engage
Bring in to class a variety of clothes items, and place these in a pile at the front of the classroom. Invite four students to play. Call out the names of several clothes items, and students race to find them in the pile and put them on. Each student says, e.g., *I'm wearing (pants).* Repeat with different students and clothes items.

Warm-up

- Greet students with the Mickey Mouse puppet, and sing the *Hello, Stars and Heroes* song (track 0.1).
- Remind students of the story from Lesson 4. Show story card 6, and students say what clothes items Maya, Cam, Peter, and Leyla are wearing.

Presentation

Video story

1 ▶ **5B Watch. Who's wearing a white skirt? Circle.**

- As a lead-in to Video 5B, ask students to look once more at the Big Picture in Lesson 1, and remind them of the movie *Mulan* and the characters. Point to Mulan and Fa Zhou, and elicit what they are wearing.
- Make the Mickey Mouse puppet stand up. Say: *Sit down, Mickey. It's video time!*
- Play the video, and students point to each picture when they see the character in the video.
- Hold up the picture cards for *white* and *skirt*, and ask: *Who's wearing a white skirt?* Play the video again, elicit the correct answer, and ask students to circle the picture.

Practice

Teaching star

Support understanding As you say what clothes items you are wearing in activity 2, invite students who are wearing the same ones to stand up and point to their own clothes item. This will allow you to check that they have understood your sentence. If any students stand up who aren't wearing the clothes item, say once more the name of the clothes item, and show the corresponding picture card. Ask these students to check whether or not they are wearing the item.

2 🎧 **5.10 Listen and color. Then say for you.**

- Students look at the picture. Ask: *What's (Leyla) wearing?,* and elicit the names of the clothes items (*T-shirt, skirt, shoes, hat*). Do the same for Cam and Peter.
- Ask: *What color is Leyla's T-shirt?* Play the first part of the audio, pausing for students to answer (*blue*). Students color Leyla's T-shirt blue.
- Play the rest of the audio, pausing for students to color the clothes in the picture.
- Describe your own clothes: *I'm wearing my (pants). My (pants) are (blue).* Students look at their own clothes and say: *I'm wearing (pants). My pants are (green).* Do the same for other clothes items you're wearing.

SUPPORT Read aloud each sentence from the audio to the class. Pause before the color word, and students look at their own clothes item and say what color their own, e.g., T-shirt, is.

STRETCH Students work in pairs, taking turns to say what they are wearing, following the model in the audio.

LESSON 5
Grammar and Speaking

1 Watch. Who's wearing a 👗? Circle.

2 Listen and color. Then say for you.

3 Listen and point. Then make and play.

Skills: I'm wearing my (T-shirt).

Audioscript (track 5.10)
1 I'm wearing my T-shirt. My T-shirt is blue.
2 I'm wearing my pants. My pants are black.
3 I'm wearing my hat. My hat is green.

3 🎧 **5.11 Listen and point. Then make and play.**

- Students use scissors to cut carefully around the dotted lines of the cut-out.
- Play the audio, pausing after the first part, and students point to the green T-shirt. Then play the next part of the audio, and students point to the blue shoes.
- Ask students to draw and color one more item of clothing in the allocated space.
- Students make the spinner by putting a paperclip in the center of the circle and placing the end of a pencil (point down) inside the paper clip. Demonstrate how to flick the paperclip so that it spins on the pencil point, and see which clothes item the spinner lands on, e.g., red pants. Say: *I'm wearing (my pants). My (pants) are (red)*.

- Play the game all together as a class. Invite a student to spin the spinner and say which clothes item they land on, e.g., *yellow sweater*. Encourage the class to say: *I'm wearing my (sweater). My (sweater) is (yellow)*.

SUPPORT Students can play the game in mixed-ability pairs. They take turns to spin the spinner, with the less confident student saying the names and colors of clothes items.

STRETCH Students can play the game in mixed-ability pairs. The more confident student makes a sentence, following the model from the audio.

Audioscript (track 5.11)
I'm wearing my T-shirt. My T-shirt's green.
I'm wearing my shoes. My shoes are blue.

Extra activity (fast finishers) Students compare what they are wearing with a partner. One student makes a sentence, e.g., *I'm wearing my (sweater)*. The other student repeats the sentence if it is true for them, or they make a new sentence if they are wearing a different clothes item.

Wrap-up
- Play *Whispers* (see Games Bank p.206). For this version, use a sentence with *I'm wearing … .*
- Sing the *Goodbye* song (track 0.7), and students say goodbye to the Mickey Mouse puppet as they leave class.

📖 Workbook   page 49

Audioscript see p.204
1 🎧 **5.4 Listen and circle.** *1 b, 2 a, 3 a, 4 a*
2 **Be Mulan. Color and say.**

Lesson 6: Myself and others

Keep trying! Student's Book page 57

Objectives

Lesson aim: identify and talk about the importance of persistence

Target language: *Good job! Keep trying!*

Recycled language: *happy, sad, nervous*

Materials: Audio; (optional) Video 5A; *Myself and others* poster; Stickers; Mickey Mouse puppet; (optional) cards for Teacher toolkit

Skills

Listening: can recognize isolated words related to familiar topics, if spoken slowly and clearly and supported by pictures or gestures (16)

Speaking: can say how they feel, using a limited range of common adjectives, e.g., *happy, cold* (22)

Writing (WB): can copy some short familiar words presented in standard printed form (10)

Teacher toolkit

Persistence
In this lesson, students explore how persistence and effort can lead to improvement. At this age, children can easily feel frustrated by things they cannot do. They are continuously learning new skills, and can experience feelings of disappointment. During the lesson, foster a growth mindset by asking students to think about how they can improve, rather than focusing on what they can't do.

Self-awareness

Engage
Set up some games on different desks around the classroom that will challenge students' motor skills, e.g., tossing a beanbag into a bucket, bouncing a ping-pong ball into a container, stacking cups, or building a tower. Students take turns to try each challenge. Encourage them to try several times (see Teaching star).

Home-school link
Encourage students to recognize when they find something difficult at home and to say to themselves: *Keep trying!* Ask them to teach their families the expressions *Keep trying!* and *Good job!*

Warm-up
- Greet students with the Mickey Mouse puppet, and sing the *Hello, Stars and Heroes* song (track 0.1).
- Show the *Myself and others* poster and review the emotions students have learned so far this year.
- Use Mickey to review the concept of persistence. Show Mickey a picture card, and make him name it incorrectly. Say: *Keep trying, Mickey!*, and make him guess incorrectly again. Repeat a few times until Mickey gets the answer right. Praise Mickey: *Good job, Micky!*

🎵 1.12 Listen and sing.
- Play the song audio, and students join in with the words and the actions.
- Ask: *How do you feel?*, and students respond with one of the emotion adjectives or point to a picture on the *Myself and others* poster.

Presentation

1 5.12 Listen and point. Then say.
- Remind students of the situations and the characters in Video 5A in Lesson 1 and the story. If required, play Video 5A and look at the story again.
- Students look at the pictures and say the names of the characters (*Peter, Mulan*). Remind students of Video 5A in Lesson 1 and the story in Lesson 4.
- Point to each picture, and students put their thumbs up or down to show how the character feels about the activity they're doing (pictures 1 and 3 – thumbs down, pictures 2 and 4 – thumbs up).
- Play the audio, and students point to the pictures. Play the audio again, pausing after each sentence for students to mime what Peter or Mulan is doing and repeat the sentence.

Audioscript (track 5.12)
1 Keep trying, Peter!
2 Good job, Peter!
3 Keep trying, Mulan!
4 Good job, Mulan!

Practice

2 Look and say.
- Point to the first photo. Mime learning to ride a bike and having some difficulty trying. Provide drama by wobbling and saying *Argh!* Students copy you, and say to them: *Keep trying!* Then point to the second photo, mime riding a bike well, and say: *Good job!*
- Do the same with the two photos showing children doing math. Use facial expression to show how each child feels (picture 3 – sad, picture 4 – happy). Elicit the sentences *Keep trying! Good job!*

Teaching star
Diversity and inclusion Some children may have physical disabilities or learning differences like dyspraxia that may make activity 3 challenging for them. Check whether or not the challenges are suitable for all the students in the class, and consider adapting the activities as necessary.

Keep trying!

LESSON 6
Myself and others

1 Listen and point. Then say.

Listen and sing.

2 Look and say.

3 Look and do. Then say. TPR

I'm a hero!

Self-management: Good job! Keep trying!

I'm a hero! Mime doing a challenging activity, e.g., roller skating (pretend to fall over, then try again). Ask students: *Do you keep trying?*, and elicit *yes/no* answers. Then students stick the sticker in their books.

Wrap-up

- Draw students' attention once more to the *Myself and others* poster, and ask them to identify the picture that reflects the lesson aim. Point to the boy in the picture and elicit *I keep trying!*
- Play *Draw it!* (see Games Bank p.206). For this version, students say to each other *Keep trying!* and *Good job!* as they play.
- Sing the *Goodbye* song (track 0.7), and students say goodbye to the Mickey Mouse puppet as they leave class.

Workbook   page 50

1 Circle *Keep trying* blue. Circle *Good job* green. Then point and say. *blue: 2, 4; green: 1, 3*
2 Who tells you *Good job*? Draw and trace.

---

3 Look and do. Then say.

- Point to the first picture. Then make a show of closing your eyes, and try to draw a circle (badly) on the board. Open your eyes, and ask: *Keep trying or good job?* Students say: *Keep trying.* Then try again two or three more times, until you draw a circle well. This time, students say: *Good job!*
- Students try the challenge in the first picture: draw a circle with their eyes closed. Say: *Keep trying!* and *Good job!*, as appropriate, and encourage students to repeat the phrases.
- Do the same with the second picture (balance a pencil on your finger) and the third picture (throw a ball of paper in the trash bin).

SUPPORT Invite different students to the front of the class to attempt each challenge. For each attempt, elicit *Keep trying!* or *Good job!* Allow students to respond with thumbs up or thumbs down if they can't remember the phrases.

STRETCH Students work in pairs, taking turns to attempt each challenge and give each other feedback, using the two phrases.

5 Lesson 7: My world

Technology: Materials Student's Book page 58

Objectives

Lesson aims: learn about materials
Target language: *cotton, leather, wool*
Recycled language: *clothes, colors*
Materials: Audio; Mickey Mouse puppet; (optional) real clothes or accessories made of cotton, leather, or wool

GSE Skills

Listening: can recognize isolated words related to familiar topics, if spoken slowly and clearly and supported by pictures or gestures (16)

Reading: can recognize single, familiar everyday words, if supported by pictures (21)

Speaking: can repeat single words, if spoken slowly and clearly (10); can repeat phrases and short sentences, if spoken slowly and clearly (16)

Writing (WB): can copy some short familiar words presented in standard printed form (10)

Teacher toolkit

Cross-curricular

In this lesson, students learn about different materials used for clothing. Cotton is a natural fiber that comes from the cotton plant. It is soft, long-lasting, and breathable, making it ideal for clothing. Wool is an animal fiber that comes from sheep and goats. Wool is highly absorbent, and woolen clothing helps provide a feeling of warmth to the wearer. Many sweaters nowadays are made from acrylic, a synthetic fiber, instead of wool. Leather is an animal product, usually coming from cows. It is highly resistant and durable. Vegan leather is a new, animal-friendly alternative.

Extend

Choose one of the materials from the lesson, and find a video online of its journey from raw material to finished product, e.g., from shearing a sheep to a knitted sweater. Play the video without sound, and try to answer any questions students may have.

Home-school link

Students find at home three clothes items, one made from cotton, one made from wool, and one made from leather. Invite them to bring one of these clothes items into the next lesson. Encourage them to tell a family member the name of the clothes item and the name of its material.

Warm-up

- Greet students with the Mickey Mouse puppet, and sing the *Hello, Stars and Heroes* song (track 0.1).
- Play *Mickey's card* (see Games Bank p.206), using the clothes picture cards.

Presentation

Teaching star

Classroom management When using realia or objects as in activity 1, ask students to sit in a circle, and pass the object around the circle. This will allow all students to see the object clearly. Decide whether students will sit on their chairs or on the floor, model the way you expect them to sit, and praise them for their patience.

1 🎧 **5.13 Listen and point. Then say.**

- If you have brought to class real clothes or materials, show them to students. If possible, let them pass the items around the class and touch them to feel the texture of the material. As you pass each item around, say: *It's (cotton)*.
- Students look at the photos. Hold up one clothes item, and students point to the photo they think matches the item's material. Repeat with other clothes items.
- Play the audio, and students point to each photo. Pause between each one, and ask students to try to find something with the same material, either something they are wearing or something in the classroom, e.g., a hat or scarf.
- Play the audio again, and students point to each photo and say the word.
- Point to each photo and elicit the word.

SUPPORT Say a word, and students repeat it and point to the corresponding photo.

STRETCH Students work in pairs, taking turns to point to a photo and say the word.

Practice

2 🎧 **5.14 Match. Listen and check. Then say.**

- Students look at the icons a, b, c below the photos. Elicit or say: *cotton, wool, leather*.
- Then point to the photo of the shoe, and ask: *Cotton, wool, or leather?* (*leather*). Students point to the *leather* icon. Use your finger to draw a line to match the clothes item and the materials icon.
- Students draw lines to match all the clothes items and the materials icons.
- Play the audio, and students listen and check their answers. Play the audio again, pausing for students to repeat the sentences.
- Hold up a picture card, say: *It's a …*, and elicit the clothes word. Then say: *It's …*, and elicit *cotton/wool/leather*.

SUPPORT Give students options to choose from for the materials. Say: *It's cotton/wool/leather.*, and students say the correct option.

STRETCH Students work in pairs, taking turns to point to a picture and say sentences.

LESSON 7
My world — Technology

Materials

1 🎧 Listen and point. Then say.

1. cotton
2. wool
3. leather

2 ✏️ 🎧 Match. Listen and check. Then say.

3 ✏️ 💬 Draw clothes. Then say.

Materials: cotton, leather, wool

Audioscript (track 5.14)
1 It's a shoe. It's leather.
2 It's a skirt. It's cotton.
3 It's a sock. It's wool.

3 Draw clothes. Then say.

- Point to the pictures, and elicit the words (*hat, T-shirt*). Then point to the drawing box, and ask: *What clothes?* Elicit the names of different clothes items.
- Draw one of the students' ideas on the board, e.g., *hat*. Add some design features, e.g., stripes or spots. Then ask: *What color?*, and color the clothes item according to students' suggestions. Say: *Look. It's a (hat). It's (wool). It's (purple and green)*.
- Students draw and color a clothes item of their own design.
- Invite a few students to show their design to the class. Ask the class to describe what they see, e.g., *It's a (T-shirt). It's (cotton). It's (blue and white)*.

SUPPORT Give students prompts to help them describe the clothes item: *It's a … . It's … .* To provide further support, give students options to choose from, e.g., *It's cotton/wool/leather*.

STRETCH Students share their designs in small groups, taking turns to describe their pictures. Monitor, supporting as necessary.

Thinking skills
Understand In activity 2, students identify different clothes items and match them to the materials of cotton, wool, and leather. The photos and artworks support identification in a new context.

Create In activity 3, students design clothes items made with the materials of cotton, wool, and leather. They describe the clothes items, identifying and naming the material and the color.

Extra activity (extension) Further develop students' higher order thinking skills by playing *Which is different?* (see Games Bank p.206). Place the *scarf, shoes, hat,* and *sweater* picture cards on the board. Students say which one is different (*shoes* – they're leather, the other items are wool).

Wrap-up

- Play *Monster munch* (see Games Bank p.206). For this version, the monster only wants to eat clothes made of cotton. Students decide whether each clothes picture card is cotton so that the monster can eat it.
- Sing the *Goodbye* song (track 0.7), and students say goodbye to the Mickey Mouse puppet as they leave class.

Workbook   page 51

1 **Look and circle.** 1 leather, 2 wool, 3 cotton
2 **Draw, trace, and say.** Students draw one item for each material.

Lesson 8: Review

Objectives

Lesson aim: review target language from Unit 5
Target language: clothes; *What's this? It's my (hat)*.
Recycled language: colors
Materials: Audio; (optional) Video 5A, Video 5B; Picture cards / Word cards (Clothes 1, 2); Stickers; Mickey Mouse puppet; a cloth; *My progress* poster

GSE Skills

Listening: can recognize isolated words related to familiar topics, if spoken slowly and clearly and supported by pictures and gestures (16)
Reading: can recognize single, familiar everyday words, if supported by pictures (21)
Speaking: can name items of clothing, if supported by pictures (22); can use a few simple words to describe objects, e.g., color, number, if supported by pictures (19)
Writing: can copy some short familiar words presented in standard printed form (10)

Teacher toolkit

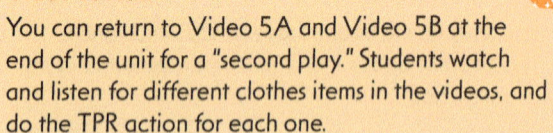

Video review
You can return to Video 5A and Video 5B at the end of the unit for a "second play." Students watch and listen for different clothes items in the videos, and do the TPR action for each one.

Remediation
Some students may need support with reading and tracing the words. Check whether students are able to hold a pencil correctly before asking them to trace the words. If students are not ready to trace, you can use a multisensory alternative such as a sand tray. Also, you can give students more practice in using a pencil by having them trace straight and squiggly lines and shapes.

Home-school link
Students use the language they've learned in the unit to describe their clothes to their families, e.g., *I'm wearing my (scarf). My (scarf) is (red). It's (wool).*

I can do it! Student's Book page 59

Warm-up
- Greet students with the Mickey Mouse puppet, and sing the *Hello, Stars and Heroes* song (track 0.1).
- Play *Memory* game (see Games Bank p.206). For this version, use the clothes picture cards. You can increase the challenge by asking questions, e.g., *What color is the (hat)?*
- Play the song audio from Lesson 3 (track 5.6), and students join in with the words and the actions. If students are confident with the words, play the karaoke version (track 5.6_karaoke).

I can do it!

1 Say and point. Then trace.
- Play *Circle it!* (see Games Bank p.206). Place the word cards on the board. Hold up a picture card, and invite a student to come to the front and draw a circle around the correct word card on the board.
- Point to each word, say it, and use your finger to trace each letter of the word in the air. Students use their own finger to do the same.
- Ask students to look at the picture of Chi-Fu and Fa Zhou, and they say what clothes items each character is wearing. Invite different students to say the words, as the rest of the class points to the correct words on the board.
- Point to the word *hat* and elicit the word. Trace the word *hat* on the board. Then students trace the word in their books. Do the same with *socks*, *pants*, and *shoes*.

Teaching star

Social and emotional learning You may need to provide differentiation activities in activity 1 for students who aren't yet comfortable with writing. Using L1, explain that all students find some things easy and other things more difficult. Tell students that if they are able to write, they should trace the words on the page, but it's also OK if they need to do the activity orally instead. Encourage students to say to each other the following expressions during the lesson: *Keep trying! Good job!*

ACHIEVE
Students name, read, and trace clothes words, and say what they are wearing.

SUPPORT
Students can trace the words in the air or in a sand tray. They can just point to the pictures and say the words.

STRETCH
Students work in pairs, taking turns to choose one of the characters and say, e.g., *I'm wearing my shoes. My shoes are brown.*, for their partner to point to the correct character in the picture.

I can do it!

LESSON 8 Review

1 🖊 Say and point. Then trace.

hat
socks
pants
shoes

2 💡🖊 Think and color. Then stick!

I can …
1
Clothes! Clothes! 2
3

✓ Unit 5!

Go online — Big Project

59

Teaching star

Growth mindset Praise students for effort and attitude rather than for their abilities. This kind of "process praise" motivates students and helps build resilience. Say: *Good job! I can see you worked hard today. I'm proud of you.*

Wrap-up

- Students reflect on which lesson or activity they most enjoyed in Unit 5. Have a class vote, and choose one activity to do again as a class, e.g., watch the video, sing the song or chant, listen to the story, or play a game.
- Draw students' attention to the *My progress* poster, and ask them to identify the picture that reflects this unit. Read aloud with students the *I can …* statements (*I can talk about clothes, I can encourage my friends to keep trying*).
- 🎵 Sing the *Goodbye* song (track 0.7), then students say *goodbye* to the Mickey Mouse puppet and tell him their favorite word from Unit 5.

📖 Workbook pages 52–53

My progress
Audioscript see p.204
1 🔊 **5.5 Listen and number.** *a 2, b 3, c 1, d 4*
2 **Act, say, and guess.**

Units W–5 My practice

1 **Color. Then point, act, and say** *I'm wearing my …*
 Find 4 backpacks and 3 posters. Say the colors. *backpacks: blue, green, purple, orange; posters: white and blue, green, blue*
2 **Draw your favorite clothes. Then say.**
Unit 5! My favorite activity: Students stick the small star sticker next to their favorite activity.

---

2 💡 **Think and color. Then stick!**
- Point to each picture, and say the *I can …* statements: *I can name clothes. I can sing a song. I can keep trying.* For each statement, give an example, and then ask: *Can you do this?* If necessary, explain in L1.
- Students demonstrate what they can do. They work in pairs, taking turns to point to and say the clothes they are wearing. Sing the song all together as a class. Students work in pairs, taking turns to act out doing something difficult and saying *Keep trying!* and *Good job!* Monitor and assess students' performance.
- Students color the stars next to what they can do. Then they stick the reward sticker to show they have completed Unit 5.

My Star and Hero! Students look at the picture of Mulan on p.4 of the Student's Book. They point to, name, and describe Mulan's clothes.
Extra activity (class game) Play *Let's dance!* (see Games Bank p.206), using the song from Lesson 3 (track 5.6).

6 Nature

Unit objectives
By the end of this unit, students can:
- talk about the things they can see in nature
- read and understand a story about working in a garden
- recognize good teamwork and learn to work in a team
- talk about symmetry

Skills development GSE
Listening: recognize what other people are describing

Speaking: talk about their bugs and things in nature; offer to help someone; describe bugs

Vocabulary
Lesson 1: ant, beetle, butterfly, ladybug
Lesson 2: flower, mushroom, pond, river, rock, tree

Grammar
Lesson 3: I can see a beetle.
Lesson 5: What color is it? It's red.

Myself and others
Teamwork In this unit, a Disney video and a story introduce the theme of teamwork. Students will learn to work together to help each other.
Language: Let's all help! Good idea.
Social awareness

Story
A good team
Help me! It's a team.

My world
Math and art: Symmetry
spots, stripes

Unit overview

a bug's life

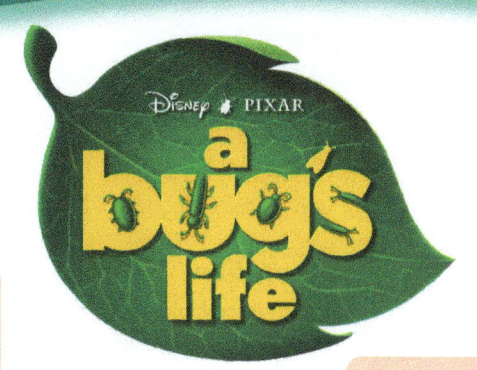

Princess Atta
The eldest daughter of the Queen of the ant colony and heir to the throne. She is nervous about her role and tries to make the colony a perfect place to live.

Dot
The younger daughter of the Queen of the ant colony, Dot is small but is destined for great things.

Flik
A nice, young ant who is always inventing contraptions to improve the colony's way of life, although his ideas don't always go to plan.

The circus bugs
Francis is a ladybug and a clown in the circus. Heimlich is a caterpillar, and he's also a clown. Dim the rhino beetle acts as a lion at the circus. Gypsy is a beautiful moth.

Flik is an inventive ant who always ends up getting into trouble. One day, after accidentally destroying the colony's crops, Flik leaves the colony and goes on a journey. He meets a group of circus bugs, who he recruits to help him save the colony.

Did you know?
The movie *A Bug's Life* is inspired by Aesop's fable *The Ant and the Grasshopper*, the story of a hungry grasshopper who spends the summer singing instead of looking for food.

Video stories
Video 6A: *Flik's adventure*
Video 6B: *I can see a beetle*

Online modules

Phonics
Words with Pp, Qq, and Rr sounds in initial position
pond, queen, rock

Big Project
Make a bug home

6 Lesson 1: Vocabulary

Student's Book pages 60–61

Objectives

Lesson aim: name bugs

Target language: ant, beetle, butterfly, ladybug

Recycled language: colors; sister, big; Who's this? What's this? It's a … Keep trying. Good job!

Receptive language: I can see … He's going on an adventure. Let's all help. The ants say …

Materials: Video 6A; Audio; Picture cards / Word cards (Bugs; Body, Disney characters); Sticker (Flik); Mickey Mouse puppet; (optional) a large tray, natural materials, plastic bugs, or foam shapes

GSE Skills

Listening: can recognize isolated words related to familiar topics, if spoken slowly and clearly and supported by pictures and gestures (16)

Reading: can recognize single, familiar everyday words, if supported by pictures (21)

Speaking: can name everyday objects, animals, or people around them or in pictures, using single words (18)

Writing (WB): can copy some short familiar words presented in standard printed form (10)

Teacher toolkit

Video summary – 6A

Flik's adventure **Videoscript see p.202**

Flik and the other ants help Princess Atta. They all work together to build a bird structure to scare off grasshoppers. It's difficult, but they keep trying, and they succeed in the end.

Engage

Set up a nature sensory tray in the classroom. Fill the tray with grass, moss, leaves, bark, and other natural materials. You could also add small pebbles or sand to provide more texture. As students progress through the unit, hide objects in the sensory tray for students to find, name, and describe, e.g., flowers, mushrooms, rocks, plastic bugs, or bug shapes cut out of EVA foam.

Teamwork

Using L1, use the video story to talk about how the ants work together in a team to make the bird and then lift the bird together. Remind students of what they learned in Unit 5 about persistence. Then play the video again, and students say *Keep trying!* and *Good job!* whenever appropriate.

Social awareness

Warm-up

- Greet students with the Mickey Mouse puppet, and sing the *Hello, Stars and Heroes* song (track 0.1).

Presentation

Video story

- Students look at the Big Picture. Introduce the movie and the characters: *This is the movie A Bug's Life. This is Flik.*
- Students count the number of bugs in the Big Picture (ten).
- Ask students to find and point to different items in the Big Picture. Ask: *Who's big? Who's small? Who's (green)?*

1 ▶ **6A Watch. What do the ants make? Circle.**

- Make the Mickey Mouse puppet stand up. Say: *Sit down, Mickey. It's video time! Let's watch!*
- Play Video 6A, and students watch and listen. Play the video again. Ask: *What do the ants make?* Then point to each of the small pictures, and say: *A butterfly, a flower, or a bird?* Ask students to point to, then circle, the correct picture.

2 ▶ **6A Check (✓) the team.**

- Try unsuccessfully to hold and show the class all six picture cards. Then invite two students each to hold two picture cards for you. Say: *We are a team.*, and high-five your team members.
- Play the video, and students high-five each other when they see the bugs working as a team.
- Point to each small picture, and ask: *Is it a team?* Students say or mime *yes* or *no*.
- Students check the correct picture.

Picture cards / Word cards (optional) Show the picture cards one by one to introduce the new vocabulary. Repeat several times, encouraging students to remember the words. Then show each word card, and elicit the words.

Practice

3 **6.1 Listen, point, and say. Then play.**

- Play the audio, pausing after each word for students to point to the bugs in the small photos. Play the audio again, pausing for students to say the words. Play the audio a third time, and students read, say, and point to the bugs.
- Invite a confident student to say a word, and the rest of the class points to the correct bug in the photos. Repeat with other students.

SUPPORT Say a word, students repeat it and point to the correct photo.

STRETCH Students work in pairs, taking turns to point to a photo for their partner to name the bug.

Audioscript (track 6.1)

1 ant // 2 beetle // 3 butterfly // 4 ladybug

6 Nature

LESSON 1 Vocabulary

1 ▶ Watch. What do the ants make? Circle.

2 ▶ Check (✓) the team.

3 🎧 💬 Listen, point, and say. Then play.
1. ant
2. beetle
3. butterfly
4. ladybug

4 🎵 Listen, chant, and act. TPR — *What's this?*

ant, beetle, butterfly, ladybug

---

4 🎵 **6.2 Listen, chant, and act.**

🐭 Give the Mickey Mouse puppet a picture card, facing away from the class. Ask: *What's this? What's this? It's a … .* Invite students to guess which bug is on the picture card.

- Display the picture cards. Play the audio, and students listen and point to the correct picture card when they hear the corresponding word.
- Devise accompanying TPR actions, and demonstrate as students copy. Play the audio again. Students join in with the chant and do the TPR actions.

Audioscript (track 6.2)
What's this? *(x2)* // It's a butterfly.
Butterfly. Butterfly. // In the sky.
What's this? *(x2)* // It's a ladybug.
Ladybug. Ladybug. // In the sky.
What's this? *(x2)* // It's a beetle.
Beetle. Beetle. // In the sky.
What's this? *(x2)* // It's an ant.
Ant. Ant. // Ants. Ants. Ants. // Arrrghhhhh!

❓ **Collect your friend** Show the picture card of Flik to help students identify the correct sticker. Students stick the sticker on p.5 in the Student's Book. Ask: *Who's this?* (Flik).

Extra activity (video extension) Play Video 6A again. Pause to hold up the *legs* picture card, and ask: *How many?* Students count the number of legs on different bugs, pausing the video where appropriate. If necessary, show a few seconds of the video so that all the bug's legs can be seen.

Wrap-up
- Play *Faster and faster* (see Games Bank p.206). For this version, use the bugs picture cards.
- 🐭 Sing the *Goodbye* song (track 0.7), and students say goodbye to the Mickey Mouse puppet as they leave class.

📝 **Workbook** — pages 54–55

1 Watch again. Then circle.
  1 Who's in the video? *a, c*
  2 What bugs do you see in the video? *a, b, c, d*
  3 Where can you see the team? *b*
2 Trace. Then point and say. *1 ant, 2 beetle, 3 butterfly, 4 ladybug*
3 Challenge! 🔍 Count the ants. Then write and say. *7*

Lesson 2: Vocabulary

Student's Book page 62

Objectives

Lesson aim: name nature items

Target language: *flower, mushroom, pond, river, rock, tree*

Recycled language: *bugs*

Materials: Audio; Picture cards / Word cards (Nature, Bugs); Stickers; Mickey Mouse puppet; (optional) photos of yourself in nature, a cloth bag

GSE Skills

Listening: can recognize isolated words related to familiar topics, if spoken slowly and clearly and supported by pictures and gestures (16)

Reading: can recognize single, familiar everyday words, if supported by pictures (21)

Speaking: can use a few simple words to describe objects, e.g., color, number, if supported by pictures (19)

Writing (WB): can copy some short familiar words presented in standard printed form (10)

Teacher toolkit

Teaching vocabulary
If possible, bring in some photos of yourself in nature to generate interest in the target vocabulary. Say, e.g., *Look! Here's a (big) (tree)! Look! I'm in a river!*

Engage
Take students outside into nature, if possible, and encourage them to notice natural features around them. You could give students a list of items, and ask them to check the items they find. Alternatively, you could take them on a virtual walk in nature, using the street view mode on an online map.

Home-school link
Encourage students to go with their families on a nature walk in a local park and point out and name the different items they see.

Warm-up

- Greet students with the Mickey Mouse puppet, and sing the *Hello, Stars and Heroes* song (track 0.1).
- Play *Where is …?* (see Games Bank p.206), using the bugs picture cards.
- Say: *Listen and chant!*, and play the chant from Lesson 1 (track 6.2). Students join in with the chant and do the actions.

Presentation

Picture cards / Word cards (optional) Show the picture cards one by one to introduce the new vocabulary. Repeat several times.

1 6.3 Listen, point, and say. Then play.

- Show the Mickey Mouse puppet the *flower* picture card. Make Mickey smell the flower, and say: *Mmm! A flower!* Students look at the photos and point to the flower.
- Say: *Listen and point.* Play the audio, and students point to the corresponding photos. Play the audio again, pausing after each word. Students point to the corresponding photo and repeat the word.
- Say a word, and students repeat it and point to the corresponding photo. Repeat with different words.

SUPPORT Say a word, and students mime an action to represent the word, e.g., smelling a flower, climbing a tree, swimming in a river, picking up a rock, being a frog on a lily pad, and eating a mushroom.

STRETCH Students work in pairs, taking turns to point to a photo for their partner to name. They can also mime an action for each word.

Practice

2 6.4 Listen, point, and stick. Then say.

- Students look at the picture and elicit the nature items they can see.
- Point to the empty sticker frames, and students say which items they think might be missing, e.g., *mushroom, flower*.
- Play the audio, pausing after the description of the mushroom and the description of the flower, for students to position the stickers in the empty frames.
- Play the audio again, and students stick the stickers in the frames. Play the audio a third time, pausing for students to point and repeat the sentences.
- Point to an item in the picture, and say: *Look! A …*, and elicit the name of the item, e.g., *mushroom*. Then say: *It's …*, and elicit the correct color and size, e.g., *It's yellow. It's small.*

Audioscript (track 6.4)

Look! A tree. It's green and brown. It's big.
Look! A pond. It's blue. It's big.
Look! A mushroom. It's yellow. It's small.
Look! A rock. It's brown. It's big.
Look! A flower. It's purple. It's small.
Look! A river. It's blue. It's big.

LESSON 2
Vocabulary

1 🎧 💬 **Listen, point, and say. Then play.**

1. flower
2. tree
3. river
4. rock
5. pond
6. mushroom

2 🎧 💬 **Listen, point, and stick. Then say.**

3 🎧 💬 **Listen and find. Then play.**

62   flower, mushroom, pond, river, rock, tree

Teaching star

Learning to learn Show students how to draw and label a picture in order to record key vocabulary. They can draw a picture scene similar to the one in activity 2 and then write or trace the words near the items.

3 🎧 **6.5 Listen and find. Then play.**

- Play the beginning of the audio, pausing after *It's big*. Students guess which item is being described. Say: *Is it a …?*, and elicit ideas. Then play the rest of the first part of the audio for students to check their ideas.
- Do the same with the other three parts of the audio.
- 🐭 Make the Mickey Mouse puppet choose and describe an item from activity 1. Students ask Mickey questions to guess what it is, e.g., *Is it a (rock)?* Make Mickey answer *yes* or *no*.

SUPPORT Provide students with prompts to complete: *Is it a …?*

STRETCH Students work in pairs, taking turns to choose and describe an item for their partner to guess.

Audioscript (track 6.5)

1. **A:** *It's green and brown.*
   B: *It's big.*
   A: *Is it a tree?*
   B: *Yes. It's a tree.*
2. **A:** *It's red and black. It's small.*
   B: *Is it a ladybug?*
   A: *Yes. It's a ladybug.*
3. **A:** *t's blue. It's big.*
   B: *Is it a river?*
   A: *No.*
   B: *Is it a pond?*
   A: *Yes. It's a pond.*
4. **A:** *It's black. It's small.*
   B: *Is it an ant?*
   A: *No.*
   B: *Is it a beetle?*
   A: *Yes. It's a beetle.*

Extra activity (class game) Play *It's in the bag* (see Games Bank p.206) with any objects that students know, e.g., classroom objects, clothes, toys. Students guess what is inside the bag by asking: *Is it a …?*

Wrap-up

- Play *Draw it!* (see Games Bank p.206). Invite a student to come to the board, and show them one of the nature picture cards. Ask them to draw the item on the board for other students to guess.
- 🐭 Sing the *Goodbye* song (track 0.7), and students say goodbye to the Mickey Mouse puppet as they leave class.

📝 **Workbook**   page 56

Audioscript see p.204

1. 🎧 **6.1 Listen and color.** *1 pond – blue, 2 rock – gray, 3 flower – purple, 4 mushroom – red, 5 tree – green and brown*
2. **Draw and trace. Then say.** *1 rock, 2 mushroom, 3 flower, 4 tree, 5 river, 6 pond*

Picture Dictionary

Students look at the Picture Dictionary on p.106 in the Student's Book and complete the activities.

6 Lesson 3: Grammar

Student's Book page 63

Objectives

Lesson aim: name things you can see
Target language: *I can see a beetle.*
Recycled language: bugs, nature
Materials: Audio; Picture cards / Word cards (Bugs, Nature); Mickey Mouse puppet; (optional) a magnifying glass (for Teacher toolkit), cardboard tubes or card, cellophane, scissors, tape

GSE Skills

Listening: can get the gist of a simple song, if supported by gestures (21); can recognize familiar words and phrases in short, simple songs or chants (18)
Speaking: can get the gist of a simple song, if supported by gestures (21); can name everyday objects, animals, or people around them or in pictures, using single words (18)

Teacher toolkit

Teaching grammar
Mime using a magnifying glass to look for something, and say: *I can see …* . Move towards one of the picture cards, and students name the item on the picture card. Do the same for all the bugs and nature picture cards.

Extend
Hide bugs and nature picture cards around the classroom. Ask students to take their notebooks and pencils and go on a trail around the classroom. They make a note of what they find by writing the words or drawing pictures.

Differentiation
Some students might not find the target structure very challenging. You can also teach the question *What can you see?*, and ask students to do the activities in pairs, taking turns to ask *What can you see?* for their partner to answer: *I can see …* .

Warm-up
- Greet students with the Mickey Mouse puppet, and sing the *Hello, Stars and Heroes* song (track 0.1).
- Make Mickey hold up each bugs and nature picture card, and elicit the word. Then ask: *What color is it?*, and students answer.

Presentation

1 Sing-along 🎵 **6.6 Listen and color. Then sing and act.**

- Point to each of the characters in the picture, and ask: *What can (Peter) see?* Students look at the picture and name the bug each character is looking at.
- Play the song audio. Students point to each bug in the picture as they hear the corresponding word in the song.
- Play the chorus and the first verse of the song again. Then pause and ask: *What color is the ant?* (*black*). Students color the ant in the picture black. Do the same with the remaining verses.
- Play the whole song a third time, and demonstrate the TPR actions. Encourage students to join in with some of the words as they do the actions. When students are confident with the words, play the karaoke version (track 6.6_karaoke), and students sing along.

> **TPR song**
> ant – run quickly on the spot
> beetle – stomp around on the spot
> butterfly – flap arms slowly
> ladybug – flap arms quickly
> During the chorus, students mime any bug.

Audioscript (track 6.6)

Bugs, bugs, bugs. Big and small. *(x2)*
I can see an ant. Small and black. *(x2)*
I can see a beetle. Big and brown. *(x2)*
Bugs, bugs, bugs. Big and small. *(x2)*
I can see a butterfly. Big and yellow. *(x2)*
I can see a ladybug. Red and black. *(x2)*
Bugs, bugs, bugs. Big and small. *(x2)*

Practice

2 6.7 Listen and find. Then say.

- Students look again at the picture in activity 1. Play the audio, pausing after each sentence for students to point to the corresponding bug.
- Play the audio again, pausing after each sentence. Students repeat the sentence and say the name of the character who can see each bug.
- Play all together as a class. Say: *I can see (a beetle).*, and students say the name of the character (*Maya*). Then invite more confident students to say a sentence for the class to complete.

Sing-along

1 🎵 **Listen and color. Then sing and act.** TPR

2 🎧 💬 **Listen and find. Then say.**

3 💬 **Guess, point, and say.**

Song: I can see a (beetle). 63

STRETCH Students work in pairs, taking turns to choose a character and say *I can see a/an …* for their partner to say the name of the character.

Audioscript (track 6.7)
1 **Cam:** *I can see a butterfly.*
2 **Peter:** *I can see an ant.*
3 **Maya:** *I can see a beetle.*
4 **Leyla:** *I can see a ladybug.*

Teaching star ✦

Creativity Foster creativity by inviting students to imagine things they can't really see. Bring to class recycled cardboard tubes, card, and cellophane. Students make a magnifying glass or a pair of binoculars to look through and tell a friend what they can "see."

LESSON 3
Grammar

3 **Guess, point, and say.**

- Use the picture cards to review the names of different bugs.
- Point to one of the magnifying glass pictures, then point to your eye. Say: *I can see (a ladybug)*.
- Say another sentence, e.g., *I can see a beetle.*, but this time, don't point to the corresponding picture. Students repeat the word (*beetle*) and point to the correct picture in their books. Repeat with other pictures.
- Invite more confident students to say: *I can see (a butterfly).*, for the rest of the class to repeat the word and point to the correct picture.

SUPPORT Point to each picture, and say: *I can see a/an …* . Students complete the sentence with the correct word.

STRETCH Students work in pairs, taking turns to point to a picture for their partner to name the item, using the structure *I can see a/an …* .

> **Extra activity (fast finishers)** Students play a game in pairs or groups with objects and pictures in the classroom. Invite a student to name something they can see, and other students find the item in the classroom.

Wrap-up

- Play *Up close!* (see Games Bank p.206), using picture cards from Units 1–6.
- 🎵 Sing the *Goodbye* song (track 0.7), and students say goodbye to the Mickey Mouse puppet as they leave class.

📓 Workbook   page 57

Audioscript see p.205

1 🎧 **6.2 Listen and put a ✓ or ✗. Then play.**
1 ✗, 2 ✓, 3 ✓, 4 ✓

2 **Match and say.** 1 b, tree; 2 d, beetle; 3 a, flower; 4 c, rock

6 Lesson 4: Story

Student's Book pages 64–65

Objectives

Lesson aim: listen to and understand a story about working in a garden

Story language: *Help me! It's a team.*

Recycled language: bugs, numbers; *I can see a butterfly. Good job!*

Receptive language: *Let's all help. Good idea!*

Materials: Audio; Picture cards / Word cards (Bugs); Story cards (Unit 6); Mickey Mouse puppet; (optional) pieces of A4 paper, small objects, e.g., erasers, small balls

GSE Skills

Listening: can understand a few basic words and phrases in a story that is read aloud (18)

Reading: can recognize single, familiar everyday words, if supported by pictures (21)

Speaking: can repeat phrases and short sentences, if spoken slowly and clearly (16)

Teacher toolkit

Story summary
The friends are working in the school garden. Both Leyla and Cam need help carrying their buckets, but Maya is busy looking for bugs. In the end, they all work together as a team to water the garden.

Extend
Connect the story to other curriculum subjects, and foster students' creative thinking skills. Students identify the problem in the story (they need to carry the water from the school building to the plants). Ask them to design another solution, e.g., connect a hosepipe, set up a sprinkler system. Encourage students to use their imaginations and be creative as they design their solution.

Teamwork
In the story, the characters are working in the garden, but not everyone is helping. The characters realize that they work best in a team. Students identify how Leyla is feeling, first when she is working alone, and then when all the friends are working as a team. Encourage students to say or act out how they themselves can work together as a team in the classroom.

Social awareness

Warm-up

- Greet students with the Mickey Mouse puppet, and sing the *Hello, Stars and Heroes* song (track 0.1).
- Hold up each bug picture card, and ask questions: *What's this? What color is it? Is it big or small? How many (legs)?*

Presentation

1 🎧 **6.8 Listen to the story. Point to a beetle, a butterfly, and a flower.**

- Make the Mickey Mouse puppet stand up. Say: *Sit down, Mickey. It's story time!*
- Point to the small pictures of bugs in the rubric, and ask students to race to find pictures of the bugs in the story as quickly as they can, doing the corresponding TPR action when they find them. (**Answers:** beetle – frame 3, butterfly – frame 1, flower – frame 6)
- Play the audio. Students listen to the story and follow in their books.
- Use the story cards to tell the story again, with or without the audio. Pause after each story frame to ask a comprehension question, e.g., *Is Leyla happy?* (no, she's grumpy) *Is Cam happy?* (no, he's grumpy) *Maya can see … .* (a butterfly / ants) *Who helps Leyla?* (Peter, Cam, and Maya).

Spot! Students find Shelly the turtle in the story. (**Answer:** frame 5)

Practice

2 🎧 **6.9 Listen and point. Then say.**

- Play the first part of the audio, then pause for students to point to the corresponding picture (picture 2). Do the same with the second part of the audio (picture 1) and the third part of the audio (picture 3).
- Play the audio again, and students repeat the lines. Encourage them to copy the intonation of the characters and make an appropriate facial expression.

Audioscript (track 6.9)
1 **Leyla:** *Maya … Help me!*
2 **Peter:** *Good job, everyone!*
3 **Maya:** *I can see an ant. Five ants.*

3 Who's the team? Circle.

- Remind students of the word *team*, and elicit that the ants in Video 6A in Lesson 1 worked together as a team to make the bird.
- Ask students to find a team in the story frames. You may wish to use the story cards for this, showing the cards one by one, and asking students to put their thumbs up (team) or down (no team).
- Students circle the people who are in the team in the story.

SUPPORT Point to each small picture, and ask: *Is (Cam) in the team?* Elicit *yes* or *no*, then students circle the pictures.

STRETCH Students act out how the four children work as a team. Encourage them to say: *Let's all help! Good job, everyone!*

LESSON 4 — Story

A good team

1 Listen to the story. Point to a 🐞, a 🦋, and a 🌼.

1. Maya: *I can see a butterfly!*
   Leyla: *Maya ... Help me!*
2. Cam: *Peter! My water.*
   Peter: *Oh, no.*
3. Maya: *I can see an ant. Five ants. It's a team.*
4. Cam: *Wow. Let's all help!*
5. Leyla: *Good idea, Cam.*
6. Peter: *Good job, everyone!*

The end

2 Listen and point. Then say.

3 Who's the team? Circle.

4 Act out the story.

Story: *Help me! It's a team.*

Teaching star

Social-emotional learning Show students story card 1, and elicit how Leyla feels (*grumpy/sad*). Do the same with story card 2, and elicit how Cam feels. Then show story card 5, and elicit that the friends are working as a team. Ask: *Are they sad/grumpy/happy?*, and elicit answers.

4 Act out the story.
- Students look at the photos of the boy and girl. Ask: *Are they a team?* Students say or mime *yes* or *no*.
- Put students in groups of four, and assign roles: Maya, Cam, Peter, and Leyla. Play the audio, and students act out the story as they listen. Students can join in with the lines, if they wish to.

Extra activity (story extension) Put students in teams of four. Give each team a piece of paper with a small object on top, e.g., an eraser (or a small ball, for added challenge). All four team members have to hold the piece of paper with one hand and transport the object to the other side of the classroom without dropping it. If the object falls, they have to start again. Encourage students to use language they have learned in this lesson, e.g., *Let's all help! It's a team. Good job!*

Wrap-up
- Invite six students to the front of the class, and give each student a story card, in random order. Give the students ten seconds to stand in the correct order of the story. Count to ten all together as a class. Then repeat with a different group of students.
- Sing the *Goodbye* song (track 0.7), and students say goodbye to the Mickey Mouse puppet as they leave class.

Workbook — page 58

Audioscript see p.205

1. 6.3 **Listen and number in order.** *a 4, b 1, c 3, d 2*
2. **Design a team hat. Then point and say.**

6 Lesson 5: Grammar and Speaking

Student's Book page 66

Objectives

Lesson aim: ask and answer about nature

Target language: *What color is it? It's red.*

Recycled language: bugs, colors; *I can see a … Who's this? Is it Flik? Yes. It's Flik.*

Receptive language: *Flik says … What color is he/she? He's/She's purple, too! Don't worry. Wow!*

Materials: Video 6B; Audio; Picture cards / Word cards (Bugs); Story cards (Unit 6); Mickey Mouse puppet; Cut-outs (Unit 6), with a cut-out model prepared; scissors; (optional) pictures of bugs colored in different colors, pasta shapes (varied)

GSE Skills

Listening: can recognize familiar words in short phrases and sentences spoken slowly and clearly, if supported by pictures or gestures (19); can identify everyday objects, people, or animals in their immediate surroundings or in pictures from short, basic descriptions, e.g., color, size, if spoken slowly and clearly (19)

Speaking: can use a few simple words to describe objects, e.g., color, number, if supported by pictures (19)

Teacher toolkit

Video summary – 6B
I can see a beetle Videoscript see p.202
One of the ants, Dot, is looking through a telescope. She sees Flik and his new friends arriving at the colony. At first, the ants are scared, but then Flik introduces them to his new friends.

Teaching grammar
Present the target structures with a game of *I spy*. Stick pictures of different-colored bugs around the classroom. Say: *I can see a (ladybug).*, and students find the ladybugs. Say: *Is it blue? Is it yellow? What color is it?*, and students repeat the question. Then answer the question, and students find the corresponding picture.

Extend
Do some research all together as a class to find out what colors the different types of bugs can be. Find photos of different species of butterflies, beetles, ants, etc. You could then ask students to work in groups to make a display showing, for example, different bugs of a particular color.

Warm-up

- Greet students with the Mickey Mouse puppet, and sing the *Hello, Stars and Heroes* song (track 0.1).
- Remind students of the story from Lesson 4. Show story card 1 and story card 3, and students say which bugs they can see in the pictures, using: *I can see … .*

Presentation

1 ▶ **6B Watch. Who's Dot? Circle.**

- As a lead-in to Video 6B, ask students to look once more at the Big Picture in Lesson 1, and remind them of the movie *A Bug's Life* and the characters. Point to Flix, and elicit that he's an ant.
- Make the Mickey Mouse puppet stand up. Say: *Sit down, Mickey. It's video time!*
- Play the video, and students point to the corresponding small pictures when they see the caterpillar, ladybug, and ant.
- Play the first part of the video again (until 0:23), and ask students to point to Dot in the small pictures.
- Students circle the correct picture. To check answers, say: *Dot is an …*, and elicit *ant*.

Practice

Teaching star

Creativity Encouraging students to think creatively can help both their language development and their thinking skills, as they apply the language they know to new contexts. Invite students to make associations between the shapes of the bugs and pasta shapes. Give students a selection of different pasta shapes, and ask them to say which bugs they can "see," e.g., farfalle bows – *butterflies*, fusilli spirals – *caterpillars*, conchiglie shells – *ladybugs*, macaroni – *ants*. Invite them to hide the pasta bugs in the sensory tray for other students to find.

2 🎧 **6.10 Listen and check (✓). Then ask and answer.**

- Students look at the first pair of pictures. Ask: *What's this?* (a beetle) *What color is it?* (red and orange / green and blue).
- Play the first part of the audio, and students point to and check the correct beetle. Do the same for the second and third pairs of pictures (*ant, butterfly*).
- Choose any one of the pictures. Invite a more confident student to ask you *What color is it?*, and answer e.g., *yellow and red*. Then invite another student to say which bug it is (*ant*).

SUPPORT Point to a bug, and ask: *What color is it?* Then say: *It's …*, and students repeat and complete the sentence with the correct two colors.

STRETCH Students work in pairs, taking turns to choose a picture and ask and answer questions about it. They can also give additional clues, e.g., *It's small. It has six legs.*

LESSON 5
Grammar and Speaking

1 ▶ ✏️ Watch. Who's Dot? Circle.

2 🎧 💬 Listen and check (✓). Then ask and answer.

3 🎧 💬 Listen and point. Then make and play.

Skills: What color is it? It's (red).

Audioscript (track 6.10)
1 **A:** I can see a beetle.
   B: What color is it?
   A: It's red and orange.
2 **A:** I can see an ant.
   B: What color is it?
   A: It's orange and brown.
3 **A:** I can see a butterfly.
   B: What color is it?
   A: It's yellow and red.

3 🎧 6.11 **Listen and point. Then make and play.**
- Students use scissors to cut carefully around the dotted lines of the cut-out.
- Show students how to fold in one bug so it can be seen through the other side of the magnifying glass. Then show them how to fold back the other bugs to hide them.
- Using the model cut-out you have prepared, fold in the ladybug. Play the audio, pausing after the first exchange, and show students your magnifying glass. Then fold in the ant, and play the second exchange.

- Students choose a bug and fold their cut-outs accordingly, so that they can see the bug through the magnifying glass. Then invite a more confident student to stand up and say: *I can see a (beetle).* Other students ask: *What color is it?*, and the student says, e.g., *It's (orange and brown).*
- Repeat the activity with different students. Then students play in groups, if appropriate.

SUPPORT Students can play the game in mixed-ability pairs. The less confident student says only the names and colors of the bug.

STRETCH Students can play the game in mixed-ability pairs. The more confident student asks *What color is it?*, as well as says full sentences, following the model from the audio.

Audioscript (track 6.11)
A: *I can see a ladybug.*
B: *What color is it?*
A: *It's red and black.*
B: *I can see an ant.*
A: *What color is it?*
B: *It's brown.*

Extra activity (fast finishers) Students play a game in pairs. Both students put a bug in their magnifying glasses by folding it over. Then they make statements or ask questions, e.g., *I can see a … What color is it? It's (purple and yellow).* If they both have the same answer (e.g., *butterfly*), they clap their hands.

Wrap-up
- Play *Yes or no?* (see Games Bank p.206). For this version, make the Mickey Mouse puppet answer the question *What color is it?* about different bugs.
- Sing the *Goodbye* song (track 0.7), and students say goodbye to Mickey as they leave class.

📖 Workbook   page 59

Audioscript see p.205

1 🎧 **6.4 Circle differences. Then listen and say.**
picture 1: tree – green and brown, mushroom – white, flower – pink; picture 2: tree – red and brown, mushroom – brown and white, flower – red; 1 picture 2, 2 picture 1, 3 picture 1

2 **Match and color. Then ask and answer.**
1 black, 2 red, 3 purple, 4 yellow

6 Lesson 6: Myself and others

Teamwork **Student's Book page 67**

Objectives

Lesson aim: recognize and talk about how to work in a team

Target language: *Let's all help. Good idea.*

Recycled language: *happy, sad, excited*

Materials: Audio; (optional) Video 6A; *Myself and others* poster; Stickers; Mickey Mouse puppet; paper, modeling dough; (optional) cards for Teacher toolkit, a small ball

GSE Skills

Listening: can recognize familiar words in short phrases and sentences spoken slowly and clearly, if supported by pictures or gestures (19)

Speaking: can produce very short fixed expressions, using gestures and asking for help when necessary (21)

Writing (WB): can copy some short familiar words presented in standard printed form (10)

Teacher toolkit

Teamwork

In this lesson, students explore different ways in which they can work as a team, and they think about how teamwork can make things better for everyone. Using L1, ask students about situations in which they work as a team, e.g., when they do group work in class, when playing a team sport such as soccer or basketball. Ask: *Do you help your team?*, and elicit answers. Point out that sometimes it's also fine to do things by ourselves.

Social awareness

Engage

Students work in a team to use modeling dough to make different words, with each student using the modeling dough to make one letter of the word.

Home-school link

Students reflect on how they can work as a team at home. Encourage them to help their families, saying: *Let's all help!* They could help with simple chores, e.g., setting the table, putting their clothes in the laundry, or helping with a younger brother or sister.

Warm-up

- Greet students with the Mickey Mouse puppet, and sing the *Hello, Stars and Heroes* song (track 0.1).
- Use Mickey to review *keep trying* from Unit 5. Put a few balls of scrunched-up paper on the floor near Mickey. Ask Mickey to clean up. Make him try to pick up the balls unsuccessfully. Say or elicit: *Keep trying, Mickey!* Then invite two or three students to help Mickey, and encourage them to notice how they are working together in a team.
- Show the *Myself and others* poster and invite students to identify the picture that shows *Keep trying!*

🎵 1.12 Listen and sing.

- Play the song audio, and students join in with the words and the actions.
- Ask: *How do you feel? Are you happy?*, and students say *yes/no* or *I'm (happy)!*

Presentation

1 Look and circle good teamwork.

- Remind students of the situations and the characters in Video 6A in Lesson 1 and the story. If required, play Video 6A and look at the story again.
- Students look at the pictures. Point to the first picture, and ask: *Are they a team?* (no). Using L1, elicit that Maya isn't helping Leyla. Do the same for the other two pictures.
- Tell students to circle the pictures showing good teamwork.

Practice

2 🎧 6.12 Listen and point. Then say and act.

- Point to the two photos and review classroom objects, furniture, and clothes. Point to different items in each photo, and ask: *What's this? What color is it? What's (he) wearing?*
- Ask students which photo shows good teamwork (photo 1). Using L1, discuss why photo 1 shows good teamwork and photo 2 doesn't (*photo 1: the children and teacher are working together to clean the classroom; photo 2: the boy is cleaning up by himself*).
- Play the audio, and students point to the correct photo.
- Play the audio again, pausing after each sentence for students to repeat.
- Put some toys or classroom objects on desks around the classroom. Students work together as a team to clean up, saying the phrases from the audio.

Audioscript (track 6.12)
A: *Let's all help.*
B: *Good idea!*

Teamwork

LESSON 6 — Myself and others

1 Look and circle good teamwork.

Listen and sing.

2 Listen and point. Then say and act. TPR

3 Work in groups. Make "TEAM." TPR

I'm a hero!

Social awareness: Let's all help! Good idea.

67

Teaching star

Support understanding Display the alphabet poster, and show students how they can make some of the letters with their bodies. Make a letter shape for each letter in the word TEAM, and say the letter sound as you do so. Encourage students to copy you and say the letter sound.

3 Work in groups. Make "TEAM."
- Point to each photo, and elicit that the children are making a letter with their bodies. Elicit what letter the boy in the first photo is making (T). Students copy the boy's posture and make a T.
- Ask students how else they can use their bodies to make the letter T, e.g., with their arms or fingers.

- Write the word TEAM on the board. Invite seven students to the front of the class, and ask them to copy the postures in the photos, to spell the word with their bodies. They can do this either standing up or sitting down. They could also make the letters using their hands. Then invite another group of students to the front of the class to form the word.
- Afterwards, elicit that students needed to work together as a team in order to do this challenge.

⭐ **I'm a hero!** ⭐ Point to the sticker picture, and elicit that the four children are working in a team to build a castle. Ask: *Is it good teamwork? Do they all help?* (yes). Students stick the sticker in their books.

> **Extra activity (class game)** Point out that good teamwork also means making sure that everyone helps. Play *Throw the ball* (see Games Bank p.206), but invite students to sit in a large circle, with some space between each student. Tell them to make sure they help each other keep the ball inside the circle, and to make sure that everyone gets a chance to roll the ball.

Wrap-up
- Invite four students to stand near the *Myself and others* poster. Say an emotion or a phrase from one of the *Myself and others* lessons (*Keep trying! Good job! Let's all help!*), and students find the corresponding picture on the poster as quickly as they can. Repeat with other students.
- Sing the *Goodbye* song (track 0.7), and students say goodbye to Mickey as they leave class.

Workbook — page 60

1 **Circle Peter's team red. Circle Leyla's team blue. Then point and say.** *Peter, Maya, Sara – red; Leyla, Cam, and two other children – blue*

2 **Who's on your team? Trace and draw.**

6 Lesson 7: My world

Objectives

Lesson aim: learn about symmetry
Target language: *spots, stripes*
Recycled language: *bugs, colors*
Receptive language: *picture*
Materials: Audio; Mickey Mouse puppet; small objects e.g., feathers, buttons, pebbles, pompoms; photos of items with spots and stripes, e.g., a red spotted mushroom, a leopard, a Dalmatian dog, a zebra, a tiger, a striped angelfish; (optional) a mirror; a soft ball

GSE Skills

Listening: can recognize isolated words related to familiar topics, if spoken slowly and clearly and supported by pictures or gestures (16)
Reading: can recognize single, familiar everyday words, if supported by pictures (21)
Speaking: can repeat single words, if spoken slowly and clearly (10); can repeat phrases and short sentences, if spoken slowly and clearly (16)
Writing (WB): can copy some short familiar words presented in standard printed form (10)

Teacher toolkit

Cross-curricular
Symmetry is usually shown by a *line of symmetry*, which divides a picture into two identical halves. Use a mirror to demonstrate the concept of symmetry. Draw and color half a simple butterfly on a piece of paper. Then place the mirror down the middle of the butterfly, so that it is reflected in the mirror as a whole butterfly. Students point out and count the features, e.g., spots and stripes.

Engage
Give students a piece of paper, and ask them to fold it in half, vertically. Tell them to draw half a picture on one side, e.g., a house, a tree, or a flower. Make sure the picture meets the center fold. Then ask them to exchange pictures with another student and complete the picture, making sure it is symmetrical.

Home-school link
Students find clothes items or other things in the home that have spots or stripes, or are symmetrical in some way. If possible, they take a photo of the item, then show it to the class in the next lesson.

Math and art: Symmetry   Student's Book page 68

Warm-up
- Greet students with the Mickey Mouse puppet, and sing the *Hello, Stars and Heroes* song (track 0.1).
- Play *Throw the ball* (see Games Bank p.206). For this version, each time a student gets the ball, they say the name of a bug.

Presentation

1 🔊 **6.13 Listen and point. Then find and say.**
- Check to see if any students are wearing clothes that show spots or stripes. If they are, bring these students to the front of the class, point to the spots or stripes on the clothes items, and pre-teach *spots* and *stripes*.
- Students look at the photos. Play the audio, and students point to each photo.
- Play the audio again, and students point to each photo and say the word.
- Demonstrate TPR actions for *spots* (make a circle with arms) and *stripes* (hold arms up in two straight lines).
- Point to each photo, and students say the word, starting off slowly, then pointing to each one more quickly.

SUPPORT Say the word, and students do the TPR action.
STRETCH Students work in pairs, taking turns to point to a photo for their partner to name.

Teaching star

Linguistic competence Some students may have trouble pronouncing the consonant clusters *sp* (spots) and *str* (stripes). Drill each consonant individually first, then gradually blend the consonants, e.g., s / t / r / st / tr / str / stripes.

Practice

2 Look and match. Then say.
- Point to picture 1 showing half a bee, and say: *Look. It has stripes.* Then students find the other half of the bee, using their finger. Do the same for picture 2, showing half a ladybug.
- Students draw lines to match the bug halves.
- Point to picture 1 again and then to picture b. Say: *Look. It's the same: stripes and stripes.* Students notice that the bee is the same on both sides. Do the same with picture 2 and picture a. Tell students that we call this *symmetry*.
- Point to each side of the ladybug, and say: *It's a ladybug. One, two, three, four spots here! One, two, three, four spots here!* Then point out the half spot on each side, and elicit that it makes one whole spot, making nine spots in total. Do the same with the bee and its stripes.
- Students count and say the number of spots and stripes on each bug.

144

LESSON 7
My world — Math and art
Symmetry

1 🎧 💬 Listen and point. Then find and say.

1. spots
2. stripes

2 💬 Look and match. Then say.

3 ✏️ 💬 Draw and color. Then say.

Symmetry: spots, stripes

68

Thinking skills

Understand In activity 2, students identify bugs from incomplete pictures and use their knowledge of symmetry to match them to their corresponding halves.

Apply In activity 3, students apply the concept of symmetry by completing a picture of a butterfly so that it is symmetrical. They describe the butterfly, identifying and naming its symmetrical features.

Extra activity (extension) Students make symmetrical faces using a variety of small objects, e.g., bottle tops, feathers, pompoms, buttons, small pebbles, or small shapes cut out of colored card.

Wrap-up

- Play *Color hunt!* (see Games Bank p.206) with patterns. Say a color and *spots* or *stripes*, and students look for related items in the classroom. These could be photos you have displayed around the classroom.
- Sing the *Goodbye* song (track 0.7), and students say goodbye to the Mickey Mouse puppet as they leave class.

📖 **Workbook** page 61

1 **Trace and match.** *1 b, spots; 2 a, stripes*
2 **Choose colors. Complete. Then say.**

3 Draw and color. Then say.

- Ask students to look at the picture of the butterfly and notice that it is incomplete. Say: *Look, a head, a body, two wings.* Point to the empty side, and tell students to draw the butterfly's head and body and wings.
- Then say: *Look, spots. Look, stripes.* Count the spots and stripes on each side together, then students draw the same number of spots and stripes on the other side.
- Draw a model butterfly on the board. Then describe it, e.g., *It's a butterfly. It's red and yellow. Look, four spots and two stripes.*
- Invite students to show their completed picture to the class and describe it.

SUPPORT Ask questions to the class as each student shows their picture: *How many spots? What color? How many stripes? What color?*

STRETCH Students work in pairs, taking turns to describe their butterfly.

6 Lesson 8: Review

I can do it! Student's Book page 69

Objectives

Lesson aim: review target language from Unit 6
Target language: bugs; nature; *What color is it? It's (brown).*
Recycled language: colors
Materials: Audio; (optional) Video 6A, Video 6B; Picture cards / Word cards (Bugs, Nature); Stickers; Mickey Mouse puppet; (optional) small word cards of the six target words for students; *My progress* poster

GSE Skills

Listening: can recognize isolated words related to familiar topics, if spoken slowly and clearly and supported by pictures and gestures (16)
Reading: can recognize single, familiar everyday words, if supported by pictures (21)
Speaking: can say single words related to familiar topics, if supported by pictures or gestures (18)
Writing: can copy some short familiar words presented in standard printed form (10)

Teacher toolkit

Video review
You can return to Video 6A and Video 6B at the end of the unit for a "second play." Students watch and copy the characters' intonation when they use the target structures: *I can see …* and *What color is it?*

Remediation
Some students may need support with reading and tracing the words. Give students the word cards to practice sight reading of the vocabulary, and they match these with the picture cards. To provide support with tracing, draw the starting point on each letter to show students where to place their pencil.

Home-school link
Invite students to point out and say to their families the names of nature items they see on their way to or from school.

Warm-up

- Greet students with the Mickey Mouse puppet, and sing the *Hello, Stars and Heroes* song (track 0.1).
- Play the game *Pass Mickey* (see Games Bank p.206) with the unit picture cards.
- Play the song audio from Lesson 3 (track 6.6), and students join in with the words and the actions. If students are confident with the words, play the karaoke version (track 6.6_karaoke).

I can do it!

1 Say and point. Then trace.

- Students look at the two pictures. Point to the word *rock* and say: *I can see a (rock).* Students point to the correct picture. Repeat with the other words.
- Ask: *What can you see?*, and elicit answers from different students with *I can see … .* The rest of the class points to the corresponding item in the picture.
- Do this stage of the activity again, but this time students find the correct word on the page and trace it with their finger.
- Students use a pencil to trace the words.

> **ACHIEVE**
> Students name, read, and trace bugs and nature words with picture prompts.
>
> **SUPPORT**
> Students match the picture cards and the word cards on the board before doing the activity.
>
> **STRETCH**
> Students trace the words, then work in pairs, taking turns to point to a word and say it.

2 6.14 Listen and find. Then play.

- Play the audio, pausing after the first sentence for students to find the butterfly in one of the two pictures. Then play the next part of the audio, pause again, and students say *yes* or *no*. Then play the answer. Do the same for the second and third exchange.
- Demonstrate the game. Say: *I can see an ant.* Give students five seconds to find the ant in the picture and say: *Picture (1).*
- Invite different students to say a sentence about one of the pictures. The rest of the class repeats the sentence, then students work with a partner to find the corresponding picture.

Audioscript (track 6.14)
I can see a ladybug. // Picture 2. // Yes!
I can see an ant. // Picture 2. // Yes!
I can see a pond. // Picture 1. // Yes!

I can do it!

LESSON 8 Review

1 ✏️ Say and point. Then trace.

tree — ant
rock — pond — beetle — ladybug

2 🎧 💬 Listen and find. Then play.

3 💡 ✏️ Think and color. Then stick!

I can ...
1. 🦋
2. 🎵 Bugs, bugs 🎵
3. 👩‍👧‍👦

✓ Unit 6!

Go online — Big Project

ACHIEVE
Students understand and say *I can see a/an …* statements.

SUPPORT
Say: *I can see a/an … .*, and use the picture cards to help elicit the name of an item from the pictures. Students work in pairs to find the item in the pictures.

STRETCH
Students play the game in pairs, taking turns to make statements and answer, following the audio as a model.

3 💡 **Think and color. Then stick!**

- Point to each picture, and say the *I can …* statements: *I can name bugs and things in nature. I can sing a song. I can work in a team.* For each statement, give an example, and then ask: *Can you do this?* Use L1 to explain, if necessary.
- Students demonstrate what they can do. They work in pairs, taking turns to say the names of different bugs and nature items. Sing the song all together as a class. Students work in pairs, taking turns to say and act out good teamwork. Monitor and assess students' performance.

- Students color the stars next to what they can do. Then they stick the reward sticker to show they have completed Unit 6.

> **My Star and Hero!** Students look at the picture of Flik on p.5 of the Student's Book. They work in pairs, taking turns to describe Flik, and say or mime how he works in a team.
>
> **Extra activity (fast finishers)** Students draw their own picture containing different bugs and nature. Invite more confident students to label their pictures with the target words.

Wrap-up

- Students reflect on which lesson or activity they most enjoyed in Unit 6. Have a class vote, and choose one activity to do again as a class, e.g., watch the video, sing the song or chant, listen to the story, or play a game.
- Draw students' attention to the *My progress* poster, and ask them to identify the picture that reflects this unit. Read aloud with students the *I can …* statements (*I can ask and answer about nature, I can work in a team*).
- 🎵 Sing the *Goodbye* song (track 0.7), then students say goodbye to the Mickey Mouse puppet and tell him their favorite word from Unit 6.

📝 Workbook — pages 62–63

My progress

Audioscript see p.205

1 🎧 6.5 **Listen and match. Then ask and answer.**
1 c, 2 b, 3 a

2 **Find, count, and write. Then say.** *a 3, b 1, c 4, d 2*

Units W–6 My practice

1 **Circle and say.** *two rocks, two flowers, one beetle*

   Find clothes. Say the colors. *dress – pink, hat – white, pants – blue, T-shirt – yellow, shoes – brown, socks – white*

2 **Draw your favorite bug.**

Unit 6! My favorite activity: Students stick the small star sticker next to their favorite activity.

7 Food

Unit objectives

By the end of this unit, students can:
- talk about the food they like and don't like
- read and understand a story about sharing food
- recognize the importance of being nice and sharing
- talk about food printing

Skills development

Listening: understand what food people like and don't like

Speaking: talk about the food they like and don't like; talk about being nice; give instructions

Vocabulary

Lesson 1: apples, cake, soup, tea
Lesson 2: cookies, ice cream, juice, noodles, pizza, sandwiches

Grammar

Lesson 3: I like pizza.
Lesson 5: I like soup. I don't like noodles.

Myself and others

Empathy In this unit, a Disney video and a story introduce the theme of empathy. Students will learn about the importance of being nice to others and sharing.

Language: nice; I can help. Let's all share. Thank you.

Self-management

Story

Lunch for Cam
hungry, lunchbox; Thanks.

My world

Art: Food prints
bell pepper, mushroom, onion; cut, paint

Unit overview

Disney
Beauty and the Beast

Gaston
A handsome young man who is popular in the village, Gaston wants to marry Belle. However, they couldn't be more different! Gaston is selfish and the person he loves the most is himself.

Beast
A prince who was turned into a monster, the Beast is a selfish and cruel man. However, the Beast is an insecure young man inside who just wants to be loved.

Belle
A young woman who loves books, Belle is different from the other people in the village. She is brave, intelligent, and nice.

Lumière and Cogsworth
Servants in the castle and best friends. Lumière takes the form of a candelabra, and Cogsworth is a clock.

Mrs. Potts
The housekeeper of the castle, Mrs Potts was transformed into a teapot. She has common sense and can be strict with the Beast. She has a son, named Chip, a small chipped teacup.

The Beast is really a prince who lives hidden away in his castle. One day, Belle, a girl from a nearby village, goes to the castle to rescue her father, who is a prisoner there. Belle takes her father's place and lives in the castle with the Beast, until eventually she learns who he really is.

Did you know?
The Beast in the movie is actually a combination of different animals. He has the head of a buffalo, the arms and body of a bear, the eyebrows of a gorilla, the jaws and mane of a lion, the tusks of a boar, the legs, teeth, and tail of a wolf, and the eyes of his human form!

Video stories
Video 7A: *Belle can help!*
Video 7B: *I like books*

Online modules

Phonics
Words with Ss, Tt, and Uu sounds in initial position
soup, tea, up

Big Project
Have a tea party!

7 Lesson 1: Vocabulary

Student's Book pages 70–71

Objectives

Lesson aim: name food

Target language: *apples, cake, soup, tea*

Recycled language: colors, clothes; *book, happy, nervous; This is Belle. Her dress is blue. Belle is happy. It's big.*

Receptive language: *Belle likes books. A present for Belle. Belle says, "Thank you." It's Beast's castle. Belle's hungry. Ouch! Dinner! Beast is hurt. Belle helps Beast. Belle is nice.*

Materials: Video 7A; Audio; Picture cards / Word cards (Food 1; Clothes 1, 2, Disney characters; Body); Sticker (Belle); Mickey Mouse puppet; (optional) pictures of food

GSE Skills

Listening: can recognize isolated words related to familiar topics, if spoken slowly and clearly and supported by pictures and gestures (16)

Reading: can recognize single, familiar everyday words, if supported by pictures (21)

Speaking: can name everyday objects, animals, or people around them or in pictures, using single words (18)

Writing (WB): can copy some short familiar words presented in standard printed form (10)

Teacher toolkit

Video summary – 7A
Belle can help! **Videoscript see p.202**
Belle goes to the Beast's castle, where she meets some unusual characters. Beast gets hurt, and Belle takes care of him. Beast is grumpy at first, but then they become friends.

Engage
During this unit, create a class cookbook containing different foods students like. As students learn new food vocabulary, they draw and color or cut out pictures of the food items and add these to the cookbook.

Empathy
nice
Use the video story to review emotions: *happy, nervous, angry,* and talk about the feelings and behavior of the characters. Show the scene where Belle is nice to Beast and, using L1, talk about how she helps him, even when he is grumpy.

Self-management

Warm-up
- Greet students with the Mickey Mouse puppet, and sing the *Hello, Stars and Heroes* song (track 0.1).

Presentation
Video story
- Students look at the Big Picture. Introduce the movie and the characters: *This is the movie* Beauty and the Beast. *This is Belle. This is Beast.*
- Hold up different clothes and body picture cards, and students find and name these items in the Big Picture.

1 ▶ **7A Watch. Who has a dress? Point.**
- Make the Mickey Mouse puppet stand up. Say: *Sit down, Mickey. It's video time! Let's watch!*
- Play Video 7A, and students watch and listen.
- Play the video again. Ask: *Who has a dress?* Students point to Belle in their books and say her name, if possible.

2 ▶ **7A Who's nice? Circle.**
- Make the Mickey Mouse puppet act sad. Demonstrate being nice, e.g., by giving him a hug. Encourage students to be nice to Mickey.
- Show students a TPR action to express *be nice*, e.g., smile and hug yourself.
- Point to each small picture, and ask: *Who's nice? Belle, Beast, or Mrs. Potts?*
- Play the video again, and students do the TPR action when they see Belle being nice.
- Then ask students to circle the correct picture.

Picture cards / Word cards (optional) Show the picture cards one by one to introduce the new vocabulary. Repeat several times, encouraging students to remember the words. Then show each word card, and elicit the words.

Practice

3 🎧 **7.1 Listen, find, and say. Then play.**
- Play the audio, pausing after each word. Students point to the food items in the Big Picture. Play the audio again, pausing for students to say the words. Play the audio a third time, and students read, say, and point to the food items.
- Invite a confident student to say a word, and the rest of the class points to the correct food item in the picture. Repeat with other students.

SUPPORT Say a word, students repeat it, then point to the correct food item in the Big Picture.

STRETCH Students work in pairs, taking turns to point to a food item for their partner to name.

Audioscript (track 7.1)
1 cake // 2 tea // 3 apples // 4 soup

7 Food

LESSON 1 Vocabulary

3 🎧 💬 Listen, find, and say. Then play.
4 🎵 Listen, chant, and act. **TPR** 🎵 *Soup, soup* 🎵

1) cake
2) tea
3) apples
4) soup

1 ▶ Watch. Who has a 👗? Point.
2 ▶ Who's nice? Circle.

Go to page 5

apples, cake, soup, tea

---

4 🎵 **7.2 Listen, chant, and act.**
- 🐭 Display the four picture cards. Make the Mickey Mouse puppet say: *Mmm, (soup)*. Students point to the correct picture card.
- Play the audio, and students point to the correct picture card when they hear each food item.
- Demonstrate the TPR actions. Play the audio again. Students join in with the chant and do the actions.

> **TPR chant**
> mmm – rub your tummy
> soup – take a sip from an imaginary spoon
> cake – take a bite of an imaginary slice of cake
> tea – hold a cup handle between your fingers and take a sip
> apples – hold an imaginary apple and take a bite

Audioscript (track 7.2)
Soup. Soup. My soup. Mmm, mmm, soup.
Cake. Cake. My cake. Mmm, mmm, cake.
Tea. Tea. My tea. Mmm, mmm, tea.
Apples. Apples. My apples. Mmm, mmm, apples.

❓ **Collect your friend** Show the picture card of Belle to help students identify the correct sticker. Students stick the sticker on p.5 in the Student's Book. Ask: *Who's this?* (Belle).

> **Extra activity (video extension)** Play Video 7A again, and students do the TPR action for each food item when they see it.

Wrap-up
- Play *Miming* (see Games Bank p.206), using the picture cards from the lesson.
- 🐭 Sing the *Goodbye* song (track 0.7), and students say goodbye to the Mickey Mouse puppet as they leave class.

📓 **Workbook** pages 64–65

1 **Watch again. Then check (✓).**
  1 What color is Belle's dress? *b* ✓
  2 What food do you see in the video? *b* ✓, *c* ✓, *d* ✓
  3 Belle is … *a*
2 **Trace and match. Then point and say.** *1 tea, 2 apples, 3 cake, 4 soup*
3 **Challenge! Draw dinner for the Beast.**

Lesson 2: Vocabulary

Student's Book page 72

Objectives

Lesson aim: name food

Target language: *cookies, ice cream, juice, noodles, pizza, sandwiches*

Recycled language: food

Materials: Audio; Picture cards / Word cards (Food 1, 2); Stickers; Mickey Mouse puppet; paper plates, magazines; (optional) empty food packaging

GSE Skills

Listening: can recognize isolated words related to familiar topics, if spoken slowly and clearly and supported by pictures and gestures (16)

Reading: can recognize single, familiar everyday words, if supported by pictures (21)

Speaking: can repeat single words, if spoken slowly and clearly (10); can use a few simple words to describe objects, e.g., color, number, if supported by pictures (19)

Writing (WB): can copy some short familiar words presented in standard printed form (10)

Teacher toolkit

Teaching vocabulary
If possible, bring in empty food packaging relating to the target vocabulary. This will help students make connections between the photos in their books and the real world. Elicit the name of the food item students think goes in each package. You could then also discuss the topic of recycling packaging appropriately.

Extend
Students create a lunch plate, using a paper plate and pictures of food cut out from magazines. Ask them to present their lunch plate to the class or to smaller groups.

Home-school link
Students take a photo, make a video, or draw a picture of their lunch at home, and name the food items to their families. They could show and describe their lunch to the class in the following lesson.

Warm-up

- Greet students with the Mickey Mouse puppet, and sing the *Hello, Stars and Heroes* song (track 0.1).
- Play *Circle it!* (see Games Bank p. 206). Draw pictures of the target vocabulary on the board, or use the food picture cards. Say one of the words, or describe it, and invite a student to come to the front and draw a circle around the correct picture or picture card.
- Say: *Listen and chant!*, and play the chant from Lesson 1 (track 7.2). Students join in with the chant and do the actions.

Presentation

Picture cards / Word cards (optional) Show the picture cards one by one to introduce the new vocabulary. Repeat several times, encouraging students to remember the words. Then show each word card, and elicit the words.

1 7.3 **Listen, point, and say. Then play.**

- Show a picture card to the Mickey Mouse puppet. Make Mickey pretend to eat the food item. Say: *Mmm, (pizza)*. Repeat with other picture cards.
- Say: *Listen and point*. Play the audio, and students point to the corresponding photos. Play the audio again, pausing after each word. Students point to the corresponding photo and repeat the word.
- Say a word, students repeat it, and then mime eating each food item, e.g., holding and biting a slice of pizza, drinking juice, licking ice cream.

SUPPORT Say each word, and students point to the corresponding photo. Start slowly, giving students time to think and respond, then gradually say the words more quickly.

STRETCH Students work in pairs, taking turns to point to a photo or mime eating a food item for their partner to name.

Practice

2 7.4 **Listen and check (✓). Then look and say.**

- Point to the first picture of a lunch tray, and elicit the different types of food students can see. Use the picture cards to prompt as necessary, asking students to find in the picture the item on each picture card. Then do the same with the second picture of a lunch tray.
- Play the audio, pausing after each food item for students to look for it on either lunch tray. Play the audio again, and students check the correct picture. Play the audio one more time, and students point and repeat the words.
- Point to one of the lunch trays, and say: *I have …*, eliciting the names of the food items from the class. Do the same with the other lunch tray.

Audioscript (track 7.4)

I have sandwiches, juice, cookies, and apples.

LESSON 2
Vocabulary

1 🎧 💬 Listen, point, and say. Then play.

1. pizza
2. juice
3. ice cream
4. noodles
5. cookies
6. sandwiches

2 🎧 Listen and check (✓). Then look and say.

3 ✏️ 💬 Draw your lunch. Then say.

cookies, ice cream, juice, noodles, pizza, sandwiches

72

Teaching star ✨

Communication Give students a reason to communicate by telling them to try to find what is the same about their lunches. Tell students to wave their hand when they hear a food item that they have in their lunchbox.

Extra activity (fast finishers) Students classify the food and drink items from Lessons 1 and 2 into healthy/unhealthy foods. They can draw pictures in their notebooks, with healthy foods on the right-hand page and unhealthy foods on the left-hand page. They can label the pictures, if possible.

Wrap-up

- Play *Up close* (see Games Bank p.206), using the food picture cards.
- Sing the *Goodbye* song (track 0.7), and students say goodbye to the Mickey Mouse puppet as they leave class.

📖 Workbook   page 66

Audioscript see p.205

1. 🎧 **7.1 Listen and check (✓).** 1 b ✓, 2 a ✓, 3 a ✓, 4 a ✓
2. **Find and circle. Then trace and say.** Students find and circle the vocabulary items in the picture. They trace the words, then point and say. *1 pizza, 2 noodles, 3 sandwiches, 4 cookies, 5 juice, 6 ice cream*

Picture Dictionary

Students look at the Picture Dictionary on p.107 in the Student's Book and complete the activities.

---

3 Draw your lunch. Then say.

- Draw on the board a large version of the lunch tray from activity 3. Invite students to choose and stick food picture cards inside the large section, and a drink in the smaller section, e.g., *tea, juice*. Say: *I have …*, and elicit the names of the food items.
- Students draw one or more food items in the larger section and a drink in the smaller section in their books. Encourage them to choose food items from this lesson and from Lesson 1.
- Invite a student to show their picture to the class and say: *I have (noodles), (cookies), and (juice)*. Ask the other students to look at their picture and, if different, say *I have …*, naming their own food and drink items.

SUPPORT Provide students with prompts to complete with single words: *I have … .*
STRETCH Students work in pairs, taking turns to describe and compare their pictures.

153

Lesson 3: Grammar

Student's Book page 73

Objectives

Lesson aim: say what food you like
Target language: *I like pizza.*
Recycled language: food
Materials: Audio; Picture cards / Word cards (Food 1, 2); Mickey Mouse puppet; (optional) colored paper

GSE Skills

Listening: can get the gist of a simple song, if supported by gestures (21); can recognize familiar words and phrases in short, simple songs or chants (18)

Speaking: can sing a simple song, if supported by pictures (22); can name everyday objects, animals, or people around them or in pictures, using single words (18)

Teacher toolkit

Teaching grammar
Use facial expression to show the meaning of *I like*. Make a happy face, and hold up a picture card. Say: *I like (cookies)*. Reinforce the meaning by saying *Mmm*, and doing an appropriate gesture.

Extend
Students create a paper pizza or sandwich with different kinds of food they like. Prepare some cut-out food shapes from colored paper, e.g., slices of bread, tomato, cheese, peppers, olives, onion, lettuce leaves, red circles to show a tomato base. Students choose the ingredients they like, and then place them on their pizza or make a sandwich.

Differentiation
Not all students will understand the difference between *I like* and *I have*, and it will be useful to help reinforce understanding. Hold a food picture card, and say: *I have (tea)*. Make a face to show you don't like tea, and move the picture card away from you. Then choose another food picture card, and say: *I have (cookies)*. Smile and gesture that you like cookies, and say: *I like (cookies). Mmm!*

Warm-up
- Greet students with the Mickey Mouse puppet, and sing the *Hello, Stars and Heroes* song (track 0.1).
- Play *Where is …?* (see Games Bank p.206) to review food vocabulary from Lessons 1 and 2.

Presentation

1 Sing-along 🎵 **7.5 Listen and point. Then sing and act.**

- Say: *Look at Leyla.* Hold up each food picture card, and ask: *Leyla has … (apples)?* Students say or mime *yes* or *no*. Do the same for Cam, Maya, and Peter.
- Play the song audio. Students point to each food item in the picture as they hear the corresponding word in the song.
- Demonstrate the TPR actions. Then play the song again, and students do the TPR actions.
- Play the song a third time, and encourage students to join in with some of the words as they do the TPR actions and dance. When students are confident with the words, play the karaoke version (track 7.5_karaoke), and students sing along.

> **TPR song**
>
> *Let's eat!* – mime eating with a knife and fork
> *I like …* – smile and rub your tummy
> *pizza, apples, juice, cake* – students do the corresponding actions from Lessons 1 and 2

Audioscript (track 7.5)

Let's eat! *(x2)* // Let's eat today.
Pizza! // I like pizza. // I like pizza for you and me!
Let's eat! *(x2)* // Let's eat today.
Apples! // I like apples. // I like apples for you and me!
Let's eat! *(x2)* // Let's eat today.
Juice! // I like juice. // I like juice for you and me!
Let's eat! *(x2)* // Let's eat today.
Cake! // I like cake. // I like cake for you and me!

Practice

2 7.6 Listen and find. Then play.

- Point to Leyla in activity 1, and say: *I like …* . Students look at the picture and say what food Leyla has on her plate (*pizza*). Do the same with Cam, Maya, and Peter.
- Play the audio, pausing after each sentence for students to point to the correct character in the picture. Play the audio again, pausing after each sentence. Students repeat the sentence and say the name of the character.
- Play this game all together as a class. Ask: *Who am I? I like …* . Say the name of one of the food items in the picture, and students say the name of the character. Then invite different confident students to ask *Who am I? I like …* for the class to name the character.

LESSON 3 Grammar

Sing-along

1 🎵 Listen and point. Then sing and act. TPR

Let's eat

2 🎧 💬 Listen and find. Then play.

3 💬 Check (✓) what you like. Then say.

Song: I like (pizza).

SUPPORT Put students into four groups: Leyla, Cam, Maya, and Peter. Say: *I like (pizza).*, and ask the corresponding group to stand up and repeat the sentence. Do for all four characters.

STRETCH Students work in pairs, taking turns to choose a character and say *I like …* for their partner to name the character.

Audioscript (track 7.6)
1 **Cam:** I like apples.
2 **Leyla:** I like pizza.
3 **Peter:** I like cake.
4 **Maya:** I like juice.

3 Check (✓) what you like. Then say.

- Use the picture cards to review the food items, and students find each one in the picture.
- Stick the picture cards on the board. Say: *I like (ice cream).*, and check next to the corresponding picture. Do the same for other food items, leaving one or two items unchecked.

- Students look at the picture in their books and check the food items they like.
- Invite different students to say *I like …* and a food item. Each time, the other students look at their answers and repeat the sentence if it is true for them.

SUPPORT Point to each item in the picture, and say: *I like …*, and students complete with the correct word.

STRETCH Students work in pairs, taking turns to talk about the food items they have checked in the picture, using *I like …* .

Teaching star ✨

Application Encourage students to apply the new language structure to vocabulary they have learned in previous units. Encourage them to think about the toys they like, and elicit: *I like my (scooter)*. Ask them to do the same with clothes and colors, e.g., *I like my purple pants*.

Extra activity (whole class) Students stand or sit in a circle. Say: *I like …* and a food item. Those students who agree with you have to change places with another student as quickly as possible. Repeat with other food items.

Wrap-up

- Play *Whispers* (see Games Bank p. 206). For this version, use a sentence with *I like …* .
- Sing the *Goodbye* song (track 0.7), and students say goodbye to the Mickey Mouse puppet as they leave class.

📝 Workbook   page 67

Audioscript see p. 206
1 🎧 **7.2 Listen and number.** a 4, b 3, c 2, d 1
2 **Look, find, and check (✓). Then say for Eric.**
2 ✓

Lesson 4: Story

Student's Book pages 74–75

Objectives

Lesson aim: listen to and understand a story about sharing food

Story language: hungry, lunchbox; Thanks.

Recycled language: food; I have two sandwiches. I like sandwiches.

Receptive language: Let's all share. I'm not hungry now.

Materials: Audio; Story cards (Unit 7); Picture cards / Word cards (Food 1, 2); Mickey Mouse puppet; (optional) a lunchbox with pictures of food or real food inside

GSE Skills

Listening: can understand a few basic words and phrases in a story that is read aloud (18)

Reading: can recognize single, familiar everyday words, if supported by pictures (21)

Speaking: can repeat phrases and short sentences, if spoken slowly and clearly (16)

Teacher toolkit

Story summary

Cam hasn't brought his lunchbox to school, but each of his friends offer to share their lunch with him. After eating, Cam realizes he doesn't need the apple, and he gives it to Shelly the tortoise.

Extend

Show story card 6, and say: *Shelly likes apples. Yes or no?* Then hold up the different food picture cards, and elicit whether tortoises like each of the food items. Elicit that we should only give some foods to animals, and that we shouldn't give them sugary foods like cake, ice cream, or juice. Students draw a picture of a tortoise and the different kinds of food they like.

Empathy

In the story, the children show empathy by sharing their lunch with Cam. Tell students to imagine they are Cam. Ask: *How do you feel?* (sad, hungry). Then elicit how the other children help Cam (by sharing their food). Make the Mickey Mouse puppet act out different situations, e.g., being sad, or having difficulty with an English activity. Invite students to act out how they can be nice to Mickey, e.g., helping him do the activity, saying *Keep trying!*, playing with him.

Self-management

Warm-up

- Greet students with the Mickey Mouse puppet, and sing the *Hello, Stars and Heroes* song (track 0.1).
- Show students Mickey's lunchbox. Say: *Look! It's Mickey's lunchbox. What food is in the lunchbox?*, and students guess what food items are inside.

Presentation

1 🔊 **7.7 Listen to the story. Who likes apples?**

- Make the Mickey Mouse puppet stand up. Say: *Sit down, Mickey. It's story time!*
- Play the audio. Students listen to the story and follow in their books.
- Use the story cards to tell the story again, with or without the audio. Pause after each story frame to ask a comprehension question, e.g., *Is Cam happy?* (no, he's grumpy/sad) *Why?* (He doesn't have his lunchbox.) *Leyla has … .* (a sandwich) *Maya has … .* (a cookie) *Peter has … .* (an apple) *Is Cam hungry?* (no).
- Point to the small picture of the apples in the rubric, and elicit the word. Point to the story, and ask: *Who likes apples?* Elicit the answer.

Spot! Students find the carrot in the story. (**Answer:** frame 4)

Practice

2 🔊 **7.8 Listen and number. Then say.**

- Play the first part of the audio, then pause. Students point to the corresponding picture, and write the number *1* in the box. Do the same with the rest of the audio.
- Play the audio again, and students act out each scene as if they were Cam.
- Play the audio a third time, and students repeat the lines. Encourage them to copy the facial expression and intonation of each of the characters.

Audioscript (track 7.8)

1 **Cam:** *Oh, no. My lunchbox!*
  Leyla: *Don't worry, Cam.*
2 **Peter:** *I have two apples.*
  Cam: *Thanks, Peter.*
3 **Cam:** *Shelly is hungry. And Shelly likes apples!*

3 Who's nice? Circle.

- Remind students of the word *nice*, and elicit that Belle was nice to Beast in Video 7A in Lesson 1.
- Ask students to look at the story frames and find the scenes where someone is being nice to another person. You may wish to use the story cards for this, showing the frames one by one, and asking students to do the action for *be nice* (smile and hug yourself).
- Students circle the people who are nice in the story.
- Ask students if they think Cam is nice in the story. Elicit yes/no answers, and then point to frame 6, where Cam gives Shelly the apple.

156

LESSON 4
Story

Lunch for Cam

1 🎧 Listen to the story. Who likes 🍎? Shelly

① Cam: Oh, no. My lunchbox!
Leyla: Don't worry, Cam.
Don't worry.

② Leyla: Let's all share. I have two sandwiches.
Cam: Wow! I like sandwiches.

③ Maya: I have two cookies.
Cam: Yippee! I like cookies.
I like cookies.

④ Peter: I have two apples.
Cam: Thanks, Peter.
Thanks, Peter.

⑤ Cam: I have one apple. I'm not hungry now.

⑥ Cam: Shelly is hungry. And Shelly likes apples!

The end

Spot!

2 🎧 ✏️ Listen and number. Then say.
2, 3, 1

3 Who's nice? Circle.

4 💬 Act out the story.

Story: hungry, lunchbox; Thanks.

Teaching star

Growth mindset Students may not be able to read the speech bubbles in the story yet. To help students develop a growth mindset, show the picture card and word card for *cookies*, then ask students to try to find the same word on p.74. Elicit that it says *cookies*, and show students how they can now read the speech bubble.

4 Act out the story.

- Students look at the photos of the boy and the girl. Ask: *How many apples?* (two). Elicit the sentence: *I have two apples.* Students repeat the sentence, then mime giving one apple to a friend.
- Put students in groups of four, and assign roles: Maya, Cam, Peter, and Leyla. Play the audio, and students act out the story.

Extra activity (story extension) Students work in pairs to act out a similar story, using other food items. Encourage students to say: *I have two pieces of (cake). I like (cake).*

Wrap-up

- Play *Talk to Mickey* (see Games Bank p.206). Make the Mickey Mouse puppet say: *I like (apples).* The student with the corresponding picture card says: *I have (two) (apples).*, and gives the picture card to Mickey. Make Mickey say: *Thank you.*
- Sing the *Goodbye* song (track 0.7), and students say goodbye to Mickey as they leave class.

📓 **Workbook**   page 68

Audioscript see p.205

1 🎧 **7.3 Listen and match. Then point and say.** 1 b, 2 c, 3 a
2 **Be nice to Cam. Draw and say *Don't worry, I have …***

7

Lesson 5: Grammar and Speaking

Student's Book page 76

Objectives

Lesson aim: talk about likes and dislikes

Target language: *I like soup. I don't like noodles.*

Recycled language: *food; books, socks; I like… Belle is grumpy.*

Receptive language: *Gaston says … Ew!*

Materials: Video 7B; Audio; Picture cards / Word cards (Food 1, 2); Stickers; Mickey Mouse puppet; Story cards (Unit 7); Cut-outs (Unit 7), with a cut-out model prepared; scissors, (optional) different types of food

GSE Skills

Listening: can recognize familiar words in short phrases and sentences spoken slowly and clearly, if supported by pictures or gestures (19); can identify everyday objects, people, or animals in their immediate surroundings or in pictures from short, basic descriptions, e.g., color, size, if spoken slowly and clearly (19)

Speaking: can use a few simple words to describe objects, e.g., color, number, if supported by pictures (19)

Teacher toolkit

Video summary – 7B

I like books **Videoscript see p.202**
Belle is walking through the village reading a book. Next, Belle is drinking tea with Mrs. Potts. Belle likes tea. Later, the Beast takes Belle to his library. Belle is happy. She likes books.

Teaching grammar
Share real information about yourself to engage students and help them connect to the structures. Show them a picture card or other picture of a food you like, and say: *I like (pizza). Mmmm.*, and do an appropriate gesture. Then contrast this by showing a picture card or other picture of a food you don't like, and say: *I don't like (cauliflower).*, and do an appropriate gesture.

Engage
Do a taste test with different healthy foods. Bring in different kinds of foods, e.g., fruits, vegetables that can be eaten raw, hummus. You could give each student a card showing pictures of the foods you have brought in, and ask students to draw an emoji next to each kind of food to show whether or not they like it. Make sure you have permission from parents, and check for any food intolerances before doing this activity.

Warm-up

- Greet students with the Mickey Mouse puppet, and sing the *Hello, Stars and Heroes* song (track 0.1).
- Remind students of the story from Lesson 4. Show story cards 2, 3, and 4, and students say: *I like (sandwiches).*

Presentation

1 🎬 **7B Watch. What doesn't Belle like? Check (✔).** *Video story*

- As a lead-in to Video 7B, ask students to look once more at the Big Picture in Lesson 1, and remind them of the movie *Beauty and the Beast* and the characters. Point to the different food items, and students say if they think Belle likes each one.
- Ask students to find books, apples and tea in the small pictures.
- Make the Mickey Mouse puppet stand up. Say: *Sit down, Mickey. It's video time!*
- Play the video, and students point to picture 1, 2, or 3, if they see the objects in the video.
- Play the video again, pausing after Belle expresses her feelings about the apples, the tea and the pink dress. Use gesture, and say: *Belle likes … Belle doesn't like …*, and elicit students' answers.
- Then ask students to check the correct pictures.

Teaching star

Support understanding Point to the picture of tea and say: *Belle likes tea. Yes or no?* Elicit students' answers. Then point to the other two pictures (soup, apples) and say: *I don't like soup. I like apples.* Ask: *Do you like soup?*, and elicit students' answers. Using L1, discuss how it is important to try new foods even if at first we might think we don't like them. Elicit from students the foods they didn't like at first, and which they got to like over time.

Practice

2 🎧 **7.9 Listen, point, and stick. Then say for you.**

- Point to the first picture, and elicit *noodles*. Point to the girl's face, and say: *I like noodles or I don't like noodles?* Elicit answers. Repeat with the picture of soup.
- Play the first sentence in the audio, and students point to the correct picture. Do the same for the second sentence.
- Point to the two empty sticker frames. Play the third sentence, and students place the correct sticker in the frame for *I don't like* (next to the girl's sad face). Then play the fourth sentence audio, and students place the correct sticker in the frame for *I like* (next to the girl's happy face).
- Students stick the stickers in their books.
- Point to one of the pictures, and tell students whether you like or don't like the food item. Then say: *And you?*, and students answer with their opinions.

158

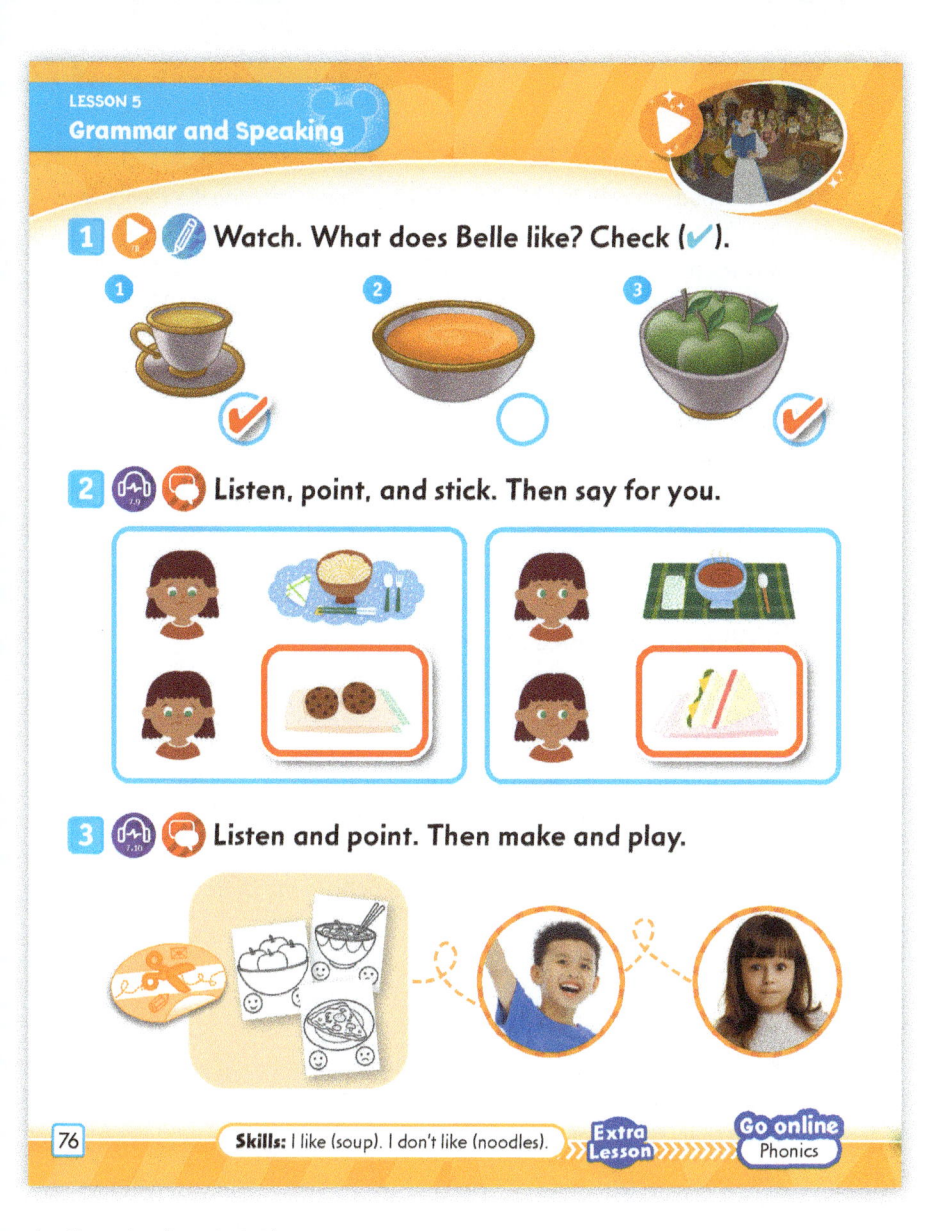

LESSON 5
Grammar and Speaking

1 Watch. What does Belle like? Check (✓).

2 Listen, point, and stick. Then say for you.

3 Listen and point. Then make and play.

Skills: I like (soup). I don't like (noodles).

SUPPORT Students can play the game in mixed-ability pairs. They take turns to pick up a card, with the less confident student saying the name of the food item and either *yes* (if they like it) or *no* (if they don't like it).

STRETCH Students can play the game in mixed-ability pairs. The more confident student says full sentences, following the model from the audio.

Audioscript (track 7.10)
A: *I like pizza. And you?*
B: *I like pizza. I like noodles. And you?*
A: *I don't like noodles. I like apples. And you?*
B: *I don't like apples.*

Extra activity (whole class) Divide the class into two groups, and invite them to stand opposite each other in two lines. Hold up a picture card, e.g., *apples*. One group chants: *I like (apples).*, then the other group chants: *I don't like (apples)*. Repeat with other picture cards. Encourage students to use facial expression and body language to reinforce the meaning of what they are chanting.

Wrap-up
- Play *Behind the doors* (see Games Bank p.206). For this version, students guess if your answer is *I like …* or *I don't like …* .
- Sing the *Goodbye* song (track 0.7), and students say goodbye to the Mickey Mouse puppet as they leave class.

Workbook page 69

Audioscript see p.205

1. 7.4 **Listen and draw** ☺ or ☹. 1 ☹, 2 ☺, 3 ☹, 4 ☺
2. **Do the maze. Find and draw** ☺ or ☹. **Then say.** cookies – ☺, soup – ☹, tea – ☹, sandwiches – ☺, cake – ☺, ice cream – ☹

Audioscript (track 7.9)
I don't like noodles.
I like soup.
I don't like cookies.
I like sandwiches.

3 7.10 **Listen and point. Then make and play.**
- Students use scissors to cut carefully around the dotted lines of the cards in the cut-out.
- Play the first part of the audio. Pause and hold up the pizza card, then color in the happy face, and say: *I like pizza.* Play the rest of the audio, then hold up the noodles card. Color in the sad face, and say: *I don't like noodles.*
- Ask students to color the correct face for each food on the cards, according to their likes and dislikes.
- Model the game with your cards. Place the cards face down on the desk. Take the top card, and say: *I like (apples). And you?* Students find their apples card. If they have the same answer, they hold up their card and say: *I like (apples).* If they don't like apples, they can shake their head and say: *I don't like apples.*

7 Lesson 6: Myself and others

Be nice Student's Book page 77

Objectives

Lesson aim: learn about being nice to others

Target language: *nice; I can help. Let's all share. Thank you.*

Recycled language: *happy, sad, excited*

Materials: Audio; Video 7A; Story cards (Units 6, 7); *Myself and others* poster; Stickers; Mickey Mouse puppet; an empty jar and cotton balls or pompoms; (optional) cards for Teacher toolkit

GSE Skills

Listening: can recognize familiar words in short phrases and sentences spoken slowly and clearly, if supported by pictures or gestures (19)

Speaking: can say how they feel, using a limited range of common adjectives, e.g., *happy, cold* (22)

Writing: can copy some short familiar words presented in standard printed form (10)

Teacher toolkit

Empathy

In this lesson, students explore empathy through different ways in which they can be nice to each other, including helping, sharing, and giving thanks. At this age, students have a basic understanding of other people's emotions, and start to develop social behavior and form stable friendships. Elicit how the people feel in the different situations in the lesson, and how we might help them by being nice.

Self-management

Extend

Set up a *Be nice!* jar. Place the jar in the classroom, and explain to students that they are going to fill the jar with small balls. To place a ball in the jar, students need to be nice to someone. Each time you see a student helping, sharing, or generally being nice to a classmate, invite them to put a ball in the jar. Continue throughout the term, and when the jar is full, celebrate.

Home-school link

Tell students to keep a record of the times they are nice to someone during the week. It could either be someone at school or someone at home. You could give students a checklist containing different ways they can be nice, e.g., help someone, share, say *Thank you*.

Warm-up

- Greet students with the Mickey Mouse puppet, and sing the *Hello, Stars and Heroes* song (track 0.1).
- Review the focus of Lesson 6 in Unit 6 (*teamwork*), using the *Myself and others* poster. Show story card 1 from Unit 6, and ask: *Does Maya help?* (no) *Is she nice?* (no). Then show story card 5, and ask: *Who helps Leyla?* (*Cam, Peter, and Maya*) *Are they nice?* (yes).

🎵 1.12 Listen and sing.

- Play the song audio, and students join in with the words and the actions.
- Ask: *How do you feel? Are you happy?*, and students respond *yes/no* or *I'm (happy)!*

Presentation

1 Who are they nice to? Match.

- Tell the first part of the story from Lesson 4, using the first two frames of the story cards and playing the corresponding audio as necessary (track 7.7). Point to the picture of Leyla, and ask: *Who does Leyla help?* Students point to the picture of Cam.
- Play Video 7A again. Point to the picture of Belle, and ask: *Who does Belle help?* Students point to the picture of Beast.
- Students draw lines to match Layla and Belle to the characters they are nice to.

Practice

2 7.11 Listen and point.

- Point to the two photos and, using L1, ask students what they think is happening in each photo. Ask: *Who helps? Who shares?*, and students point to the different people in each photo.
- Say: *Listen and point.*, then play the audio, and students point to the correct photos.
- Play the audio again, pausing after each sentence for students to repeat it and point to the person who is speaking in each picture.

Audioscript (track 7.11)

1 I can help. // Thank you.
2 Let's all share. // Thank you.

Teaching star

Support understanding 🐭 Use the Mickey Mouse puppet to demonstrate the concept of sharing and to teach the word *share*. Give Mickey some crayons. Ask: *Do you want a crayon?* Offer a crayon to a student, but make Mickey take the crayon for himself. Say: *Mickey, be nice and share with (Mariam).* Then make Mickey hand out the crayons to different students.

160

Be nice

LESSON 6 — Myself and others

1 Who are they nice to? Match.

2 Listen and point.

3 Choose and act. TPR

Self-management: nice; I can help. Let's all share. Thank you.

77

I'm a hero! Point to the sticker picture, and elicit that Peter is sharing his apple. Ask: *Is Peter being nice?* (yes) *Are you nice?* Then students stick the sticker in their books.

Extra activity (fast finishers) Students look back through Units 1 to 6 and identify any situations where people are being nice (Unit 1 – the children invite Maya to sit with them, Unit 2 – Leyla asks Cam to play with her, Unit 3 – Sara is nice to Shelly, Unit 4 – Leyla's mom helps Leyla, Unit 5 – the children encourage each other to keep trying).

Wrap-up

- Draw students' attention once more to the *Myself and others* poster. Call out expressions, e.g., *Keep trying! I'm not grumpy. It's OK. Let's all help. Let's all share.* Students find pictures on the poster where someone might say each expression.
- Sing the *Goodbye* song (track 0.7), and students say goodbye to the Mickey Mouse puppet as they leave class.

Workbook page 70

Audioscript see p.205

1 7.5 **Who's nice? Circle. Then listen and point.** *Maya, Cam*

2 **Trace and draw. Then say.**

3 Choose and act.

- Review how we can be nice, using the *Myself and others* poster. Elicit students' ideas in L1, and provide useful language in English, e.g., *share my food/toys/crayons/book, help my friend/brother/mom, say "Thank you," smile, hug my friend.*
- Point to one of the photos in activity 2, and invite two students to act out the situation. Encourage them to use the expressions from the activity 2 audio, prompting as necessary. Say: *Look! They're (sharing). They're nice.*
- Students work in pairs to choose a situation and act it out.
- Invite confident students to act out their situation in front of the class. Encourage the other students to use the phrases from activity 2 to say how the student is being nice: *I can help. / Let's all share.*

161

Lesson 7: My world

Art: Food prints Student's Book page 78

Objectives

Lesson aims: learn about food prints
Target language: bell pepper, mushroom, onion; cut, paint
Recycled language: food, colors, shapes
Materials: Audio; Mickey Mouse puppet; vegetables, a knife and paints (see Cross-curricular), a vegetable print (see Teaching star); a cloth bag; (optional) a picture of vegetables

GSE Skills

Listening: can recognize isolated words related to familiar topics, if spoken slowly and clearly and supported by pictures or gestures (16)
Reading: can recognize single, familiar everyday words, if supported by pictures (21)
Speaking: can repeat single words, if spoken slowly and clearly (10); can repeat phrases and short sentences, if spoken slowly and clearly (16)
Writing (WB): can copy some short familiar words presented in standard printed form (10)

Teacher toolkit

Cross-curricular
This type of printing is called "relief printing." The texture of the printed surface is visible on the paper. If you choose to do the art project, the materials you will need are: non-shiny paper such as construction paper, poster paints or tempera, and firm vegetables. To save paint, make a stamp pad by adding paint to a damp sponge.

Extend
Students make food art. Cut the vegetables in half for students. They paint the cut side of the vegetable or dip it in paint, then press it face-down onto a piece of paper. Tell students to print it several times and notice how the print mark fades as they progress.

Home-school link
Students make more food art at home with different fruits and vegetables. Ask them to bring in their prints and say: *Look! It's a (potato).*

Warm-up
- Greet students with the Mickey Mouse puppet, and sing the *Hello, Stars and Heroes* song (track 0.1).
- Play *It's in the bag* (see Games Bank p.206). Put a fruit or vegetable inside a cloth bag. Students take turns to put their hand in the bag and try to guess the food item inside.

Presentation

1 🎧 **7.12 Listen and point. Then say.**

- Show students a picture of different vegetables. Point to each type of vegetable, and say: *I like (bell peppers). I don't like (onions).* Encourage students to point and say *I like* and *I don't like* about different vegetables.
- Ask students to look at the photos, and pre-teach the words.
- Play the audio, and students point to the corresponding photos. Play the audio again, and demonstrate TPR actions: *bell pepper* (mime eating a slice of a pepper, and make a *crunch* sound), *onion* (mime chopping and crying), *cut* (mime chopping with a knife), and *paint* (mime painting with a brush). Play the audio a third time, and students repeat the words and do the TPR actions.

SUPPORT Say the words, and students do the TPR action.
STRETCH Students work in pairs, taking turns to say one of the words for their partner to do the corresponding TPR action.

Practice

2 🎧 **7.13 Look and match. Then listen and say.**

- Ask students to look at the half vegetable photos on the left and to find the onion (picture 1). Then ask them to look at the half vegetable photos on the right and to find the onion (picture b). They draw a line to match the half onions. Do the same with the apple and the bell pepper.
- Play the first part of the audio, and students point to the corresponding picture. Then play the first part again, and students act out cutting, painting, and printing the onion on their desks. Do the same for the second and third parts of the audio, with the apple and the bell pepper.
- Play the audio again, and students repeat the sentences as they do the TPR actions.

Audioscript (track 7.13)
1 Cut the onion. Paint the onion. Look! It's an onion.
2 Cut the apple. Paint the apple. Look! It's an apple.
3 Cut the bell pepper. Paint the pepper. Look! It's a pepper.

LESSON 7
My world

Food prints

1 🎧 💬 **Listen and point. Then say.**

1. bell pepper
2. onion
3. cut
4. paint

2 ✏️ 🎧 **Look and match. Then listen and say.**

3 ✏️ 💬 **Look and number in order. Then say.**

Food prints: bell pepper, mushroom, onion; cut, paint

78

Thinking skills

Understand In activity 2, students identify food items from incomplete pictures and match them to their corresponding halves. They identify the actions and demonstrate them, using mime.

Apply In activity 3, students apply their knowledge of the process involved in food printing by putting the actions in order chronologically. They describe the process, identifying the actions in the pictures and naming them.

Teaching star ✨

Creativity Show students a vegetable print you have prepared. Then ask them to imagine what other things the print could be, e.g., a flower, a tree, a hat, a ladybug. Show students how we can combine prints to make a picture.

Extra activity (extension) Students find different items from nature that could be used to make prints, e.g., leaves, bark, rocks. Then they give each other instructions to make prints, e.g., Paint the (leaf) (yellow). Look! It's a (yellow) (leaf). Encourage students to make a picture with different numbers and colors of prints.

Wrap-up

- Play *Follow the leader* (see Games Bank p.206) For this version, students say actions from the lesson, e.g., *cut the bell pepper, paint the bell pepper*.
- Sing the *Goodbye* song (track 0.7), and students say goodbye to the Mickey Mouse puppet as they leave class.

📋 Workbook   page 71

1 Number. Then trace, point, and say. *a 3, b 2, c 1*

2 Trace, color, and match. Then say. *1 b, 2 a, 3 c*

---

3 Look and number in order. Then say.

- Point to the second picture, and ask: *How many mushrooms?* Invite students to count, and elicit that there are two mushrooms (one mushroom is cut into two halves).
- Ask students to look at the three pictures. Say: *One. Cut the mushroom.* Students point to the correct picture and write *1* in the box. Then say and students point and write accordingly: *Two. Paint the mushroom. Three. Look! It's a mushroom.*
- Point to the pictures in order, and elicit: *Cut (the mushroom). Paint (the mushroom). Look! It's a (blue) mushroom.*

SUPPORT Say the sentences, and students point to the pictures and mime.

STRETCH Students work in pairs, taking turns to say the instructions for their partner to point to and mime.

Lesson 8: Review

I can do it! Student's Book page 79

Objectives

Lesson aim: review target language from Unit 7

Target language: food; *I like … I don't like …*

Materials: Audio; (optional) Video 7A, Video 7B; Picture cards / Word cards (Food 1, 2); Stickers; Mickey Mouse puppet; *My progress* poster

GSE Skills

Listening: can recognize isolated words related to familiar topics, if spoken slowly and clearly and supported by pictures and gestures (16)

Reading: can recognize single, familiar everyday words, if supported by pictures (21)

Speaking: can say single words related to familiar topics, if supported by pictures or gestures (18)

Writing: can copy some short familiar words presented in standard printed form (10)

Teacher toolkit

Video review
You can return to Video 7A and Video 7B at the end of the unit for a "second play." Students watch and put their thumbs up when they see something they like, and they put their thumbs down when they see something they don't like.

Remediation
Encourage students to develop learner autonomy by asking them to identify any areas in which they lack confidence. Ask students to show you any words or structures they are having difficulty with, then give them additional help and provide further practice, by playing *Mickey's card* (see Games Bank p.206), by playing matching games with picture cards and word cards, or by listening to and singing the song from Lesson 3 (track 7.5).

Home-school link
Students make more food art at home with different fruits and vegetables. Ask them to bring in their prints and say: *Look! It's a (potato)*.

Warm-up

- Greet students with the Mickey Mouse puppet, and sing the *Hello, Stars and Heroes* song (track 0.1).
- Play the game *Monster munch* (see Games Bank p.206). For this version, the monster only wants to eat words with five letters or more. Use this as an opportunity to practice spelling.
- Play the song audio from Lesson 3 (track 7.5), and students join in with the words and the actions. If students are confident with the words, play the karaoke version (track 7.5_karaoke).

I can do it!

1 7.14 **Listen and color. Then trace.**

- Point to the picture, and say: *I can see (tea)*. Then elicit *I can see …* about each of the food items.
- Ask: *What color is the apple?* Play the first part of the audio, then pause for students to color the apple red. Play the rest of the audio, pausing for students to color the corresponding food item in the picture.
- Check answers by saying: *I can see an (apple). It's …*, and elicit the correct color.
- Students trace the words in their books. Encourage them to say the word as they trace it.

ACHIEVE
Students name, read, and trace food words, and color a picture when listening to simple instructions.

SUPPORT
Pause the audio after the first sentence. Students find the food item. Then play the second sentence, and pause for students to color the food item. Do the same with all the pictures.

STRETCH
Students work in pairs, taking turns to say *I can see … It's …* for their partner to point to.

Audioscript (track 7.14)

I can see an apple. It's red. // I can see an ice cream. It's pink. // I can see soup. It's green. // I can see tea. It's brown. // I can see a cake. It's yellow. // I can see juice. It's orange.

2 Draw ☺ or ☹ for you. Then say.

- Point to a food item in the picture in activity 1, and say: *I like (juice). And you? I don't like (tea). And you?*, making a happy face and a sad face as appropriate.
- Students draw the faces on the emojis to show whether or not they like each food item.
- Students work in pairs, taking turns to point to different food items in the picture and say *I like … / I don't like … And you?* for their partner to answer.

- Students color the stars next to each objective they can do. Then they stick the reward sticker to show they have completed Unit 7.

My Star and Hero! Students look at the picture of Belle on p.5 of the Student's Book. They imagine they are Belle, saying *I like…* and *I don't like…*, then say or mime how they are nice to others.

Extra activity (class survey) Stick a happy face on one side of the classroom and a sad face on the other side of the classroom. Show students a food picture card, and they go to either side of the classroom, according to whether they like or don't like the food item. Count the number of students on each side of the classroom, and keep a tally on the board.

Wrap-up

- Students reflect on which lesson or activity they most enjoyed in Unit 7. Have a class vote, and choose one activity to do again as a class, e.g., watch the video, sing the song or chant, listen to the story, or play a game.
- Draw students' attention to the *My progress* poster, and ask them to identify the picture that reflects this unit. Read aloud with students the *I can …* statements (*I can say what food I like or don't like, I can be nice*).
- Sing the *Goodbye* song (track 0.7), and students say goodbye to the Mickey Mouse puppet, then tell him their favorite word from Unit 7.

Workbook — pages 72–73

My progress

Audioscript see p.205

1. 7.6 **Listen and number.** *a 2, b 1, c 4, d 3*
2. **Play and say.**

Units W–7 My practice

1. **Color the food. Then say.**
   Find, circle, and say. bugs – ladybug, butterfly; clothes: T-shirt, pants, shoes, dress; toys: kite, yo-yo, ball; family: mom, dad, brother, sister
2. **Draw your favorite food.**

Unit 7! My favorite activity: Students stick the small star sticker next to their favorite activity.

ACHIEVE
Students talk and ask about the items in the picture they like and dislike.

SUPPORT
Make *I (don't) like …* statements about the items in the picture for students to answer.

STRETCH
Students make *I (don't) like …* statements about food and other items.

3 Think and color. Then stick!

- Point to each picture, and say the *I can …* statements: *I can name food. I can sing a song. I can be nice.* For each statement, give an example, and then ask: *Can you do this?* If necessary, explain in L1.
- Students demonstrate what they can do. They work in pairs, taking turns to say the names of different foods. Give students the opportunity to write the words on the board. Sing the song all together as a class. Students work in pairs, taking turns to say and act out being nice. Monitor and assess students' performance.

8 Animals

Unit objectives

By the end of this unit, students can:
- talk about animals and what they can do
- read and understand a story about sports day
- recognize when they need to ask for help
- talk about animal needs

Skills development GSE

Listening: recognize animal and action words, if spoken slowly and clearly and supported by pictures or gestures

Reading: recognize key words and basic phrases in a short, simple cartoon story

Speaking: describe animals and what they can do; ask for help; say what animals need

Writing: copy short, familiar words for actions

Vocabulary

Lesson 1: bird, elephant, lion, monkey, zebra
Lesson 2: climb, fly, run, swim, walk

Grammar

Lesson 3: I can swim.
Lesson 5: Monkeys can climb.

Myself and others

Asking for help In this unit, a Disney video and a story introduce the theme of asking for help. Students will learn to identify situations when they need to ask for help.

Language: I can do it. I need help.

Self-awareness

Story

Sports day
glasses, hero, shoes; Now I can run. Here you are.

My world

Science: Animal needs
food, home, water

Disney THE LION KING

Unit overview

Mufasa
A big, strong lion and the king of the Pride Lands. Mufasa is a wise king, but he also loves playing games with Simba.

Simba
A lion cub who grows up during the movie. Simba is adventurous, playful, and bold.

Zazu
A red-billed hornbill bird who acts as advisor to Mufasa. He's loyal and always tries to protect Simba.

Nala
Simba's best friend, Nala is a female lion cub. She's smart, strong, and a good friend.

Timon
Timon is a meerkat. He and his friend Pumbaa, a warthog, take care of Simba.

Rafiki
An elderly mandrill monkey and friend of Mufasa. Rafiki is a wise, eccentric shaman who helps Simba make the decision to return to the Pride Lands.

Simba is heir to the throne in the animal kingdom. When Simba's father dies, Simba leaves his community because he feels responsible for his father's death. However, when an old friend finds him, he convinces Simba to come home.

Did you know?
The Lion King's original title was King of the Jungle. However, there was one problem – lions don't live in the jungle!

Video stories
Video 8A: *Run, Simba!*
Video 8B: *Monkeys can climb*

Online modules

Phonics
Words with Vv and Ww sounds in initial position and Xx sound in final position
vest, walk, fox

Big Project
Do an animal performance

8 Lesson 1: Vocabulary

Student's Book pages 80–81

Objectives

Lesson aim: name animals

Target language: bird, elephant, lion, monkey, zebra

Recycled language: family, numbers, nature; ants, big, small, angry; I can see … Where's Zazu?

Receptive language: Simba says, "I can jump!" Mufasa says, "Simba, go home." Help! I need help. Run!

Materials: Video 8A; Audio; Picture cards / Word cards (Animals, Disney characters); Sticker (Simba); Mickey Mouse puppet; (optional) A3 card, paper, scissors, glue

GSE Skills

Listening: can recognize isolated words related to familiar topics, if spoken slowly and clearly and supported by pictures and gestures (16)

Reading: can recognize single, familiar everyday words, if supported by pictures (21)

Speaking: can name everyday objects, animals, or people around them or in pictures, using single words (18)

Writing (WB): can copy some short familiar words presented in standard printed form (10)

Teacher toolkit

Video summary – 8A
Run, Simba! Videoscript see pp.202–203
Simba is the heir to the throne in the animal kingdom. He goes exploring with his friend, Nala. They find themselves in danger, and Mufasa rescues them.

Engage
During the unit, make a class lapbook about animals, with each student creating one section of the lapbook. Each student can choose an animal, draw, and write about it using the structures and vocabulary they learn in this unit, then stick their work in the lapbook.

Asking for help
Use the video story to review the concept of helping others. Show students the ASL (American Sign Language) sign for *asking for help*: hold one hand flat with your palm facing up, then make a "thumbs up" sign with your other hand and bring it down to your palm. While watching, students do the sign when they see someone in need of help.

Self-awareness

Warm-up
- Greet students with the Mickey Mouse puppet, and sing the *Hello, Stars and Heroes* song (track 0.1).

Presentation

Video story

- Students look at the Big Picture. Introduce the movie and the characters: *This is the movie The Lion King. This is Simba and Nala. This is Zazu* (the bird) / *Rafiki* (the monkey).
- Students count the number of animals in the Big Picture (ten animals, including three butterflies).
- Review symmetry by asking students to notice the patterns and colors on the butterflies.

1 ▶ 8A Watch. Who jumps? Circle.

- Make the Mickey Mouse puppet start jumping. Say: *Don't jump, Mickey! Sit down, please. It's video time! Let's watch!*
- Play Video 8A, and students watch and listen.
- Point to the small pictures, and ask: *Who jumps?* Play the video again, and students jump when they see Simba jump. Then students circle the picture.

2 ▶ 8A Who asks for help? Check (✓).

- Show students the ASL sign for asking for help (see Teacher toolkit).
- Play Video 8A again, and students do the ASL sign when they see someone ask for help. Pause at 2:58, and elicit the phrase Simba uses (*Help! I need help.*).
- Point to each small picture, and ask: *Who asks for help? Simba or the hyenas?* Students check the correct picture.

Picture cards / Word cards (optional) Show the picture cards one by one to introduce the new vocabulary. Repeat several times, encouraging students to remember the words. Then show each word card, and elicit the words.

Practice

3 🎧 8.1 Listen, find, and say. Then play.

- Play the audio, pausing after each word. Students point to the animals in the Big Picture. Play the audio again, pausing for students to say the words. Show students a TPR action for each animal (see activity 4). Play the audio a third time, and students read and say the word, then do a TPR action.
- Divide the class into two groups. Hold up a picture card. One group says the name of the animal, and the other group does the TPR action. Continue with different picture cards, asking the groups to take turns.

SUPPORT Call out the name of an animal. Students point to the animal in the Big Picture, then do the TPR action.

STRETCH Students work in pairs, taking turns to point to an animal for their partner to name and mime.

Audioscript (track 8.1)
1 elephant // 2 lion // 3 zebra // 4 bird // 5 monkey

168

8 Animals

LESSON 1 Vocabulary

1. elephant
2. lion
3. zebra
4. bird
5. monkey

1 Watch. Who jumps? Circle.

2 Who asks for help? Check (✓).

3 Listen, find, and say. Then play.

4 Listen, chant, and act. **TPR**
🎵 Elephants! 🎵

bird, elephant, lion, monkey, zebra

---

4 🎵 **8.2 Listen, chant, and act.**

- Display the five picture cards. Make the Mickey Mouse puppet make an animal noise, and students point to the correct picture card.
- Play the audio, and students listen and point to the correct picture card when they hear each animal sound.
- Review the TPR actions. Play the audio again. Students join in with the chant and do the actions.

TPR chant

elephant – use your arm as a trunk
zebra – trot on the spot, and move arms up and down
bird – flap your arms like wings
monkey – bend arms at the elbow, with hands to armpits
lion – roar like a lion

Audioscript (track 8.2)

Elephants! Elephants! I like elephants. // Oooooo. Oooooo.
Zebras! Zebras! I like zebras. // Hee-Haw. Hee-Haw.
Birds. Birds! I like birds. // Tweet-tweet. Tweet-tweet.
Monkeys! Monkeys! I like monkeys. // Oh ah. Oh ah.
Lions! Lions! I like lions. // Grrrrr!

Collect your friend Show the picture card of Simba to help students identify the correct sticker. Students stick the sticker on p.5 in the Student's Book. Ask: *Who's this?* (*Simba*).

Extra activity (video extension) Play Video 8A again, with the screen off, so it's audio only. When students hear each animal sound, they do the TPR action.

Wrap-up

- Play *Miming* (see Games Bank p.206), using the word cards.
- Sing the *Goodbye* song (track 0.7), and students say goodbye to the Mickey Mouse puppet as they leave class.

📝 Workbook pages 74–75

1 **Watch again. Then answer.**
   1 **Number in order.** *a 2, b 1, c 3*
   2 **What animals do you see in the video? Check (✓).**
      a ✓, b ✓, c ✓, d ✓, e ✓
   3 **Who helps Simba? Circle.** *b (Mufasa)*
2 **Trace and match. Then point and say.** *1 elephant, 2 zebra, 3 monkey, 4 bird, 5 lion*
3 **Challenge! Join the dots. Then guess the animal.** *1 zebra, 2 lion, 3 bird*

8 Lesson 2: Vocabulary

Student's Book page 82

Objectives

Lesson aim: name actions
Target language: *climb, fly, run, swim, walk*
Recycled language: animals
Materials: Audio; Picture cards / Word cards (Animals, Actions 2); Mickey Mouse puppet; (optional) card/paper, scissors, popsicle sticks or pencils

GSE Skills

Listening: can understand basic action words, e.g., *clap, stamp, jump, walk* (15)

Reading: can recognize basic action words, e.g., *clap, stamp, jump, walk* (21)

Speaking: can describe the size of everyday objects, using a basic phrase, e.g., *It's big.* (23); can use language related to basic actions, e.g., *clap, stamp, jump, walk* (21)

Writing (WB): can copy some short familiar words presented in standard printed form (10)

Teacher toolkit

Teaching vocabulary
Model the action words using TPR mimes, making sure you choose suitable mimes for the students' age, e.g., mime *swimming* with a front crawl stroke, which students will recognize rather than breast stroke. As you teach each action word, extend and review by asking students to say where animals sometimes do these actions, e.g., *swim in a river, fly above the trees*.

Engage
Students make mini-puppets that they can use to show the action words. They could draw and cut out an animal puppet, or you could give them pictures of Simba, Zaza, and Rafiki to cut out. Students stick the pictures onto popsicle sticks to make the puppets. They use the puppets to show the actions.

Home-school link
Students keep a record of all the actions they do during the week. You could give them a chart to complete with a list of the five actions, and they check in the list each time they do an action.

Warm-up

- Greet students with the Mickey Mouse puppet, and sing the *Hello, Stars and Heroes* song (track 0.1).
- Play *What's missing?* (see Games Bank p.206). For this version, use the animals picture cards.
- Say: *Listen and chant!*, and play the chant from Lesson 1 (track 8.2). Students join in with the chant and do the actions.

Presentation

Picture cards / Word cards (optional) Show the picture cards one by one to introduce the new vocabulary. Repeat several times, encouraging students to remember the words. Then show each word card, and elicit the words.

1 8.3 Listen, point, and say. Then play.

- Show one of the picture cards, say: *(Run), Mickey!*, and make the Mickey Mouse puppet do the action. Repeat with other picture cards.
- Say: *Listen and point*. Play the audio, and students point to the corresponding photos. Play the audio again, pausing after each word. Students point to the corresponding photo and repeat the word.
- Then say a word, and students repeat it and point to the corresponding photo. Repeat with different words.

SUPPORT Say a word, students repeat it and then mime the action.

STRETCH Students work in pairs, taking turns to say an action word for their partner to say the name of the animal that is doing that action in the photo.

Practice

Teaching star

Support understanding Make sure students know how to write numbers so that they can put the pictures in order in activity 2. Stick four picture cards on the board: *fly, walk, climb, swim*. Name the picture cards in random order, e.g., *one – climb, two – fly, three – swim, four – walk*. Show students how to write the number *1* next to the *climb* picture card. Then elicit the numbers for the other picture cards, and write them on the board.

2 8.4 Listen and number. Then point and say.

- Point to the first picture from the video, and say: *Look! They're ants. They walk.* Students walk like ants. Do the same with the other pictures.
- Play the audio, pausing after each word for students to point to the correct picture. Play the audio again, and students number the pictures in the correct order. Play the audio one more time, and students point and repeat the words.

Audioscript (track 8.4)
1 fly // 2 walk // 3 climb // 4 run

170

LESSON 2
Vocabulary

1 🎧 💬 **Listen, point, and say. Then play.**

1. run
2. fly
3. climb
4. walk
5. swim

2 🎧 ✏️ **Listen and number. Then point and say.**

2, 4, 1, 3

3 **Say and act.** TPR

climb, fly, run, swim, walk

82

Extra activity (fast finishers) Students say or write the actions for each animal, e.g., *bird – fly, walk, swim* (depending on the type of bird).

Wrap-up
- Play *Mickey says* (see Games Bank p.206). Ask the Mickey Mouse puppet to give instructions to the class for students to follow. Demonstrate each action as Mickey says it. Use the actions from the lesson.
- Sing the *Goodbye* song (track 0.7), and students say goodbye to the Mickey Mouse puppet as they leave class.

Workbook   page 76

Audioscript see p.205

1 8.1 Listen and check (✓). Then say.
   1 a ✓, 2 b ✓, 3 a ✓, 4 b ✓

2 **Match and trace. Then say and act.** *1 fly, 2 walk, 3 climb, 4 run*

Picture Dictionary
Students look at the Picture Dictionary on p.108 in the Student's Book and complete the activities. (**Answers:** walk, run, swim)

---

3 Say and act.
- Point to each photo, and elicit which action each child is doing (*swim, jump, climb*).
- Make the Mickey Mouse puppet act out each of the actions, and elicit the action words from students.
- Invite individual students to tell Mickey what action to do, then ask other students to make Mickey do the action.
- Display the action picture cards on the board. Point to a picture card, elicit the word, then students mime the action. Repeat with different picture cards.

SUPPORT Invite a student to act out one of the pictures, and the rest of the class says the action word.

STRETCH Students work in pairs, taking turns to say an action word for their partner to mime.

8 Lesson 3: Grammar

Student's Book page 83

Objectives

Lesson aim: say what you can do
Target language: *I can swim.*
Recycled language: animals, actions; *I'm (small).*
Materials: Audio; Picture cards / Word cards (Animals, Actions 2, Bugs); Stickers; Mickey Mouse puppet; (optional) lots of pictures of animals (including multiple copies)

GSE Skills

Listening: can recognize familiar words and phrases in short, simple songs or chants (18); can understand basic action words, e.g., *clap, stamp, jump, walk* (15)

Speaking: can recite a short, simple rhyme or chant (16); can use language related to basic actions, e.g., *clap, stamp, jump, walk* (21); can talk about things they can or can't do, using a simple fixed expression (28)

Teacher toolkit

Teaching grammar

Use TPR actions to present *I can …* . Mime doing each of the Lesson 2 actions (except *fly*) successfully, and say: *I can (run).* Then mime doing some of these actions successfully and some of these actions unsuccessfully, e.g., attempting to run but stopping, showing that you are out of breath. For each action, say: *I can (run).* Students say *yes* if you mime doing the action successfully, and they say *no* if you mime doing the action unsuccessfully.

Extend

Foster critical thinking skills through a classification activity. Put students into groups, and give each group pictures of different animals. They classify the animals according to the actions the animals can do. Make sure you provide multiple copies of some animal pictures so that the animal can be placed in more than one category.

Differentiation

Provide different types of support and scaffolding to ensure students understand the animal descriptions. For example, hold up or point to picture cards, use mime and exaggerated facial expression, and display the answer options during an activity.

Warm-up

- Greet students with the Mickey Mouse puppet, and sing the *Hello, Stars and Heroes* song (track 0.1).
- Play *Pass Mickey* (Games Bank p.206), using the animals and actions picture cards.

Presentation

1 Sing-along 🎵 **8.5 Listen and point. Then sing and act.**

- Point to the picture of Leyla, and elicit the name of the action she is doing (*swim*). Do the same with the pictures of Maya (*climb*), Cam (*jump*), and Peter (*run*).
- Play the song audio. Students point to each character as they hear the corresponding action word in the song.
- Demonstrate the TPR actions. Then play the song again, and students do the TPR actions.
- Play the song a third time, and encourage students to join in with some of the words as they do the TPR actions and dance. When students are confident with the words, play the karaoke version (track 8.5_karaoke), and students sing along.

> **TPR song**
> swim – mime swimming front crawl
> climb – mime climbing a tree
> jump – jump high in the air
> run – run on the spot

Audioscript (track 8.5)

I can swim, swim, swim. *(x2)* // I can swim in the river. // I can swim, swim, swim.
I can climb, climb, climb. *(x2)* // I can climb in the trees. // I can climb, climb, climb.
I can jump, jump, jump. *(x2)* // I can jump on the rocks. // I can jump, jump, jump.
I can run, run, run. *(x2)* // I can run with my kite. // I can run, run, run.

Practice

2 8.6 Listen and find. Then say.

- Students look again at the pictures in activity 1. Point to Leyla, and say: *I can …*, to elicit *swim*. Do the same with Maya, Cam, and Peter.
- Play the audio, pausing after each sentence for students to point to the correct character.
- Play the audio again, pausing after each sentence. Students repeat the sentence and say the name of the character.
- Play as a class. Ask: *Who am I? I can (jump).*, and students say the name of the character (*Cam*). Then invite more confident students to say: *I can (run).*, and other students name the character.

Audioscript (track 8.6)

1 **Peter:** *I can run.*
2 **Cam:** *I can jump.*
3 **Maya:** *I can climb.*
4 **Leyla:** *I can swim.*

Sing-along

1 🎵 **Listen and point. Then sing and act.** TPR

🎵 I can swim 🎵

LESSON 3 Grammar

2 🎧 Listen and find. Then say.

3 🎧 Listen, point, and stick. Then say and guess.

Song: I can (swim). I'm (small).

83

SUPPORT Students do the corresponding TPR action after you say each sentence with *I can …*.

STRETCH Students work in pairs, taking turns to describe the animals for their partner to guess. Encourage them to say the color, size, and body parts, as well as what action the animal can do.

Audioscript (track 8.7)
I can fly. I'm small. … I'm a bird.
I can climb. I like bananas. … I'm a monkey.
I can walk. I'm black and white. … I'm a zebra.
I can swim. I'm big. … I'm an elephant.

Teaching star ✦

Creativity Allowing students to be creative can help develop their language and thinking skills, as they take risks by imagining new possibilities. Encourage students to let their imaginations go wild in the Extra activity below. They can use their prior knowledge to help them decide what their animal will look like (e.g., the animal will need wings to be able to fly), but encourage them to use their imaginations freely and creatively.

Extra activity (fast finishers) Students draw a picture of an imaginary animal, with the body parts of different animals, e.g., an elephant's head, a zebra's body, a bird's wings, and a lion's legs. They present their animal to the class, saying what actions it can do.

---

3 🎧 **8.7 Listen, point, and stick. Then say and guess.**

- Use the picture cards to review *bird*, *zebra*, *elephant*, and *beetle*, and students find each one in the picture.
- Point to the empty sticker spaces, and students say which two animals they think are missing, e.g., *monkey*, *lion*, *butterfly*, *bird*.
- Play the audio, pausing after each sentence for students to point to the sticker they think is being described. When the animal is named, students place their stickers in the correct spaces. Play the audio again, and students stick the stickers.
- Play the first part of the audio one more time, pausing after each sentence for students to point and repeat the words.
- Describe one of the animals, e.g., *I can run. I have four legs. I'm black and white. I'm a …* . Students say the name of the animal. Do the same with the other animals.

Wrap-up

- Play *Which is different?* (see Games Bank p.206). For this version, choose animal picture cards.
- 🎵 Sing the *Goodbye* song (track 0.7), and students say goodbye to the Mickey Mouse puppet as they leave class.

📖 **Workbook** page 77

Audioscript see p.205

1 🎧 **8.2 Listen and number.** a 1, b 3, c 4, d 2
2 Put a ✔ **for you. Then say.**

173

Lesson 4: Story

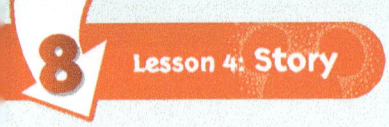

Student's Book pages 84–85

Objectives

Lesson aim: listen to and understand a story about school sports day

Story language: *glasses, hero, shoes; Now I can run. Here you are.*

Recycled language: *actions; Good job, Leyla!*

Receptive language: *Yippee! I can help. Don't worry! Thanks! Let's all help.*

Materials: Audio; Story cards (Unit 8); Mickey Mouse puppet; (optional) a hard-boiled egg (or a table tennis ball) and a spoon

GSE Skills

Listening: can understand a few basic words and phrases in a story that is read aloud (18)

Reading: can recognize single, familiar everyday words if supported by pictures (21)

Speaking: can repeat phrases and short sentences, if spoken slowly and clearly (16); can talk about things they can or can't do, using a simple fixed expression (28)

Teacher toolkit

Story summary
Leyla can't take part in Sports Day because she's hurt her hand. As the other children take part in their races, Leyla helps each child. In the end, the teacher gives Leyla a prize for being the Sports Day hero!

Engage
If possible, set up outdoors an egg and spoon race and a sack race. Alternatively, have an indoor race, where students have to find and bring back specific picture cards or word cards. Encourage students to say to each other *Good job!*, and to ask for help if they need it.

Asking for help
In the story, Leyla helps her friends when they ask for help. Using L1, ask students why Leyla gets a medal at the end of the story (Leyla's nice, and she helps everyone). Ask students if they sometimes ask for help and if they help other people. Then ask them how they feel when they help someone, e.g., *happy, proud.*

Self-awareness

Warm-up

- Greet students with the Mickey Mouse puppet, and sing the *Hello, Stars and Heroes* song (track 0.1).
- Give Mickey a spoon with an egg on it. Tell students that Mickey has to carry the egg to the other side of the classroom. Ask: *Can he do it?*, and elicit *yes* or *no*. Then make Mickey carry the egg on the spoon, either successfully or unsuccessfully. Encourage students to say *Keep trying!* or *Good job!*

Presentation

1 🎧 **8.8 Listen to the story. Who can run? Who can jump?**

- Make the Mickey Mouse puppet stand up. Say: *Sit down, Mickey. It's story time!*
- Play the audio. Students listen to the story and follow in their books.
- Use the story cards to tell the story again, with or without the audio. Pause after each story frame to ask a comprehension question, e.g., *Peter can run. Yes or no?* (yes) *Where are Peter's glasses?* (on the ground) *Maya can walk with the egg and spoon. Yes or no?* (yes) *Who helps Peter, Maya, and Cam?* (Leyla) *Who is the hero?* (Leyla).
- Point to the small pictures in the rubric, and elicit the action words. Ask: *Who can run?* (Peter) *Who can jump?* (Cam).

Spot! Students find the monkey and the lion in the story. (**Answers:** the monkey is on Maya's T-shirt, the lion is on the boy's T-shirt in frame 2)

Practice

2 🎧 **8.9 Who says it? Listen, circle, and say.**

- Students look at the pairs of small pictures and identify each of the characters.
- Play the first part of the audio, pausing for students to point to the corresponding character (*Peter*). Do the same with parts two and three.
- Play the audio again, pausing after each sentence for students to circle the correct character. Play the audio a third time, and students repeat the lines and mime the actions.

Audioscript (track 8.9)
1 **Peter:** *I can run.*
2 **Leyla:** *I can help.*
3 **Maya:** *My shoes! I need help.*

3 Who needs help? Check (✓).

- Remind students of Video 8A from Lesson 1. Using L1, elicit who needed help (Simba and Nala).
- Show each story card, and students look in the picture for someone who needs help. When they find someone who needs help, they do the TPR action for *asking for help* (see Lesson 1).
- Students point to the people in the small pictures who need help in the story. Then they check these characters.

174

LESSON 4 Story

Sports day

1 Listen to the story. Who can 🏃 [Peter]? Who can 🤸 [Cam]?

1 Ms. Smart: Welcome to Sports Day!
Peter: I can run.
Cam: I can jump.
(I can run.)

2 Peter: Oh, no. My glasses.
Leyla: I can help.
Peter: Thanks! Now I can run.

3 Maya: My shoes! I need help.
Leyla: Don't worry.
Maya: Thanks. Now I can walk.
(Thanks.)

4 Cam: I need help!
Leyla: Here you are.
Cam: Thanks! Now I can jump.
(Now I can jump.)

5 Leyla: Look at Ms. Smart. Let's all help.

6 Ms. Smart: Good job, Leyla. You're the hero today!
Leyla: Wow! Thanks, Ms. Smart.
(Good job, Leyla.)

The end

Spot!

2 Who says it? Listen, circle, and say.

3 Who needs help? Check (✓).

4 Act out the story.

Story: glasses, hero, shoes; Now I can (run). Here you are.

Teaching star

Linguistic competence To help students with the correct intonation of the phrases in activity 4, play the audio of the sentences in the speech bubbles several times, pausing for students to repeat. First, students repeat each sentence at normal volume, then they whisper it, and finally, they say the sentence loudly.

4 Act out the story.

- Students look at the photos of the boy and the girl. Say: *Now I can …*, and elicit an action verb *(jump)*.
- Choose one student to role-play Leyla, and put the other students into three groups. Each group will act out a different race from the story: running race / egg and spoon race / sack race.
- Play the story audio, and each group acts out their scene, saying their lines from the speech bubbles. The student playing Leyla goes to "help" the other students in each group.
- At the end, all the students applaud and congratulate Leyla, saying: *Good job!*

Extra activity (story extension) Students mime trying but failing to do an action, e.g., running and falling over. They ask another student to help them, and then say: *Now I can (run).*

Wrap-up

- Play *Follow the leader* (see Games Bank p. 206).
- Sing the *Goodbye* song (track 0.7), and students say goodbye to the Mickey Mouse puppet as they leave class.

Workbook   page 78

Audioscript see p.205

1 8.3 **Listen and number in order.** *a 2, b 1, c 4, d 3*

2 Who needs help? Check (✓). Then act and say with a friend.
1 ✓

8 Lesson 5: Grammar and Speaking

Student's Book page 86

Objectives

Lesson aim: describe animal abilities
Target language: *Monkeys can climb.*
Recycled language: animals, actions
Receptive language: *Don't worry. Where's …? Here's …*
Materials: Video 8B; Audio; Picture cards / Word cards (Animals, Actions 2); Story cards (Unit 8); Mickey Mouse puppet; Cut-outs (Unit 8), with a cut-out model prepared; scissors; (optional) a ball

GSE Skills

Listening: can recognize familiar words in short phrases and sentences spoken slowly and clearly, if supported by pictures or gestures (19); can understand basic action words, e.g., *clap, stamp, jump, walk* (15)

Speaking: can describe the size of everyday objects, using a basic phrase, e.g., *It's big.* (23); can use language related to basic actions, e.g., *clap, stamp, jump, walk* (21)

Teacher toolkit

Video summary – 8B

Monkeys can climb **Videoscript see p.203**
Many different animals live in the savannah, and each one can do different actions. A grown-up Simba and Nala can run and jump, and they can swim together in a watering hole.

Teaching grammar

To help students make connections between the grammar and the real world, search online to find and show videos of real animals doing different actions, e.g., a monkey climbing, a lion running.

Extend

Students do some research about the actions different animals can do. Allow students to choose an animal they want to find out more about, e.g., the elephant. Elicit questions, and go online to find the answers together in class. Alternatively, when students are at home, they research, with an adult's help, to find out what a specific animal can do. In the next lesson, they can share with the class what they have found out, e.g., *Elephants can walk. Elephants can run. Elephants can swim.*

Warm-up

- Greet students with the Mickey Mouse puppet, and sing the *Hello, Stars and Heroes* song (track 0.1).
- Remind students of the story from Lesson 4. Show story cards 2, 3, and 4, and students say: *Peter can run. Maya can walk. Cam can jump.*

Presentation

Video story

1 ▶ **8B Watch. Circle for Simba.**

- As a lead-in to Video 8B, ask students to look once more at the Big Picture in Lesson 1, and remind them of Video 8A and the characters. Point to the different animals, and students say what actions they can do.
- Ask students to look at each of the small pictures and say the corresponding action words (*jump, run, climb, fly*).
- Make the Mickey Mouse puppet stand up. Say: *Sit down, Mickey. It's video time!*
- Play the video, and students do a TPR action when they see each action in the video.
- Ask: *What can Simba do?* Play the video again, pausing at 1:16 (*run*), 1:33 (*jump*), and 1:39 (*swim*). Say: *Simba can …*, and elicit the action verbs.
- Students circle the correct pictures. Note: adult male lions don't usually climb trees because they are too big and heavy.

Practice

2 🎧 **8.10 Match. Then listen, check, and say.**

- Point to the picture of the ladybug, and elicit its name. Say: *Ladybugs can … .* Then point to the pictures of the actions, and elicit the words (*climb, fly, run*). Use your finger to show students how to match the ladybug with the three pictures. Say: *Ladybugs can climb/fly/run?* Elicit answers, then show how to draw the line with your pencil (*fly*).
- Students draw lines to match the pictures of the animals with the pictures of the actions. Point out that some animals can do more than one action.
- Play the audio, and students check their answers. Play the audio again, pausing after each sentence for students to say the sentence.

Audioscript (track 8.10)
1 Ladybugs can fly.
2 Monkeys can climb. And monkeys can run.
3 Zebras can run.

Teaching star

Diversity and inclusion If any students find cutting out difficult and are likely to take a long time to do this, cut out the cards for them. This will give these students more time to practice the vocabulary and structures, and to develop their communicative competence.

LESSON 5
Grammar and Speaking

1 Watch. Circle for Simba.

2 Match. Then listen, check, and say.

3 Listen and say. Then make and play.

Skills: (Monkeys) can (climb).

86

---

3 🎧 **8.11 Listen and say. Then make and play.**

- Students use scissors to cut carefully around the dotted lines of the cut-outs.
- Place your cut-outs face down on the desk in front of you. Make sure you know where the cards for *zebra* and *fly* are, as you will need these for the example.
- Play the first part of the audio, then pause. Turn over the cards for *zebra* and *fly*. Play the next part of the audio, then repeat the sentence: *Zebras can fly.* Ask: *Yes or no?*, and elicit answers.
- Students place their cards on their desk, with the animal cards on one side of the desk and the action cards on the other. Invite a student to turn over an animal card and say the name of the animal. Then invite another student to turn over an action card and say the name of the action. Elicit the sentence from the class, and students answer *yes* or *no*. Repeat the activity several times with different students.

SUPPORT Students can play the game in mixed-ability pairs. They turn over two cards, and the less confident student responds to their partner's sentence with either *yes* or *no*.

STRETCH Students can play the game in mixed-ability pairs. The more confident student uses the cards to make a sentence, e.g., *(Monkeys) can (swim)*, for their partner to respond *yes* or *no*.

Audioscript (track 8.11)
A: *Zebras. Fly.*
B: *Zebras can fly.*
A: *No. It's false.*

Extra activity (class game) Play *Mickey's card* (see Games Bank p.206). For this version, give the Mickey Mouse puppet an animal picture card and an action picture card, but hide them from the class. Students take turns to guess the sentence, e.g., *Zebras can swim*.

Wrap-up
- Play *Throw the ball* (see Games Bank p.206). Ask students to sit or stand in a circle, and throw or roll a ball to each other. Each time they get the ball, students make a sentence, e.g., *Monkeys can climb*.
- Sing the *Goodbye* song (track 0.7), and students say goodbye to the Mickey Mouse puppet as they leave class.

Workbook page 79

Audioscript see p.205
1. 🎧 **8.4 Listen and check (✓).** zebra ✓, ✗, ✗; butterfly ✗, ✗, ✓; lion ✓, ✓, ✗
2. **Follow. Then say.** *Monkeys can climb. Elephants can swim. Birds can fly. Lions can run.*

Lesson 6: Myself and others

Asking for help Student's Book page 87

Objectives

Lesson aim: learn to ask for help
Target language: *I can do it. I need help.*
Recycled language: *I can …*
Materials: Audio; (optional) Video 8B; *Myself and others* poster; Stickers; Mickey Mouse puppet; colored card, pictures of people with different disabilities, paper, crayons, scissors, glue, flip sign you have prepared

GSE Skills

Listening: can recognize familiar words in short phrases and sentences spoken slowly and clearly, if supported by pictures or gestures (19)
Speaking: can say how they feel, using a limited range of common adjectives, e.g., *happy, cold* (22)

Teacher toolkit

Asking for help

In this lesson, students explore different situations in which they might need to ask for help. At this age, students are starting to be autonomous, and need to know when to ask for help. By exploring how they feel when they need help, students will start to understand when they can offer to help others. Encourage students to think of situations when they need help and say, using L1, how they felt when they needed help and when someone helped them.

Self-awareness

Engage

Show pictures of people with various disabilities or mobility issues: a wheelchair user, a blind person, a cane user, a deaf person. Students think about which everyday activities might be challenging for these people, and what help they might need. e.g., when they are getting dressed, catching a bus, or crossing the road.

Home-school link

Remind students to ask for help at home when they need it. Encourage them to say *I need help* and then *I can do it!* when they manage to complete a challenging activity.

Warm-up

- Greet students with the Mickey Mouse puppet, and sing the *Hello, Stars and Heroes* song (track 0.1).
- Use the *Myself and others* poster to review being nice and sharing. Elicit that one way of being nice is by helping people. Using L1, encourage students to suggest different ways they can help people, e.g., helping at home, helping a classmate do an activity, helping in class by handing out materials, etc.

🎵 **1.12 Listen and sing.**

- Play the song audio, and students join in with the words and the actions.
- Ask: *How do you feel today?*, and students respond with *I'm …* and an emotions adjective.

Presentation

1 🔊 **8.12 Listen and point. Then say.**

- Students look at the picture of Simba in the Big Picture in Lesson 1 and say what he can do, e.g., *walk, run, swim*. If necessary, play Video 8B once more.
- Ask students to look at the pictures of Simba and the course characters. Ask: *Who needs help?*, and elicit answers (*Simba and Maya*).
- Play the audio, and students point to the corresponding pictures. Play the audio again, pausing after each sentence for students to repeat.
- Point to the second picture, and ask: *Does Simba need help?* (*no*) Say: *I'm Simba. I can do it!*, and students repeat and act out Simba pouncing.

Audioscript (track 8.12)

1 Simba says, "I need help."
2 Simba says, "I can do it."
3 Maya says, "I need help."

Practice

Teaching star

Social-emotional learning Use the pictures to initiate a discussion and help students understand that people have differing abilities. For example, some people may be able to tie their shoelaces, but other people may not – they may not have learned yet, or they may have a physical disability that makes this activity difficult. Try to foster a positive classroom environment where students offer to help each other when they see a classmate having difficulties.

2 Point and say.

- Point to the first photo, and make the Mickey Mouse puppet say: *I can do it*. Make Mickey look both left and right, and then pretend to cross the road. Do the same with the other photos, making Mickey say: *I need help!*, with tying his shoelaces and putting up a tent. With the last photo, make Mickey say: *I can do it!*, and say: *Mickey can make a pizza. It's yummy!*

178

Asking for help

LESSON 6
Myself and others

1 Listen and point. Then say.

2 Point and say.

3 Make a flip sign. Then play.

Self-awareness: I can do it. I need help.

- Invite a few students to act out in front of the class one of the scenarios elicited at the start of this activity. The other students use their flip signs to respond.
- ⭐ **I'm a hero!** ⭐ Point to the sticker picture, remind students of the story, and elicit that Leyla is helping her friends. Ask: *Is Leyla helping?* (yes) *Do you help?* Then students stick the sticker in their books.

> **Extra activity (whole class / fast finishers)**
> Invite students to write some simple math equations on the board. Give students time to look and think, then use their flip signs to show if they can solve it, or if they need help.

Wrap-up
- Draw students' attention once more to the *Myself and others* poster. Invite students to find any pictures where one person is helping another person.
- Sing the *Goodbye* song (track 0.7), and students say goodbye to the Mickey Mouse puppet as they leave class.

Workbook — page 80

1 Color for you. Then say.
2 Who helps you? Draw.

- Show students a TPR action for *I can do it!* (silent applause or "jazz hands" – shake both hands in the air) and the action for *I need help* (see Teacher toolkit in Lesson 1).
- Point to each photo, and say or elicit the expressions, supporting students as necessary.
- Using L1, ask students about other situations in which they need help. Elicit ideas, prompting as necessary, e.g., buttoning clothes, making a sandwich, reading and writing.

3 Make a flip sign. Then play.
- Point to the photo of the flip sign, then show students the flip sign you have made. Show students both sides of the flip sign, and elicit: *I need help. / I can do it!*
- Students draw pictures for their flip signs, e.g., a happy face (*I can do it!*) and a hand (*I need help.*). Tell them to use red to color the *I can do it!* side and green to color the *I need help* side. Students may need help sticking the sign together.
- Point to one of the photos in activity 2, and students place their sign on their desk to show if they can do it, or if they need help.

8 Lesson 7: My world

Science: Animal needs Student's Book page 88

Objectives

Lesson aims: learn about animal needs
Target language: *food, home, water*
Recycled language: *animals; need*
Materials: Audio; Picture cards / Word cards (Bugs; Nature; Food 1, 2; Animals; Actions 2); Mickey Mouse puppet; photos or videos of lions in their habitats and their lifestyles, A3 card; (optional) a bottle of water and some cheese (or a picture)

GSE Skills

Listening: can recognize isolated words related to familiar topics, if spoken slowly and clearly and supported by pictures or gestures (16)

Reading: can recognize single, familiar everyday words, if supported by pictures (21)

Speaking: can repeat single words if, spoken slowly and clearly (10); can repeat phrases and short sentences, if spoken slowly and clearly (16)

Writing (WB): can copy some short familiar words presented in standard printed form (10)

Teacher toolkit

Cross-curricular

Some students may not have much prior knowledge about the animals in the lesson and may only have seen lions and monkeys in a zoo. Show students a map and pictures of each animal's habitat, or show videos that help students understand where each animal lives and the type of food it eats.

Extend

Place the animal picture cards around the classroom. Students use their hands to make imaginary binoculars, or they can make toy binoculars by taping together two toilet paper tubes. Students "explore the savannah" through their binoculars, and they say what the animals need: *I can see a (bird). (Birds) need water. (Birds) need food.*

Home-school link

If students have a pet at home, ask them to tell or ask their families about what it needs, e.g., food, water. Alternatively, they can ask a friend or neighbor about their pet's needs.

Warm-up

- Greet students with the Mickey Mouse puppet, and sing the *Hello, Stars and Heroes* song (track 0.1).
- Ask students if they asked for help at home, and encourage them to share their responses with the class.
- Play *Up close* (see Games Bank p.206) with several animal picture cards.

Presentation

1 8.13 Listen and point. Then say.

- Use the Mickey Mouse puppet to pre-teach the concepts of a home, food, and water. Say: *Mickey is a mouse.* Tell students that the classroom is Mickey's home. If you keep Mickey in a specific place in the classroom, ask students to point to his "home." Then say: *Mickey needs food* (show students the cheese) *and water* (show students the bottle of water).
- Show students the *bird* picture card. Then point to each photo, and read aloud each of the sentences.
- Play the audio, and students point to each photo. Show students TPR actions for *home* (make a triangle over your head with your arms, like a roof), *water* (mime drinking), and *food* (mime eating). Play the audio again, and students repeat the sentences and do the TPR actions.

SUPPORT Read out the sentences again, and students do the TPR actions.

STRETCH Students work in pairs, taking turns to say a target word (*home/water/food*) for their partner to do the TPR action.

Practice

2 Circle for lions. Then say.

- Show students the *lion* picture card. Say: *Lions need ...,* and elicit *a home, water, food*. If you have photos or videos of lions and their lifestyle and habitat, show them now as examples.
- Point to the photo of the lions, and say: *Lions need a home.* Then point to each photo one by one, and students mime or say if it's a lion's home. Do the same for *Lions need water* and *Lions need food*.
- Students circle the photos showing what lions need.
- Say: *Lions need a home / water / food.*, and students point to the correct photos.

Teaching star

Classroom management Varying classroom dynamics can help engage students. You could allow students to choose how they approach the last step of activity 3: they could describe their picture to a partner, or they could present it to a larger group. You could also work with a group of students to provide support where necessary.

180

LESSON 7
My world — Science

Animal needs

1 🎧 💬 Listen and point. Then say.

1. Birds need a home.
2. Birds need water.
3. Birds need food.

2 💬 ✏️ Circle for lions. Then say.

3 ✏️ 💬 Draw for monkeys. Then say.

Animal needs: food, home, water

88

Thinking skills

Understand In activity 2, students identify and circle the various needs of a lion, using prior knowledge of a lion's habitat and lifestyle. The photos support identification in a new context.

Create In activity 3, students use prior knowledge to identify the needs of a monkey and draw a series of pictures. They describe their pictures, identifying and naming a monkey's needs.

Extra activity (extension) Draw a Venn diagram on the board for monkeys and lions. Elicit what monkeys and lions have in common, and what their differences are. Complete the Venn diagram all together as a class.

Wrap-up

- Say true or false sentences about animals, using the picture cards from Units 6 and 7, e.g., *Monkeys need cake. Yes or no?* Students respond with the TPR action for *yes* or *no*. Try to include humor by saying unusual sentences, e.g., *Elephants can fly.*
- Sing the *Goodbye* song (track 0.7), and students say goodbye to the Mickey Mouse puppet as they leave class.

📝 Workbook — page 81

1 **Look and circle. Then say.** *1 a, Birds need home.; 2 b, Butterflies need water.; 3 a, Lions need food.*

2 **Trace and draw for you.**

3 **Draw for monkeys. Then say.**

- Show students the *monkey* picture card. Say: *Monkeys need …,* and elicit *a home, water, food.*
- Point to the photos in activity 2, and ask students if they show a monkey's home. Elicit ideas about where monkeys live (in or near trees). Do the same with a monkey's food and water. Draw the monkey's home, food, and water on the board.
- Students draw pictures of their ideas in the spaces provided.
- Students compare their drawings with a partner. Encourage them to point and say: *home, water, food.*

SUPPORT Say: *Monkeys need a home / water / food.*, and students point to their corresponding drawings.

STRETCH Students present their drawings to the class, saying: *Monkeys need … .*

Lesson 8: Review

Objectives

Lesson aim: review target language from Unit 8
Target language: animals, actions; *I can …*
Materials: Audio; (optional) Video 8A, Video 8B; Picture cards / Word cards (Animals, Actions 2); Stickers; Mickey Mouse puppet; (optional) students' flip signs from Lesson 6; *My progress* poster

GSE Skills

Listening: can understand basic action words, e.g., *clap, stamp, jump, walk* (15)

Reading: can recognize single, familiar everyday words, if supported by pictures (21)

Speaking: can use language related to basic actions, e.g., *clap, stamp, jump, walk* (21)

Writing: can copy some short familiar words presented in standard printed form (10)

Teacher toolkit

Video review
You can return to Video 8A and Video 8B at the end of the unit for a "second play." Play the videos on mute (without sound), and students say the target vocabulary when they see the related items in the videos.

Remediation
Students display the flip signs they made in Lesson 6 while they are working on activity 1. Walk around the classroom, and pay attention to students' flip signs. If possible, ask students questions, or point to pictures and words in their books to elicit the target language. Make a note of how each student is coping, and plan for additional practice where necessary.

Home-school link
Students share what they've learned in the unit with their families. Encourage them to say what they know about animals they have as toys or animals in story books, e.g., *Lions can run. Lions need a home.*

I can do it! Student's Book page 89

Warm-up
- Greet students with the Mickey Mouse puppet, and sing the *Hello, Stars and Heroes* song (track 0.1).
- Play the game *Which is different?* (see Games Bank p.206).
- Play the song audio from Lesson 3 (track 8.5), and students join in with the words and the actions. If students are confident with the words, play the karaoke version (track 8.5_karaoke).

I can do it!

1 Choose, trace, and say.

- Before the lesson, place the action picture cards on the board, with the word card below each one. Point to each picture card, and elicit: *I can (walk).* For *fly*, shake your head and say, with a sad expression: *I can't fly.*
- Point to the first picture, and say: *Zebras can run. Zebras can fly. Run or fly?* Students say the correct word and do the corresponding TPR action. Do the same with the other animals and action verbs.
- Tell students to trace only the correct action word. Check answers by saying: *(Zebras) can …*, and elicit the correct action word.

ACHIEVE
Students name, read and write action verbs, and say what animals can do.

SUPPORT
Do the activity all together as a class. First say: *(Zebras) can (run).*, and elicit *yes* or *no* answers. When students answer *yes*, encourage them to trace this word in their books.

STRETCH
Students work in pairs, taking turns to point to an animal for their partner to make a sentence about it, e.g., *Elephants can walk.*

2 What can you do? Say.

- Hold up an action picture card, and say: *I can …*, and elicit the action verb, e.g., *swim.* Then ask: *And you?*, and students say *yes* or *no*. Repeat with other actions.
- Students work in pairs, taking turns to say and act out a sentence about what they can do. Encourage students to name other things they can do, using mime where they don't have the vocabulary to describe the actions.

ACHIEVE
Students say what they can do, using *I can …* and action verbs.

SUPPORT
Make statements using *I can …* and TPR actions. Students repeat the sentence and do the TPR action if it is true for them.

STRETCH
Students write *I can …* and *I can't …* sentences that are true for them, then work in pairs to read aloud their sentences.

I can do it!

LESSON 8 Review

1 ✏️ 💬 Choose, trace, and say.

1. run / fly
2. fly / climb
3. climb / walk
4. fly / climb

2 💬 What can you do? Say.

3 💡 ✏️ Think and color. Then stick!

I can ...
1.
2. I can swim
3.

✓ Unit 8!

Go online — Big Project

- Students color the stars next to each objective they can do. Then they stick the reward sticker to show they have completed Unit 8.

My Star and Hero! Students look at the picture of Simba on p.5 of the Student's Book. They imagine they are Simba and say what he can do and what his needs are.

Extra activity (whole class) Give students some challenges to complete, e.g., jump 20 times, run on the spot for 30 seconds, walk backwards to the door. Encourage them to say: *I can do it!*

Wrap-up

- Students reflect on which lesson or activity they most enjoyed in Unit 8. Have a class vote, and choose one activity to do again as a class, e.g., watch the video, sing the song or chant, listen to the story, or play a game.
- Draw students' attention to the *My progress* poster, and ask them to identify the picture that reflects this unit. Read aloud with students the *I can ...* statements (*I can say what animals can or can't do, I can ask for help*).
- Sing the *Goodbye* song (track 0.7), and students say goodbye to the Mickey Mouse puppet, then tell him their favorite word from Unit 8.

Workbook — pages 82–83

My progress

Audioscript see p.205

1. 🎧 8.5 **Listen and match. Then point and say with a friend.** 1 b, 2 a, 3 d, 4 c
2. **What can they do? Circle the odd one out. Then say.** 1 zebra, 2 elephant, 3 tortoise

Units W–8 My practice

1. **What can lions do? Look and check (✓). Then say.** 1 ✓, 2 ✓, 4 ✓, 5 ✓
   Circle your favorite animal. Then say.
2. **Trace. Then find, count, and say.** a 6, b 3, c 8

Unit 8! My favorite activity: Students stick the small star sticker next to their favorite activity.

Teaching star

Growth mindset Tell students to be honest when they color the stars in activity 3. If they don't feel very confident about one of the *I can ...* statements, they can either not color the star or color only a part of it. They can come back later and color the star when they feel more confident that the *I can ...* statement is true for them.

3 💡 **Think and color. Then stick!**

- Point to each picture, and say the *I can ...* statements: *I can name actions. I can sing a song about the things I can do. I can help other people.* For each statement, give an example, and then ask: *Can you do this?* If necessary, explain in L1.
- Students demonstrate what they can do. They work in pairs, taking turns to say the names of animals and what they can do. Give students the opportunity to write the words on the board. Sing the song all together as a class. Students work in pairs, taking turns to say and act out situation where they need to ask for help and then help each other. Monitor and assess students' performance.

9 In the city

Unit objectives

By the end of this unit, students can:
- talk about things in a city
- read and understand a story about being brave on a school trip
- recognize how they can be brave, and learn what to do when they aren't feeling brave
- talk about road safety

Skills development GSE

Listening: recognize things in a city from descriptions, if spoken slowly and clearly and supported by pictures or gestures

Reading: recognize key words and basic phrases in a short, simple cartoon story

Speaking: describe things in a city; talk about being brave; explain how to cross the road

Writing: copy short, familiar words describing things in a city

Vocabulary

Lesson 1: car, house, street, train
Lesson 2: fast, long, new, old, short, slow

Grammar

Lesson 3: It's a fast car.
Lesson 5: It's a train. It's very fast.

Myself and others

Being brave In this unit, a Disney video and a story introduce the theme of being brave. Students will explore different ways of being brave, and will learn what to do when they aren't feeling brave.

Language: That's brave. I'm very brave.

Self-awareness

Story

A school trip
snake; Are you OK? Be nice!

My world

Social Science: Road safety
Go. Look left/right. Stop. Wait.

Disney ZOOTOPIA

Unit overview

Nick
A smart red fox who is great at tricking people. Nick ends up as Judy's sidekick as they work together to solve a case.

Gideon
A red fox who lives in Judy's hometown. Gideon is bigger than the other children and uses his size to bully them. He later apologizes for his bad behavior.

Finnick
A tiny fennec fox and Nick's friend and fellow trickster.

Judy
A young female rabbit who has always dreamed of becoming a police officer. Judy is independent, has a big heart, and tries to make the world a better place.

Zootopia is the city home to all kinds of different animals. Judy Hopps is a young police officer who is finding her new job more difficult than she expected. However, Judy is determined to be an excellent cop.

Video stories
Video 9A: *Good job, Judy!*
Video 9B: *It's a long street*

Did you know?
The Mayor of Zootopia, Lionheart, was inspired by Mufasa from *The Lion King*!

Online modules

Phonics
Words with Yy and Zz in initial position
yellow, zebra

Big Project
Design a car

9 Lesson 1: Vocabulary

Student's Book pages 90–91

Objectives

Lesson aim: name things in a city
Target language: car, house, street, train
Recycled language: colors, clothes, family; big, small; Be nice. Good job!
Receptive language: Be careful! Judy wants to be a police officer. Judy is brave. Ouch! Dinner! It's a long street. It's long.
Materials: Video 9A; Audio; Picture cards / Word cards (City; Clothes 1, 2, Disney characters); Stickers (Judy); Mickey Mouse puppet; (optional) students' small toys

GSE Skills

Listening: can recognize isolated words related to familiar topics, if spoken slowly and clearly and supported by pictures and gestures (16)
Reading: can recognize single, familiar everyday words, if supported by pictures (21)
Speaking: can name everyday objects, animals, or people around them or in pictures, using single words (18)
Writing (WB): can copy some short familiar words presented in standard printed form (10)

Teacher toolkit

Video summary – 9A
Good job, Judy! **Videoscript see p.203**
Judy is a young rabbit who wants to be a police officer. One day, she sees Gideon, a fox, take her friends' raffle tickets, and she bravely confronts him. Later, Judy becomes a police officer and has her first adventure.

Engage
Ask students to bring to class various items to help create a small world city street on a spare table in the classroom, e.g., toy cars, trains, small toy houses, small dolls or figures, toy trees. You could make some buildings by covering empty juice cartons with paper and drawing on windows. During the unit, students rearrange the city street and describe what they see, e.g., *I can see a train. It's long. It's green.*

Being brave
Use the video story to talk about the feelings and behavior of the characters. Elicit how Judy feels in different scenes and how she expresses her emotions, especially when she's being brave at the police academy.
Self-awareness

Warm-up
- Greet students with the Mickey Mouse puppet, and sing the *Hello, Stars and Heroes* song (track 0.1).

Presentation
- Students look at the Big Picture. Introduce the movie and the characters: *This is the movie Zootopia. This is Judy. This is Nick.*
- Ask: *What is Judy wearing? What is Nick wearing?* Elicit answers, using the clothes picture cards for support.

1 9A **Watch. Circle Judy's hat.**
- Make the Mickey Mouse puppet stand up. Say: *Sit down, Mickey. It's video time! Let's watch!*
- Play Video 9A, and students watch and listen.
- Play the video again. Point to each hat picture, and ask: *Is it Judy's hat?* Students respond *yes* or *no*, then they circle the correct hat in their books.

2 9A **Who's brave? Check (✓).**
- Show students a TPR action to express *be brave*, e.g., put your hands on your hips, and make a "superhero" pose.
- Play Video 9A again, and students do the TPR action when they see someone being brave [0:51–1:01; 1:20–1:48].
- Point to each small picture, and ask: *Who's brave?* Students point to the characters they think are brave. Then they check the correct pictures.

Picture cards / Word cards (optional) Show the picture cards one by one to introduce the new vocabulary. Repeat several times, encouraging students to remember the words. Then show each word card, and elicit the words.

Practice

3 9.1 **Listen, point, and say. Then play.**
- Play the audio, pausing after each word. Students point to the city items in the small pictures. Play the audio again, pausing for students to say the words. Play the audio a third time, and students read and say the word.
- Students work in pairs, taking turns to point to a picture for their partner to name.

SUPPORT Say a word, students repeat it, and they point to the correct picture.

STRETCH Students work in pairs, taking turns to describe a picture for their partner to name, e.g., *It's big. It's yellow.*

Audioscript (track 9.1)
1 street // 2 house // 3 car // 4 train

9 In the city

LESSON 1 Vocabulary

1 ▶ ✏️ Watch. Circle Judy's hat.

2 ▶ Who's brave? Check (✓).

3 🎧 💬 Listen, point, and say. Then play.
1. street 2. house 3. car 4. train

4 🎵 Listen, chant, and act. TPR — *This is a street*

Go to page 5

car, house, street, train

---

4 🎵 **9.2 Listen, chant, and act.**

🐭 Display the four picture cards. Make the Mickey Mouse puppet say: *This is a (train)*. Students point to the correct picture card.

• Play the audio, while students listen. When they hear the word for each city item, they point to the correct picture card.

• Devise accompanying TPR actions, and demonstrate as students copy. Play the audio again, and students join in with the chant and do the actions.

Audioscript (track 9.2)
This is a street. A street. A street.
This is a house. A house. A house.
This is a car. A car. A car.
This is a train. A train. A train.
A street, a house, a car, a train. (x2)

❓ **Collect your friend** Show the picture card of Judy to help students identify the correct sticker. Students stick the sticker on p.5 in the Student's Book. Ask: *Who's this?* (Judy).

> **Extra activity (video extension)** Put students into three groups. Play Video 9A, and each group acts out a role, either Judy, Gideon, or the weasel.

Wrap-up

🐭 Play *Talk to Mickey* (see Games Bank p.206). For this version, make the Mickey Mouse puppet say the word in a sentence, e.g., *I can see a car*.

🐭 Sing the *Goodbye* song (track 0.7), and students say goodbye to Mickey as they leave class.

📘 **Workbook** pages 84–85

1 **Watch again. Then check (✓).**
  1 Who's small? *Judy* ✓
  2 What do you see in the video? a ✓, b ✓, c ✓, d ✓
  3 When is Judy brave? b ✓
2 **Look and trace. Then point and say.** *1 street, 2 car, 3 house, 4 train*
3 **Challenge! Find the police clothes. Circle and say.** *a (hat), b (pants), c (shoes)*

187

9 Lesson 2: Vocabulary

Student's Book page 92

Objectives

Lesson aim: name adjectives

Target language: *fast, long, new, old, short, slow*

Recycled language: *city; elephant, lion, tortoise; pencil, ruler; teddy bear; bed, chair, desk, poster; socks*

Materials: Audio; Picture cards / Word cards (Adjectives, City; Room; Toys; School items; Clothes 1, 2; Animals); Mickey Mouse puppet; (optional) old and new items, long and short items

GSE Skills

Listening: can recognize isolated words related to familiar topics, if spoken slowly and clearly and supported by pictures and gestures (16)

Reading: can recognize single, familiar everyday words, if supported by pictures (21)

Speaking: can use a few simple words to describe objects, e.g., color, number, if supported by pictures (19)

Writing (WB): can copy some short familiar words presented in standard printed form (10)

Teacher toolkit

Teaching vocabulary
If possible, bring in a few old and new items students know, e.g., toys, classroom objects, animals. Make sure the items are obviously either new or old. Use these items to distinguish between the concepts of *old* and *new*, e.g., *Look at this ball. It's new. Look at that ball. It's old.* Do the same with long and short items.

Engage
Put students into groups, and give each group one of the vocabulary words (*fast, long, new, old, short, slow*). Each group makes a poster to show their word, using pictures of different objects. They can draw pictures or cut out photos from magazines.

Home-school link
Students use the vocabulary words to describe objects at home to their families. They could bring one of the objects to class and say: *It's my (doll). It's (old).*

Warm-up
- Greet students with the Mickey Mouse puppet, and sing the *Hello, Stars and Heroes* song (track 0.1).
- Play *Faster and faster* (see Games Bank p. 206), using the picture cards from Lesson 1 and from previous units.
- Say: *Listen and chant!*, and play the chant from Lesson 1 (track 9.2). Students join in with the chant and do the actions.

Presentation

Picture cards / Word cards (optional) Show the picture cards one by one to introduce the new vocabulary. Repeat several times, encouraging students to remember the words. Then show each word card, and elicit the words.

1 🎧 **9.3 Listen, point, and say. Then play.**

- Say: *Listen and point.* Play the audio, and students point to the corresponding photos. Play the audio again, pausing after each word. Students point to the corresponding photo and repeat the word.
- Say a word, and students repeat it and point to the corresponding photo.

SUPPORT Say a word, students point to the corresponding photo. Then say the word again for them to repeat.

STRETCH Students work in pairs, taking turns to say an adjective for their partner to find and say the opposite word, e.g., *old – new*.

Practice

2 🎧 **9.4 Listen and put a ✓ or ✗. Then play.**

- Point to the picture of the ruler, and say: *It's a ruler.* Hold up the *long* and *short* picture cards, and ask: *Long or short?* (*long*) Say: *It's a ruler. It's long.* Play the first part of the audio, and students repeat. Give them time to think about whether the sentence is correct or not, then elicit a thumbs-up response. Show students how to put a check in the circle.
- Play the second part of the audio, and students repeat the sentence. Point to the second picture, and elicit a thumbs-down response. Show students how to put an x in the circle.
- Play the remaining sentences, pausing for students to repeat and put their thumbs up or down, then put checks and x's in the circles next to the pictures.
- Point to one of the pictures, and make a true or false statement about it, using the adjectives, e.g., (picture 2) *It's new.* Elicit a thumbs-up or thumbs-down response from the class (thumbs-up).

Audioscript (track 9.4)

1 It's long. // 2 It's old. // 3 It's fast. // 4 It's short. // 5 It's old. // 6 It's slow.

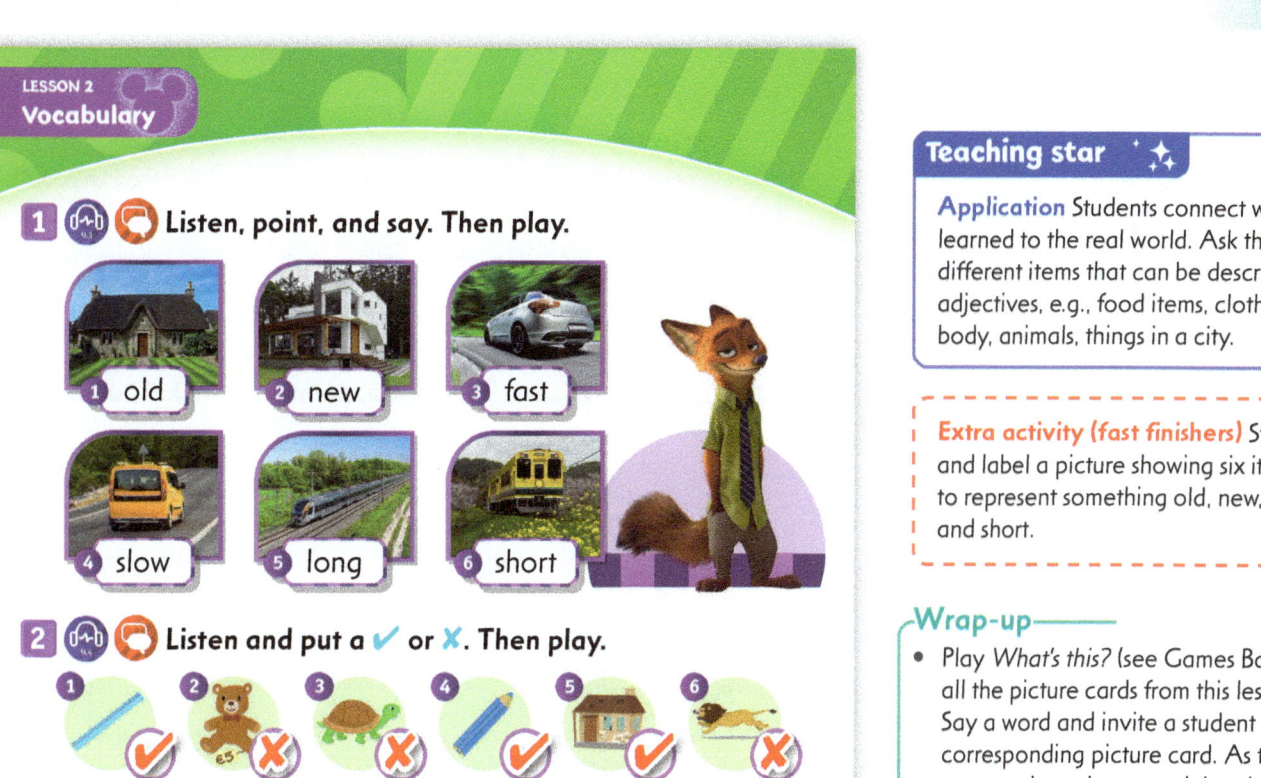

LESSON 2
Vocabulary

1 🎧 💬 **Listen, point, and say. Then play.**

1. old
2. new
3. fast
4. slow
5. long
6. short

2 🎧 💬 **Listen and put a ✓ or ✗. Then play.**

1. ✓ 2. ✗ 3. ✗ 4. ✓ 5. ✓ 6. ✗

3 💬 **Play. Say and guess.**

fast, long, new, old, short, slow

92

3 Play. Say and guess.

- Choose an item from the picture, and describe it, e.g., *It's long. It's green. It's fast.* Students raise their hands, then invite a student to guess the item (*train*).
- Play the game all together as a class. Describe different items, and students point to the item in the picture. Encourage the whole class to call out the answer simultaneously. If they are correct, say: *Good job!* If their answer is wrong, say: *Keep trying!*

SUPPORT Students compare their answer in pairs before they share it with the class.
STRETCH Students play the game in pairs, taking turns to describe an item in the picture for their partner to guess.

Teaching star ✨

Application Students connect what they have learned to the real world. Ask them to think of different items that can be described using the adjectives, e.g., food items, clothes, parts of the body, animals, things in a city.

Extra activity (fast finishers) Students draw and label a picture showing six items, each item to represent something old, new, fast, slow, long, and short.

Wrap-up

- Play *What's this?* (see Games Bank p.206). Place all the picture cards from this lesson face-down. Say a word and invite a student to find the corresponding picture card. As the student turns over each card to reveal the picture, ask him/her to say the word. Ask the class to say *yes* or *no*. Repeat with different students.
- Sing the *Goodbye* song (track 0.7), and students say goodbye to the Mickey Mouse puppet as they leave class.

📝 Workbook   page 86

Audioscript see p.205

1. 🎧 **9.1 Listen and color.** *1 blue, 2 yellow*
2. **Look, trace, and circle. Then say.** *1 long, 2 fast, 3 old*

Picture Dictionary

Students look at the Picture Dictionary on p.109 in the Student's Book and complete the activities. (***Answers:*** *new – old, fast – slow, long – short*)

9 Lesson 3: Grammar

Student's Book page 93

Objectives

Lesson aim: describe objects
Target language: *It's a fast car.*
Recycled language: city
Materials: Audio; Picture cards / Word cards (City, Adjectives); Stickers; Mickey Mouse puppet; a ball; (optional) colored card

GSE Skills

Listening: can recognize familiar words and phrases in short, simple songs or chants (18)
Speaking: can recite a short, simple rhyme or chant (16); can use a few simple words to describe objects, e.g., color, number, if supported by pictures (19)

Teacher toolkit

Teaching grammar
To help students put the parts of a sentence in order correctly, make cards for each of the adjectives in one color and each of the nouns in a different color. Then make cards in a third color for *It's* and *a*. Show students how they can use different adjectives and nouns to make a sentence, e.g., *It's a fast car.*

Extend
Ask students to look out of the window, or take students to the street outside. Ask them to name what they can see, including things in the city (*street, house, car*), people (family vocabulary) and their clothes items, things from nature (*tree, flower*), and actions people are doing (*walk, run*). Encourage students to use adjectives to describe these things, e.g., *It's a long street. It's a fast car. It's an old house.*

Differentiation
Some students may find it difficult to remember to say both the adjective and the noun in a sentence. Give students small word cards showing individual adjectives and nouns. As students listen, they find each word, and then place the corresponding cards on their desk, with the adjective, e.g., *long*, on the left and the noun, e.g., *street*, on the right. This visual cue will help students when they say the sentence, e.g., *It's a long street.*

Warm-up

- Greet students with the Mickey Mouse puppet, and sing the *Hello, Stars and Heroes* song (track 0.1).
- Play *Throw the ball* (see Games Bank p.206) to review vocabulary from Lessons 1 and 2.

Presentation

1 Sing-along 🎵 **9.5 Listen, point, and stick. Then sing and act.**

- Say: *Look at Cam's picture. It's a …*, and elicit *street*. Then say: *It's a street. It's …*, and elicit the adjective *long*. Use the picture cards to prompt, if necessary. Do the same with Peter. Then point to the empty sticker spaces, and students look at their stickers and say what pictures they think Leyla and Maya have drawn.
- Play the song audio, pausing after each verse for students to place the stickers in the correct spaces. Play the song again, and students stick the stickers.
- Review the TPR actions you devised in Lesson 1. Then play the song a third time, and encourage students to join in with some of the words as they do the TPR actions and dance. When students are confident with the words, play the karaoke version (track 9.5_karaoke), and students sing along.

Audioscript (track 9.5)

It's a long street. It's a long street. It's a long street.
It's my town! It's my town!
It's an old house. It's an old house. It's an old house.
It's my town! It's my town!
It's a fast car. It's a fast car. It's a fast car.
It's my town! It's my town!
It's a new train. It's a new train. It's a new train.
It's my town! It's my town!

Practice

2 9.6 Listen and find. Then say.

- Point to the picture of Cam in activity 1, and elicit: *It's a long street.* Do the same with Peter, Leyla, and Maya.
- Play the audio, pausing after each sentence for students to point to the correct picture. Play the audio again, pausing after the first sentence for students to repeat it, then elicit the name of the character who drew the picture. Do the same for all the sentences.
- Invite more confident students to say the sentence for one of the pictures, and the class points to the correct picture.

SUPPORT Say each sentence, and students point to the corresponding picture. Encourage them to repeat the sentence or just the adjective + noun, e.g., *old house*.

Sing-along

1 🎵 **Listen, point, and stick. Then sing and act.** TPR

🎵 It's my town 🎵

2 🎧 **Listen and find. Then say.**

3 💬 **Look and find five differences. Then say.**

Song: It's a (fast) (car).

STRETCH Students work in pairs, taking turns to point to a picture for their partner to say the sentence.

Audioscript (track 9.6)
1 **Leyla:** It's an old house.
2 **Peter:** It's a fast car.
3 **Cam:** It's a long street.
4 **Maya:** It's a new train.

Teaching star ✨

Linguistic competence Model sentence stress in activity 3 by emphasizing the adjective to highlight the difference, e.g., It's a **fast** car. It's a **slow** car. Exaggerate the stress to make it clear. Drill the sentences, asking students to copy your intonation.

LESSON 3 Grammar

3 Look and find five differences. Then say.

- Point to the picture on the left, and say: *It's a long train.* Then point to the picture on the right, and say: *It's a short train. It's different.* Repeat each sentence again, and students point to the corresponding picture.

- Invite a more confident student to point to one of the pictures and make a sentence about it, e.g., *It's an old house.* Then the rest of the class looks at the other picture, finds the house, and notices how it is different. Students raise their hands to answer and make an opposite sentence: *It's a new house.* (**Answers:** It's a long train. It's a short train. It's an old house. It's a new house. It's a fast car. It's a slow car. It's a big tree. It's a small tree. It's a small pond. It's a big pond.)

SUPPORT Make a sentence about the picture on the left, e.g., *It's an old house.* Then students look at the picture on the right. Ask: *Is it an old house?* Students answer *yes* or *no*.

STRETCH Students work in pairs, taking turns to make opposite sentences about each of the pictures and find all five differences, e.g., *It's an old house. / It's a new house.*

Extra activity (fast finishers) Students look at the children's pictures in activity 1. They draw their own picture, and then make up a new verse for the song, e.g., *It's a new house.*

Wrap-up

- Play *Follow the leader* (see Games Bank p. 206). For this version, students mime a fast car, a long train, and other actions.
- 🎵 Sing the *Goodbye* song (track 0.7), and students say goodbye to the Mickey Mouse puppet as they leave class.

📝 **Workbook** page 87

Audioscript see p. 205

1 🔊 **9.2 Listen and circle.** 1 a, 2 b, 3 a, 4 b
2 **Help Judy find Nick. Say what you see.** *It's a new house. It's a fast car. It's a slow car.*

9 Lesson 4: Story

Student's Book pages 94–95

Objectives

Lesson aim: listen to and understand a story about being brave on a school trip

Story language: *snake; Are you OK? Be nice!*

Recycled language: *cry; It's a long snake! Leyla is brave. It's a fast car. I'm nervous. I'm sad.*

Receptive language: *Come on, Peter. Are you OK, Peter?*

Materials: Audio; Story cards (Unit 9); Picture cards (Characters); Mickey Mouse puppet; (optional) pictures of amusement park attractions

GSE Skills

Listening: can understand a few basic words and phrases in a story that is read aloud (18)

Reading: can recognize single, familiar everyday words if supported by pictures (21)

Speaking: can repeat phrases and short sentences, if spoken slowly and clearly (16)

Writing (WB): can copy some short familiar words presented in standard printed form (10)

Teacher toolkit

Story summary
The children are on a school trip to the amusement park. All of them have mixed feelings about some of the activities at the amusement park, but each child is brave in a different way.

Extend
Brainstorm other amusement park attractions, using pictures as prompts, e.g., rollercoasters, slides, bumper cars, water rides. Students can use L1 to describe any other attractions. Then invite students to say which attractions they like and don't like, and whether or not they feel brave about going on them. You could also ask students to imagine they are the story characters, and they say: *I'm brave/nervous/excited.*

Being brave
In the story, Peter doesn't think he is brave because he doesn't want to go on the rollercoaster. However, he shows bravery in other situations. Draw students' attention to how Peter is brave in the school playground. Point out that there are lots of different ways of being brave, and students act out some ways of being brave.

Self-awareness

Warm-up
- Greet students with the Mickey Mouse puppet, and sing the *Hello, Stars and Heroes* song (track 0.1).
- Tell students that Mickey is going on a school trip. They can use L1 to guess where Mickey is going. Then show students story card 2, and tell them that Mickey is going to the amusement park.

Presentation

1 🎧 **9.7 Listen to the story. Point to an old house and a fast car.**

- Make the Mickey Mouse puppet stand up. Say: *Sit down, Mickey. It's story time!*
- Play the audio. Students listen to the story and follow in their books.
- Use the story cards to tell the story again, with or without the audio. Pause after each story frame to ask a comprehension question, e.g., *Is Maya happy?* (no, she's sad) *Is she brave?* (yes) *Does Leyla like snakes?* (no) *Is she brave?* (yes) *Is Peter nervous?* (yes) *Is he sad?* (yes) *Why?* (He thinks he isn't brave.) *Is Peter brave?* (yes).
- Point to the small pictures in the rubric, and elicit *house* and *car*. Students find the old house and the fast car in the story. (**Answers:** frames 1 and 3).

Spot! Students find the rainbow in the story. (**Answer:** in frame 6).

Practice

2 🎧 **9.8 Listen and match.**

- Play the first part of the audio, then pause. Students find the small picture of Peter, then point to the corresponding picture (b). Demonstrate how to draw a line matching picture 1 with picture b, then students draw a matching line in their books. Do the same with the rest of the audio.

Audioscript (track 9.8)

1 **Boy:** *It's a yo-yo.*
  Peter: *Hey! Be nice!*
2 **Leyla:** *Wow! It's a long snake!*
  Peter: *Leyla is brave.*
3 **Cam:** *Come on, Peter. It's a fast car.*
  Peter: *No, thanks, Cam. I'm nervous.*

3 Who's brave? Circle.

- Remind students of the word *brave*, and elicit that Judy was brave in Video 9A in Lesson 1. Students do the TPR action for *brave* (put hands on your hips).
- Show each story card, and students find the scenes where someone is being brave (frames 1, 2, 3, and 6).
- Tell students to circle the people who are brave in the story.
- Say each character's name, and students stand up if they chose that character and act out the situation where the character is being brave.

192

LESSON 4 Story

A school trip

1 Listen to the story. Point to 🏠 and 🛹.

① Peter: Wow. Maya doesn't cry. That's brave.

② It's a long snake!
Leyla: Wow! It's a long snake!
Peter: Leyla is brave.

③ Cam: Come on, Peter. It's a fast car.
Peter: No, thanks, Cam. I'm nervous.

④ No.
Ms. Smart: Are you OK, Peter?
Peter: No. I'm sad. I'm not brave.

⑤ Hey!
Boy: It's a yo-yo.
Peter: Hey! Be nice!

⑥ Wow, Peter!
Maya: Wow, Peter! That's brave.
Peter: Thanks, Maya.

The end

spot!

2 Listen and match.

3 Who's brave? Circle.

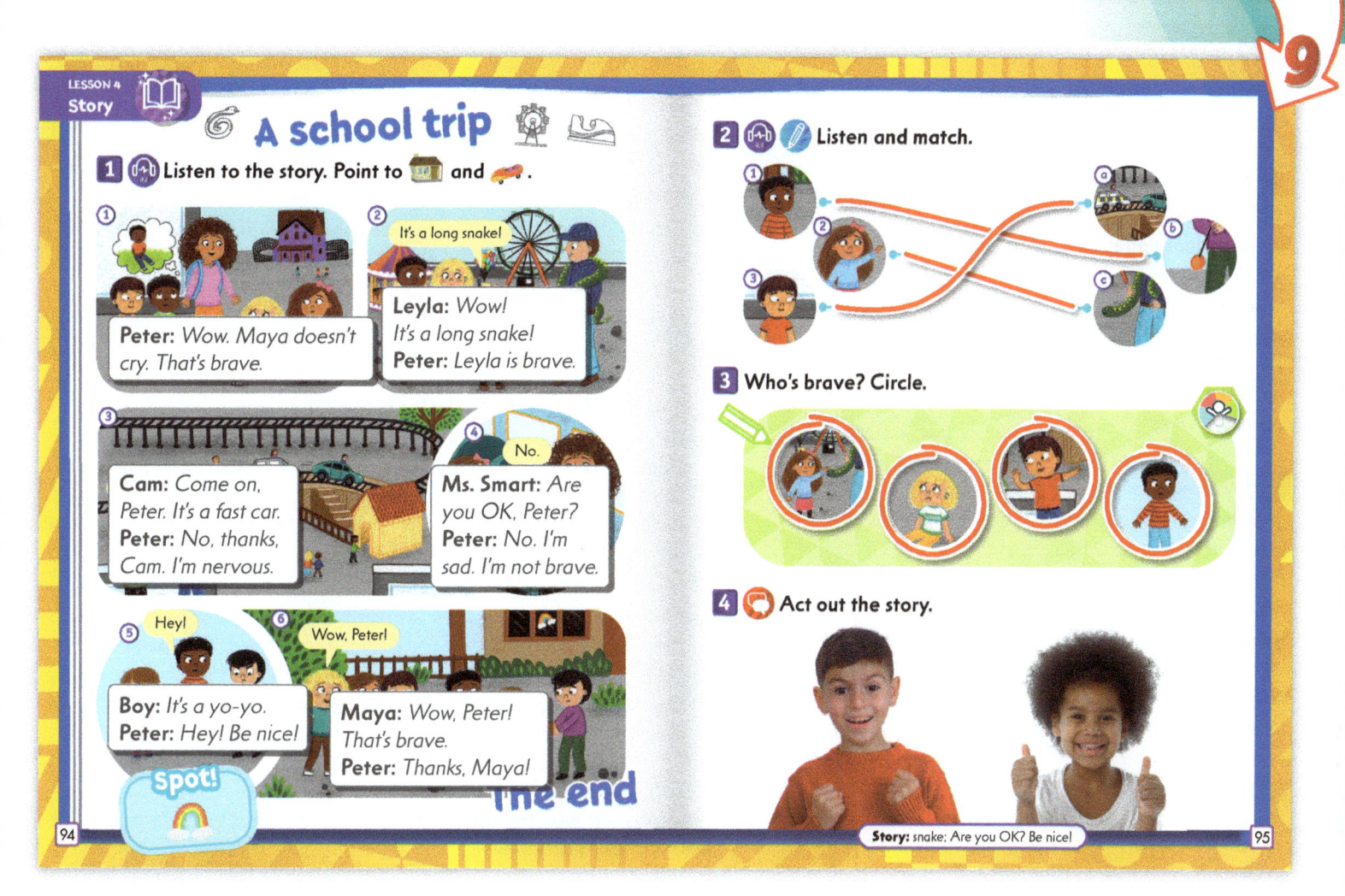

4 Act out the story.

Story: snake; Are you OK? Be nice!

Teaching star

Growth mindset Some students may prefer not to talk as they act out the story. Tell them this is OK, but encourage them to be brave and to say some of the words as you play the audio. When a quieter student is brave enough to talk, say: *Good job! You're brave!*

4 Act out the story.

- Students look at the photos of the boy and the girl. Say: *They can do it! They're brave.*
- Tell students to choose one of the characters: Maya, Leyla, Peter, Cam, Ms. Smart, Boy. Then play the audio, and students act out their scene. Encourage students to repeat the lines for their character as they role-play.

Extra activity (story extension) Place the character picture cards for the four characters in different parts of the classroom. Say sentences from the story, e.g., *It's a long snake!*, and students go to the correct picture card. With large classes, play in groups.

Wrap-up

- Play *Behind the doors* (see Games Bank p.206). Hold your hands in front of your face like two closed doors. Make a face showing an emotion, behind your hands. Ask students to guess the emotion. Then open the two doors and show students your expression. Invite students to play the game in pairs or small groups.
- Sing the *Goodbye* song (track 0.7), and students say goodbye to the Mickey Mouse puppet as they leave class.

Workbook   page 88

Audioscript see p.205

1 **9.3 Listen and check (✓). Then point and say.** *1 a ✓, 2 b ✓*

2 **Match and trace. Then say.** *1 c, 2 a, 3 b*

9 Lesson 5: Grammar and Speaking

Student's Book page 96

Objectives

Lesson aim: describe things in the city
Target language: *It's a train. It's very fast.*
Recycled language: colors, city, adjectives; *What's this?*
Receptive language: *Be careful, Nick. Brrr. Popsicles!*
Materials: Video 9B; Audio; Picture cards / Word cards (City, Adjectives); Mickey Mouse puppet; Story cards (Unit 9); Cut-outs (Unit 9), with a cut-out model prepared; scissors

GSE Skills

Listening: can identify everyday objects, people, or animals in their immediate surroundings or in pictures from short, basic descriptions, e.g., color, size, if spoken slowly and clearly (19)

Speaking: can use a few simple words to describe objects, e.g., color, number, if supported by pictures (19)

Writing (WB): can copy some short familiar words presented in standard printed form (10)

Teacher toolkit

Video summary – 9B
It's a long street **Videoscript see p.203**
Judy is at work when she sees Finnick, a very small fox. Judy follows Nick and Finnick to a cold, snowy place, where she discovers Nick and Finnick's secret plan.

Teaching grammar
Place in a row on the board the city picture cards. Then place the adjectives picture cards in a second row. Point to one picture card in the top row, and elicit: *It's a (train)*. Then point to one adjective picture card in the bottom row, and elicit: *It's (long)*. Repeat with other pairs of picture cards.

Extend
Play scenes from the different videos in Units 1 to 9, and students describe what they see, using the target structures, e.g., *It's a (train). It's very (fast). I can see a ….*

Warm-up

- Greet students with the Mickey Mouse puppet, and sing the *Hello, Stars and Heroes* song (track 0.1).
- Remind students of the story from Lesson 4. Show story card 4. Say: *It's a fast car!* Students stand behind you in a line, with their hands on the shoulders of the person in front of them. Pretend you are all on a rollercoaster, moving up, moving down, and turning from side to side.

Presentation

1 9B **Watch. What color is the car? Check (✓).**

- As a lead-in to Video 9B, ask students to look once more at the Big Picture in Lesson 1, and remind them of Video 9A and the characters. Point to the picture, and elicit: *It's a long street. It's a fast/slow car. It's an old house. / It's a new house.* Then point to different vehicles in the picture, and ask: *What color is the car?*
- Make the Mickey Mouse puppet stand up. Say: *Sit down, Mickey. It's video time!*
- Point to each color splotch, and elicit the color word. Then point to the small picture of the car, and ask: *What color is the car?*
- Play Video 9B, and students point to the correct color splotch. Then students check the circle next to it.

Practice

Teaching star

Learning to learn Demonstrate how to use actions to help students remember the rhythm of each sentence, e.g., *It's* (clap hands) *a* (slap right thigh) *train* (slap left thigh). *It's* (clap hands) *very* (hold up right palm, then left palm) *fast* (slap both thighs). Encourage students to use this technique whenever they have to remember a longer phrase or sentence.

2 9.9 **Listen and number. Then play.**

- Students look at the pictures and name the things they see.
- Play the first part of the audio, and students point to the correct picture. Do the same for the remaining parts of the audio.
- Play the audio again, pausing for students to number the pictures. Play the audio a third time, and students repeat the sentences as they point to the pictures.
- Provide sentence starters to prompt students: *It's a … It's very …*, and students complete each sentence with a noun and an adjective, for their partner to point to the corresponding picture.

SUPPORT Describe one of the pictures, and students repeat the sentence as they point to the picture.

STRETCH Students work in pairs, taking turns to describe a picture for their partner to point to.

LESSON 5
Grammar and Speaking

1 ▶ Watch. What color is the 🚗? Check (✓).

2 🎧 ✏️ Listen and number. Then play.

3 🎧 💬 Listen and point. Then make and play.

Skills: It's a (train). It's very (fast).

Audioscript (track 9.9)
1 It's a train. It's very fast.
2 It's a car. It's very fast.
3 It's a street. It's very short.
4 It's a car. It's very old.

3 🎧 **9.10 Listen and point. Then make and play.**

- Students use scissors to cut carefully around the dotted lines of the cut-outs. Then they place their dominoes face up on their desks.
- Place all the cut-out picture dominoes on your desk, face up. Play the audio, and hold up the corresponding card (with a small house). Play the audio again, and students find the same card on their desks.
- Point to the other picture on your domino, and say: *It's a street. It's short.* Ask: *Can you see a street?* Find the other domino with a short street, and place it next to the first domino so that the two pictures are next to each other. Students do the same.

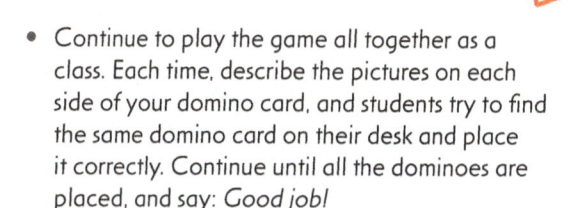

- Continue to play the game all together as a class. Each time, describe the pictures on each side of your domino card, and students try to find the same domino card on their desk and place it correctly. Continue until all the dominoes are placed, and say: *Good job!*

SUPPORT Students can play the game in mixed-ability pairs with one set of cards and each student taking four cards. The less confident student says single words to describe the thing in the city, e.g., *train, long*.

STRETCH Students can play the game in mixed-ability pairs. The more confident student says full sentences to describe the thing in the city, e.g., *It's a train. It's very long.*

Audioscript (track 9.10)
It's a house. It's very small. // Yes.

> **Extra activity (fast finishers)** When students have finished playing, they cut their dominoes in half so that each picture is on a separate card. Then they can work in pairs to play a card game, e.g., taking turns to put down single cards to find matching pairs.

Wrap-up
- Play *Draw it!* (see Games Bank p. 206). For this version, ask students to guess short phrases, e.g., *I can see a short train.*
- Sing the *Goodbye* song (track 0.7), and students say goodbye to the Mickey Mouse puppet as they leave class.

📝 Workbook   page 89

1 **Match. Then say.** *1 c, 2 a, 3 b*
2 **Circle the odd one out. Then say.** *1 It's very old. 2 It's very small. 3 It's very long.*

Lesson 6: Myself and others

Being brave **Student's Book page 97**

Objectives

Lesson aim: identify brave actions and behaviors
Target language: *That's brave. I'm very brave.*
Recycled language: *happy, sad, excited, nervous, grumpy*
Materials: Audio; (optional) Video 9A; *Myself and others* poster; Stickers; Mickey Mouse puppet; Story cards (Unit 9); the mood-o-meter from Unit 3; (optional) cards for Teacher toolkit

Skills

Listening: can recognize familiar words in short phrases and sentences spoken slowly and clearly, if supported by pictures or gestures (19)
Speaking: can say how they feel, using a limited range of common adjectives, e.g., *happy, cold* (22)

Teacher toolkit

Being brave

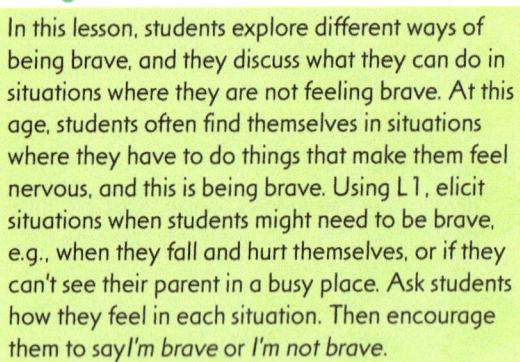

In this lesson, students explore different ways of being brave, and they discuss what they can do in situations where they are not feeling brave. At this age, students often find themselves in situations where they have to do things that make them feel nervous, and this is being brave. Using L1, elicit situations when students might need to be brave, e.g., when they fall and hurt themselves, or if they can't see their parent in a busy place. Ask students how they feel in each situation. Then encourage them to say *I'm brave* or *I'm not brave*.

Self-awareness

Engage

Use the 'mood-o-meter' you made in Unit 3 to help students show how brave they feel about the different activities and situations discussed in the lesson. Stick a photo above the mood-o-meter, showing someone brave, e.g., a superhero, or Merida from the movie *Brave*. Invite individual students to go and move the arrow as you discuss the activities in the lesson, according to how brave they feel about it.

Home-school link

Encourage students to keep a bravery diary. They can draw a picture any time they feel that they were brave or they weren't brave. Invite a few students to share their diaries with the class during each lesson, saying: *I'm (not) brave.*

Warm-up

- Greet students with the Mickey Mouse puppet, and sing the *Hello, Stars and Heroes* song (track 0.1).
- Use the *Myself and others* poster to review the focus of asking for help. Remind students of how Simba needed help, then ask: *Is Simba brave?*, and elicit answers.

🎵 **1.12 Listen and sing.**

- Play the song audio, and students join in with the words and the actions.
- Ask: *How do you feel?*, and students respond, e.g., *I'm (happy)!*

Presentation

1 🎧 **9.11 Listen and point. Then say.**

- Remind students of the story from Lesson 4. Hold up the story cards, and tell the story together, encouraging students to join in with the words. Then ask: *Who's brave?*, and elicit answers.
- Point to the picture of Judy, and ask: *Is Judy brave?* If necessary, play Video 9A again before eliciting answers (yes – Judy is brave when she stands up to Gideon and when she chases the thief).
- Point to the other pictures, and ask: *Brave or not brave?* Students say the words or do the TPR action for *brave* (hands on hips) or *not brave* (hands covering face).
- Play the audio, and students point to the pictures. Play the audio again, and students repeat the sentences.

Audioscript (track 9.11)
1 That's brave, Judy.
2 That's brave, Maya.
3 That's brave, Leyla.
4 That's brave, Peter.

Practice

2 **What do you do when you don't feel brave? Circle.**

- Remind students of Simba from *The Lion King* in Unit 8 and how he needed to ask for help. Point out that Simba was in a dangerous situation, and being brave wasn't the best option for him.
- Point to each picture, and scaffold the meaning of each action, using mime (1 laugh, 2 ask for help, 3 imagine the scary thing / creature as something small and nice, 4 ask a friend to go with you).
- Model the activity by miming being scared, and say: *I don't feel brave. I (ask my friend to come with me).*
- Students circle one or more pictures according to what they do when they don't feel brave.

Being brave

LESSON 6 — Myself and others

1 Listen and point. Then say.

Listen and sing.

2 What do you do when you don't feel brave? Circle.

3 How do you feel? Color and tell a friend.

not brave | brave | very brave

I'm a hero!

Self-awareness: That's brave. I'm (very) brave.

97

- Model the activity with the scenario shown in the first photo. Say: *It's very big! I'm nervous.* Then say: *I feel very brave / I feel brave / I don't feel brave,* according to how you feel about it. Then color in the boxes (or move the arrow if you made a card mood-o-meter).
- Give students time to think about the scenario in each photo and color in the boxes.
- Students work in pairs to compare their mood-o-meters, saying *brave / very brave / not brave.* Encourage them to say how they feel in each scenario and what they do when they don't feel brave, e.g., *ask for help.*

★ **I'm a hero!** ★ Point to the sticker picture, and ask: *Is Peter brave?* (yes) *Are you brave?* Students stick the sticker in their books.

> **Extra activity (class game)** Students stand up. Describe a situation where students might need to be brave, using picture cards and gesture to support meaning, e.g., *I can see a big lion. / It's a long snake. / It's a monster. / I can fly. / I climb a big tree.* Students mime and say *brave / very brave / not brave.*

Wrap-up
- Point to the *being brave* picture on the *Myself and others* poster, and students say if they feel brave, very brave, or not brave. If they don't feel brave, they say what they do.
- Sing the *Goodbye* song (track 0.7), and students say goodbye to the Mickey Mouse puppet as they leave class.

Workbook — page 90

Audioscript see p.205

1 🎧 **9.4 Listen and color for Leyla. Then point and say.** *1 one box, 2 three boxes, 3 two boxes*

2 **Make a bravery badge. Color the stars for you.**

Teaching star ✦

Social-emotional learning Discuss how being brave can mean different things for different people. Being brave is about confronting our fears, and something that isn't scary for one person may be terrifying for another. Ask students how they can be nice and show concern for each other when they don't feel brave, using the pictures in activity 2.

3 How do you feel? Color and tell a friend.

- If you have made a mood-o-meter (see Teacher toolkit), show students how it works. Alternatively, you could draw the mood-o-meter on the board. Each picture has three boxes to color in, one for each section of the mood-o-meter: three boxes — very brave, two boxes — brave, one box — not brave.

Lesson 7: My world

Objectives

Lesson aims: learn about road safety
Target language: *Go. Look left/right. Stop. Wait.*
Recycled language: *street, car; left, right*
Materials: Audio; Picture cards (City, Adjectives); Mickey Mouse puppet; model or template of traffic lights, card, scissors; (optional) picture of traffic lights and crosswalks

GSE Skills

Listening: can recognize isolated words related to familiar topics, if spoken slowly and clearly and supported by pictures or gestures (16)
Reading: can recognize single, familiar everyday words, if supported by pictures (21)
Speaking: can repeat single words, if spoken slowly and clearly (10); can repeat phrases and short sentences, if spoken slowly and clearly (16)
Writing (WB): can copy some short familiar words presented in standard printed form (10)

Teacher toolkit

Cross-curricular
This lesson is all about road safety. Discuss the road safety rules in your country, and make sure students know which way to look first before they cross the road.

Extend
Create a song or chant about road safety with the class, with accompanying TPR actions, e.g., *What color is the light? It's red. Stop!* (lift your arm straight in front of you with your palm flat) *What color is the light? It's yellow. Wait!* (lift your arm to the side with your hand slightly raised) *What color is the light? It's green. Go! Go! Go!* (walk on the spot).

Home-school link
Ask students to notice how they use the roads safely with their families. Ask them to draw pictures of one or more situations where they practice road safety, e.g., waiting at a crosswalk, wearing a seatbelt when they are in a car.

Social Science: Road safety   Student's Book page 98

Warm-up
- Greet students with the Mickey Mouse puppet, and sing the *Hello, Stars and Heroes* song (track 0.1).
- Play *Where is ...?* (see Games Bank p.206) using the unit picture cards.

Presentation

1 🎧 **9.12 Listen and point. Then say.**
- Before the lesson, set up a space at the front of the classroom between you and the students, to represent a street. You could place some strips of paper along the "street" as road markers.
- Use the Mickey Mouse puppet to introduce the idea of crossing the road safely. Stand with Mickey at the other side of the "street." Invite two students to stand at either end of the street and act out driving cars along the street. Make Mickey attempt to cross the road. Say: *No, Mickey! Stop! Look*. Make Mickey look left and right (see Cross-curricular overview in Teacher toolkit), then cross the road safely.
- Students look at the photos. Pre-teach each of the words and phrases.
- Play the audio, and students point to the corresponding photos. Play the audio again, and students do TPR actions with you. Play the audio a third time, and students repeat the words or phrases and do the TPR actions.

SUPPORT Say the words or phrases, and students do the TPR action.
STRETCH Students work in pairs, taking turns to say one of the words or phrases for their partner to do the corresponding TPR action.

Practice

2 🎧 **9.13 Number in order. Then listen and check.**
- Point to the picture, and ask students what the animals should do when they cross the road. Elicit ideas, asking students to say the words or phrases, or point to the photos in activity 1.
- Point to and read aloud each word. Students do the TPR actions.
- Ask students what the animals should do first. Point to each word, say it, and elicit *yes* or *no*. Hold up one finger, and say: *Stop*. Hold up a second finger, and elicit what the animals should do next (*Wait.*). Do the same for the remaining actions.
- Students number the words from 1 to 4.
- Play the audio, and students do the TPR actions and check their answers.

Audioscript (track 9.13)
First you stop.
Then you wait.
Look left and look right, and look left.
Then you can go.

Teaching star

Classroom management In activity 3, use the street you set up in the classroom for activity 1. Depending on how large the "street" is, invite one group at a time to act out the role-play game in activity 3.

LESSON 7
My world — Social Science

Road safety

1 🎧 💬 **Listen and point. Then say.**

1. Stop.
2. Go.
3. Wait.
4. Look right.
5. Look left.

2 🎧 ✏️ **Number in order. Then listen and check.**

- [4] Go.
- [1] Stop.
- [2] Wait.
- [3] Look.

3 ✏️ 💬 **Make. Then act.** TPR

"Look left and look right."

Road safety: Go. Look left / right. Stop. Wait.

Thinking skills

Apply In activity 2, students identify and number the instructions in order to help the animals cross the road safely. The picture supports identification in a new context.

Create In activity 3, students make their own set of traffic lights to support them with giving road safety instructions. They use their traffic lights to give and follow instructions.

Extra activity (extension) Turn the focus to driving, and elicit ideas about how we can be safe in a car, e.g., driving slowly, looking out for obstacles or people, not listening to loud music or talking on the phone.

Wrap-up
- Play *Mickey says* (see Games Bank p.206), using the language from the lesson.
- Sing the *Goodbye* song (track 0.7), and students say goodbye to the Mickey Mouse puppet as they leave class.

Workbook — page 91

1 **Trace. Color green or red. Then say.** *1 red, 2 red, 3 green*

2 **Color and circle. Then say.** *1 red, stop; 2 red, wait; 3 green, go*

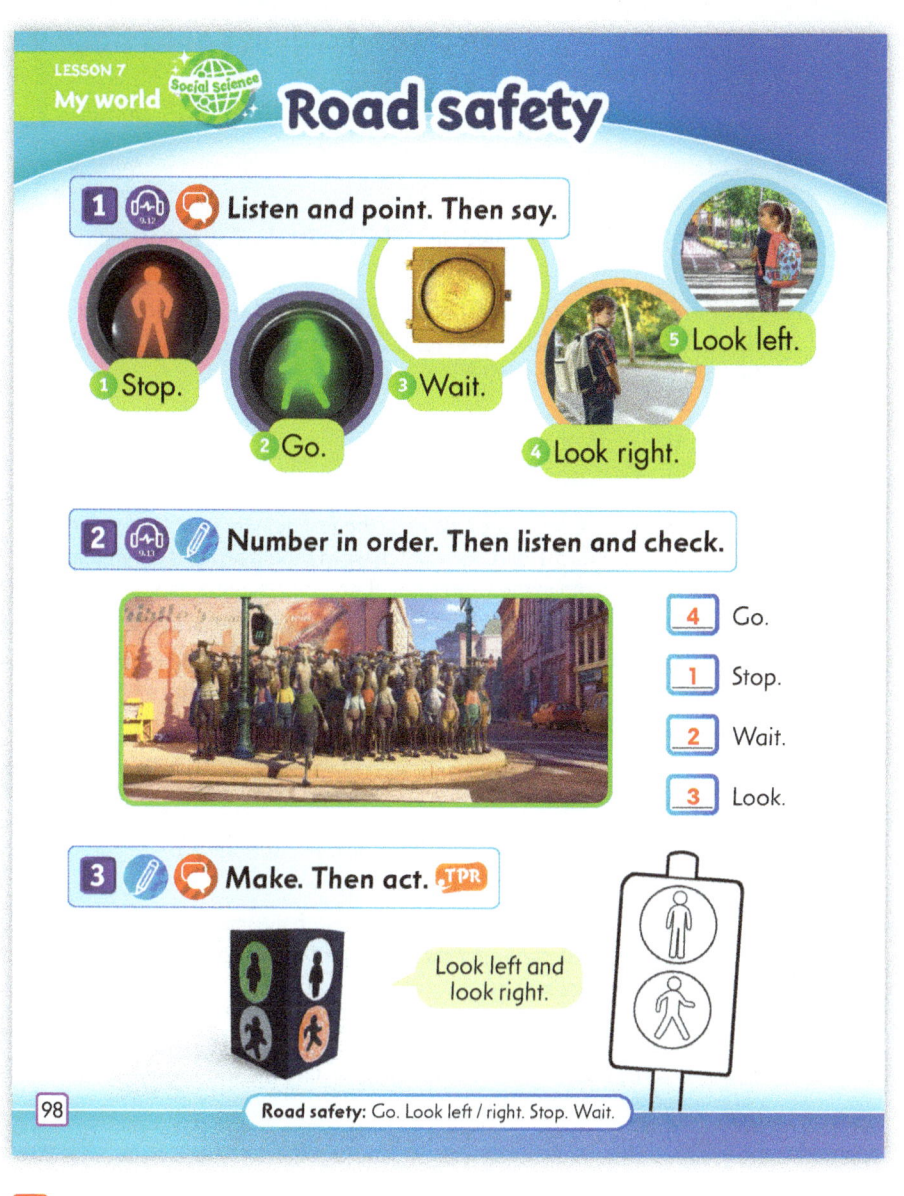

---

3 Make. Then act.

- Before the lesson, make a model of the traffic lights. Fold a piece of card in half, then draw and stick traffic lights on each side, as shown in the photo. Alternatively, make a traffic light template for each student.
- Point to the picture of the traffic lights on the right, and elicit what color each light should be (top – red, bottom – green). Then students color the traffic lights, as a model.
- If possible, give students a template with circles to cut out. Students draw two standing figures and two walking figures in the circles. Then they color one traffic light green and another red. Students cut out the circles, then stick the lights onto their piece of card.
- Call out instructions, using the verbs in activity 1, and students point to the correct traffic light.
- Invite three students to the front of the class. One student operates the traffic lights, another gives instructions according to the traffic lights, and the third student crosses the road.
- Students play the game in groups of three.

9 Lesson 8: Review

Objectives

Lesson aim: review target language from Unit 9
Target language: city, adjectives; *It's a …*
Materials: Audio; (optional) Video 9A, Video 9B; Picture cards / Word cards (City, Adjectives); Stickers; Mickey Mouse puppet; (optional) small word cards for the vocabulary; *My progress* poster

GSE Skills

Listening: can recognize isolated words related to familiar topics, if spoken slowly and clearly and supported by pictures and gestures (16)
Reading: can recognize single, familiar everyday words, if supported by pictures (21)
Speaking: can say single words related to familiar topics, if supported by pictures or gestures (18)
Writing: can label simple pictures related to familiar topics by copying single words (16)

Teacher toolkit

Video review
Play Video 9A and Video 9B again. Invite students to the front of the class, and give each student a word card. Encourage the rest of the class to describe what they see in the video. If a student at the front hears their word, they hold up their word card.

Remediation
Show students the picture cards in pairs: an old house, a new house, a fast car, a slow car, a long train, a short train. With each pair of items, say the adjective + noun, e.g., *an old house*, and students repeat the phrase and point to the correct picture cards. Play the song from Lesson 3 (track 9.5) for additional support and practice.

Home-school link
Ask students to make a city street at home using recycled milk and juice containers. They can draw windows on the containers and place them along a "street." They can use small dolls and toy cars, and describe their street to their families as they play.

I can do it! Student's Book page 99

Warm-up
- Greet students with the Mickey Mouse puppet, and sing the *Hello, Stars and Heroes* song (track 0.1).
- Play the game *Circle it!* (see Games Bank p.206), using picture cards and word cards.
- Play the song audio from Lesson 3 (track 9.5), and students join in with the words and the actions. If students are confident with the words, play the karaoke version (track 9.5_karaoke).

I can do it!

1 Trace and write.
- Students look at all the photos. Point to the first activity item, and say: *mmm house*. Point to photo 1 and elicit which word should replace *mmm* (*old*). Point to the word *old* in the word pool, then point again at the word gap.
- Do the same with the other activity items, pointing to the words, the word gaps and the word pool, and eliciting the correct words to complete the gaps.
- Students trace and write the words in their books.

> **ACHIEVE**
> Students read and write adjectives and things in a city to describe pictures.
>
> **SUPPORT**
> Do the activity all together as a class. For each missing word, point to the word in the word pool, and students point to the same word, then copy it into their books.
>
> **STRETCH**
> Students work in pairs to look at the picture, find the missing word, then write and trace in their books.

2 9.14 Listen and find. Then say.
- Play the audio, pausing after each sentence for students to point to the correct photos. Play the audio again, and students repeat the sentences.
- Students work in pairs, taking turns to say a sentence about one of the photos for their partner to point to.

Audioscript (track 9.14)

It's a long train. It's very long.
It's an old house. It's very old.
It's a fast car. It's very fast.
It's a slow car. It's very slow.
It's a new house. It's very new.
It's a short train. It's very short.

LESSON 8 Review

I can do it!

1 ✏️ Trace and write.

long old slow car house

1. old house
2. new house
3. long train
4. short train
5. fast car
6. slow car

2 🎧 👁️ Listen and find. Then say.

3 💡✏️ Think and color. Then stick!

I can ...
1. 🏠
2. 🎵 It's my town 🎵
3. 🦸

✅ Unit 9!

Go online — Big Project

- Students color the stars next to each objective they can do. Then they stick the reward sticker to show they have completed Unit 9.

My Star and Hero! Students look at the picture of Judy on p.5 of the Student's Book. They imagine they are Judy and act out being brave.

Extra activity (class survey) As this is the final lesson in the book, ask students which unit was their favorite. They write the number of the unit on a small slip of paper, fold it up, and put it into a bag or hat. Take out all the votes, count them up, and reveal how many students liked each unit.

Wrap-up

- Draw students' attention to the *My progress* poster, and ask them to identify the picture that reflects this unit. Read aloud with students the *I can …* statements (*I can describe things in the city, I can be brave*).
- Tell students *Good job!*, and give them a round of applause for completing the book. Encourage them to say *Good job!* to each other.
- 🎵 Sing the *Goodbye* song (track 0.7), and students say goodbye to the Mickey Mouse puppet for the last time this year.

Workbook   pages 92–93

My progress

Audioscript see p.205

1. 🎧 **9.5 Listen and draw. Who does Ms. Smart see? Circle.** *1 b, 2 c, 3 a*
2. **Who does Ms. Smart see? Play with a friend.**

Units W–9 My practice

1. **Look and number. Then say.** *(from top to bottom) 4, 1, 3, 2*

   Color the animals. Circle the food. Then say. *color: monkey, zebra, elephant; circle: apple, ice cream, sandwich*

2. **Draw your house. Then say.**

Unit 9! My favorite activity: Students stick the small star sticker next to their favorite activity.

ACHIEVE
Students understand descriptions of things in a city and match them to pictures. They use adjectives to describe things in a city.

SUPPORT
Students say individual words (e.g., *train*, *long*) or make very simple sentences (e.g., *It's a train. It's long.*).

STRETCH
Students identify and describe items in different pictures across the units in their books.

3 💡 **Think and color. Then stick!**

- Point to each picture, and say the *I can …* statements: *I can name things in a city. I can sing a song. I can be brave.* For each statement, give an example, and then ask: *Can you do this?* If necessary, explain in L1.
- Students demonstrate what they can do. They work in pairs, taking turns to say the names of or describe different things in a city. Give students the opportunity to write the words on the board. Sing the song all together as a class. Students work in pairs, taking turns to say and act out being brave. Monitor and assess students' performance.

Videoscript

Welcome

Lesson 1 Video 0A *Say hello with Nemo!*
Look! It's Nemo and Marlin. Nemo is orange, white, and black. It's time for school. Wow! Look at the fish. Red and purple, green and blue. Wow! Ha-ha! This is Nemo. Say *hello* Nemo. Pearl says: "Hi! I'm Pearl. I'm pink." Wow! It's the teacher. He's blue and white. He says, "Hello!" Nemo says, "Bye!"

Unit 1

Lesson 1 Video 1A *Merida's family*
This is Merida. Mm! Shh! Look! Merida's family. This is Dad. And Merida's brothers. They love stories. This is Mom. Merida's brothers love cake. Who's this? Oh! It's Merida's mom. She's a bear now. Oops! Ouch! Look! Here's Merida. Wow! Merida's happy!

Lesson 5 Video 1B *Who's this?*
Look! A forest. This is Merida and this is mom. It's fun! Where's Merida? Merida! And who's this? Oh! This is dad. Wow! A present! Oops! Where is it? Here!

Unit 2

Lesson 1 Video 2A *At school with Mike*
This is Mike. This is Mike's school. Wow! Wee! Let's play! Come on, Mike! Here's Mike's room. Uh! Who's this? Oh, it's Randall. Mike and Randall are friends. Where's Randall? Oh, there he is! Look! A bed, a desk, and posters. Mike's happy. Who's this? Sulley! Mike is grumpy. Sulley! Hahaha!

Lesson 5 Video 2B *Is it a bed?*
It's Mike and Sulley's new house. It's big. Hello! Is it a table? Yes. It's small. Look! Oops! Mm. Thanks. It's Mike and Sulley's room. Is it a bed? Yes, it's a bed. Ouch! It's small. Mike and Sulley are grumpy. O-oh! Good night, Mike. Good night, Sulley.

Unit 3

Lesson 1 Video 3A *Bonnie's toys*
This is Woody. Woody is Bonnie's toy and her friend. Oh, no! Bonnie's sad. Look! It's Mom and Dad. Dad says: "Let's go, Bonnie." Oh! Where's Woody? There he is. In Bonnie's backpack. It's Bonnie's school. It's big. Look at the children! This is the teacher. Bonnie says: "Bye, Mom!" Bonnie's nervous. Let's make a toy. Oh, no! What's Woody doing? Crayons! A pencil. It's blue. Bonnie says: "Hmm. Let's make a toy." Who's this? Wow! It's Forky! Bonnie's happy. And Woody's happy. And look! It's Mom and Dad! Yeah!

Lesson 5 Video 3B *How many?*
Look! It's Bonnie. How many backpacks? One. One backpack. How many beds? One. One bed. It's big. Look! How many toys? Two. Two toys. It's Woody and Forky. Woody says: "Good night."

Unit 4

Lesson 1 Video 4A *Wake up, Elsa!*
Look! A castle. It's big. This is Elsa. Shh! Who's this? It's Anna. Anna is Elsa's sister. Anna says: "Wake up, Elsa! Come on, let's play!" Wee! Wow! Snow! Yippee! Is it a ball? No, it's a snowman. A body, a head, a nose, and two arms. He's white. Hello, Olaf! Let's dance. Wee!

Lesson 5 Video 4B *It's a nose*
Hi, Sven! He's excited. Look! It's Anna and Kristoff. What's this? It's Sven's head. Who's this? Olaf! What's this? It's a nose. It's big. One head, one body, and how many arms? Two arms. Olaf says: "Hi, Sven!" Ah! Be careful, Olaf!

Unit 5

Lesson 1 Video 5A *Keep trying, Mulan!*
This is Mulan. Mm! Oops! Who's this? It's Mulan's dad. Look! Mulan's skirt is white. Wow. Mulan is a soldier now. Mulan's sad. Mulan says: "Goodbye, Mom. Goodbye, Dad." Shh… Look! Mulan's shoes are black. Good morning! It's Mushu. Look. Mulan's pants are brown. Breakfast! Let's go! Look! Mulan's socks are white. Keep trying! Oh, no! Ouch… Keep trying, Mulan! Wow! Yippee! Good job, Mulan!

Lesson 5 Video 5B *I'm wearing my pants*
Who's this? It's Mulan's mom. It's Mulan. Mulan says, "I'm wearing my skirt. My skirt is white." Mulan's mom says, "Come on, Mulan." Wow! Now Mulan says, "I'm wearing my shirt. My shirt is blue." Hmm. Let's play. Mulan is a soldier. She's nervous. Mulan says, "Help me, Mushu!" Mushu says, "Let's go!" Look! Mulan says, "I'm wearing my pants. My pants are brown." Oh, Mulan! Hahaha

Unit 6

Lesson 1 Video 6A *Flik's adventure*
I can see ants. This is Flik. He's going on an adventure. Who's this? They're Flik's friends. Mm. I can see a red and black ladybug. What's this? It's a bird! Atta says, "Let's all help!" The ants all help. The ants say, "Yeah!" Wow! Look at the bird! Keep trying. Good job, team!

Lesson 5 Video 6B *I can see a beetle*
I can see an ant. What color is it? It's purple. Oh! It's Dot! Look. Who's this? Is it Flik? Yes. It's Flik. Flik says, "Hello, Dot." Ahhhh. I can see a beetle. It's Dim. What color is he? He's purple, too! And who's this? It's Gypsy. She's blue, purple, red, and orange. Flik says, "Hello!" Flik says, "Don't worry." Wow!

Unit 7

Lesson 1 Video 7A *Belle can help!*
This is Belle. Her dress is blue. Look. A book. Belle likes books. A present for Belle! Wow! It's the Beast's castle. It's big. Phillipe is nervous. Belle says, "Don't worry, Phillipe." Oh. It's Mrs. Potts. Look! Lumiere and Cogsworth. Belle's hungry. Lumiere says, "Come on, Belle. "Ouch! Dinner! Wow! Look! Soup. Tea. And cake! Belle is happy. Oh, no! The Beast is hurt. Belle helps the Beast. Ouch! Belle is nice. The Beast says, "Thank you, Belle."

Lesson 5 Video 7B *I like books*
Look! I can see Belle. And I can see some red apples. Does Belle like apples? Yes, she does. She likes apples and books. Oh! Who's this? This is Mrs. Potts. Mm, tea! Does Belle like tea? Belle says, "Yes, I like tea. Thank you." Oh! A pink dress. Belle says, "No, I don't like this dress." Look. It's Belle and the Beast. Belle says, "Oh my! So many books!" Is Belle happy now? Yes, she is. Belle likes books.

Unit 8

Lesson 1 Video 8A *Run, Simba*
Look at the animals! I can see ants and zebras. And an elephant! It's big. Look. A bird. Look! I can see a monkey. It's Rafiki. And a lion. It's Mufasa, Simba's dad. And Simba! He's small. It's Zazu. He's a bird. Simba says, "I can jump!" Mufasa says, "Simba, go home." Look. It's Nala. Nala is Simba's friend.

Wow. Zazu says, "Go home." "Oh, no!" Simba says. Run! Oh, no! "Help!" Simba says. "I need help!" It's Mufasa! Mufasa is angry. Simba says, "I'm sorry, Dad."

Lesson 5 Video 8B *Monkeys can climb*
I can see a tree. It's a monkey. Hello, Rafiki. Wow! Monkeys can climb! Yummy! It's Timon. It's Nala. Nala says, "Where's Simba?" Here's Simba. Wow. Lions can run. Lions can jump! And lions can swim! Aaaa! Brrr.

Unit 9
Lesson 1 Video 9A *Good job, Judy!*
Who's this? It's Judy. She's small. It's Judy's mom and dad. Judy's hat is blue. Who's this? It's Gideon. He's big. Oh! Where's Judy? Be careful. Judy says, "Be nice, Gideon." Judy wants to be a police officer. Judy is small. And Judy is brave. Ouch. Judy is a police officer now. Look at the cars! It's a long street. Oh, no! A train! It's long. Good job, Judy!

Lesson 5 Video 9B *It's a long street*
It's a long street. It's *very* long! Look! It's a red car. It's Finnick. He's very small. And Nick. Be careful, Nick. It's a brown van. It's very old. Brrr. What's this? Mmm. Popsicles! Nick says, "Thank you."

Workbook audioscript

Welcome

Lesson 2 activity 2, page 3
Track 0.1
Hello. I'm Maya.

Unit 1

Lesson 1 activity 2, page 5
Track 1.1
Blue: Mom
Green: Brother
Red: Sister
Black: Dad

Lesson 2 activity 2, page 6
Track 1.2
1 It's purple.
2 It's blue.
3 It's red.
4 It's green.
5 It's yellow.
6 It's orange.

Lesson 3 activity 1, page 7
Track 1.3
1 **A:** Are you five?
  B: Yes. I'm five.
2 **A:** Are you two?
  B: No. I'm three.
3 **A:** Are you six?
  B: Yes, I'm six.

Lesson 4 activity 1, page 8
Track 1.4 – see SB Starter Track 1.8

Lesson 5 activity 1, page 9
Track 1.5
1 **A:** Who's this?
  B: Sister.
2 **A:** Who's this?
  B: Dad.
3 **A:** Who's this?
  B: Mom.
4 **A:** Who's this?
  B: Brother.

Lesson 8 activity 1, page 12
Track 1.6
1 **A:** Who's this?
  B: This is my dad.
2 **A:** Who's this?
  B: This is my mom.
3 **A:** Who's this?
  B: This is my sister.
4 **A:** Who's this?
  B: This is my brother.

Unit 2

Lesson 1 activity 2, page 15
Track 2.1
Green: poster
Yellow: chair
White: bed
Brown: desk

Lesson 2 activity 1, page 16
Track 2.2
1 puppet
2 scooter
3 teddy bear
4 kite
5 yo-yo
6 ball

Lesson 3 activity 1, page 17
Track 2.3
1 It's a ball. It's big. It's yellow.
2 It's a kite. It's small. It's pink.
3 It's a teddy bear. It's big. It's brown.
4 It's a bed. It's small. It's blue.

Lesson 4 activity 1, page 18
Track 2.4 – see SB Starter Track 2.7

Lesson 5 activity 1, page 19
Track 2.5
1 **A:** Is it a ball?
  B: No.
  A: Is it a yo-yo?
  B: Yes. It's a yo-yo.
2 **A:** Is it a teddy bear?
  B: No.
  A: Is it a puppet?
  B: Yes. It's a puppet.
3 **A:** Is it a kite?
  B: No.
  A: Is it a scooter?
  B: Yes. It's a scooter.

Lesson 8 activity 2, page 22
Track 2.6
1 **A:** Is it a kite?
  B: No.
  A: Is it a ball?
  B: Yes. It's a ball.

Workbook audioscript

2 **A:** *Is it a kite?*
B: *No.*
A: *Is it a puppet?*
B: *Yes. It's a puppet.*

3 **A:** *Is it a teddy bear?*
B: *No.*
A: *Is it a yo-yo?*
B: *No.*
A: *Is it a poster?*
B: *Yes. It's a poster.*

Unit 3

Lesson 1 activity 2, page 25
Track 3.1
1 It's a backpack. It's orange.
2 It's a book. It's red.
3 It's a ruler. It's yellow.
4 It's a marker. It's blue.
5 It's a pencil. It's purple.
6 It's a crayon. It's green.

Lesson 2 activity 1, page 26
Track 3.2
1 Rulers. One, two, three, four, five, six, seven.
2 Markers. One, two, three, four, five, six, seven, eight.
3 Pencils. One, two, three, four, five, six, seven, eight, nine.
4 Crayons. One, two, three, four, five, six, seven, eight, nine, ten.

Lesson 3 activity 1, page 27
Track 3.3
1 I have a ruler. I have two pencils. I have four markers.
2 I have two pencils. I have a marker. I have three crayons.
3 I have four markers. I have a crayon. I have two rulers.

Lesson 4 activity 1, page 28
Track 3.4 – see SB Starter Track 3.7

Lesson 5 activity 1, page 29
Track 3.5
1 **A:** *How many pencils?*
B: *One, two, three, four, five, six, seven. Seven pencils.*
2 **A:** *How many crayons?*
B: *One, two, three. Three crayons.*

3 **A:** *How many rulers?*
B: *One, two, three, four. Four rulers.*

Lesson 7 activity 2, page 31
Track 3.6
1 Five plus three is eight.
2 Six minus four is two.

Lesson 8 activity 1, page 32
Track 3.7
1 I have six pencils.
2 I have eight crayons.
3 I have two markers.
4 I have a backpack.

Unit 4

Lesson 1 activity 2, page 35
Track 4.1
1 hand
2 body
3 head
4 leg
5 nose
6 arm

Lesson 2 activity 1, page 36
Track 4.2
1 shake
2 touch
3 clap
4 stomp

Lesson 3 activity 1, page 37
Track 4.3
Girl: *Clap your hands. Don't stomp your feet. Don't shake your head.*
Boy: *Don't clap your hands. Stomp your feet. Shake your head.*

Lesson 4 activity 1, page 38
Track 4.4 – see SB Starter track 4.7

Lesson 5 activity 1, page 39
Track 4.5
1 **A:** *What's this?*
B: *Anna says, "It's my nose."*
2 **A:** *What's this?*
B: *Kristoff says, "It's my leg."*
3 **A:** *What's this?*
B: *Elsa says, "It's my hand."*

Lesson 8 activity 1, page 42
Track 4.6
1 Maya, shake your leg.
2 Cam, touch your nose.
3 Leyla, stomp your feet.

Unit 5

Lesson 2 activity 2, page 46
Track 5.1
1 It's a hat. It's red.
2 It's a sweater. It's yellow.
3 It's a coat. It's brown.
4 It's a scarf. It's green.

Lesson 3 activity 1, page 47
Track 5.2
1 My socks are white.
2 My sweater is green.
3 My shoes are yellow.
4 My hat is blue.

Lesson 4 activity 1, page 48
Track 5.3 – see SB Starter track 5.7

Lesson 5 activity 1, page 49
Track 5.4
1 I'm wearing my pants. My pants are green.
2 I'm wearing my T-shirt. My T-shirt is blue.
3 I'm wearing my hat. My hat is pink.
4 I'm wearing my shoes. My shoes are black.

Lesson 8 activity 1, page 52
Track 5.5
1 I'm wearing my T-shirt. My T-shirt is green.
2 I'm wearing my hat. My hat is yellow.
3 I'm wearing my shoes. My shoes are red.
4 I'm wearing my pants. My pants are blue.

Unit 6

Lesson 2 activity 1, page 56
Track 6.1
1 It's a pond. It's blue.
2 It's a rock. It's gray.
3 It's a flower. It's purple.
4 It's a mushroom. It's red.
5 It's a tree. It's green and brown.

Lesson 3 activity 1, page 57
Track 6.2
1. I can see a flower.
2. I can see a rock.
3. I can see a tree.
4. I can see a ladybug.

Lesson 4 activity 1, page 58
Track 6.3 – see SB Starter track 6.7

Lesson 5 activity 1, page 59
Track 6.4
1. **A:** I can see a tree.
   B: What color is it?
   A: It's red and brown.
   B: Picture 2.
2. **A:** I can see a mushroom.
   B: What color is it?
   A: It's white.
   B: Picture 1.
3. **A:** I can see a flower.
   B: What color is it?
   A: It's pink.
   B: Picture 1.

Lesson 8 activity 1, page 62
Track 6.5
1. **A:** I can see a butterfly.
   B: What color is it?
   A: It's yellow and pink.
2. **A:** I can see a butterfly.
   B: What color is it?
   A: It's red and black.
3. **A:** I can see a butterfly.
   B: What color is it?
   A: It's purple and blue.

Unit 7

Lesson 2 activity 1, page 66
Track 7.1
1. I have noodles. Mmm.
2. I have sandwiches. Mmm.
3. I have juice. Mmm.
4. I have cookies. Mmm.

Lesson 3 activity 1, page 67
Track 7.2
1. I like apples.
2. I like juice.
3. I like cake.
4. I like cookies.

Lesson 4 activity 1, page 68
Track 7.3 – see SB Starter track 7.7

Lesson 5 activity 1, page 69
Track 7.4
1. I don't like soup.
2. I like cake.
3. I don't like tea.
4. I like apples.

Lesson 6 activity 1, page 70
Track 7.5
1. **Maya:** I can help.
   Ms. Smart: Thank you.
2. **Cam:** Let's all share.
   Leyla: Thank you.

Lesson 8 activity 1, page 72
Track 7.6
1. I like juice.
2. I don't like pizza.
3. I like apples.
4. I don't like noodles.

Unit 8

Lesson 2 activity 1, page 76
Track 8.1
1. swim
2. fly
3. climb
4. walk

Lesson 3 activity 1, page 77
Track 8.2
1. I can climb.
2. I can run.
3. I can jump.
4. I can walk.

Lesson 4 activity 1, page 78
Track 8.3 – see SB Starter track 8.7

Lesson 5 activity 1, page 79
Track 8.4
1. Zebras can swim.
2. Butterflies can fly.
3. Lions can swim. Lions can climb.

Lesson 8 activity 1, page 82
Track 8.5
1. I can run. I'm yellow.
2. I can climb. I'm brown.
3. I can swim. I'm big.
4. I can fly. I'm small.

Unit 9

Lesson 2 activity 1, page 86
Track 9.1
1. It's a train. It's old. It's short. It's slow. It's blue.
2. It's a train. It's new. It's long. It's fast. It's yellow.

Lesson 3 activity 1, page 87
Track 9.2
1. It's a fast car.
2. It's a long car.
3. It's an old scooter.
4. It's a new house.

Lesson 4 activity 1, page 88
Track 9.3 – see SB Starter track 9.4

Lesson 6 activity 1, page 90
Track 9.4
1. I'm not brave.
2. I'm very brave.
3. I'm brave.

Lesson 8 activity 1, page 92
Track 9.5
1. It's a fast car. It's very fast. It's an old house. It's very old. It's a slow car. It's very slow.
2. It's a fast car. It's very fast. It's an old house. It's very old. It's a short train. It's very short.
3. It's a fast car. It's very fast. It's a long train. It's very long. It's a new house. It's very new.

Workbook audioscript 205

Games Bank

Picture/Word card games

Faster and faster Display the picture cards in a row on the board. Point to each one and elicit the word. Start off slowly, giving students time to think. Then point to each picture card more quickly, getting faster and faster as students become more confident.

Monster Munch Draw a picture of a monster on the board. Tell students that your monster is hungry. But today it only wants to eat certain words, e.g., food words or words with at least five letters. Show students picture cards. Ask them to decide whether the monster can eat each one.

Up close Cut out a magnifying glass-shaped hole into a piece of colored card. The card should be at least as big as the picture cards. Place a picture card behind the piece of card so that students can only see part of the picture. Ask students to guess what the picture is.

What's missing? Place the picture cards face-up so that all students can see them. Ask students to say the words one by one. Then turn one of the picture cards face-down, and ask students to say the words one by one again, including the word for this card. Continue, turning another card after each round, and see if students can remember the words for the face-down picture cards.

What's this? Place all the picture cards face-down. Say a word and invite a student to find the corresponding picture card. As the student turns over each card to reveal the picture, ask him/her to say the word. Ask the class to say *yes* or *no*. Repeat with different students.

Where is …? Place the picture cards around the classroom. Say a word and ask students to find and point to the correct picture card.

Which is different? Place four picture cards from the same set on the board plus one picture card from a different set on the board. Ask students to say which one is different.

Pencil and drawing games

Circle it! Draw pictures of the target vocabulary on the board, or use the picture cards. Say one of the words, or describe it, and invite a student to come to the front and draw a circle around the correct picture.

Draw it! Ask a student come to the board and show them an object they know in their Student Book, e.g., book, cake, bear, tree. The student draws the object on the board for the other students to guess.

TPR (Total Physical Response) games

Color hunt Say a color. Ask students to look for items of that color in the classroom, point at them or count them. Repeat with other colors.

Follow the leader One student stands at the front and says and does a series of actions, e.g., *stomp my feet, clap my hands, jump,* for the other students copy.

Let's dance! Play the song and ask students to make up a dance. Start by making up a funny dance move and ask the students to copy you. Then invite students to make up a new dance move. Each time, one student comes to the front, makes up a dance move and everyone copies.

Song/Chant activities

Let's listen! Provide students with a word from the song/chant that they have to listen for. Play the recording, and children stand up and sing/chant or sit down when they hear the word.

Stand in order Ask a few students to come to the board, and give them picture cards with items from the song/chant. Children listen to the lyrics and stand in the order in which the words from their cards appear.

Sing my part Divide the class into groups, and give each group a section of the song/chant to remember. Play the song/chant, and each group stands up and joins in when they hear their part.

Guessing games

Behind the doors Hold your hands in front of your face like two closed doors. Behind your hands, make a face showing an emotion. Ask students to guess the emotion. Then open the two doors and show students your expression. Invite students to play the game in pairs or small groups.

It's in the bag Put an object inside a cloth bag. Ask students to take turns to put their hand in the bag and try to guess what's inside.

Speaking and listening games

Memory game Put several objects on a desk. Point to each one and elicit its name. Then cover the objects with a cloth. Ask students to try to remember all the objects. You can add challenge by asking questions, e.g., *What color is the (marker)?*

Miming Show a student a word from the unit (a number, a family member, or an emotion). The student mimes the word, and the other students guess.

Throw the ball Ask students to sit or stand in a circle, and throw or roll a ball to each other. Each time they get the ball, they say a word.

Whispers Sit with students in a circle, and whisper a word to the student on your left. Ask him/her to whisper the word to the student on their left, and so on, around the circle, until it reaches the student on your right. Ask the students on your right to say the word – is it correct?

Mickey Mouse puppet games

Hello, Mickey! Model the game by introducing yourself to the Mickey Mouse puppet. Shake Mickey's hand or give him a high five, and say: *Hello, Mickey! I'm (name)*. Then students sit in a circle, taking turns to introduce themselves to Mickey.

Mickey's card Give the Mickey Mouse puppet a picture card, but hide it from the class. Students take turns to guess what is on the picture card.

Mickey says … Ask the Mickey Mouse puppet to give instructions to the class for students to follow. Demonstrate each action as Mickey says it.

Pass Mickey! Sit in a circle. Ask students to pass the Mickey Mouse puppet around the circle. Count as they pass him around or play music. When you get to ten (or pause the music), the students stop passing Mickey around. Hold up a picture card from the unit and ask the student holding Mickey to say the word.

Talk to Mickey Ask four students to come to the front of the class and give each student a picture card. Invite a different student to whisper a word to the Mickey Mouse puppet, e.g., *brother*. Mickey says the word in a target structure. The student with that picture card responds appropriately.

Yes or no? Give the Mickey Mouse puppet a picture card, and ask him to say the word. Sometimes, Mickey says the wrong word. Students say *Yes!* if the word is correct and *No!* if it's incorrect.

The Mickey Mouse puppet is a recognizable, friendly character that can have a particularly stimulating effect on children learning English. He is a symbol of playing and having fun, which is a great starting point for creating a positive attitude in children towards learning a foreign language. The Teacher's Book lesson notes are written to include the Mickey Mouse puppet in particular, repetitive situations. These can be introducing students to the lesson, singing the *Hello, Friends!* song together with the class, initiating games, helping students realize their language achievements, and saying goodbye at the end of the class. In this way, the puppet also plays the role of a friend who provides students with a sense of predictability and encourages linguistic confidence in classes.

The lesson notes contain specific instructions of how to use the Mickey Mouse puppet to interest and engage students, although you may also wish to introduce him in your own way! Here are some more suggestions for how to use the puppet during your lessons:

- Make Mickey part of the class experience. You may want to invite him to listen to a story, join a game or a song, and get him to have fun with the class.
- Make Mickey greet every child at the start of the lesson. This will make all students feel welcome and will encourage them to say hello.
- Use Mickey to model new language. You can have short conversations with him to ask questions and give answers.
- Use Mickey to revise language at the start of the class. He can help you ask questions to students.
- Use Mickey to model good behavior. In the conversations you have with him, make sure you treat each other very kindly.
- Use Mickey to praise students and show encouragement.
- Use Mickey to say goodbye to students, making sure he addresses each student by name.

My teacher progress journal

1 Which unit(s) engaged my students the most? Why?
_____
_____

2 Which lessons and activities did my students enjoy most? Why?
_____
_____
_____

3 Which lessons or activities did students find most challenging? What helped them?
_____
_____

4 Which Personal and Social Skills did my students develop? Check (✓).
   Social awareness ○   Self-awareness ○   Self-management ○
   Relationship skills ○   Responsible decision-making ○

5 Which way of working did my students enjoy the most? Rate from 1 (not much) to 5 (a lot).
   individually ○   in pairs ○   in groups ○   in larger teams ○   whole class ○

   Reflect on reasons why.
   _____
   _____
   _____

6 Which **Teacher toolkit** ideas were most helpful? Which would I reuse in the future?
_____
_____
_____

7 Which **Teaching star** tips were most helpful? Which would I reuse in the future?
_____
_____
_____

8 Which resources were most useful?
_____

9 Is there anything I will do differently next year?
_____
_____
_____
_____

> Why not share what works for you with other teachers? Ask questions to learn from them, too!